Economic Policy and the History of Economic Thought

This book discusses key issues in economic policy in the context of the history of economic thought.

Most of the current and past academic controversies in economics are, explicitly or implicitly, centred around the application and form of economic policy. This is particularly evident in the post-WWII period, with the appearance of economic policy as a distinguishable subfield, but important elements of various economic policy issues can be found throughout the history of economic thought. This book discusses various topics in economic policy – such as questions over state spending and taxation, income redistribution, and the role of money – with each chapter focusing on a particular period or major school of economic thought ranging from the 'prehistory' of economics up to the present day. Specific chapters of the volume cover the main schools of economic thought from different national and theoretical traditions, incorporating mercantilism, the Physiocratic School, the German Historical School, Marxism, the Austrian School, institutional economics, Keynesian economics, behavioural economics and more.

This book will be of great interest to readers of the history of economic policy as well as the history of economic thought, macroeconomics and economic history more broadly.

Stavros Drakopoulos obtained a BA in economics from the Athens University of Economics and Business, and an MSc and a PhD in economics from the University of Stirling, UK. Having served academic appointments at the Universities of Glasgow and Aberdeen, he is currently Professor of Economics in the Department of Philosophy and History of Science of the National and Kapodistrian University of Athens, Greece. His research interests include Economic Methodology and History of Economic Thought, Labour Economics, Health Economics and the Economics of Subjective Well-Being. He has 52 publications in refereed journals, 5 books, and 15 chapters in edited books.

Ioannis Katselidis obtained a BA from the University of Piraeus, an MSc from the University of Birmingham, and an MSc and a PhD from the Athens

University of Economics and Business. He has been an Adjunct Lecturer at the Athens University of Economics and Business, the National and Kapodistrian University of Athens and the Hellenic Naval Academy, among others. He was also a Research Fellow at the Center of Planning and Economic Research (KEPE). In addition, he has published scientific papers in various refereed journals, and he has also participated in many Greek and international academic conferences. His research interests include History and Philosophy of Economic Analysis and Labour Economics and Policy.

Routledge Studies in the History of Economics

Metaphors in the History of Economic Thought
Crises, Business Cycles and Equilibrium
Edited by Roberto Baranzini and Daniele Besomi

Liberalism and the Philosophy of Economics
Tsutomu Hashimoto

An Economic Philosophy of Production, Work and Consumption
A Transhistorical Framework
Rodney Edvinsson

The Early History of Economics in the United States
The Influence of the German Historical School of Economics on Teaching and Theory
Birsen Filip

Economic Methodology, History and Pluralism
Expanding Economic Thought to Meet Contemporary Challenges
Edited by Ioana Negru and Penelope Hawkins

Monetary Economics, Banking and Policy
Expanding Economic Thought to Meet Contemporary Challenges
Edited by Penelope Hawkins and Ioana Negru

Modern Japanese Economic Thought
An Intellectual History to 1950
Kiichiro Yagi

Economic Policy and the History of Economic Thought
Edited by Stavros Drakopoulos and Ioannis Katselidis

For more information about this series, please visit: www.routledge.com/series/SE0341

Economic Policy and the History of Economic Thought

Edited by
Stavros Drakopoulos and
Ioannis Katselidis

Routledge
Taylor & Francis Group
LONDON AND NEW YORK

First published 2023
by Routledge
4 Park Square, Milton Park, Abingdon, Oxon OX14 4RN

and by Routledge
605 Third Avenue, New York, NY 10158

Routledge is an imprint of the Taylor & Francis Group, an informa business

British Library Cataloguing-in-Publication Data
A catalogue record for this book is available from the British Library

ISBN: 978-1-032-13196-2 (hbk)
ISBN: 978-1-032-13197-9 (pbk)
ISBN: 978-1-003-22809-7 (ebk)

DOI: 10.4324/9781003228097

Typeset in Bembo
by codeMantra

Contents

Contributors

Sheila Dow's research focuses on the methodology and history of economics, money and banking, regional finance and macroeconomics. In addition to her academic career, she has worked as an economist and served as an adviser in the government sector. Her recent books include *Foundations for New Economic Thinking* (2012), and *The General Theory and Keynes for the 21st Century* and *Money, Method and Post-Keynesian Economics for the 21st Century* (both co-edited with J. Jespersen and G. Tily, 2018).

Stavros Drakopoulos obtained a BA in economics from the Athens University of Economics and Business, and an MSc and a PhD in economics from the University of Stirling, UK. Having served academic appointments at the Universities of Glasgow and Aberdeen, he is currently Professor of Economics in the Department of Philosophy and History of Science of the National and Kapodistrian University of Athens, Greece. His research interests include Economic Methodology and History of Economic Thought, Labour Economics, Health Economics and the Economics of Subjective Well-Being. He has 52 publications in refereed journals, 5 books, and 15 chapters in edited books.

Peter E. Earl (MA, PhD, Cambridge) is an honorary associate professor in the School of Economics at the University of Queensland, Australia, where he worked from 2001 until his retirement in 2020. He has been a behavioural economist since the late 1970s and is a past co-editor of the *Journal of Economic Psychology*. His latest book is *Principles of Behavioral Economics: Bringing Together Old, New and Evolutionary Approaches* (Cambridge University Press, 2022).

George Gotsis is Professor of Philosophy and History of Economics at the Department of History and Philosophy of Science, National and Kapodistrian University of Athens (NKUA), Greece. He holds two PhD degrees in Political Science from Panteion University and in Economics from NKUA, respectively. His main research interests comprise, among others, History of Economic Ideas, Religion in Business and Faith at Work, Entrepreneurship and Religion, and Intercultural Business Ethics. He has extensively published in peer-reviewed journals and edited volumes. He has also co-authored a book (with Dr Gerasimos Merianos) entitled *Managing Financial Resources in Late Antiquity* (London: Palgrave MacMillan, 2018).

Harald Hagemann is Professor Emeritus of Economics at the University of Hohenheim in Stuttgart, a life member of Clare Hall, University of Cambridge, Honorary Past President of the European Society for the History of Economic Thought and Honorary Chairman of the German Keynes Society. In 1999–2000, he was Theodor Heuss Professor at the New School for Social Research in New York. He is the author and editor of numerous books and articles on the history of economic thought and the emigration of economists from Nazi Germany.

Arne Heise is Professor of Economics at the Department of Socioeconomics at Hamburg University, Germany, and the director of its Center for Economic and Sociological Studies (CESS). He has held professorships at the University of Cologne, Vienna University of Economics and Business, Austria and Izmir Economics University, Turkey, and he was a guest fellow at St. Edmunds College of the University of Cambridge, UK. His main research areas are Macroeconomics, European Integration and the Socioeconomics of Economics.

Ioannis Katselidis obtained a BA from the University of Piraeus, an MSc from the University of Birmingham, and an MSc and a PhD from the Athens University of Economics and Business. He has been an Adjunct Lecturer at the Athens University of Economics and Business, the National and Kapodistrian University of Athens and the Hellenic Naval Academy, among others. He was also a Research Fellow at the Center of Planning and Economic Research (KEPE). In addition, he has published scientific papers in various refereed journals, and he has also participated in many Greek and international academic conferences. His research interests include the History and Philosophy of Economic Analysis and Labour Economics and Policy.

Atsushi Komine received his Master's and PhD in Economics from Hitotsubashi University, Japan. Since 2008, he has been Professor of the History of Economic Thought at Ryukoku University, Kyoto, and he is now Dean of the Faculty. From 2001 to 2002 and from 2009 to 2010, Dr. Komine was an Honorary University Fellow of Exeter University and a Visiting Fellow of Clare Hall, Cambridge University, respectively. His contributions to the history of economic thought include his monograph on Keynes (*Keynes and His Contemporaries*, Routledge, 2014), and his edited books on peace and war, and on text mining, among others.

Charalampos Konstantinidis is Associate Professor of Economics and Graduate Programme Director of the Master's programme in Applied

Economics at the University of Massachusetts Boston. His research interests lie in political economy with a particular emphasis on the political economy of agriculture and food. He holds a PhD in Economics from the University of Massachusetts Amherst.

Peter T. Leeson is the Duncan Black Professor of Economics and Law at George Mason University.

Robert McMaster is Professor of Political Economy in the Adam Smith Business School at the University of Glasgow. From 2005 to 2017, he co-edited the *Review of Social Economy*. His recent publications include a co-authored book with John Davis, *Health Care Economics*, and four-volume Routledge Major Works Series, *Social Economics: Critical Concepts in Economics*, co-edited with Wilfred Dolfsma, Ellen Mutari, Deb Figart and Mark White. He has published in numerous journals, including *American Journal of Public Health*, *British Journal of Management*, *Cambridge Journal of Economics*, *Economic Geography*, *Economy and Society*, *Journal of Business Ethics* and *Journal of Institutional Economics*, among others.

Cosma Orsi holds a PhD in both Political Philosophy and History of Economic Doctrines. After teaching history of economic thought in Italy (Catholic University of Milan and University of Milano Bicocca), Switzerland (Università della Svizzera Italiana), and Denmark (Roskilde University), he is currently a researcher at the University of Catania. He is the author of scholarly essays published in international journals about the relationship between economic theory and public policy.

Cosimo Perrotta is formerly Full Professor of History of Economic Thought at the University of Salento (Italy) and Council Chair of the European Society for the History of Economic Thought (2002–2006). He is Honorary Member of STOREP (The Italian Association for the History of Political Economy). He received Ernest Lluch Prize in 2019. He is reviewer/referee for all the main international journals of his discipline. He has published with many of the main publishers in economics. He has been invited/key speaker at the Universities of: Cambridge UK, New South Wales (Sydney), Duke (Durham, NC, U.S.), Stuttgart, Frankfurt, Sophia Un. (Tokyo); Waseda Un. (Tokyo), UNAM (Mexico City); Colegio de México (Mexico City); Athens, Coimbra (Portugal), Volos (Greece), Napoli, Milano Statale, Torino, La Sapienza (Rome), Roma Tre (Rome), Valencia, Fukuoka (Japan), Kyoto, etc.

Simona Pisanelli is a researcher at the University of Salento (Lecce, Italy). Her research interests lie in the field of the History of Economic Thought, with a focus on the French and Scottish Enlightenment. She has published the monograph *Condorcet et Adam Smith. Réformes économiques et progrès social au siècle des Lumières* (Classiques Garnier 2018), several chapters in collected volumes, and articles in journals, most recently in the *European Journal of*

History of Economic Thought. She is a member of several European societies of the History of Economic Thought and collaborates with journals and research groups in this field.

Louis Rouanet is an Assistant Professor of economics at Western Kentucky University. He completed his PhD in economics at George Mason University in Summer 2021. His scholarly work focuses on applying public choice and rational choice to different historical contexts and has been published in the *Journal of Economic History*, the *European Review of Economic History*, *Public Choice*, and the *Southern Economic Journal*, among others.

Andriana Vlachou is a Professor at the Athens University of Economics and Business. She received her PhD in Economics from the University of Massachusetts. Her fields of teaching and research include Marxian Economics, History of Economic Thought and Environmental and Resource Economics. She has published articles in *Cambridge Journal of Economics*, *Capitalism Nature Socialism*, *Energy Economics*, *Energy Policy*, *Journal of Policy Modeling*, *Review of International Political Economy*, *Review of Radical Political Economics*, *Rethinking Marxism*, *Science & Society*, *Southern Economic Journal* and others. She has also authored or edited several books, including *Contemporary Economic Theory: Radical Critiques of Neoliberalism* (Macmillan 1999) and *Economic Crisis and Greece* (with N. Theocarakis and D. Milonakis, Gutenberg and The Greek Scientific Association of Political Economy 2011, in Greek). She is an editor-at-large of *Capitalism Nature Socialism*.

Michel S. Zouboulakis, PhD (Economics) University of Paris 1, is Professor of the History and Methodology of Economics, Department of Economics, University of Thessaly, Greece. He published *La science économique à la recherche de ses fondements. La tradition épistémologique ricardienne, 1826–1891* (Paris: PUF, 1993), a textbook on Economic Methodology (University of Thessaly Press, 2007), a monograph *The Varieties of Economic Rationality: From Adam Smith to Contemporary Behavioural and Evolutionary Economics* (London: Routledge 2014) and *National Defence and National Debts* (Athens: Gutenberg, 2021, co-authored with Prof. C. Kollias). He has also published over 75 articles in peer-reviewed journals and collective volumes.

1 Introduction

Stavros Drakopoulos and Ioannis Katselidis

Since the last three decades and compared to the 1970s and even to the 1980s, the history of economic thought as a distinct subdiscipline has experienced a decline as an integral part of economics education in many leading universities (see also Roncaglia 2014). Recently, however, this area of study has enjoyed a noticeable comeback in terms of papers published in non-specialist journals, international conference attendance, and a number of books published in the field. It has been argued that this revival was an important part of the response to the financial crisis of 2008 and the resulting re-examination of both the content and the teaching of economics (Dow 2020: 21–22). There are clear signs that the profession is starting to rediscover its value. Even before the financial crisis, there were many sound arguments supporting its role and usefulness in economics. One of the most well-known defences of the history of economic thought as a subject is Mark Blaug's powerful statement:

> No idea or theory in economics, physics, chemistry, biology, philosophy and even mathematics is ever thoroughly understood except as the end-product of a slice of history, the result of some previous intellectual development.
>
> (Blaug 2001: 156)

Other authors have emphasized the role of the discipline in the understanding of the nature of economics research and its relationship to other sciences, and also the contribution of the history of economic thought to the comprehension of past and current theoretical and methodological disputes (Mirowski 1989; Roncaglia 1996, 2014; Weintraub 2002; Schabas 2006; Marcuzzo 2008; Dow 2009). For Steven Kates, without history of economic thought, economics is a lesser subject, less penetrating, less interesting, and of much less social value (Kates 2013). Contemporary economic methods and the epistemology of economics in general, are better understood when supplemented with the study of the history of economics (Marcuzzo and Rosselli 2002; Dow 2020). Further, in the last two decades, the history of economic thought is increasingly connected to the wider field of the history of science and it

DOI: 10.4324/9781003228097-1

is already contributing to the understanding of the evolution of scientific discourse (Schabas 2002; Emmett 2010). Historians of economic thought also stress that one of the main benefits of studying the field is its valuable function for the further comprehension of contemporary economic theories and how contemporary economics has absorbed particular economic ideas. By the same token, it is reasonable to maintain that the history of economic thought is also important for the understanding of the historical and theoretical background of various economic policies, especially of economic policy controversies and disputes.

Economic policy prescriptions are an essential aspect of economics as a discipline. Most of the current and past academic controversies in economics are explicitly or implicitly aimed at the applications and forms of economic policies. Alfred Marshall's renowned definition of economics as "the study of mankind in the ordinary business of life" and his interest in policy clearly imply the close relationship between the two (Marshall 1890: 1). Marshall's successor A. C. Pigou had a general preference for discussion of economic policies that he deemed particularly pressing and urgent in relation to the British society of his era (Aslanbeigui and Oakes 2015). John Maynard Keynes' belief that "the political problem of mankind is to combine three things: economic efficiency, social justice, and individual liberty" visibly points to his great concern for economic policy (Keynes 1926: 311). The close connection between economic thought and economic policy is particularly evident after the post-WWII period. Although economic policy as a distinguishable academic subfield appeared in that period, one can find key elements of various economic policy issues in the history of economic thought. For instance, discussions concerning state spending and taxation, income redistribution, and the role of money can be located in most classical economists' writings but also in many pre-classical and even ancient economic discourses.

The connection between economic policy and history of economic ideas is also present but not always immediately noticeable when we refer to the pre-modern era. Topics that are considered to fall under the modern conception of what constitutes economic policy, such as taxation, state lending and borrowing, and issue of coinage, are found even in ancient societies. Direct and indirect taxation, duties, rents from public lands, and public expenditures in the ancient city-states of Athens and Sparta are representative examples (Bitros and Karayiannis 2010). Taxation policies, debasement of coinage, and price controls are clearly discernable at various periods in ancient Rome (Temin 2006). Consequently, ancient authors wrote about the notions of the division of labour, value and prices, surplus, abundance, and of the nature of money, among others (Lowry 1987; Leshem 2016). Thus, it is not surprising that the origins of contemporary economic thought can be traced back to the ancients (Backhouse 2004). Even past economic ideas which have been seemingly discredited can sometimes be implicit but nevertheless detectable in modern policy debates. For instance, the late twentieth-century economic policies such as income and wage policies that were popular as inflation remedy in the 1970s can be conceptually linked to the pre-mercantilist medieval and guild-economy philosophy of the "just price" (Johnson 1974: 2; see also Taylor 1981).

It is generally accepted that policy-makers are guided by the prevailing economic theories which are in turn formed by specific theoretical traditions. In the historical context, there have been various disagreements both among economists and policy-makers with respect to the appropriate policy agendas and the related economic policy measures. The alleged failure of neoclassical macroeconomics to predict the economic downturn and to provide effective policy prescriptions for the recent economic crisis is one contemporary example here (Stiglitz 2018; Chatelain and Ralf 2020). The long controversy regarding the microfoundations of macroeconomic theory and its policy suggestions is another example (Mirowski 2013; Duarte and Lima 2014; Denis 2016). Undoubtedly, there is a close connection between theory, policy, and economic reality.

A central theme that can be distinguished in the modern history of economic thought is the debate concerning the operation of the free markets and the role of the state. One intellectual tradition argues that free markets work best toward improving social welfare and economic progress, and therefore markets should be given free rein. In the last decades, this intellectual tradition became dominant and the ensuing economic policies were in favour of minimal government intervention in market economies. Another intellectual tradition, as in the case of John Maynard Keynes and his followers, has pointed to the inherent instability of the free markets and to the need for governments' intervention in the economy in order to correct various imbalances caused by markets' functioning. The general agreement toward the use of active fiscal and monetary policy by government authorities after the Great Depression in 1929 indicated the prevalence of this tradition in the early post-WWII decades (Acocella et al. 2016). After a break of several decades, it seems that many policy-makers' responses after the 2008 financial crisis suggest that the pendulum of economic ideas may have started to return toward its side (Eichengreen 2020). Similarly, the current debate concerning appropriate economic policies to face the increasing environmental challenges can also be linked to relevant ideas in the history of economic thought (Pearce 2002; Sandmo 2015). It is also telling that environmental economics specialists also recognize the usefulness of the history of economic ideas in the sense "that examining our early history can give us a broader perspective on current environmental problems and may also influence our research priorities in a positive way" (Sandmo 2015: 43). In any case, it is clear that the study of economic policy in the context of the history of economic thought is necessary for the better understanding of current and past economic policies and policy controversies. In this framework, the principal aim of this edited book is to shed light on the interaction between economic theories and economic policy through the lens of the history of economics. It covers various approaches by different and diverging schools of thought which have appeared in different times and at different places.

This book discusses topics of economic policy in the context of the history of economic thought. It consists of 14 chapters each focusing on a particular period or major school of economic thought. The book follows a broad chronological order in examining the topic under consideration. Its purpose is to offer a comprehensive historical dimension to the relation between economic approaches and economic policies starting from the prehistory of economics and up to twenty-first-century developments. It does not claim to include every strand of economic discourse, but it attempts to represent the most well-known and influential schools of economic thought. In particular, the chapters of this volume cover the main schools of economic thought from different national (e.g. Austrian, German, French) and theoretical (e.g. Classical, Marxian, Institutional, Austrian, Keynesian, Behavioural) traditions, highlighting various aspects of the issue under examination during distinct time periods and places.

As was mentioned above, the chapters of the book are organized chronologically, something which is rather standard in most history of economics textbooks. In brief, the first three chapters discuss the pre-classical ideas on economic policy including ancient Greek and Roman but also encompassing non-Western traditions. The relevant views of Mercantilist and Physiocrat authors are discussed next. Chapters 5 and 6 turn to the classical political economy tradition and examine the views of David Ricardo, Thomas Malthus, and Karl Marx. Economic policy ideas of leading marginalists and early neoclassical economists are presented in Chapter 7. The following three chapters focus on non-mainstream schools of economic thought: German Historical School, old Institutionalism, and Austrian economics. Keynes and his legacy on economic thought and policy are the subjects of Chapters 11 and 12. The ensuing two chapters discuss post-war heterodox approaches and the contributions of behavioural economics. The final chapter closes with one of the major current issues in terms of economic policy which is the role of fiscal policy after the great recession. Although there are many aspects of the history of economic policy and of economic ideas which are not covered by the present volume, there is a conscious attempt to encompass a wide array of streams of thought. Hopefully, it will contribute toward a more thorough understanding of the major intellectual currents in the history of economic ideas and policies.

Chapter Outlines

The opening chapter by George Gotsis focuses on the so-called prehistoric era of economics. It intends to provide a framework that seeks to capture issues of economic policy underlying ancient and medieval economic ideas, by exploring policy implications derived from various streams of thought on economic phenomena. After briefly discussing classical, Hellenistic, and

Roman conceptions of economic activities, this chapter adopts a comparative approach by reviewing policy implications as integral to certain non-Western traditions and more specifically, to Confucian virtue ethics, embedded in different societal and cultural contexts. The aim here is to identify potential convergence and divergence on policy issues between distinct traditions of thought. It also seeks to demonstrate commonalities between Eastern and Western approaches to policy issues and suggest plausible reasons for elaborating parallel or competing views on a variety of phenomena such as household management, economic motivation, state intervention, tax and monetary reforms, redistributive initiatives, and price control.

Cosimo Perrotta focuses on mercantilism in the third chapter. In the period under examination, the new economy (capitalism) – based on private investment and the pursuit of profit – took off and replaced the feudal economy. This chapter starts by discussing the nature of mercantilism and of the historical factors which contributed to its emergence. Perrotta then examines mercantilism's first period, when its principles were elaborated, and how these principles became hegemonic. He proceeds to discuss the main policies of mercantilism including its policy suggestions toward employment and wages, and toward the poor. He continues by arguing how the subsequent mainstream economic thought marginalized mercantilism mainly because its development project saw public interest and public policy as central. Consequently, Perrotta contends that this neglect has been a great loss for economic thought given that the criticisms to mercantilism – since Physiocracy and Adam Smith onwards – always had a simplistic approach and reduced all the problems to being favourable or not favourable to economic freedom.

Chapter 4 by Simona Pisanelli examines Physiocracy and fiscal reform, and focuses on the chimera of the *impôt unique*. Pisanelli starts by arguing that despite its limited space-time range (France 1756–1777), the Physiocratic School has left a decisive mark on the history of economic thought. By investigating the cause and nature of national wealth and the methods to increase it, François Quesnay and the other members of the Physiocracy identified the agricultural sector as the only source of produit net. Based on this economic viewpoint, they drew up proposals for economic policy aimed at reforming the productive structure of a backward society, perceiving the advantages of a capitalist re-organization of agriculture. This chapter also maintains that among the reforms proposed by the Physiocrats, the most radical was that of the *impôt unique* on landowners' rent, replacing the various direct and indirect taxes. Despite its undeniable charm, this proposal was destined to fail, both because of the resistance of the privileged classes that would have been affected, and because of some indisputable "technical" limits.

Cosma Orsi's Chapter 5 discusses the post-Smithian views on poverty and poor relief. Orsi starts by arguing that by the end of the eighteenth century, the English social legislation shifted from a safety net devised to deal with emergencies to a social security system implemented to cope with the threat of unemployment and poverty. It was based on the innovative mechanism of the Speenhamland system – a form of outdoor relief resting on an ex-ante logic of aid – and ended in 1834 when the New Poor Law replaced at once the Speenhamland system. Economic writers like Frederick Morton Eden, David Ricardo, and Thomas Robert Malthus played a fundamental role in such an architectonic shift. Orsi examines the extent that the contributions in the field of political economy were used as a map for the legislator who designed and implemented the social legislation of 1834. The author shows that what influenced their views on poverty and poor relief rested not only on their understanding of economic development but also on their idea that individual motivation was the only drive for the poor to escape their condition. Following this train of thought, this chapter enquires about their arguments in favour of a Friendly Society and Saving Banks for the lower classes. This work looks at an issue almost forgotten by historians of economic ideas, namely the relationship between economic theorizing and social legislation.

Charalampos Konstantinidis and Andriana Vlachou are the authors of Chapter 6 which is on Karl Marx's critical views on economic policy. This chapter starts by pointing out that while Karl Marx's critique of political economy is fairly well-known, its relation to economic policy in capitalism is relatively understudied. Konstantinidis and Vlachou proceed to examine Marx's economic writings, particularly *Capital*, to show that Marx's analysis displays a nuanced understanding of the shaping and workings of economic policy in capitalism. In particular, Marx's analysis of economic policy and regulation in cases such as the Factory Acts and the Enclosure Acts displays an understanding of economic policy and state regulation as outcomes of class struggle and rivalries between and within classes, including intra-capitalist rivalries. At the same time, economic policy and regulation emerge as key factors that secure and shape the conditions of existence for the extraction, appropriation, and distribution of surplus value at an expanded scale in capitalism. As such, Marx's understanding of economic policy offers valuable insight into the shaping of policy and the role of the state in contemporary capitalism.

Economic policy in Marginalist and early neoclassical economics is the subject of Chapter 7 by Michel Zouboulakis. Economics after 1870 made a significant turn thanks to the so-called "Marginal Revolution" which is usually associated with the simultaneous discovery of the concept of marginal utility and the application of differential calculus in economic theory. Both innovations have been possible mainly because of the redefinition of the scope of economic analysis, from the social conditions of production, distribution, and accumulation of wealth, to the subjective factors of exchange, or, in brief, from Political Economy to Economics. Yet, the period of 1873–1896 is marked by the Long Depression, during which the world economy faced constantly falling prices, falling interest rates and profit rates, generating massive business failures, and rising unemployment rates. Economic growth returned slowly after the substantial re-organization of labour and capital, the rise of protectionism, and the push of imperialistic expansion to its limits.

Zouboulakis attempts to tackle how the turn to more abstract theorizing has affected the economist's view on burning economic policy issues. He considers the views on the economic policy of some exceptional economists such as W.S. Jevons, L. Walras, V. Pareto, A. Marshall, I. Fisher, K. Wicksell, and A.C. Pigou covering 50 years from 1871 to 1920s, in major topics with respect to international trade and monetary policy, as well as taxation and public economics.

Harald Hagemann discusses the German Historical School (GHS) on Economic Policy in Chapter 8. This chapter covers the main areas to which representatives of the GHS made important contributions: social policy, development policy, trade policy, fiscal policy, and monetary policy. The discussion covers major aspects of the GHS: the older HS (Roscher, Knies, Hildebrand), the younger HS (Schmoller and his followers), and the youngest HS (Weber, Sombart). Emphasis on productive forces (including human capital) had a long tradition in German economics as well as an evolutionary perspective, reflected in a stages theory of economic development, and an empirical-statistical approach. The term Staatswissenschaften (state sciences) expresses the typical German symbiosis of state and economy, in contrast to the more theoretical and abstract British classical political economics. Trade policy always was a controversial issue, most strongly when disputes between free traders and protectionists in 1879 led to the greatest crisis in the Verein für Socialpolitik. The Verein had been founded in 1872/1873 in opposition to laissez-faire liberalism as well as to the revolutionary ideas of Marxism. Under the towering influence of Schmoller, an ethical-normative approach was taken and social policy was attributed to the state. Wagner, who like Schmoller was a great admirer of Bismarck, believed in the implementation of distributive justice by the government. Hagemann also argues that although Schmoller was politically a conservative, he nevertheless was an advocate of progressive income taxation and of taxes on wealth and inheritance.

In Chapter 9, the co-editors of this volume turn to the old Institutional School. Apart from the criticism of the narrow conception of economic welfare only in terms of efficiency and satisfaction of consumer interests, the role of institutional and non-market factors in the functioning of an economic system was a core theme of the old institutional economists. The old institutionalists focused on issues related to justice, human self-development, and labourers' welfare. Drakopoulos and Katselidis maintain that the institutionalist conception of the labour market functions is an indicative example of the uniqueness of the old Institutional approach. In contrast to the standard framework, labour market functioning does not depend only on the price mechanism, but is also affected by other key factors and parameters such as social norms, several psychological factors, and various labour institutions. After presenting the origins and method of the School, this chapter briefly compares old Institutionalism and early neoclassical economics focusing on labour market issues. It also discusses the old institutional approach with respect to collective action and labour market policy. This chapter concludes with the Ross-Dunlop debate on labour unions and the case of minimum wages policy in order to emphasize the relevance of early institutional ideas in analyzing contemporary labour market issues.

Chapter 10 by Peter Leeson and Louis Rouanet examines the relationship between Austrian economics and economic policy. It maintains that from very early in the history of the Austrian School, its members have consistently argued for a liberal position on the freedom of markets and the limits of government intervention. Apart from the grand debates over liberalism and socialism, other topics that are discussed involve the understanding of the details of business cycles and of monetary policy. The authors start by stressing that the early Austrian economists were not much concerned with policy in their academic writings, and that their policy views were not appreciably different from those of other early marginalists. Only after the socialist calculation debate did a later generation of Austrian economists progressively develop a distinctive approach to economic policy. That approach considers economic policies and institutions in light of their (in)congruity with broad principles, most notably the idea that knowledge is dispersed and incomplete. Leeson and Rouanet maintain that in the 1960s and 1970s, several insights of the later Austrian School were integrated into other "schools," such as Public Choice and New Institutional Economics. The integration, however, was not total, and an emphasis on "knowledge problems" in the context of economic policies and institutions remains a distinctive feature of the contemporary Austrian School.

Given Keynes' major influence on post-war economic policies, Chapters 11 and 12 focus on his economic thought and economic policy vision. Sheila Dow in Chapter 11 starts by arguing that Keynes made a unique contribution to thought about economic policy in three important respects. First, he spearheaded a new line of thought on macroeconomic theory and policy-making which involved a more active role for the state. Second, he was actively engaged at the centre of economic policy-making in the UK in both the domestic and international spheres. Third and drawing on his work in philosophy, the content of his macroeconomics, and his experience of policy-making, Keynes developed a distinctive approach to the relationship between theory and policy. This chapter focuses on this third aspect, illustrating it by exploring how Keynes addressed issues such as domestic and international monetary reform. Contextualizing his thought with respect to the prevailing policy discourse, Dow argues that Keynes' methodology as a theorist was geared toward facilitating policy application. Employing practical reason, Keynes paid particular attention to policy context in order to identify how the theory might need to be modified for application rather than seeking universal application. In a further departure from the emerging positivism in economics, Keynes kept on the surface the nature and implications of his political philosophy and also the role of social institutions.

In the same vein, Atsushi Komine examines the visionary legacy of Lord Keynes in Chapter 12. This chapter claims that Lord Keynes has left us two types of legacy. First, there is counter-cyclical demand simulation in the short run (pragmatism). Problems of unemployment, monopoly, and inequality could not perish even after Keynesian policies were launched. Instead, these problems survived and took on worse forms after the 1990s (the subprime/Lehman shock in 2007/2008, Big Five's and Alibaba's overwhelming market powers, and Piketty's influential work). Second, there is "socialization of investment" in the long run (idealism). This side, considered less serious until now, is loyal to Keynes' original statements. Henceforth, we must consider not only the magnitude of financial expenditure but also its contents, avoiding military Keynesianism while investing in the Green New Deal. Komine's conclusion is that these two types of Keynesian policies would be able to evolve so as to keep pace with the drastic transformation of modern capitalism.

After the two chapters on Keynes and Keynesian policies, Chapter 13 turns to the Post-War Heterodox Approaches to Economic Policy. Robert McMaster describes heterodox economics with reference to a range of schools of thought, including, but not limited to, Austrianism, Institutionalism, Post Keynesianism, and Radical Political Economy. Based on this, it is apparent that there is no single "heterodox" approach to economic policy. Indeed, policy stances transcend distinctions between heterodoxy and the mainstream, with, for example, Austrianism demonstrating a close ideological affinity to the Chicago School. This chapter attempts to provide an overview in tracing the evolution of heterodox approaches to economic policy, which emerged partly in response to developments in mainstream thinking, such as the macro consensus around New Keynesianism and neoliberalism, which was severely challenged by the 2007–2008 financial crisis. In doing so, McMaster refers to the trajectory of Post Keynesianism, arguably the most prominent heterodox school. The emergence of two high-profile policy-rich approaches, one nested in Post Keynesianism (modern monetary theory, MMT), and the other, stratification economics (SE) are discussed as illustrative of heterodox alternatives to neoliberalism.

Peter Earl, in Chapter 14, concentrates on the policy challenges from the point of view of behavioural economics, a contemporary school of economic thought which attracts increasing attention by the profession. It explores the co-evolutionary relationship between behavioural economics and economic policy via a series of short case studies that cover a wide range of policy areas and aspects of both "old" and "new" approaches to behavioural economics. First, it considers Katona's work on the macroeconomic significance of shifting consumer confidence and its significance for Keynesian demand-management policies. Second, it considers the rise and fall of the behavioural theory of the firm and X-efficiency theory and their relationship with Japanese management systems and neoliberal/managerialist policies of microeconomic reform. Third, it examines behavioural approaches to non-price competition in relation to problems of de-industrialization in the UK from the 1970s onwards. Fourth, it considers the "heuristics and biases" underpinnings of the libertarian-paternalist "nudge" approach to economic policy and contrasts the nudge philosophy with more education-based "boost" approaches to enhancing consumer well-being. Finally, Earl considers the potential role of behavioural insights in relation to contemporary environmental challenges.

The last chapter by Arne Heise examines the role of fiscal policy after the crisis and high public debts also caused by the impact of the Corona pandemic. In particular, this chapter attempts to shed some light on these developments in economic policy-making and explore the future of fiscal policy. This chapter starts by indicating the failure of the model known as New Consensus Macroeconomics (NCM). In the models that made up NCM, fiscal policy played no role – or, to be more precise, fiscal policy had to follow a balanced-budget rule, with the task of stabilizing an economy over the business cycle entrusted entirely to monetary policy (following a Taylor rule). And in the midst of the global financial crisis, Carmen Reinhart and Kenneth Rogoff (2010) proposed the figure of 90% of GDP as a threshold level for public debt which, if exceeded, would harm economic growth, leaving fiscal austerity as the best way to trigger economic recovery. Only a decade later, the economics profession now appears to have taken a very different view on fiscal policy: in order to cope with the next economic crisis, resulting from the coronavirus pandemic, most economists recommend an active fiscal policy stance and even a huge increase in debt-to-GDP levels. Heise's discussion attempts to shed some light on these developments in economic policy-making and also ponders on the future of fiscal policy.

It is hoped that the contents of this volume will contribute to the ongoing discussion concerning the relationship between economic policy and economic thought, and promote further interest to this important issue. In addition, an investigation of the various currents in the history of economic thought that is focused on economic policies might assist in further understanding current controversies pertaining to economic policies. In its pursuit, this volume brings together an international set of expert authors from Europe, North America, Australia, and Japan who aim to enrich our conception of the relationship between economic thought and economic policy.

Bibliography

Acocella, N., Bartolomeo G.D. and A. Hughes Hallett (2016). *Macroeconomic Paradigms and Economic Policy: From the Great Depression to the Great Recession*. Cambridge: Cambridge University Press.

Aslanbeigui, N. and Oakes, G. (2015). *Arthur Cecil Pigou*. Basingstoke: Palgrave Macmillan.

Backhouse, R. (2004). *The Ordinary Business of Life: A History of Economics from the Ancient World to the Twenty-First Century*. Princeton, NJ: Princeton University Press.

Bitros, G.C. and Karayiannis, A.D. (2010). 'Morality, Institutions and the Wealth of Nations: Some Lessons from Ancient Greece', *European Journal of Political Economy*, 26: 68–81.

Blaug, M. (2001). 'No History of Ideas, Please, We're Economists', *Journal of Economic Perspectives*, 15(1): 145–164.

Chatelain, J.-B. and Ralf, K. (2020). 'How Macroeconomists Lost Control of Stabilization Policy: Towards Dark Ages', *European Journal of the History of Economic Thought*, 27(6): 938–982.

Denis, A. (2016) 'Microfoundations', *Review of Political Economy*, 28(1): 134–152.

Dow, S. (2009). 'History of Thought and Methodology in Pluralist Economics Education', *International Review of Economics Education*, 8(2): 41–57.

Dow, S. (2020). 'The Methodological Role of the History of Economic Thought', in Marcuzzo, M., Deleplace, G. and Paesani, P. (eds.), *New Perspectives on Political Economy and Its History*. London: Palgrave Macmillan, pp. 21–37.

Duarte, P.G. and Lima, G.T. (eds.) (2014). *Microfoundations Reconsidered: The Relationship of Micro and Macroeconomics in Historical Perspective*. Cheltenham, Edward Elgar.

Eichengreen, B. (2020). 'Keynesian Economics: Can It Return If It Never Died?', *Review of Keynesian Economics*, 8(1): 23–35.

Emmett, R.B. (2010). 'History of Economics and History of Science: A Comparative Look at Recent Work in Both Fields', in Biddle, J.E. and Emmett, R.B. (eds.) *A Research Annual (Research in the History of Economic Thought and Methodology)*, Vol. 28, Part 1. Bingley: Emerald Group Publishing Limited, pp.71–94.

Johnson, H. (1974). 'Mercantilism: Past, Present and Future', *The Manchester School of Economic & Social Studies*, 42(1): 1–17.

Kates, S. (2013). *Defending the History of Economic Thought*. Cheltenham: Edward Elgar.

Keynes, J.M. (1926 [1973]) 'Liberalism and Labour', in *Essays in Persuasion. Collected Writings*, Vol. IX. London: Macmillan for the Royal Economic Society, pp. 307–11.

Leshem, D. (2016). 'What Did the Ancient Greeks Mean by Oikonomia', *Journal of Economic Perspectives*, 30(1): 225–231.

Lowry, T. (1987). *The Archeology of Economic Ideas*. Durham, NC: Duke University Press.

Marcuzzo, M.C. (2008). 'Is History of Economic Thought a 'Serious' Subject?', *Erasmus Journal for Philosophy and Economics*, 1(1): 107–123.

Marcuzzo, M.C. and Rosselli, A. (2002). 'Economics as History of Economics: The Italian Case in Retrospect', in E.R. Weintraub (ed.) *The Future of the History of Economics*. Durham, NC: Duke University Press, pp. 98–109.

Marshall, A. (1890 [1959]). *Principles of Economics*. London: Macmillan.

Mirowski, P. (1989). *More Heat than Light: Economics as Social Physics, Physics as Nature's Economics*. Cambridge: Cambridge University Press.

Mirowski, P. (2013). *Never Let a Serious Crisis Go to Waste: How Neoliberalism Survived the Financial Meltdown*. London: Verso.

Pearce, D. (2002). 'An Intellectual History of Environmental Economics', *Annual Review of Energy and the Environment*, 27: 57–81.

Reinhart, C.M. and Rogoff, K.S. (2010). 'Growth in a Time of Debt'; *American Economic Review*, 100(2): 573–578.

Roncaglia, A. (1996). 'Why Should Economists Study the History of Economic Thought?', *European Journal of the History of Economic Thought*, 3(2): 296–309.

Roncaglia, A. (2014). 'Should the History of Economic Thought Be Included in Undergraduate Curricula?', *Economic Thought*, 3(1): 1–9.

Sandmo, A. (2015). 'The Early History of Environmental Economics', *Review of Environmental Economics and Policy*, 9(1): 43–63.

Schabas, M. (2002). 'Coming Together: History of Economics as History of Science', in E. R. Weintraub (ed.), *The Future of the History of Economics*. Durham, NC: Duke University Press, pp. 208–225.

Schabas, M. (2006). *The Natural Origins of Economics*. Chicago, IL: The University of Chicago Press.

Stiglitz, J. (2018). 'Where Modern Macroeconomics Went Wrong', *Oxford Review of Economic Policy*, 34(1–2): 70–106.

Taylor, T. (1981). 'Incomes Policy: Justice and Freedom', *Employee Relations*, 3(5): 14–15.

Temin, P. (2006). 'The Economy of the Early Roman Empire', *Journal of Economic Perspectives*, 20(1): 133–151.

Weintraub, E.R. (ed.) (2002). *The Future of the History of Economics*. Durham, NC: Duke University Press.

2 Economic Policy in the Prehistory of Economics

A Comparative Framework

George Gotsis

Introduction

Beyond conventional approaches, one possible way of examining economic policy is to identify its potential antecedents through the lenses of history. The first issue that resonates with this perspective is to assess whether economic history has an added value in elucidating aspects of policy advice that remain underexplored, or have not yet been the object of intellectual scrutiny. The historical narratives of the past in particular are in a position to unravel policy incidents, the implications of which have been unnoticed in the mainstream, namely orthodox economic theory. Exploring such incidents would proffer a better understanding of modes of economic organization of the past that can enrich our knowledge of how premodern economies were operating in many significant respects. Economic policy in many of these cases was embedded in prevailing modes of thought, social structures and widely held beliefs, as these factors reflect historical, geographical and political contingencies.

Undoubtedly, there is a paucity of research in considering economic policies of a remote past through the lenses of the historian of economic thought and more specifically, in exploring policy issues in other than a strictly European context. The present study is intended to fill this gap, by commenting on certain policy implications that originate in indigenous philosophical worldviews, in particular in various streams of reasoning associated with the Confucian tradition that permeates typical East Asian economies such as those of China, Korea and Japan. In so doing, we employ a twofold comparative approach: first, by differentiating between three respective economies, and second, by comparing the Confucian moral tradition with that of the ancient Greek moral philosophy which is the cornerstone of subsequent developments in medieval and premodern economic ideas. Worthy to mention is that both Aristotelian and Confucian traditions are deemed as two typical cases of virtue ethics systems, centred on the priority of virtue in economic life.

This study is structured as follows. In the first section, we offer a review of the basic premises upon which the Ancient Greek and Roman economic ideas were based and discuss two typical cases of policy implementation in the Ancient Mediterranean world. We also provide a brief review of policy

DOI: 10.4324/9781003228097-2

implications in the thought of medieval scholastics. Through a subsequent change of focus on research interest epitomized in a shift in analytical locus, we proceed to review in more detail the anthropological premises of Confucian ethical ideas centred on issues such as economic motivation, virtue in economic life, rational self-interest, utility or profit-seeking. In the third section, three typical case studies embodying different concerns on policy issues are examined and reviewed. Finally, in the discussion section, we employ a twofold strategy: assessing the prospects of potential convergence and divergence between Eastern and Western streams of thought, on the one hand, and highlighting the rich diversity of policy solutions embedded in distinct societal, historical and cultural contexts, on the other.

The Locus of Research Interest: Virtuous Economic Behaviour in the West

Policy Implications in Ancient Greek and Roman Economic Thought

The ancient Greek concept of *oikonomia*, of effective household management, imbued with moral connotations, originates in Xenophon's Oeconomicus and is further elaborated in Aristotle's Politics (1253b23–28, 1259b18–21, 1278b37–39) as a sort of admonition offered to aristocratic men about the specific ways they should adopt to properly rule their wives, children and slaves. The rationale behind these instructions was that the notion of household was a constituent element of the societal order; household codes were assumed to govern city affairs, given that the ancient city was conceived in terms of an extended household (Aristotle, Politics 1253b1–4. Cf. Plato, Protagoras 318E–319A; Meno 71E; Gorgias 520E).

Similar implications are identified in other writings of the Classical and Hellenistic era, among which Dio Chrysostom's fragmentary *On Household Management* (LCL vol. 5, 348–351), Dionysius of Halicarnassus' *encomium of Rome*, in which Roman household relationships are vigorously praised (*Roman Antiquities* 2.25.4–26.4), as well as in Seneca's discussion of the respective relationships (*Ep.* 94.1–3). The concept of household management was shared by Jewish authors of the early Roman Empire. For instance, Josephus (*Against Apion* 2.181) focuses on the value of piety (*eusebeia*) as a unifying principle shaping domestic, religious and civil duties, and permeating all obligations in life.

The household management tradition was an administrative, not a market, approach to economic phenomena, its prime aim being the efficient management of resources for the achievement of desired objectives. Accordingly, the economy was not so much considered an autonomous sphere of interactions governed by market arrangements, but as a sub-system subordinated to political functions, as well as to forms of belonging, solidarity and commitment. Economic activities including taxation debts, forced extraction of goods or labour, production, distribution and trade, all were governed by power-structured institutional relationships. Typical economic decisions were substantially linked with and shaped by these institutions demarcating existing markets: by imposing, reinforcing or perpetuating social norms, these extra-market factors were able to constrain appropriate economic behaviour. The *oikonomia* tradition places an emphasis upon efficacious decision-making in situations involving allocation of scant resources: in this respect, a properly managed estate required both human capital and organizational efficiency (Lowry, 2003, pp. 11–14). In respective importance, personal competence, skills and expertise as conducive to economic efficiency were adequately taken into consideration (Aristotle, *Nicomachean Ethics* 1098a29–37, 1103a35–b5).

Economic transactions were practiced both in the family and in the marketplace through selling or buying goods and services, or hiring labour. Hence, the practice of thrift, of stewardship of property and wealth, was not simply encouraged, but mostly mandated in administering limited resources. On the contrary, wealth pursued for its own sake rather than being a means of serving a virtuous living was viewed as morally shameful, insofar as economic motivation oriented towards limitless increase of riches, tended to deteriorate into unnatural chrematistics. On the one hand, avarice was considered a root of injustice (Aristotle, *Rhetoric* 1368b15–20). On the other hand, the pursuit of wealth, indulgence in insatiable desires and consumption of luxury goods entailed moral depravity as detrimental to virtue (Aristotle, *Rhetoric* 1372b10–15, 1378b–1379a; *Politics* 1267a10–15. Cf. Plato, *Laws* 831D–918C).

In the ancient Greek *oikonomia* tradition, we conduct a virtuous life by demonstrating virtue when generating wealth: This primary emphasis on virtuous management permeates Xenophon's Oeconomicus, Pseudo-Aristotle's (Theophrastus) (*Oeconomica*, book 1), the Epicurean philosopher Philodemus of Gadara (*On the Household Economy*), and the Neopythagorean philosopher Bryson (*Oikonomikos Logos*, Management of the Estate). This model of proper stewardship of wealth is based upon the premise that all participants in household management affairs, master, wife and slaves, are urged to behave prudently, espousing virtue in conformity to their status (Leshem, 2014, p. 210). Through the primary virtue of soundness of mind (*sophrosyne*), the ancient Greek moral philosophers attempted to constrain the endless pursuit of gratification of human desires. Basic needs have to be satisfied in a context of an ethical economy that yields surplus, whereas the nature of such a surplus generated through household management reflects the quality of *oikonomia*, of administering limited resources within the sphere of the *oikos* (Leshem, 2016, p. 232).

Virtue was associated with the ideal of self-sufficiency, of not indulging in conspicuous consumption denoting an economic behaviour inimical to the cultivation of virtue. Equally importantly, schools of thought such as the Stoics and the Cyrenaic school argued in favour of considering the two extremes, wealth and poverty, as *adiaphora*, as indifferent to achieving a state of happiness and self-fulfilment (Perrotta, 2003, pp. 206, 209, 211). Beyond the realm of the household, ancient Greek philosophers considered certain policy issues that the polis had to face: the sources of municipal revenue, the omnipresence of urban poverty, the economic impact of war and peace and the competing demands between private enterprises and state intervention (Fitzgerald, 2019). The Athenian democracy was effective in realizing this ideal, primarily through supervising the efficient operation of markets without imposing price controls, as well as by assigning to wealthy citizens the obligation to undertake specific *liturgies*, the provision of public services through donations and funding of construction projects in view of furthering social welfare. Bitros and Karayiannis (2010) infer that under a proper institutional framework, the Athenian state performed all those tasks pertinent to contemporary policy-making.

From a macro-economic point of view, research interest on policy issues embraces a variety of specific cases, among which we examine two particular incidents of late Roman state intervention to coordinate market mechanisms and to address failure in the efficient operation of markets. *First*, the Roman Emperor Diocletian issued in 301 AD the *edictum de pretiis*, an edict setting maximum prices for basic commodities, the violation of which incurred death punishment. These price controls were the corollary of Diocletian's belief that the rampant inflation of the era was primarily due to speculation and hoarding behaviours, rather than debasement of currency (Kallmes, 2018). Both Diocletian and Constantine I advanced economic reforms intended to control immoderate prices and ensure social stability. The effect of such policies on stabilizing economic fluctuations was insignificant, as the imposition of maximum prices resulted in an underground economy that abolished the policy measures introduced.

Second, the endeavour of Emperor Julian to set maximum prices on grain during a famine in Antioch in 361/2 AD, was severely impeded by the speculating behaviour of the regional influential elites who cancelled the imperial policy measures through buying the cheap imported grain and then selling it at exorbitant prices. Not infrequently, wealthy landowners engaged in hoarding grain, insofar as this surplus yielded higher levels of profit in times of food shortages. During such periods, the reactions of lower strata were directed against members of the elites who failed to address expectations of public generosity and civic virtue. For instance, during a riot in the city of Prusa in the late first century AD, the prosperous landowner Dio Chrysostom was accused by the populace of hoarding grain, instead of channelling the surplus to the local market. Dio appeared to frustrate public expectations according to which prominent citizens had to contribute capital to the common fund (Merianos and Gotsis, 2018, p. 78).

Julian sought to enlarge the tax base by abolishing certain tax exempts enjoyed by the wealthy, yet to no avail (Merianos and Gotsis, 2018, p. 103). Despite these shortcomings, the early Roman Empire witnessed a period of economic prosperity during which large-scale production, exploitation of comparative advantage in competitive markets, mobility of resources and institutional stability reduced informational asymmetries and transactions costs, and induced a modest rate of economic growth (Temin, 2006; Kessler and Temin, 2007).

Policy Implications in Medieval Scholasticism

The economic ideas of medieval schoolmen in Western Europe were highly influenced by the Aristotelian virtue ethics tradition. Moral justification of profit-seeking was inserted within a code of ethics comprising tenets on prohibiting hoarding, fraud, usury and illicit means of negotiation. Economic arrangements yield a legitimate profit only because of just price variations depending upon alterations in needs and demand over time and place. Profit was justified on the basis of labour, expenses and risk (Peter Olivi, *Tractatus de emptionibus*, Q.6; Duns Scotus, *Opera Omnia*, vol.18, IV, 15, 2). Profit derived by differentials in just prices was allowed under the condition that commercial activities were not motivated by seeking financial gain, given the negative perceptions of avarice and greed in the Thomistic tradition.

The problem of the definition of the just price was solved in the context of an Aristotelian approach to economic exchanges, in which commutative justice was treated in terms of *estimatio communis*, or common estimation by virtuous persons, a concept developed on the grounds of Roman Law considerations of mutual agreement between contracting parties. The just price implies a kind of estimation that allows a certain latitude, precisely because its formation presupposes bargaining that precludes every means of economic compulsion. Monopolies were viewed as sinful because they entailed compulsion, while merchants were warned against making contracts that involved or imposed an excessive price for the buyer (Antonin of Florence, *Confessionale: De mercatoribus*, f.92r). Thomas Aquinas believed that the state should perform the economic functions of provision for the needy, maintenance of population and securing freedom and safety of exchanges. Accordingly, the right of the public authorities to regulate prices, and the concomitant attempt to control the price of labour during labour shortages, was moderated by a principle of free bargaining over the level of the just wage (or collective bargaining in the case of associations) involving a notion of justice based on proportion rather than strict arithmetical equality (Drakopoulos and Gotsis, 2004, p. 25).

Among the medieval schoolmen, Nicole Oresme addressed the widespread problem in fourteenth-century France concerning the progressive debasement of national currencies by their respective governments. The primary function of money consists in its use as a medium of exchange, a function disrupted by the debasement process, which converts money into an object of borrowing and lending. Oresme broadened the explanatory potential of previous medieval commentators on these issues by assessing the rationale for debasement, its different techniques and its devastating effects: devaluation of the purchasing power of money, inflation, loss of confidence in money as a medium of exchange and loss of monetary stability. The practices of debasement were conceived as a means of extracting negative interest on behalf of the sovereign rulers, and thus as a form of usury (precluding consent of the contracting parties, imposed on the subjects of a kingdom). Debasement yielded illicit profits to the ruler since they were extracted from the political community to whom money belonged. Accordingly, debasement was a form of economic coercion impossible to endure for long: it served mainly as a temporary measure for raising money funds for the common good. Debasement as an instrument of monetary policy was based upon perceptions of money as a kind of loan granted to governments by free people who acquired it through their labour (Oresme, *De moneta*, ch. 6, p. 10, ed. C. Johnson; Drakopoulos and Gotsis, 2004, p. 27).

The scholastics confronted the expanding practice of usury in later medieval societies in an ambivalent way: condemning lending at interest if it was oriented at consumption, but encouraging the same practice if it served productive engagements. Usury as a socially detrimental activity contradicted the basic postulates of medieval economic ethics thus, it was invested with negative connotations as a morally repugnant institution, tolerated only in the cases of *damnum emergens* (an abrupt loss suffered by the creditor by the inability of the debtor to return the loan in due time), and *lucrum cessans* (anticipating the opportunity cost of lending, by identifying opportunities for deriving profits by placing capital on a joint venture).

After discussing virtuous management primarily, yet not exclusively, in the Aristotelian and Thomistic traditions, we proceed to a shift in analytical locus by examining policy implications in the Confucian streams of moral philosophy. Our aim is to explore potential convergence and divergence between these streams of philosophical reasoning on the one hand, as well as to indicate the rich diversification within the Confucian ethical views, on the other.

A Change of Focus: Economic Evidence from East Asian Traditions of Thought

The Premises of Neo-Confucian Thought: Tensions between Virtue and Self-Interest

Like the Aristotelians and Thomists in the West, the Confucians supported a close relationship between virtue and economic behaviour. Moral excellence permeates the writings of an eminent scholar of the Fujian school, Zhu Shi (1130–1200). For him, the virtue of benevolence pertains to the heavenly realm, whereas selfishness is reflective of mundane pursuits, being an impediment to the fulfilment of our noblest aspiration, which is moral perfection (Shun, 2010, p. 182). Zhu Shi advocates a strong sense of moral duty and underscores a particular set of moral priorities based on self-restraint (Arghirescu, 2020, p. 491), thus acknowledging self-interest subject to moral constraints (Wang, 2015, p. 165). In his famous comments on Confucian classics, he emphasizes the preponderance of morality over profit-seeking, a view consonant to the Confucian focus on moral responsibility (Chun, 2012, pp. 285 and 292).

An emphasis on moral cultivation remained a distinct feature of prominent scholars during later periods, as a practical response to the ongoing prosperity that entailed amelioration of the status of entrepreneurial classes. Wang Yangming (1471–1529), a distinguished scholar during the Ming dynasty (1368–1644), lived in such conditions of economic growth claiming that virtuousness should be a core human attribute. Individuals governed by greediness succumb to covetousness, this resulting in a broadening gap between human praxis and knowledge of good and right (Knapp, 2012, p. 166).

In late medieval China and beyond, a group of scholars adopted a different view on the role of self-interest in economic life. Among them, Li Zhi (1527–1602) during the Ming dynasty (1368–1644) claims that the pursuit of self-interest emanates from human nature insofar as individuals act in accordance with this motive in economic engagements. Li Zhi's arguments on the utilitarian roots of our innate requirements are manifest in his affirming of individuality. Self-interest arises as a corollary of this mindset (Zhang, 2021, p. 443). He thus contended that avoiding harm and seeking benefit was a proclivity inherent to human nature (Zhang, 2021, p. 411).

Wang Fuzhi (1619–1692), another Neo-Confucian scholar during the early Qing dynasty (1644–1911), advances the view that the pursuit of self-interest can be morally legitimized, under the constraint that self-interest is not degenerated into a purely egoistic proclivity that urges us to satisfy our ambitions to the detriment of others. Refraining from selfish desires by adhering to ethical constraints necessitates moral cultivation: the heavenly principles can by no means be viewed in isolation from mundane goal-setting. Based on this premise, the root of the economic problem is not an integral part of the human condition, taken for granted that flourishing is a basic constituent of nature, and human desires facilitate this very process (Miller, 2012, p. 365).

In Huang Zongxi's (1610–1695) view, the denial to seek self-interest in economic occupations is far from being a rational choice, whereas for Gu Yanwu (1613–1682), the pursuit of self-interest becomes a premise of administrative activities (Wang, 2015, pp. 185–186). Li Guangdi (1642–1718), a prominent scholar of about the same period, adopted a moderate stance with respect to enlightened self-interest, yet his views substantially differ from earlier developments associated with Zhang Zhai (1020–1077), Cheng Yi (1033–1107) and Zhu Shi. For this group of scholars, corrupt behaviour originated in a lack of self-control that entailed gratification of desires detrimental to others' well-being.

A radical approach to economic motivation is found in Dai Zhen (1724–1777), a Qing dynasty scholar, who advocated rational self-interest as a particular type of self-love that has to be demarcated with respect to selfishness, the latter failing to consider the perspectives of others (Tiwald, 2010, pp. 418–419; Tiwald, 2011). Dai Zhen's views were based on more realistic psychological assumptions centred on the need for empathy, yet he did not seem to account for issues of social cooperation arising from such altruistic tendencies (Terjesen, 2013, p. 207).

The cultivation of virtues was a core issue in the reasoning of Japanese Neo-Confucians. Matsunaga Sekigo (1592–1657), a prominent philosopher of the Edo period, suggested that selfish desires should be substantially constrained in view of promoting benevolence. For him, human failure was the social corollary of self-interested dispositions. Instead, humans should embrace the virtuous mindset in accordance with the doctrine of the mean shared by both Aristotelian and Confucian traditions, the tendency to avoid excess and follow the middle way. In this respect, the virtue of propriety assumes social connotations insofar as both state and household management aim at fostering peace and economic prosperity (Tucker, 2014, p. 55).

This debate is reiterated in the writings of the distinguished philosopher Ogyū Sorai (1666–1728). In his view, humans are endowed with talents and capacities in varying degrees: Confucian conventions comprise a component of social stability secured through attaining virtue. Such rituals originate in the kindest aspirations of noble men to promote social harmony and are not reduced to binding precepts authoritatively imposed upon humans because of their perverted nature, as Xun zi contended in warring states China (476–221 BC).

A group of Japanese scholars shared the belief that self-interest cannot be denounced a priori. Among them, Dazai Shundai (1680–1747) viewed human nature as having a primary inclination towards self-interest. In sharp contrast to the argument of Ogyū Sorai on the detrimental effects of market conditions, Dazai considered self-interest not a root of worsening of the economic status of the commoners, but rather a byproduct of our wisdom to refrain from pain and pursue pleasure, the two main human instincts (Flueckiger, 2014, p. 224). In his thought arises a perennial conflict between virtue and natural disposition to gratify desires, this anthropological premise being accountable for his policy doctrine according to which authorities should follow the way of *wu we*i, of acting by non-acting, the Taoist non-interventionism in economic affairs.

A few decades later, Kaio Seiryo (1755–1817) conceded that practical reason tends to assume utilitarian connotations. Desires are entrenched in human nature that it is impossible to eradicate them. Self-interest, originating in love for one's self, cannot be subdued by the binding principles of social conventions. In the complex reality of contractual relations, profit-seeking dominates mundane pursuits, not values-based codes of conduct (Ansart, 2014, pp. 201–205). In this respect, Seireyo seeks to bridge the gap between subjective desires and public interest: the former were justified if they were channelled to the promotion of public welfare, furthering not the ruler's benefit, but the well-being of all under heaven (Ansart, 2014, p. 202). Economically detrimental activities were significantly curtailed because of the institutional arrangements that reflected the omnipotence of the virtue of propriety. Compliance with rituals was mandatory, otherwise, the ensuing sanctions imposed upon those who violated social order were expected to make individuals less prone to indulge in selfish motives inimical to others' well-being. This view remains at odds with that held by Oshio Haihachiro (1793–1837) who envisaged a society grounded on the virtues of sincerity and honesty, in conformity to Confucian ideals.

Three Exemplary Cases of East Asian Economic Policy Reforms

The Song Dynasty Economic Reforms: In Defence of State Intervention

As already argued, the Song dynasty era (960–1279) witnessed an ardent debate on whether the motive of self-interest can be socially sanctioned. For Zhou Dunyi (1016–1073), an eminent scholar of the Lianzi School during the Northern Song dynasty (960–1127), the elucidation of the exact relationship between morality and self-interest is found to be at the forefront of his moral philosophy. In his view, humans are urged to refrain from self-interested pursuits, in compliance with the universal precepts of justice. Zhang Shi (1133–1181), another distinguished scholar of the Southern Song dynasty (1127–1279), differentiates between actions dictated by moral righteousness, and activities focusing solely on promoting self-interested pursuits. In this perspective, economic justice was in alignment with the precept of heaven, whereas the pursuit of individual benefit was tantamount to the gratification of selfish desires perceived as threatening social cohesion. More specifically, this type of morality was supportive of public policies that fostered impartiality in view of improving community bonds and societal welfare. Public morality nurtures humaneness, which is in turn reflected in policies promoting quality of life and social justice (Arghirescu, 2020, pp. 489–490).

A group of Neo-Confucian scholars during the Song dynasty, Li Gou (1009–1059), Chen Liang (1143–1194) and Ye Shi (1150–1223) in particular, was holding the belief that deriving utility from satisfying one's needs was far from being denounced. On the contrary, the emphasis on utility did not contravene the cultivation of morality, in conformity to the principles set forth by the Yongjia school of Neo-Confucian philosophy. Early Chinese precursors of utilitarian views advocated a clear delineation between market and state, arguing in favour of certain restrictions on state intervention in economic life, in view of reinforcing competitive market forces. Beyond Ye Shi, proponents of these views were Qiu Jun (1421–1495), a scholar on the art of governance who claimed that the state should intervene in markets only in times of an impending crisis, as well as Huang Zongzi (1610–1695) and Tang Zhen (1630–1704). In this vein of reasoning, deterioration of public management and ineffective administration was primarily due to the fact that men of virtue refrained from engaging in these occupations that appeared as contravening the rule of morality: as a result, individuals of ambiguous moral character occupied state positions (Wang, 2015, pp. 180–181).

A second group of scholars supported the policy reforms inaugurated by the Northern Song dynasty, the most eminent proponents of which were Wang Anshi (1021–1086) and Lu Zuquian (1137–1181). These scholars acknowledged the fact that the state was not deprived of the ability to exploit the emerging opportunities from rapid economic growth, expansion of monetary economy and proliferation of lucrative commercial exchanges. In so doing, the administrative authorities had any plausible cause of shaping state monopolies, insofar as augmenting state profits was viewed as the ultimate goal of an economically efficient policy. Lu Zuquian, for instance, was not hesitant in defending state enrichment as a socially sanctioned goal, fact that was reminiscent of later theoretical developments associated with the rise of mercantilist policies in early modern Europe (Marchal, 2010, pp. 209–210).

Wang Anshi never ceased to insist that public management and more precisely, policies seeking to strengthen effective demand through public expenditure were critical in reducing unemployment rates. This objective would be feasible through policy-making intended to support state investment through large-scale financial projects. These views were at odds with the ideas of both Zhu Shi and the Cheng brothers who systematically opposed the reformations introduced by the Song dynasty on the grounds of the argument that such policies encouraged the pursuit of self-interest through engaging in profitable, yet morally ambiguous behaviours. In their opinion, these policies encouraged motives inimical to the manifestations of virtue.

Interestingly, Wang Anshi highly valued public investment in infrastructure that enabled the unfolding of latent productive capacities. Moreover, he rejected policies of fiscal austerity by placing an emphasis on the need for public expenditure as a means of economic expansion. To address the lack of sufficient resources for undertaking such policies, he suggested a type of management that aimed at motivating farmers to raise agricultural produce by reforming the loan system through introducing low-interest-rate loans, in view of restricting outright exploitation. In this respect, state intervention in the functioning of markets was a prerequisite for addressing economic stagnation and depression, as well as for alleviating poverty. These views on unemployment relief through state control may be considered a predecessor of Keynesian theories on the necessity of intervening in the operation of markets. Zhao and Drechsler (2018, p. 1252) plausibly arrived at the conclusion that in order to address issues of economic instability, Wang Anshi restored the Chinese state into a countervailing power to the private sector. In so doing, he managed to control interest rate and consumption by increasing government spending on investment, as well as by supporting the inducement to invest and the propensity to consume in order to enable a state of full employment. These endeavours are reminiscent of Keynes' policy doctrines implemented in Western economies centuries later.

Beyond fiscal policies, Zhao Shen (1127–1194 AD), reigning as Emperor Xiaozong (1162–1189), introduced a monetary policy to stabilize the value of money. Anticipating, albeit intuitionally, the quantity theory of money, Emperor Xiaozong made use of both gold and silver to maintain an appropriate quantity of paper money in circulation, a type of policy which exerted a major influence on subsequent reforms, in particular in late imperial China (Xueyi, Yaguang, and Whalley, 2013, p. 103). This proliferation of monetary transactions especially during the Mongol Yuan dynasty (1279–1368) was not sustainable (Onge, 2017). In 1430, the Ming dynasty made the Chinese economy dependent upon imported silver as the principal medium of exchange. As Wang Fuzhi (1619–1692) claimed, silver coinage should be supported because of its longer duration and easiness of storing compared to bronze coins, whereas Gu Yanwu (1613–1682) was opposing the restoration of paper money as an auxiliary mode of currency complementing bronze coinage (Horesh, 2013, p. 390). Paper money dominated the monetary transactions in the late Qing dynasty (1842–1911), a period in which China witnessed an acute outflow of silver due to an adverse balance of payments (Horesh, 2020).

Economic Policy Reforms in Late Joseon: In Defence of State Beneficence

Korean scholars made a significant contribution to issues of administrative ethics. Philosophers like Jeong Dojeon (1342–1398), Jo Gwangjo (1482–1520) and Sŏ Kyŏngdŏk (1489–1546) expanded their scope on problems of public administration, focusing on the need for establishing an ideal state grounded on social harmony. Sŏ Kyŏngdŏk claimed that humans seek to find an equilibrium situation, avoiding pain and discomfort in their social interactions. This is practically feasible by maintaining rituals and adhering to social conventions that realize our innate disposition towards refraining from psychological burden and attaining a state of inner harmony (Kim, 2019, pp. 142–144).

During the early seventeenth century, Korean society witnessed drastic changes due to both external and internal factors, fact that necessitated policy reforms in many significant respects. Japanese and Manchu invasions to Korea in 1592 and 1636, respectively, resulted in a progressive deterioration of standards of living, a situation severely aggravated by economic stagnation, corruption and extant inequalities in income and wealth distribution. In such a rapidly changing environment Korean literati such as Kim Chip (1574–1656), Song Junkil (1606–1672), Song Siyŏl (1607–1689), Pak Sech'ae (1631–1695) and Yun Chŭng (1629–1714) placed an emphasis on the need for cohesiveness achieved through attendance of Confucian propriety, yet ritual order alone did not suffice to stabilize the economy. Korean society was in need of more drastic policy measures that would be able to alleviate extreme poverty, mitigate sharp inequalities and create the prerequisites for economic prosperity.

In this direction, a group of scholars among which Kim Yuk (1580–1658), Yu Hyòngwòn (1622–1673), Yi Ik (1681–1763), Bak Jiwon (1737–1805) and Bak Jega (1750–1815) focused on the priority of practical learning (in Korean, *Silhak*) over metaphysical contemplation. For the scholars of the *Silhak* School, the introduction of economic reforms was more than evident. Kim Yuk was the main proponent of a major tax and fiscal reform known as *daedongbeop*. Yu Hyòngwòn, just to mention another one of these scholars, claimed that the ongoing economic transformations of the era necessitated administrative reforms that would meet the challenges emerging from rapid monetization of the economy, high degree of division of labour and more importantly, lack of coordination of market transactions (Palais, 2015). Rather than stressing the need for economic efficiency, this reform was justified on the grounds of Confucian ethical principles that emphasized benevolence as a sound foundation of policy reforms (Yoo, 2014).

The previous tribute system incurred transaction costs and illegal profit-making reflected in the process of tax collection. Under the new taxation system of abolishing tributary payment, the peasantry had to pay taxes in kind, this system relieving the needy from excessive tax burden. After the adoption of *daedongbeop*, there was a significant expansion in state granaries the inspection of which was assigned to the *hwangok*, a state institution of civilian famine relief. This premodern welfare state substantially differs from Western counterparts primarily in that "the Confucian welfare system was perceived as an outcome of the ruler's benevolence rather than of the people's entitlement" (Kang and Choi, 2016, p. 435), fact that explicates its potential limits. Albeit this managerial ethic was advanced to balance intervention in, and support for, the market, it was heavily dependent upon the ruler's benefaction in terms of a more equitable distribution of wealth (Kang and Choi, 2017, p. 127). Kang and Choi (2016, p. 431) plausibly noticed that lessening people's tax burden was entrenched in the Confucian ideal of state beneficence: establishment of financial agencies and granary construction was viewed as a manifestation of the *minben* ideal, a participatory human rights community that nurtures dignity and self-respect.

The most eminent scholar of the Joseon period was Dasan Jeong Yakyong (1762–1836), an ardent supporter of an in-depth reform of the rigid institutional structures of the era. More specifically, his views on the political art of statecraft (*Gyeongron*) involved the planning of a transparent and resilient bureaucratic system accounting for the rationalization of contractual relationships and more importantly, for addressing the peril of economic stagnation (Baek and Lee, 2014; Lee, 2016, pp. 190–191). For Dasan, public management reflected the Confucian virtue of moral integrity, refraining from extravagance in state expenses, and displaying thrift in administering scant resources. This policy aimed at the attainment of social stability understood in terms of a subtle balance between virtues on the one hand, and the need for considering pragmatic aspirations evidenced in economic engagements, on the other (Kim, 2020).

Economic Policy Reforms in Edo Japan: The State as Balancing Competing Interests

During the Edo period, Sai On (1682–1761), a prominent state official in the kingdom of Ryukyu, contended that morality was not inimical to the goal of material prosperity. Inspired by Neo-Confucianism, Sai On placed an emphasis on the moral excellence of government officials, yet he never ceased to acknowledge the need for considering the self-interested motivation that permeated everyday occupations (Smits, 2014, p. 135). Moreover, it seemed that he was aware of the difficulties accompanying any attempt to regulate economic activities. This pragmatist thought helped him adopt a more positive stance towards the profit motive, fact that revealed the potentialities, but also the limits of Japanese Neo-Confucianism (Smits, 2014, p. 137).

Economic activities in late feudal Japan were undertaken by prominent elite families of landlords who contributed to economic growth, prosperity and accumulation of wealth, subject to the rigid political constraints of economic isolationism (McNabb, 2016, pp. 191–192). The enclosure decree of the Edo period (1636), in combination with the prevailing negative attitudes towards the activities of middle-status merchants, was posing an impediment to social welfare. Perceptions of dishonest merchants, corrupt state officials and close entrepreneurial networks based on kinship or strategic alliances, worsened the situation. Oh and Koh (2016, p. 407) extrapolate the conclusion that in Edo Japan the state resorted to policy measures to perpetuate particular authority structures and social networks that ultimately controlled state institutions. Accordingly, varying ethical discourses were employed in order to justify group interests within the public realm which entailed changes in economic institutions reflecting consecutive shifts from one mode of production to another (manorial, market, mercantile, entrepreneurial).

In such an ambiguous environment, Confucian literati provided permeating insights on the need for introducing coping mechanisms to meet emerging challenges. Policies of state non-interventionism were proclaimed by certain scholars of the era. Dazai Shundai (1680–1747) for instance, devoted a significant part of his philosophical essays to providing suggestions on the economic organization of feudal Japan, considering entrepreneurial activities as the source of creating surplus and generating wealth. These goals were realized by getting a comparative advantage in a politically limited non-domestic trade either through exchanges primarily with other Confucian countries, mainly Korea and China, or through transfer of surplus from areas of affluence to geographical areas facing scarcity problems (Smits, 2014, p. 136).

The changing socio-political landscape of late Edo Japan urged policy reforms intended to establish a more liberal institutional framework, the main goal of which being not the promotion of self-interested aspirations of the rising entrepreneurial class, but its perceived contribution to the strengthening of the nation's welfare and international power (Sagers, 2006, p. 93). The global challenges of the period necessitated policy reforms, yet the Confucian conviction that state officials should act by channelling self-interest to socially beneficial outcomes did not decline. In fact, the Confucian tenets according to which the scholarly elites assumed a moral obligation to protect the lower social strata and in particular the indigent and needy, had not lost their influence on the intellectual scene of the era (Sagers, 2006, p. 105).

However, it was with Ogyū Sorai (1666–1728) that this line of reasoning was challenged. According to Sorai, policy reforms should be evaluated not on the grounds of their adherence to universal principles, but on their appropriateness to address persistent challenges (Sagers, 2006, pp. 21–22). This adjustment of economic policies to the logic of circumstances resulted in a gradual process of decoupling political economy from the ethical authority of Confucian ideals. The intellectual legacy of Ogyū Sorai was appropriated by scholars like Fukuzawa Yukizhi (1836–1901), Nishi Amane (1829–1897) and Tsuda Mamichi (1829–1903) who were in a position to close the gap between Confucian virtue ethics and the preponderance of public utility (Paramore, 2016, p. 126). The endeavour of reconciliation of Japanese Neo-Confucianism with advanced market structures culminated in the writings of Shibusawa Eiichi (1840–1931), in particular in his portrayal of the ideal, innovative, ethical entrepreneur (Sagers, 2018).

Discussion and Concluding Comments: An East-West Perspective

In this study, we included a discussion of aspects of policy-making in the philosophical thought of Neo-Confucian *literati* in three distinct streams of thought, Chinese, Korean and Japanese Neo-Confucianism. We noticed a rich diversity of ideas regarding economic motivation among these scholars, yet we can divide them into two major groups, despite the wide heterogeneity in basic premises regarding the justification of economic activities. The first group favours a virtues-based approach to economic motivation according to which virtue is grounded on conceptions of the good life, a mode of thinking familiar to Western and more specifically, to Aristotelian and Thomistic approaches to the economic sphere, as indicated in the first section of this chapter. The second group of scholars adopts a more pragmatic stance on economic motives, acknowledging the role of enlightened self-interest in orientating economic behaviours. Yet, both groups seem to realize that the pursuit of self-interest should be socially beneficial, thus channelling profit-seeking to the promotion of public welfare.

We in turn examined three case studies on policy-making in three typical societies of the Confucian cluster, China, Korea and Japan. We argued that among those cases, the introduction of *daedongbeop in* seventeenth-century Joseon was a policy deeply entrenched in core Confucian values of genuine concern for prosperity and social welfare. Undoubtedly, the enactment of this policy reform originated in pragmatic reasons, yet its ideological justification reflected typical Confucian perceptions of good government. On the contrary, economic policies in Edo Japan were subject to constant adjustment to the prevailing interests that dominated production and distribution of goods. As a result, pragmatic concerns and more specifically, balancing competing interests or supporting certain groups while discouraging others, affected the scope and prospects of policy-making. Wang Anshi's policy reforms in Song dynasty China in support of government expenditure on public investment reflected the same concern for social welfare as in Korea Joseon, yet its ideological basis cannot be reduced to Confucian ideals of virtuous administration: it stemmed from affirming the desirability, feasibility and efficiency of state intervention in the emerging market structures of the era.

In this respect, two important issues arise that are worthy of further consideration. The first revolves around the role of virtue in economic life, underscored by both Aristotelianism and Confucianism. Confucian virtues are enacted in socially beneficial governance structures that facilitate self-fulfilment. This ideal emerges in situations commensurate with the principle of social harmony that is feasible when human action is dictated by the doctrine of the mean. Through refraining from excess, human thriving stems from harmonizing individual and civil interests, given that for the Confucians the state acts as an extended family that enables economic prosperity (Berthrong, 2010, p. 172). Through similar lenses, Li Guangjin (1549–1623) of the School of Principle expanded on these issues, by perceiving the ideal merchant as a concealed scholar, in support of a more positive evaluation of trade activities (Fu, 2020).

As noted earlier, virtuous economic behaviour was highlighted in the context of ancient Greek economic ideas. Tensions between virtue and wealth were mitigated through benevolence, an act of channelling surplus to networks of friendship in view of allowing leisure time devoted to politics or engaging in philosophical contemplation by seeking *eudaimonia*. Moreover, the surplus generated through the administration of the *oikos* was channelled to acts of civic benefaction, from which the entire political community substantially benefited (Leshem, 2013, p. 51). Despite the efficiency and competency notions akin to modern management, the ancient art of *oikonomia* was subordinated to ethical concerns, governed by an administrative ethics conducive to higher goals. The attainment of self-sufficiency (*virtuous autarkeia*) facilitates human thriving. *Oikonomike techne* was a sort of ruling art that reduced macroeconomics to an implementation of microeconomics at a higher scale (Alvey, 2011, p. 721).

Interestingly, a similar administrative ethics is typical of the Neo-Confucian stream of thought. For instance, the Korean philosopher Li Eonjeok (1491–1553), drawing on the Confucian doctrine of the mean, of following the middle road between two extremes, contends that the art of managing state affairs was the logical consequence of household management tradition, an idea reminiscent of the Aristotelian notion of *oikonomia*. For Yi Hwang (1551–1570), the virtue of wisdom remains the foundation of good government: this scholar underscores the importance of moral dignity, sharing the Confucian belief that intrinsic motivation was more effective than social sanctions or coercive mechanisms of political surveillance. In this vein of reasoning, Yi Yi (1538–1584) insisted on reforms aiming at ameliorating the moral character of state officials. Refraining from selfish desires remains the cornerstone upon which administering public affairs should be based (Jeong, 2016, pp. 78–79).

Certain strands of thought in Chinese moral literature appear to be more tolerant of the self-interested nature of individuals than their ancient Greek counterparts. For Ye Shi (1150–1223), public management must be minimized, through encouraging people to pursue their own agendas (Ma, 2014, p. 162). Though certain policies have been the object of both traditions, ancient Chinese reasoning is more replete with macro-economic policy implications than the ancient Greek economic thought. This is explained by the fact that the household management tradition, which is microeconomic in nature, occupies dominant position in the thought of the Greeks. Undoubtedly, ancient Greek ideas are not bereft of issues that refer to the macro-level, yet Confucian traditions are more concerned with problems of inflation, unemployment, total expenditure and economic stability due to their wider scope focusing on the empire level.

Worthy to mention is the heterogeneity of policy recommendations of Confucian scholars. Beyond Wang Anshi's support for state intervention, other literati took a different stance: Mencius (372–288 BC), for instance, was an ardent proponent of freedom in economic exchanges, claiming that natural law dictates human activity. He thus discouraged mandatory state intervention in economic affairs, insofar as such policies would induce more harm than benefit to the entire society (Ma, 2014, p. 156). In this respect, the ruler should secure an equitable distribution of income through moderate taxes and government expenditures. The famous historian of the Western Han dynasty Sima Qian (ca 145–89 BC) denounced excesses in state intervention, insofar as undertaking profitable engagements should be left to private entrepreneurs (Ma, 2014, p. 159). He contended that in the absence of state intervention, the market could effectively operate: if the state refrained from hindering business activities, prosperity would be secured (Sun, 2014, pp. 108–109). Sun (2014, p. 110) pointed out that pervasive profit-seeking revealed the ceaseless pursuit of wealth and the need for social betterment as driving forces sufficient to maintain division of labour by decentralized exchange.

Like the Western scholastics, the Ming dynasty scholar Qiu Jun (1421–1495) condemned state monopolies because such policy measures resulted in higher prices, lower quality of goods, decrease in consumption and deterioration of people's well-being (Ma, 2014, p. 164). In this respect, economic policies should motivate people to increase production, ensuring a more equitable allocation of wealth. Confucian scholars appeared in certain instances to be more efficacious than their Western counterparts in influencing state decisions because the Neo-Confucians often held official positions in the administrative mechanisms of the era. This fact facilitated them to better implement their policy doctrines under enlightened monarchy.

The second issue to be examined is the relative weight attributed to ethical and pragmatic concerns with respect to policy reforms. Employing a comparative framework, we infer that in Edo Japan, the justificatory basis of such reforms was grounded in pragmatic reasons reflecting the complexity of the economic structures of the era. Administrative policies had to harness aspirations of economic agents perceived as threatening existing hierarchies of power. Rapid social mobility viewed as potentially subversive of established hierarchies and rigid power structures was far from being countenanced or approved. On the contrary, in Joseon Korea, the advancement of economic reforms was deemed a moral obligation of the ruling class, a duty embedded in the overarching ideological entity shaped by Confucian ideals of virtuous governance. In Song dynasty China, imperial officials reasoned that engaging in commerce was integral to the immanent pattern of the cosmos, given that such occupations were viewed as enduringly supportive of general well-being. However, the attempt to embed financial transactions in moral learning fell short of being sustainable in the long run (De Pee, 2018).

Wang Anshi's advocacy of state intervention in Song dynasty China reveals the ongoing transformations in a rapidly changing environment that had to be addressed by the imperial court for reasons of both stability and economic prosperity. Wang Anshi was deemed an expert in financial management, like Liu Yan (718–780 AD) who had pursued a prudent monetary policy under the Tang dynasty (619–907 AD). At that time, a set of policy measures intended to increase state revenues by reducing the economic power of influential groups was initiated. In fact, economic interactions were undergoing an internal change due to a variety of factors: expansion of monetary economy, innovation in economic exchanges through the introduction of paper money, adjustments in fiscal policy, addressing unemployment and so forth.

The Northern Song imperial court increased money circulation, without affecting the price level. Dong and Gong (2014) identified this paradox and noticed that a steady increase in the velocity of money, comparable to that of early modern Europe, was accompanied by an increase in total output, reflecting a process of economic development. Liu (2015) argues that the Song dynasty inaugurated a sustainable tax state under three aspects: monetization of the economy, indirect taxation and professionalization in tax administration. What ensued was the transition to a fiscal state on the basis of a new relationship between public revenues, expenditure, and credit instruments (Liu, 2015, p. 73), having a significant impact on economic growth (Von Glahn, 2020). Policy reforms embodied contingent and historical factors: policies encouraging increased output through public expenditure to alleviate poverty co-existed with policies supportive of free market by stimulating individuals to behave accordingly (Zanasi, 2015).

In sum, we argued that policy measures based on values that fostered an entwinement between private interests and morality were far from being uncommon in the premodern East Asian economies. Both Aristotelian and Confucian traditions involve remarkable examples of widely differing programmes for economic policy based on varying behavioural assumptions and theoretical premises, which share the core features of a coherent discourse worthy of meticulous comparative consideration. Further research on policy issues stemming from these comprehensive worldviews that will substantially broaden and deepen our understanding of the intercultural encounter of East and West, is appreciated and warmly encouraged.

Bibliography

Ansart, O. (2014). The philosophical moment between Ogyū Sorai and Kaiho Seiryō: Indigenous modernity in the political theories of eighteenth-century Japan? *In*: Huang, C. and Tucker, J.(eds.), *Dao Companion to Japanese Confucian Philosophy* (pp.183–214). Dordrecht: Springer.

Alvey, J.E. (2011). The ethical foundations of economics in ancient Greece, focusing on Socrates and Xenophon. *International Journal of Social Economics, 38*(8):714–733.

Arghirescu, D. (2020). Zhu Xi's ideal of moral politics: Theory and practice. *In*: Ng, K. and Huang, Y. (eds.), *Dao Companion to Zhu Xi's Philosophy* (pp.465–497). Cham: Springer.

Back, Y. (2016). Sages and the rest of us: The views of Zhu Xi and Jeong Yakyong. *In*: Back, Y. and Ivanhoe, P.J. (eds.), *Traditional Korean Philosophy: Problems and Debates* (pp.147–176). London: Rowman and Littlefield.

Baek, M. and Lee, Y. (2014). Chŏng Yagyong's political philosophy: Kyŏngse Yup'yo and Mongmin Simsŏ's arguments on state governance. *Sungkyun Journal of East Asian Studies, 14*(1):111–141.

Baker, D. (2019). What is Korean about Korean Confucianism? *In*: Ro, Y. (ed.), *Dao Companion to Korean Confucian Philosophy* (pp.47–71). Dordrecht: Springer.

Berthrong, J. (2010). Zhu Xi's cosmology. *In:* Makeham, J. (ed.), *Dao Companion to Neo-Confucian Philosophy* (pp.153–175). Berlin: Springer.Bitros, G.C. and Karayiannis, A.D. (2010). Morality, institutions and the wealth of nations: Some lessons from ancient Greece. *European Journal of Political Economy, 26*(1):68–81.

Chun, S. (2012). *Major Aspects of Chinese Religion and Philosophy: Dao of Inner Saint and Outer King*. Berlin/Heidelberg: Springer.

De Pee, C. (2018). Circulation and flow: Immanent metaphors in the financial debates of northern Song China (960–1127 CE). *History of Science, 56*(2):168–195.

Dong, B. and Gong, J. (2014). Velocity of money and economic development in medieval China: The case of Northern Song. *Review of Development Economics, 18*(2):203–217.

Drakopoulos, S. and Gotsis, G.N. (2004). A meta-theoretical assessment on the decline of scholastic economics. *History of Economics Review, 40*:19–45.

Fitzgerald, J.T. (2019). Early Greek economic thought. *In:* Hollander, D.B., Blanton, T.R and Fitzgerald, J.T. (eds.), *The Extramercantile Economies of Greek and Roman Cities: New Perspectives on the Economic History of Classical Antiquity* (pp.29–50). London: Taylor and Francis.

Flueckiger, P. (2014). Human nature and the way in the philosophy of Dazai Shundai. *In:* Huang, C.C. and Tucker, J.A. (eds.), *Dao Companion to Japanese Confucian Philosophy* (pp.215–232). Dordrecht: Springer.

Fu, C.R. (2020). Scholars in disguise: The Cheng-Zhu neo-Confucian reappraisal of the merchant class in late Ming. *Ming Studies, 82*:23–47.

Horesh, N. (2013). 'Cannot be fed on when starving': An analysis of the economic thought surrounding China's earlier use of paper money. *Journal of the History of Economic Thought, 35*(3):373–395.

Horesh, N. (2020). The monetary system of China under the Qing dynasty. *In:* Battilossi, S., Cassis, Y. and Yago, K (eds.), *Handbook of the History of Money and Currency* (pp.549–570). Singapore: Springer.

Jeong, W. (2016). Does the neo-Confucianism of the Chosŏn dynasty belong to the Cheng-Zhu school? Rethinking the intellectual history of Chosŏn through the philosophical tradition of Yi I (1538–1584). *Journal of Korean Religions,* 7(1):67–92.

Kallmes, K. (2018). Imperial monetary policy and social reaction in third century Rome. *Journal des Economistes et des Etudes Humaines, 24*(1). https://doi.org/10.1515/jeeh-2017-0002.

Kang, S. and Choi, J. (2016). Confucian business ethics in Korea: Pre-modern welfare state. *Asia Pacific Business Review, 22*(3):422–438.

Kang, S. and Choi, J. (2017). Business ethics and government intervention in the market in Joseon. *In:* Oh, I. and Park, G.S. (eds.), *The Political Economy of Business Ethics in East Asia: A Historical and Comparative Perspective* (pp.113–130). Amsterdam: Elsevier.

Kessler, D. and Temin, P. (2007). The organization of the grain trade in the early Roman Empire. *Economic History Review, 60*(2):313–332.

Kim, J.Y. (2019). Sŏ Kyŏngdŏk and the rise of the philosophy of *Ki* 氣. *In*: Ro, Y. (eds.) *Dao Companion to Korean Confucian Philosophy* (pp.135–158). Dordrecht: Springer.

Kim, S. (2020). Reversing the stream: Virtue politics and moral economy in Neo-Confucian Korea. *Dao, 19*(1):69–90.

Knapp, K. (2012). The Confucian tradition in China. *In:* Nadeau, R.L. (ed.), *The Wiley Blackwell Companion to Chinese Religions* (pp.147–169). Oxford: Blackwell.

Lee, H.S. (2016). The neo-Confucianism of the Joseon dynasty: Its theoretical foundation and main issues. *Asian Studies, 4*(1):165–194.

Lee, Y. and Baek, M. (2018). Spirit of Confucianism and characteristics of Zhu Xi learning in Chosŏn Korea, focusing on Confucius, Zhu Xi and Yi Hwang. *Taiwan Journal of East Asian Studies, 15*(2):101–127.

Leshem, D. (2013). Oikonomia redefined. *Journal of the History of Economic Thought, 35*(1):43–61.

Leshem, D. (2014). The ancient art of economics. *European Journal of the History of Economic Thought, 21*(2):201–229.

Leshem, D. (2016). Retrospectives: What did the ancient Greeks mean by oikonomia? *Journal of Economic Perspectives, 30*(1):225–231.

Liu, W.G. (2015). The making of a fiscal state in Song China, 960–1279. *Economic History Review, 68*(1):48–78.

Lowry, S.T. (2003). Ancient and medieval economics. *In*: Samuels, W.J., Biddle, J.E. and Davis, J.B. (eds.), *A Companion to the History of Economic Thought* (pp.11–27). Oxford: Blackwell.

Ma, T. (2014). Confucian thought on the free economy. *In:* Lin, C., Peach, T. and Fang, W. (eds.), *The History of Ancient Chinese Economic Thought* (pp.153–165). London: Routledge.

Marchal, K. (2010). Lu Zuqian's political philosophy. *In:* Makeham, J. (ed.), *Dao Companion to Neo-Confucian Philosophy* (pp.197–222). Berlin: Springer.

McNabb D.E. (2016). Tokugawa isolation, commerce, and industry, 1603–1868. *In*: *A Comparative History of Commerce and Industry* (Vol. I, pp.181–197). New York: Macmillan.

Merianos, G. and Gotsis, G. (2018). *Managing Financial Resources in Late Antiquity: Greek Fathers' Views on Hoarding and Saving.* London: Palgrave MacMillan.

Miller, J. (2012). Nature. *In:* Nadeau, R.L. (ed.), *The Wiley Blackwell Companion to Chinese Religions* (pp.349–368). Oxford: Blackwell.

Perrotta, C. (2003). The legacy of the past: Ancient economic thought on wealth and development. *European Journal of the History of Economic Thought, 10*(2):177–229.

Oh, I. and Koh, Y. (2016). The state as a regulator of business ethics in Edo Japan: The Tokugawa authority structure and private interests. *Asia Pacific Business Review, 22*(3):397–410.

Onge, P.S. (2017). How paper money led to the Mongol conquest money and the collapse of Song China. *Independent Review, 22*(2):223–244.

Palais, J.B. (2015). *Confucian Statecraft and Korean Institutions: Yu Hyongwon and the Late Choson Dynasty.* Washington, DC: University of Washington Press.

Paramore, K. (2016). *Japanese Confucianism: A Cultural History.* Cambridge: Cambridge University Press.

Sagers, J.H. (2006). *Origins of Japanese Wealth and Power: Reconciling Confucianism and Capitalism, 1830–1885.* New York: MacMillan.

Sagers, J.H. (2018). *Confucian Capitalism: Shibusawa Eiichi, Business Ethics, and Economic Development in Meiji Japan.* London: Macmillan.

Shun, K. (2010). Zhu Xi's moral psychology. *In:* Makeham, J. (ed.), *Dao Companion to Neo-Confucian Philosophy* (pp.177–195). Berlin: Springer.

Smits, G. (2014). Making destiny in the kingdom of Ryukyu. *In*: Huang, C. and Tucker, J. (eds.), *Dao Companion to Japanese Confucian Philosophy* (pp.109–140). Dordrecht: Springer.

Sun, G.Z. (2014). The economics of the division of labour in early Chinese literature: With particular comparison to the ancient Greek thought. *The European Journal of the History of Economic Thought, 23*(1):102–126.

Temin, P. (2006). The economy of the early Roman Empire. *Journal of Economic Perspectives, 20*(1):133–151.

Terjesen, A. (2013). Is empathy the 'one thread' running through Confucianism. *In:* Angle, S. and Slote, M. (eds.), *Virtue Ethics and Confucianism* (pp.201–208). London: Routledge.

Tiwald, J. (2010). Dai Zhen on human nature and moral cultivation. *In:* Makeham, J. (ed.), *Dao Companion to Neo-Confucian Philosophy* (pp.399–422). Berlin: Springer

Tiwald, J. (2011). Dai Zhen's defense of self-interest. *Journal of Chinese Philosophy, 38*(S1):29–45.

Tucker, J.A. (2014). The meanings of words and Confucian political philosophy: A study of Matsunaga Sekigo's *Ethics. In:* Huang, C.C. and Tucker, J.A. (eds.), *Dao Companion to Japanese Confucian Philosophy* (pp.31–68). Dordrecht: Springer.

Von Glahn, R. (2020). Modalities of the fiscal state in imperial China. *Journal of Chinese History, 4*(1):1–29.

Wang, X. (2015). *On Moral Capital*. Berlin/Heidelberg: Springer.
Xueyi, Z., Yaguang, Z. and Whalley, J. (2013). Monetary theory and policy from a Chinese historical perspective. *China Economic Review, 26*(1):89–104.
Yoo, K.J. (2014). Foundation and management of the Joseon dynasty: Revisiting Jeong do-Jeon's political philosophy based on the royal record of Joseon dynasty. *Asian Studies, 2*(2): 127–143.
Zanasi, M. (2015). Frugality and luxury: Morality, market, and consumption in late imperial China. *Frontiers of History in China, 10*(3):457–485.
Zhang, X. (2021). *History of Chinese Philosophy in the Ming Dynasty*. Singapore: Springer.
Zhao, X. and Drechsler, W. (2018). Wang Anshi's economic reforms: Proto-Keynesian economic policy in Song dynasty China. *Cambridge Journal of Economics, 42*(5):1239–1254.

3 Mercantilism

A Project for Development

Cosimo Perrotta

Introduction

In this chapter, we will consider the economic policy of early Modern Age.[1] In that period the new economy (capitalism) – based on private investment and the pursuit of profit – took off and replaced the feudal economy. The economists of that period are generically called mercantilists, following Smith's expression "the mercantilist system" (Smith 1776, book IV, ch. 1). The chapter has the following structure: we will first discuss the nature of mercantilism (Section 1), then hint at the historical factors which generated it (Section 2). In Section 3, we examine mercantilism's first period when the principles were elaborated; in Section 4, we see how these principles became hegemonic. Then we will examine three major developments of later mercantilism (Section 5) and conclude on the importance of mercantilist-like policies today (Section 6).

What Mercantilists Really Thought

Mercantilism was not, properly, a school of thought. Rather it was a coherent set of norms of economic policy, with precise goals. Although this approach was dominant only during the seventeenth century, it was active at least for two and a half centuries, from Starkey (1529–1530), who first fixed some basic principles, up to Steuart (1767), who provided a systematic theory. Even after Steuart, late followers can be found up to the first decades of the nineteenth century.

The mercantilist policies aimed at extending manufactures in order to absorb the huge unemployment of the time and to enrich the country. Manufactures were aggregates of numerous wage workers in which the multi-task work of the old artisan was divided among several people (increasing division of labour). They derived from the old workshops first flourished during the Middle Ages in the most active trade centres like the Flanders and Centre-North Italy. They were no more managed by an artisan but by a merchant, who did not work directly in the process (see, for example, Pirenne 1933, ch. 7; Cavalli 1974, ch. 4).

DOI: 10.4324/9781003228097-3

In the sixteenth and seventeenth centuries, population increase had to be favoured to expand production. Skills had to be promoted, in order to raise productivity and make the country prevail in foreign competition. Infrastructures had to be implemented and improved so that transport could become easier, in order to foster development and extend employment. Mercantilists were mainly concerned with these issues (for a detailed documentation, see Perrotta 2004, ch. 8). They wanted policies to increase population (ibid.: 168–170); to raise skills and attract the best foreign artisans (ibid.: 171–176); to create new roads, canals, and ports; and to make many rivers navigable. Finally, an essential aspect of such growth was the increase in exports (see below).

In the mercantilist strategy, foreign trade was central but only in connection with the increase in domestic production. On the one hand, mercantilists strongly supported the import substitution policy, that is the policy of producing at home the products which were previously imported (at least the more important ones). On the other hand, they supported the increase in exports, to give an outlet to the growing production. This strategy implied efforts to obtain a favourable balance of trade, in which total exports were higher than total imports.

Mercantilism was born to contrast the bullionist authors (flourished in fifteenth and sixteenth centuries), who wanted to forbid the export of precious metal money. It was the bullionists, not the mercantilists, who used to confuse wealth with precious metal money. Mercantilists argued that exporting money in order to increment trade would make money return in greater quantities. They were well aware that money was the essential means to increase investments. Then – although they used a bullionist terminology – they saw money as capital, not as a treasury to be hoarded.

Then, mercantilism was an organic project for economic development. It was conceived as national policy in the bigger states of western Europe. It also was – as many historians have stressed – a political project for power (see, for example, Furniss 1920). But such power was mainly seen as a consequence of economic development. The mercantilist approach did not derive from theoretical research; it always kept an empirical nature. Except for Giovanni Botero, each mercantilist author concentrated on their own state, and competition between states was an essential feature of this approach. Until the end of the seventeenth century, economists' reflection was stimulated not by the dialogue with other authors, even less with foreign authors, but by experience. Actually, many economic analyses were not written by intellectuals but by merchants (like Edward Misselden, Thomas Mun, Diego Dormer) or public officials (like Luis Ortiz, Barthélemy de Laffemas, Mateo Lisón y Viedma, Antonio Serra, etc.).

In the eighteenth century, although some mercantilist authors – like John Cary, Jean-François Melon, François de Forbonnais, James Steuart and many others – provided remarkable and sophisticated analyses, the prevalent view gradually became hostile to mercantilism. First, Bernard Mandeville and other authors criticised the idea of a permanently favourable trade balance, arguing that the loser country would have soon stopped exchange (Mandeville 1714, remark L). Then, David Hume provided a stringent analysis proving that the belief (attributed to mercantilists) that the country should accumulate as much precious metal money as possible was wrong because inflation would have soon caused an outflow of that money (Hume 1752: 322–327). François Quesnay and Victor de Riqueti, Marquis de Mirabeau accused mercantilists of not being free traders and of praising manufactures – which, in Quesnay's and Mirabeau's mind, were unproductive (see Quesnay 1757–1758; Mirabeau, *Philosophie rurale*, 1763).

The most accurate and devastating criticism came from Adam Smith, whose critique of mercantilism occupies one-fourth of his enormous book *Wealth of Nations* (Smith 1776, book IV, esp. chs. 1–8). Smith hinted that mercantilists confused wealth with money (book IV, ch. 1) and attacked the restrictions posed to imports and the policy of import substitution (IV.2). He criticised all the types of trade restrictions: the policy of the favourable balance of trade (IV.3), the support to selected exports (IV.5) and the commercial treatises based on privileges for single countries (IV.6). He also attacked the formation of monopolies protected by the state (IV.7.iii) and finally accused mercantilists of supporting the interests of merchants, not those of consumers and workers, because – by allowing restrictions to free trade and competition – they favoured the high costs of consumption goods (IV.8).

Some of Smith's accusations are right, but most of them are unfair and misleading. Certainly, the economy of the eighteenth century had to get rid of trade restrictions and monopolies protected by the state, because they had grown too strong. Nonetheless, free competition helps development only when the exchangers (individuals or countries) are more or less at the same level. The development economists of the 1940s–1960s have proved that backward economies are exploited when they freely exchange with developed economies (for example, Prebisch 1949; Singer 1950; Myrdal 1957; Furtado 1961; Balogh 1963). Not by chance, in the 1960s the former colonial countries rediscovered the import substitution policy, the need for certain trade protection and the role of the state in promoting development (see Perrotta 2016c).

Anyway, Smith's treatment discredited mercantilism in the following centuries. Since then, most economists blindly repeat Smith's accusations, nearly always without reading the mercantilist literature. So it happened that some ambiguous hints by Smith became dogmas, and mercantilists were, and are, accused of the ideas they had always rejected, like the confusion of wealth with money, i.e. chrysohedonism (see, for example, Lauderdale 1804, ch. 3: 35; Say 1828–1829; Senior 1828: 35–44, 1836: 657; Allen 1966: 67), the zero-sum economy (see, for example, J.S. Mill 1848: 4–5; McLeod 1872, III.10–11: 68–70), and an economy based on rents (see, for example, Ekelund and Tollison 1981: 5–15). Moreover, these criticisms pushed economists to neglect some important acquisitions of mercantilism, like the difference in productivity among the various sectors of production, or the importance of state intervention during structural crises.

This blindness persists despite the brilliant analyses, which appreciate mercantilists, provided by numerous insightful scholars in the last two centuries, like for example Friedrich List and the representatives of the Historical School (List 1841, §27 and 29; Heyking 1880, ch. I; Eisenhart 1881, ch. 3; Schmoller 1884: 49–52; Oncken 1902: 154–158). Other scholars devoted entire books to mercantilism with acute analyses. To mention just a few, Jean Morini-Comby (1930), Edgar Johnson (1937), Philip Buck (1942), Joseph Spengler (1960), etc. Other historians, although committed to free trade, have appreciated many aspects of mercantilism (see, for example, Eli Heckscher (1931) and Joyce Appleby (1978).

★

Of course, even around the sixteenth century, not all economists were advocating mercantilism. In Italy, Bernardo Davanzati (1588) provided excellent analyses of commerce and money without having any perception of mercantilist policies. The same happened to a long series of authors who analysed the nature of credit or of money (see, for example, De Santis 1605; Montanari 1687).

In Spain, the economic crisis began as early as the middle of the sixteenth century. Only the mercantilists were aware of it. But they were derided because many vested interests did not want any change. On the other hand, there was a mass of authors, the so-called "arbitristas", who untiringly proposed to the authorities remedies (which were often unlikely) for the economic crisis. Other authors, like Miguel Caxa de Leruela (1631), defended the interests of breeders.

In England, at the end of the seventeenth century, several authors disagreed with some mercantilist assumptions, like the favourable balance of trade (Bernard Mandeville), or the control of foreign trade (Dudley North, Nicholas Barbon. See below).

France is the most interesting example. While Barthélemy de Laffemas, minister of Henri IV, strongly promoted the mercantilist policy (see below), another minister of the same king, Maximilien de Béthune, duke of Sully, projected an opposite policy in which development was based on the modernisation of agriculture and on great landowners (see Sully 1638, tome II, chs. 2, 25 and 44). The great landowners, however, always impeded any modernisation in agriculture up to the French Revolution. The anti-mercantilist tradition continued later with Pierre Boisguilbert, whose view of the economy – based on landowners' consumption – inspired Richard Cantillon (see below) and Quesnay (see, for example, Boisguilbert 1695). Quesnay even declared himself a follower of Sully (Quesnay 1767).

The Historical Premises of Mercantilism

The precondition for a project of power and development was the formation of a big state, which could provide the resources for a development policy. In the late Middle Ages trade had increased, especially in the commercial cities (or regional states) of Central-northern Italy, Provence, Flanders, the Hanseatic League, and Catalunya. But at the end of the fifteenth century, trade had grown so much that the small political entities were no more able to face the keen international competition.

Not only manufacture needed to expand, but merchants had to organise themselves in big companies, protected and supported by a strong state and a homogeneous society. At the beginning of the sixteenth century, only the national states dominated the economy, i.e. England, Holland, France, Spain and Portugal (on the national states, see Toynbee 1953, V.75). They had one dominant language and religion, one government and a common tradition of stable social relationships (see Cipolla 1974, V.31).

On the contrary, Northern-Central Italy was still divided into small states due to the influence of the papacy.[2] Florence, Venice, Genoa and Milan kept being economically strong, but their scope was limited and gradually they became subordinate to the bigger foreign states (see Cipolla 1974, V.31.3.2). Consequently, Italy did not have a mercantilist project for national development. It only had two great, isolated, mercantilist thinkers, Botero and Serra (see below).

Germany too failed unification, probably due to the influence of the medieval empire. However, it kept a good economic level, thanks to the cameralist authors. The latter supported the economic tasks of public administration. They theorised a just proportion among the production sectors and a balance in the number of workers among the professions (see, for example, Becher 1668). The cameralist approach had the merit of considering the economy as a whole, which also included the governance and political programmes (see Schiera 1980). However, it also had a static view of society, without any aspiration to progressive change and economic development. In the end, Germany too remained out of the race for the capitalist takeoff.

On the other hand, development in the big states was not granted (see Piuz 1997, I.5). It depended on the alliance between the two protagonists of modern economy: the sovereign and merchants, with the support of artisans, professionals, intellectuals and bureaucracy. The sovereign and the modern classes had a common enemy to defeat, i.e. feudal landlords, who still kept their grip on agriculture (see, for example, Bevilacqua 1996: 168–170).

Against the productive classes, the feudal class tried to hinder any initiative for modernisation, that is urban expansion, abolition of the infinite number of duties on transports and economic activities, limitation of the jungle of privileges, extension of manufactures, common rules and common measures, infrastructures and improved transportations (see, for example, De Maddalena 1980, sections 2–4). Against the sovereign, landlords wanted to keep their feudal jurisdiction and control of the national army. On the contrary, the sovereign needed to be independent of landlords and to directly control bureaucracy, justice, the army, and economic policy. The monarch also needed ample monetary resources in order to develop these sectors, something that only merchants could supply (see, for example, Heckscher 1931, I.1 and I.8).

Thus, an alliance between the state and merchants was necessary for development. In the countries where such alliance was implemented, mercantilism flourished, development policy started and capitalism had its takeoff. This is the case of Holland and England (see, for example, Bairoch 1997, I.III.1). Later, France joined them, once it got rid of the endless religious civil wars. On the contrary, in the countries where this alliance failed, the economy started declining. This is the case of Spain, Portugal and Southern Italy, which were still dominated by feudal landlords (on the complex relationship between bourgeoisie and landlords, see Braudel 1977, II: 80–82).

In Portugal, despite its worldwide commercial network, the economic basis remained essentially feudal. Southern Italy's kingdom never experienced any kind of capitalist development since its birth (XII c.). In Spain, an entrepreneurial bourgeoisie had emerged. However, the re-conquest of Arab Spain and the conquest of America gave the upper hand again to feudal landlords. Iberian big landowners hindered the growth of manufacture and exported to Latin America a kind of feudal system. Moreover, they used native Americans and Africans as slaves in American mines and plantations (on the divide between Southern and Northern European countries, see Braudel 1977, III).

The decisive divide for the capitalist takeoff was given by the wool trade policies. Wool trade, in the fifteenth and sixteenth centuries, was the driving force of economic development. Spain and England were the producers of the best wool in Europe, while the demand for wool was increasing more and more. The demand came from the textile manufacture of Florence and other Italian cities, Lyon, the Flanders, Barcelona, etc. These cities worked the imported wool, refined it and sold it – mainly abroad – at a much higher price. In order to increase the export of raw wool, both British and Spanish landlords seized the common land which belonged to the villages through the so-called *enclosures*, and transformed it into pastures and expelled peasants (on the XVI c. economic transformations, it is still useful Marx 1867, chs. 26–31). Thus, the cities were invaded by the former peasants, who became beggars. But the final results of such processes, as we will see below, were very different in the two countries (see Perrotta 2004, chs. 6–7).

The Founding Phase

The mercantilist thought first developed in England in the sixteenth century, but some scattered anticipations can be found in the fifteenth century. Some Italian authors, among whom Diomede Carafa was the most relevant, criticised the bullionist policy and maintained that the sovereign should encourage private investment and private welfare. Another writer who anticipated some mercantilist ideas was the Albertine author, a merchant from the Saxon region (Carafa 1476: 272–273, 282–291; Albertine author 1530–1531: 214–216; see also Perrotta 2000).

Starkey's *Dialogue* is an outstanding analysis, which already contains nearly all the basic principles of mercantilism. This Oxford professor of philosophy begins with defending the enclosures of the common land, because – he says – agriculture needs to become more efficient. However, he strongly opposes the free export of raw wool (the enclosures aimed precisely at increasing the production of wool). Foreigners, he exclaims, pay very cheap our raw products, refine them and then sell them again to us at a much higher price. At the same time, he complains that the country is crowded of unemployed beggars. By exporting raw wool, he writes, we give work to the foreign poor while ours are starving. Our wool must be worked and refined at home; we should build up workhouses in which our poor can work and gain a living (see Starkey 1529–1530: 34, 60–62, 113–117).

Starkey expressed a feeling which was widespread in Britain and shared not only by merchants and urban workers but also by the gentry and by other authors (see, for example, Hales 1549 and Coke, mid XVI c.). In the same years of Starkey's work, the Tudor sovereigns were carrying on the same policy. They fought successfully against landlords. Two fundamental laws deserve to be mentioned in this long struggle. Henry VIII's law of 1531–1532 imposed on big landowners to devote a section of their land to grow flax or hemp, and prohibited the export of raw wool. All these raw products had to be worked at home to give beggars relief and put them to work (the text of the law is in Eden 1797, vol. III, p. CCXLIII. For other laws by Henry VIII, see ibid., vol. I: 82–86. See also Jordan 1959: 83–91 and Solar 1995: 3–15).

Henry's daughter, queen Elizabeth I, issued many laws in the same direction; the most complete being that of 1601 (see the text in Eden 1797, III, pp. CLXVII–CXCIII). Elisabeth's laws provided a series of norms which drew an organic policy of – we can say – "productive assistance". Parishes were made responsible for collecting alms for the poor. Such alms were initially voluntary, but soon they became taxes aimed at financing the workhouses. Then parishes were also in charge of sheltering the poor, building up workhouses, putting the able-bodies to work and paying overseers for surveillance. Tudors' organisation of the poor was the first large-scale application of the mercantilist policy (see Starkey 1529–1530: 115ff). Thanks to it, England rapidly substituted imports, developed its economy and put the basis for the capitalist takeoff, which made that country great in later centuries (see Jordan 1959, ch. IV).

In Spain, on the contrary, landlords kept the absolute freedom of exporting raw wool (see Giginta 1587: 44–45). In the meantime, they expelled with fraud or violence most of the independent farmers and bought their land at very low prices (see Lysón y Viedma 1622); hindered the formation of manufactures (see Ortiz 1558); impeded the organisation of beggars and the implementation of workhouses (see below). Thus, when gold and silver started to arrive from America in huge quantities, there was no possibility of investing them productively. Consequently, terrible inflation destroyed what remained of the economy, and American gold was used to buy foreign products. The result was that the other European countries enriched through the Spanish gold (see, for example, Mun 1623: 12–13, 54–55; Cantillon 1730, II.6), while Spain became increasingly poor. It missed development for more than four centuries (see Hamilton 1932: 202–203; Viñas y Mey 1970: 420; Vicens Vives 1972).

The mercantilists' marginalisation in Spain is evident in the debate about the organisation of the poor (see Luis Vives 1526; Juan Medina 1545; Giginta 1584; Pérez de Herrera 1595 and, above all, the king's decree *Real Cédula* 1540). The text of the *Cédula* (see Campomanes 1775–1777, vol. I: 250–258) supported the policy of collecting alms and putting the poor in workhouses, to solve the problem of unemployment and begging. But a number of authors – from Soto to Villavicencio – strongly defended the freedom of the poor to go and beg everywhere; and, we would say, also the freedom of the landlords to exploit the poor without restraint (Medina 1545; Soto 1545; Villavicencio 1564).[3]

Against the feudal hegemony, Spanish mercantilists asked the government to expand manufacture, process raw materials inside the country and protect the economy from excessive imports. Luis Ortiz (1558) made an impressive list of manufactured goods (mostly, necessary goods for everyday life) that Spain did not produce and imported from abroad. He appealed to the state to forbid the export of money (but only in the sense of investing it at home in productive activities); to build up manufactures and provide work to the poor; to impede the export of raw products and work them inside.

The same proposals for a policy of import substitution were also made by a long series of mercantilists (see, for example, Cellorigo 1600; Moncada 1619; Martínez Mata 1650; Álvarez Osorio 1686; Uztáriz 1724; Muñoz 1769; Campomanes 1774, etc.). Cellorigo provided a devastating criticism of Spanish "false" economy, all based on rents and on a mountain of papers, like juros, censos, and other loans at interest granted by rents. He stressed that wealth is not made of money, it is made of products. The delusion that sees money as wealth, he wrote, has ruined Spain (Cellorigo 1600: 1, 21–22, 29). But in Spain, the hegemony of the nobles was so deep-rooted that mercantilists were derided and despised.

At the turn of the sixteenth century, Botero and Laffemas reaffirmed the strategy of mercantilism. Botero, a great erudite, accustomed to the Jesuits' international experience, stated that – to increase wealth – manufactures, new inventions, skill and industriousness were more important than soil fertility. He added that, with development, industry prevails over agriculture (Botero 1589, VIII.3: 246–250).

Like the other mercantilists, Botero supported population increase, but this had to be accompanied by a correspondent increase in production (ibid. book

VII, and VIII.1). He also formulated the argument – repeated by Mun and others – against the bullionist idea of forbidding the export of precious metal money: if a state exports much and imports less, it can enrich because it gets more gold from abroad (Botero 1618: 23; see also Perrotta 2012).

Barthélemy de Laffemas, a former tailor of king Henri IV, then his minister, had a poor education but a sharp mind. His main concern was to extend silk production through a policy of import substitution. He tried to plant, with scarce success, mulberries everywhere in France, in order to nourish the silkworms with their leaves. Laffemas collided with the powerful merchants of Lyon, who were big importers of silk. At the same time, he strived to improve the techniques of production and to attract to the country the best foreign artisans. He also tried to modernise the other manufacture and to reform guilds, by reviving discipline, encouraging professional selection, and inspiring pride for belonging to the guild (see Laffemas 1597; see also Perrotta 2022).

However, his great efforts were not very successful. Besides, the sudden death of the king (1610), stabbed by a fanatic catholic, rapidly led Laffemas' policy to an end. A few years later, Montchrétien picked up the flag of mercantilism, but he did not even mention Laffemas.

The Conquest of Hegemony

At the beginning of the seventeenth century, bullionists had disappeared, the mercantilist approach spread and became the new canon. In ten years (1613–1623), the main representatives of the national mercantilist projects wrote their main works and gave mercantilism its complete features.

Antonio Serra analysed the economic flaws of the kingdom of Naples, then possessed by the Spanish king. This state, writes Serra, is terribly backward, with no manufacture nor trade. The few economic activities of the state are in the hands of foreign merchants, mostly from Northern Italy. The central-northern Italian cities, which were still very dynamic, were presented by Serra as a model to imitate for the "lazy" southern people. Due to the lack of manufacture, he writes, we import nearly all manufactured products from abroad. His long list of imported goods is as impressive as that of Ortiz (Serra 1613: 127–141, passim). This is the very cause of our money's weakness in international trade and of the permanent scarcity of money inside. It is the import of manufactured products that brings money abroad (ibid.: 133). Thus, Serra asked for an import substitution policy, like Starkey, Laffemas and Ortiz (although he ignored their writings).

Serra reveals another aspect of mercantilism. Not only he confirms that competitiveness depends on the strength of manufacture, but he also shows that weak production makes the country lose steadily its resources in favour of foreigners. In sum, Serra effectively points to the existence of underdevelopment. Actually, Southern Italy's economy was then squeezed by the convergence of three connected forces: landowners and their rents, foreign merchants and the Spanish government (Serra 1613: 147–153, passim. On Serra, see also Perrotta 2016a and Tiran 2016).

Antoine de Montchrétien appealed to the king for an overall mercantilist policy: pushing entrepreneurs to increase manufacture (Montchrétien 1615: 88–89, 133, passim); giving relief to the poor and putting them in the workhouses (ibid.: 122, 238, passim); attracting the best foreign artisans (71–72); protecting French merchants abroad but limiting the freedom of trade in France to foreign merchants (128–129, 178, 182, passim).

Montchrétien was also the founder of French colonial policy. He asked the king to build a powerful commercial fleet and a naval army to conquer new territories throughout the world (141–212). Besides, he attacked the landlords' absenteeism and criticised excessive inequality (79–80, 234–235); asked to give public appointments on the basis of merits and stated that institutions must be submitted to the law (261, 277). He also criticised merchants for cheating the poor (402–403). His attitude to defend the rights of the poor is a positive exception in the first phase of mercantilism. Montchrétien too supported an import substitution policy, which implied to export luxury and manufactured goods, and to import only raw materials and wage goods: 114, 382 (on Montchrétien, see also Perrotta 2016b; Sunna 2017; Tiran 2017).

Sancho de Moncada, like Cellorigo, saw beggars as unemployed and indicated the cause of inflation in American gold. Cellorigo and Moncada anticipated Mun in maintaining that the discovery of the western Indies was the cause of Spain's poverty (Cellorigo 1600: 22; Moncada 1619: 101, 141–144). Moncada effectively described the mechanism of the dependence on foreign goods and its negative consequences. But, like Martinez Mata and many other Spanish authors, he also blamed foreigners as the cause of Spain's disaster. Somehow he considered unavoidable such things as excessive luxury (100, 160–161), the great number of monks (135), *censos* and *juros* (101) and even the Moors' expulsion: 159–160 (Moncada 1619; Martínez Mata 1650–1660).

Thomas Mun represents the peak of this great elaboration. His main book, *England's Treasure by Forraign Trade*, written in 1623 but published only in 1664 by his son, is the *summa* of mercantilism. In it he explains in the clearest way all the basic principles of the mercantilist policy. He first showed Spain as a negative model. This country, he writes, does not use its money to invest; moreover, it impedes other countries to trade with its colonies. Since Spain does not produce, despite being "the source of money", it is forced to use money to buy from abroad what it needs. So the other countries enrich at its expense. Spain is the best example of how wealth can be wasted instead than invested (Mun 1623: 14, 22–24, 54–55). This is exactly the opposite of what some historians of economic thought such as Ekelund and Tollison have understood. These authors blame mercantilists for the parasitism which they strongly opposed (Ekelund and Tollison 1981).

Contrary to Spain, Mun adds, Tuscany has enriched itself because it lets money freely flow, like the sower who disperses corn to get a greater quantity of it (Mun 1623: 17–19). But he warns that trade enriches the country only at the condition of stimulating internal production. We should avoid excessive imports, grow as many products as we can and use them as raw materials. Italians enrich by working with Spanish raw silk (12–13, 52–53); and the Dutch enrich thanks to fishery and a great commercial fleet: 73–82 (on Mun, see also Perrotta 2014).

Mun too somehow perceived the dualism between developed and underdeveloped economies, so well analysed by Serra. Also, he was afraid of the competitive strength of Holland. He wrote that the Dutch behaved towards Britain as Northern Italy's merchants behaved towards Southern Italy (81). But such a comparison was rather exaggerated; Britain was by no means underdeveloped.

Farther Developments

In this section, we will only hint at the three most interesting developments of mercantilist thought after Mun.

Productive Labour

William Petty was the great pioneer of many later economic analyses, such as quantitative analysis, demography, value, the source of profit, the role of labour, etc. However, he remained a mercantilist, and provided to this approach one of the most precious acquisitions: the distinction between more or less productive works. He discussed this issue in a number of writings, scattered over more than three decades (we only mention here Petty 1644–1645: 185, 190–191; Petty 1671: 238–239; Petty 1676: 269–271). This issue is a typical mercantilist theme. Those authors were always in quest of the most productive sectors. Petty considered manufacturing to yield more than agriculture, and commerce more than manufacturing. Several mercantilist authors had already hinted at the differences in productivity among jobs (see, for example, Pedro de Valencia 1618 and Montchrétien 1615). Note that Petty did not engage in theoretical distinctions as Quesnay and Smith did on this subject. He only wanted to find more productive employment for wealth.

After Petty, this subject was treated by a great many authors (see Perrotta 2004, ch. 9). Two different approaches gradually emerged. In the first one, the authors stressed the need to have a proportion among production sectors according to their economic productivity. Particularly important is the distinction underlined by Cantillon: luxuries producers cannot be considered as productive as the producers of agricultural or manufactured daily goods (Cantillon 1730, I.12, I.16). This approach culminated in Genovesi's analysis (still neglected). Genovesi showed that the productiveness of intellectual labour depends on the level of social evolution and economic development (Genovesi 1768–1770, see above all chs. 9–11). This implies an evolutionary view, in which the more skilled works and the more refined consumption products become productive and socially necessary as long as economic development goes on (see Perrotta 2018b).

The second approach was expressed by authors who defined as productive any labour which yielded some return. Smith expressed the most important analysis of this approach and obscured all the previous statements on the issue of productive labour. However, Smith's definition required productive labour to be material and this created controversies even among his followers (see Perrotta 2018a, chs. 4–6).

Balance of Trade

In the eighteenth century, free traders considered the mercantilist theory of the favourable balance of trade as naïve. But they neglected the difference between types of imported and exported goods which was implied in that theory since its emergence. According to mercantilists, imports should be confined to the products which helped to increase production, namely raw materials and wage goods, while exports should consist of products which had exhausted their ability to activate labour, like luxury goods and finished non-wage goods.

To this theory, Cantillon and Steuart provided the more stringent arguments. Cantillon explained that in the exchange of Champagne's wine with Brabant's lace, Champagne loses twice while Brabant gains twice, because the first renounces to a wage good (wine) which can feed workers, and acquires lace, whose only utility is to adorn the rich ladies (unproductive consumption). Brabant, on the contrary, acquires a good which is useful for its workers while giving in exchange a good which has already exhausted its productive potentialities; as the classical economists will say, it does not enter any more the production process (Cantillon 1730, I.15–16, III.1).

Steuart formulated the general rule of foreign exchange by using the distinction, first used by Petty, between nature or land or matter (i.e. natural resources) and labour as the two components of products. All products contain matter and labour in different proportions. The country loses, in terms of production potential, when it exports matter, while it gains when it exports labour. This is because if labour has already activated employment at home, then this employment has already been paid for by the foreign purchaser. Thus the country is advantaged when it exports goods with much labour and little matter. For the same reason, the country is advantaged when it imports goods which contain a great quantity of matter and a little quantity of labour, so they can activate new production (Steuart 1767, II.24).

Wages

In the sixteenth and seventeenth centuries, international trade was based, for a big part, on luxury goods. Its main target was aristocracy, but also landed bourgeoisie and the professionals. Besides, wages were as low as possible and mercantilists justified this fact with the necessity of impeding workers' debauchery or lack of discipline. This means that wages could not express a sufficient demand on the market. Thus, the supply of goods increased more than demand, and such a growing gap could drive accumulation to a standstill.

Actually, in the last decades of the seventeenth century, the commerce directed to elites was going to saturate its narrow market, despite the frantic changes in fashion (about which the rich were particularly keen). This is a permanent tendency of capitalist accumulation. To mention only the most important crises due to low wages, we can refer to the gluts noted by Malthus and Sismondi in the first decades of the nineteenth century, the 1930s crisis and the crisis of our times.

Thus, at the turn of the eighteenth century, English mercantilists rapidly changed direction. Dudley North warned against an economy only concerned with elementary needs, and Barbon praised the "needs of the mind" (North 1691: 528–529; Barbon 1690: 14, 21–22, 32–36). But the decisive change was the awareness that wages had to be increased. Mercantilists realised that – as *The British Merchant* put it – the best consumers of English commodities were English people (*The British Merchant* 1713, vol. I: 141).

Martyn and Defoe expressed the new tendency in terms of foreign trade. Martyn affirmed that production costs should not be hindered by lowering wages but by increasing productivity (Martyn 1701, chs. 12–15). Defoe stated that English production costs could not compete in the international market with those of China and India. The latter's costs were very low due to low wages and the wretched conditions of their workers. England could only compete in the opposite direction: thanks to high wages – the highest in the world – English workers could produce goods of higher quality (Defoe 1728: 59–67). Smith revived Defoe's reasoning, without acknowledgement (Smith 1776, I.viii.36).

The new view about wages expressed by mercantilists paved the way for the general support of high wages by the Enlightenment authors (see the insightful analysis by Karayiannis and Katselidis 2014). High wages greatly enhanced development in the XVIII c. Europe and accumulation grew fast thanks to the increase in the general welfare. However, wages started diminishing again in the 1770s due to the industrial revolution. In the factory, a deep technical transformation created a huge substitution of human labour with new machines. Most artisans and manufacturing workers lost their labour, unemployment soared and wages dropped under the subsistence level. The last achievement of the mercantilist theory – a growth based on wage increase – went lost.

Conclusion: The Mercantilist Teaching

Mercantilism was born to give an outlet to the feudal economy's final crisis in urban areas and to the need for capitalist takeoff. The privatisation of the common land and the crisis of artisan economy (both caused by the international trade expansion) had led to huge unemployment. Thus mercantilists promoted a radical employment policy by implementing manufactures, creating infrastructures, supporting a competitive conquest of foreign markets, specialising production. All this implied a shift of attention to the more productive goods – like wage goods and highly skilled products – and to the more productive jobs.

Precisely these kinds of policies, *mutatis mutandis*, were needed in the later structural crises and the consequent unemployment, during the industrial revolution, the 1920s–1930s and the present years. But in the industrial economy, far from adopting employment policies, profits were largely based on the reduction of wages under the subsistence level. This fact hindered the investment increase that accumulation needed.

Consequently, up to the 1930s, there were frequent underconsumption crises, stagnation and growing unproductive investments. Roosvelt's and Keynes' policies (and World War II) restated a policy of mercantilist flavour, based on a demand-led expansion and the growth of human capital (welfare state). However, the consequent strong increase in skill and productivity led in the 1980s to the saturation of traditional markets and the need to expand a post-industrial economy, based on the growth of human capital and immaterial production. Yet, here too, enterprises are preferring to take advantage of unemployment and increase profits through low wages. Once again the mercantilist teaching has been discarded.

Notes

1 I thank Stavros Drakopoulos and Ioannis Katselidis for their careful and very useful comments and suggestions. I also thank Graham Sells for his thorough revision of the English text. Any errors are mine alone.

2 The popes, in order to keep their own independence, managed to impede Italy's unification (even only of the Center-North) for more than a thousand years (eighth to nineteenth centuries).

3 Particularly dramatic was the controversy between the Augustinian abbot Juan de Medina and the Dominican Domingo de Soto, professor at Salamanca. Soto even made the Council of Trento prohibit the organisation of the poor.

Bibliography

The date after the author's name indicates the first publication or the work's completion.

Albertine author (1530–1531) Gemeine Stymmen Von der Müntze & Apologie, in Walter Lotz, ed., *Die drei Flugschriften über den Münzstreit der sächsischen Albertiner und Ernestiner um* 1530, Leipzig: Duncker und Humblot, 1893.

Allen, William (1966) La posizione dei mercantilisti e i primi sviluppi della teoria del commercio internazionale, in R. Eagly, ed., *Eventi, ideologia e teoria economica*, trans. from English, Milano: Angeli, 1977.

Álvarez Osorio, Miguel (1686) Extensión política y económica, in P. Campomanes, ed., *Apéndice a la educación popular* (4 vols), Madrid: Sancha, 1775–1777, vol. I: 7-206.

Appleby, Joyce (1978) *Economic Thought and Ideology in Seventeenth Century England*, Princeton, NJ: Princeton U.P.

Bairoch, Paul (1997) *Storia economica e sociale del mondo*, trans. of *Victoires et déboires. Histoire économique et sociale du monde du XVIe siècle à nos jours*, Torino: Einaudi, 1999.

Balogh, Thomas (1963) *Una società di ineguali*, trans. from English (*Unequal Partners*), Torino: Einaudi.

Barbon, Nicholas (1690) *A Discourse of Trade*, reprint, Baltimore, MD: Johns Hopkins U.P., 1905.

Becher, Johann (1668) *Politische Discurs*, Glashutten im Taunus: Auvermann, 1972.

Bevilacqua, Piero (1996) *Latifondo*, entry of *Enciclopedia delle scienze sociali* (vol. V), Roma: Istituto dell'Enciclopedia italiana.

Boisguilbert, Pierre (1695) *Le Détail de la France*, in Daire, Eugène, ed., *Économiste financiers du dix-huitième siècle*, Paris: Guillaumin, 1843.

Botero, Giovanni (1589) *Della Ragion di Stato*, Torino: UTET, 1948.

——— (1618) *Delle relationi universali. Parte Seconda*, posthumous, Venezia: Vecchi.

Braudel, Fernand ((1977) *La dinamica del capitalismo*, trans. from French, Bologna: il Mulino, 1981.

British Merchant (1713), *or Commerce Preserved* (3 vols.), Charles King ed., reprint, London: Osborne, 1748.

Buck, Philip (1942) *The politics of Mercantilism*, reprint, New York: Octagon Books, 1964.

Campomanes, Pedro (1774) *Discurso sobre el fomento de la industria popular*, Madrid: Instituto de Estudios Fiscales, 1975.

——— ed. (1775–1777) *Apéndice a la educación popular* (4 vols), Madrid: Sancha.

Cantillon, Richard (1730) *Essai sur la nature du commerce en général*, London: Macmillan, 1931.

Carafa, Diomede (1476) I doveri del principe, in Tommaso Persico ed., *Gli scrittori politici napoletani dal '400 al '700* (1899), reprint, Bologna: Forni, 1974: 261–296.

Cavalli, Alessandro (1974) *Le origini del capitalismo*, Torino: Loescher.

Caxa de Leruela, Miguel (1631) *Restauración de la antigua abundancia de España…*, Madrid: Instituto de Estudios Fiscales, 1975.

Cellorigo, Martín González (1600) *Memorial de la política necesaria a la República de España …*, Valladolid: Bostillo.

Cipolla, Carlo M. (1974) *Storia economica dell'Europa pre-industriale*, Bologna: il Mulino.

Coke, John (mid XVI c.) *Debate between the heralds of England and France*, Paris: Firmin-Didot, 1877.

Davanzati, Bernardo (1588) Lezione delle monete, in Filippo Argelati ed., *De monetis Italiae dissertationes* (vol. 4th, 1752: 157–167), Milano: Regia Curia.

Defoe, Daniel (1728) *Plan of the English Commerce* ..., reprint, New York: Kelley, 1967.

De Maddalena, Aldo (1980) Il mercantilismo, in L. Firpo ed. *Storia delle idee politiche, economiche e sociali* (vol. IV.1: 637–704), Torino: UTET.

De Santis, Marc'Antonio (1605) Discorso intorno agli effetti che fa il cambio in Regno, in Raffaele Colapietra ed., *Problemi monetari negli scrittori napoletani del Seicento* (1973: 110–141), Roma: Accademia dei Lincei.

Eden, Sir Frederic (1797) *The State of the Poor. A History of the Labour Classes in England* (3 vols), London: J. Davies.

Ekelund, Robert B., jr and Tollison, Robert D. (1981) *Mercantilism as a Rent-Seeking Society*, College Station, TX: A.& M. University Pr.

Eisenhart, Hugo (1881) *Geschichte der Nationalökonomie* (2nd ed. 1901), Jena: Fischer.

Furniss, Edgar (1920) *The Position of the Laborer in a System of Nationalism*, reprint, New York: A. Kelley, 1965.

Furtado, Celso (1961) *Development and Underdevelopment*, trans. from Portuguese, Berkeley: Un. of California Press, 1964.

Genovesi, Antonio (1768–1770) *Lezioni di economia civile*, Milano: Vita e Pensiero, 2013.

Giginta, Miguel (1584) *Cadena de oro*, Perpiñán: Sansón Arbus.

——— (1587) *Atalaya de Charidad*, Zaragoza: Portmaris.

Hales, John (1549) [or Thomas Smith] *A Discourse of the Common Weal of This Realm of England*, Cambridge: Cambridge U. P., 1893.

Hamilton, Earl J. (1932) El mercantilismo español antes de 1700, in *El florecimiento del capitalismo*, Madrid: Revista de Occidente, 1948, trans. from English.

Heckscher, Eli (1931) *Mercantilism* (2nd ed., 1955), London: Allen & Unwin, trans. from Swedish.

Heyking, Edmund (1880) *Zur Geschichte der Handelsbilanztheorie*, Part I, Berlin: Puttkammer & Mühlbrecht.

Hume, David (1752) *Of the Balance of Trade*, in Idem [1964: 330–345].

——— (1964) *Essays Moral, Political and Literary*, in Idem, *The Philosophical Works*, 1882–86, reprint, Aalen: Scientia, 1964.

Johnson, Edgar Augustus Jerome (1937) *Predecessors of Adam Smith*, reprint, New York: A. Kelley, 1965.

Jordan, Wilbur (1959) *Philanthropy in England, 1480–1660*, London: Greenwood, 1978.

Karayiannis, Anastassios and Katselidis, Ioannis (2014), Wages and work effort in English economic thought, 1670–1770, *European Journal of the History of Economic Thought*, 1/2: 230–251.

Laffemas, Barthélemy (1597) *Règlement général pour dresser les manufactures en ce royaume*, Paris: Monstroeil.

Lauderdale, James (1804) *Ricerche sulla natura ed origine della pubblica ricchezza*, trans. from English, Biblioteca dell'Economista, I.5, Torino: Pomba, 1854.

List, Friedrich (1841) *The National System of Political Economy*, trans. from German. London: Longmans & Green, 1909. Online: Library of Economics and Liberty.

Lysón y Viedma, Mateo (1622) *Discursos y apuntamientos*, no place, no publisher, (read in Madrid, Biblioteca Nacional).

Mandeville, Bernard (1714) *Remarks*, in Idem *The Fable of the Bees*, Oxford, Clarendon, 1924.

Martínez Mata, Francisco (1650–60) *Del remedio de la despoblación, pobreza de España*, Madrid: Moneda y Credito, 1971.

Martyn, Henry (1701) Considerations on the East-India Trade, in John R. McCulloch, ed., *A Select Collection of Early English Tracts on Commerce*, London: Political Economy Club, 1856: 541–629.

Marx, Karl (1867) *Capital I*, Moscow: Progress Publishers 2015, online.

McCulloch, John R. (1856) *A Select Collection of Early English Tracts on Commerce*, London: Political Economy Club.

McLeod, Henry (1872) *Principi di filosofia economica*, trans. from English, Biblioteca dell'Economista, III.3, Torino: UTET, 1877.

Medina (Robles), Juan (1545) De la orden en la limosna, in Soto, Domingo, ed., *Deliberación en la causa de los pobres*, Madrid: Instituto de Estudios políticos, 1965.

Mill, John Stuart (1848) *Principi di economia politica*, trans. from English, Torino: UTET, 1953.

Mirabeau, Victor de (1763) *Philosophie rurale* (2nd ed., 1764, 3 vols.), reprint, Aalen: Scientia, 1972.

Moncada, Sancho de (1619) *Restauración política de España*, Madrid: Instituto de Estudios Fiscales, 1974.

Montanari, Geminiano (1687) *Della moneta*, in Pietro Custodi, *Scrittori classici italiani di economia politica* (1803–16), reprint, Roma: Bizzarri, 1965–69, O. Nuccio ed., parte Antica, vol. 3.

Montchrétien, Antoine de (1615) *Traicté de l'oeconomie politique*, François Billacois, ed., Genève: Droz, 1999.

Morini-Comby, Jean (1930) *Mercantilisme et protectionnisme*, Paris: Alcan.

Mun, Thomas (1623) England's Treasure by Forraign Trade, in McCulloch, John R., ed., *A Select Collection of Early English Tracts on Commerce*, London: Political Economy Club, 1856: 115–209.

Muñoz, Antonio [Ramos, Enrique] (1769) *Discurso sobre economía política*, Madrid: Ibarra.

Myrdal, Gunnar (1957) *Economic Theory and Under-developed Regions*, London: Duckworth.

North, Dudley (1691) Discourses upon Trade, in McCulloch, John R., ed., *A Select Collection of Early English Tracts on Commerce*, London: Political Economy Club, 1856: 505–540.

Oncken, August (1902) *Geschichte del Nationalökonomie* (2 vols), Leipzig: Hirschfeld.

Ortiz, Luis (1558) Memorial a Felipe II, *Anales de Economía*, 63, Enero 1957: 117–200.

Pedro de Valencia (1618) *Contra la ociosidad*, in Idem, *Escritos sociales*, Madrid: Escuela Social, 1945.

Pérez de Herrera, Christobal (1595) *Discursos morales y políticos*, Madrid: Biblioteca Nacional.

Perrotta, Cosimo (2000) *Einleitung zum Münzstreit der sächsischen Albertiner und Ernestiner um 1530*, in B. Schefold (ed.), *Die drei Flügschriften, über den Münzenstreit* (101–156), Düsseldorf: Wirtschaft und Finanzen.

——— (2004) *Consumption as an Investment*, London, New York: Routledge.

——— (2012) "Giovanni Botero", entry of *Enciclopedia Italiana – Il contributo italiano alla storia del pensiero – Economia*, ed. by Vera Negri Zamagni and Pier Luigi Porta, Roma: 281–286.

——— (2014) "Thomas Mun's *England's Treasure by Forraign Trade*: the 17th c. Manifesto for Development Economics", *History of Economics Review*, 59, Winter 2014: 94–106.

——— (2016a) Serra and underdevelopment, in R. Patalano & S. Reinert, eds., *Antonio Serra and the Economics of Good Government* (2016: 214–233), Basingstoke: Palgrave-Macmillan.

——— (2016b) Montchrétien Founder of Political Economy, *History of Economic Thought & Policy*, 2–2016: 73–84.

——— (2016c) The brilliant fifties: International trade as a cause of underdevelopment, in D. Gualerzi and C. Sunna eds., *Development Economics in the XXI century* (51–70), Abingdon, New York: Routledge.

——— (2018a) *Unproductive Labour in Political Economy*, London, New York: Routledge.

——— (2018b) Evolution and development, categories of Genovesi's economics, *The European Journal of the History of Economic Thought*, 2018/4: 605–626.

——— (2022) Laffemas, founder of French mercantilism, *Revue d'histoire d'économie politique*, n° 14, 2022/2: 207–230.

Petty, William (1644–1645) Miscellaneous, in Petty, *The Petty Papers. Some Unpublished Writings* (1967), reprint, New York: Kelley [1927], II.

——— (1671) Political Observations, in Petty, *The Petty Papers. Some Unpublished Writings* (1967), reprint, New York: Kelley [1927], II: 226–239.

——— (1676) *Political Arithmetick*, in Petty, *Economic Writings* (2 vols.), [1899], I: 233–313, reprint, New York: Kelley, 1963 and 1964.

——— (1899) *Economic Writings* (2 vols.), reprint, New York: Kelley, 1963 and 1964.

——— (1927) *The Petty Papers. Some Unpublished Writings* (1967, 2 vols. in one), reprint, New York: Kelley.

Pirenne, Henri (1933) *Storia economica e sociale del Medioevo*, trans. from French, Milano: Garzanti.

Piuz, Anne-Marie (1997) Le economie tradizionali in Europa, in Bairoch (1997: 77–122).

Prebisch, Raúl (1949) El desarrollo económico de la América Latina y algunos de sus principales problemas, reprint in *Desarrollo Económico*, 26, 1986: 479–502.

Quesnay, François (1757–1758) Hommes, in Quesnay, ed., *Oeuvres économiques complètes …* (2 vols), Paris: INED, 2005: 257–323.

——— (1767) *Maximes générales du gouvernement économique d'un royaume agricole*, in his *Oeuvres*: 565–596, tome I.

——— (2005) *Oeuvres économiques complètes …* (2 vols), Paris: INED, 2005.

Say, Jean-Baptiste (1828–1829) *Corso completo d'economia politica pratica*, trans. from French, Biblioteca dell'Economista, Torino: UTET, 1855.

Schiera, Pierangelo (1980) La concezione amministrativa dello Stato in Germania (1550–1750), in L. Firpo ed., *Storia delle idee politiche, economiche e sociali*, Torino: UTET.

Schmoller, Gustav (1884) *The Mercantile System and its Historical Significance*, reprint New York: A. Kelley 1967, trans. from German.

Senior, Nassau W. (1828) *Three Lectures on the Transmission of the Precious Metals from Country to Country and the Mercantile Theory of Wealth*, in his *Selected Writings on Economics*, reprint, New York: Kelley, 1966.

——— (1836) *An Outline of the Science of Political Economy*, reprint, New York: Kelley, 1965. Online, Mises Institute from Library of Congress.

Serra, Antonio (1613) *A Short Treatise on the Causes that Can Make Kingdoms Abound in Gold and Silver even in the Absence of Mines*, trans. from Italian, London, New York, Delhi: Anthem Press, 2011.

Singer, Hans W. (1950) The distribution of gains between investing and borrowing countries, *American Economic Review*, 40:2: 473–485.

Smith, Adam (1776) *Inquiry into the Nature and Causes of the Wealth of Nations*, Edwin Cannan, ed., London: Methuen, 2 vols, 1904, online: Maryville Univ.

Solar, Peter (1995) Poor relief and English economic development before the industrial revolution, *Economic History Review*, 1995: 1–22.

Soto, Domingo (1545) *Deliberación en la causa de los pobres*, Madrid: Instituto de Estudios políticos, 1965.

Spengler, Joseph (1960) *Mercantilistes, physiocrates et théorie de la croissance*, in B. Hoselitz, ed., *Théories de la croissance économique* (1960), Paris: Dunod, 1970, trans. from English: 1–136.

Starkey, Thomas (1529–1530) *A dialogue between Pole and Lupset*, London: Royal Historical Society & University College, 1989.

Steuart, James (1767) … *Principles of Political Oeconomy* (1966, 2 vols), Chicago, IL: Chicago U. P.

Sully, Maximilien, duc de (1638) *Mémoires des sages et royales économies d'Etat de Henry le Grand* (1st vol.), Amsterdam: Clearetimelee et Pistariste, 1638.

Sunna, Claudia (2017) A. de Montchrétien and development economics, *History of Economic Thought & Policy*, 2017/1: 101–113.

Tiran, André (2016) Real and monetary factors in the de Santis-Serra controversy, in R. Patalano & S. Reinert, eds., *Antonio Serra and the Economics of Good Government* (2016: 191–213), Basingstoke: Palgrave-Macmillan.

——— (2017) A. de Montchrestien and Antonio Serra: Two founders of political economy, *History of Economic Thought & Policy*, 2017/1: 89–100.

Toynbee, Arnold (1953) *Il mondo e l'Occidente*, trans. from English, Palermo: Sellerio, 2014.

Uztáriz, Gerónimo (1724) *Theórica y práctica de Comercio y de Marina*, Madrid: Sanz, 1742.

Vicens Vives, Jaime (1972) *Historia de España y America social y económica* (2 vols), Barcelona: Vicens Vives.

Villavicencio, Laurencio (1564) *De Oeconomia sacra circa pauperum curam* …, Paris: Sonnio.

Viñas y Mey, Carmelo (1970) *Notas sobre primeras materias, capitalismo industrial y inflación en Castilla durante el siglo XVI*, in *Anuario de Historia Económica y Social*, Enero 1970, Madrid, Univ. de Madrid, 1970: 339–421.

Vives, Juan Luis (1526) *Del socorro de los pobres*, in Idem, *Obras completas* (1947, vol. 1), Madrid: Aguilar.

4 Physiocracy and Fiscal Reform

The Chimera of the *Impôt Unique*

Simona Pisanelli

Introduction

As is well known, François Quesnay (1694–1774), personal physician to Madame Pompadour at the court of Louis XV, did not take an interest in economic matters until late in his life. This did not prevent him from making a systematic and influential contribution to the widespread debate on grain that developed in France in the second half of the eighteenth century. Quesnay was in close contact with the circle of the *philosophes*, but it was only after his meeting with Victor Riqueti de Mirabeau that the physiocratic school was born. Struck by the reading of Mirabeau's *Ami des hommes, ou Traité de la population*, published in 1756 and immediately well received by the French public, Quesnay summoned the author to court (22 July 1757) (Orain and Steiner 2016, 31). In turn, Mirabeau was so impressed by his meeting with Quesnay that he declared that he had become a Physiocrat during his first conversation with the court physician.[1] In fact, from the day of their first meeting, Quesnay and Mirabeau were meeting constantly, thereby establishing a fruitful and continuous collaboration.[2]

Actually, Pierre Samuel Dupont de Nemours was the first who used the title *Physiocratie*, collecting the main writings of Quesnay and other authors belonging to his circle. Dupont de Nemours' intention was to present the new discipline not as a mere "*science of wealth*" but as "the *science of natural law* applied [...] to civil societies," as "the science of *constitutions*" and, again, as "the science of enlightened justice" (Dupont [1815] 1848: 369; *my translation*), that could accelerate the general process of reorganisation of French society. His operation of promoting Quesnay's school was undoubtedly successful: not only did the term "physiocracy" attract the attention of the public of the time, but it also gained a central place in the language of the history of economic thought (Weulersse 1910, I, 128; Hoselitz 1968, 651–652).

The juridical and economic foundations on which the physiocratic school was based were respectively the idea of a "natural order" as a model on which to shape the "positive order",[3] and the key role of the development of agriculture, which the Physiocrats considered the only sector capable of producing a surplus. From the latter stemmed the proposal of the *impôt unique*, the

DOI: 10.4324/9781003228097-4

cornerstone of the fiscal reform promoted by François Quesnay and Victor Riqueti de Mirabeau,[4] and later supported by other authors, who gradually joined the group of *Économistes* (Mercier de la Rivière, Dupont de Nemours, and Guillaume François Le Trosne[5]).

This chapter consists of three sections. In the first, I will show how the Physiocrats attempted to translate their knowledge of political economy into practical economic policies. In the second section, I will point out the theoretical and practical obstacles that prevented the Physiocrats from implementing the *impôt unique*. Finally, in the third section some brief conclusions will be presented.

From Political Economy to Economic Policy: *produit net* and *impôt unique*

The Physiocrats' analysis starts from the observation of the poor productivity levels of French agriculture compared to those of England. The comparison with England was inevitable, not only because of its geographical proximity to France but also because it highlighted the economic backwardness of large areas of French agriculture, which showed no signs of capitalist organisation.

Praising the English agricultural system, Quesnay writes in his *Grains*: "In England, the great landlords dwell in their lands part of the year, and have greatly carried forward the improvement of their goods; for in this kingdom agriculture is the source of their wealth" (Quesnay [1757–1758a] 2005, 307; *my translation*). While in England, and before that in Flanders, new agronomic techniques were being tried out, in France this process was slowed "by institutions, by the remnants of the seigniorial regime, by economic policy, by the fiscal regime" (Ardant 1972, 69).

Furthermore, the dualism of the French economy was evident: Southern France still had a feudal production structure (*petite culture*), whereas Northern France was characterised by a capitalist agricultural production structure (*grande culture*) (Quesnay [1756] 2005, 129ff., espec. 131; Quesnay [1757] 2005, 163–173; Candela and Palazzi 1979, xi; Zagari 1972, 65). Quesnay regarded technical progress in agriculture and capital accumulation as two elements that automatically implied positive effects and, by allowing the transition from *petite* to *grande culture*, constituted the bridge between a poor economy and a prosperous one (Vaggi 1987, 154)[6]:

> Land cultivated with the aid of animal labour employs fewer men than land cultivated by men with their arms; and land cultivated with horses employs even fewer men than land cultivated with oxen. But for the cultivation of grains the fewer men it employs, the more advantageous it is to the state.
>
> (Quesnay [1757–1758a] 2005, 298; *my translation*)

Based on this belief, the Physiocrats pursued two objectives: to intervene in the agricultural sector, increasing its productivity and, at the same time, to widen the economic system to ensure an increase in national wealth.

As a consequence, they aimed to translate the general discussions about the need to revive the French economy that circulated in Parisian salons into tangible proposals, moving from the level of economic analysis to the definition of concrete economic policies (Ridolfi 1973, xi). The institution of the single tax, "which frees the agricultural entrepreneur from tax burdens", was only one of the economic policies that the Physiocrats tried to promote. The ideal society that Quesnay described in his economic tables, showing the relations between social classes and the functioning of the economy, would only have been possible once all the economic reforms that he and his collaborators hoped for had been implemented:

> the universal application of large-scale capitalist agriculture; the establishment of free trade in corn, which ensures the 'proper price' for agricultural produce; [...] the complete fulfilment by the class of proprietors of their duty to provide the advances necessary for the improvement of their land, the development of transport facilities, etc.
>
> (Meek [1962] 2003, 298; see also Weulersse 1910, II, 151, 153, 160)

The Physiocrats ascribed great practical importance to the tax system because, according to their vision, they believed that the distribution of taxes was the main cause of the misery of the people of their time. The introduction of a single tax would help give impetus to a general fiscal reform, beyond the significant effects it would have on increasing national wealth. Even if, today, we attribute poverty more to inadequate production and misdistribution of wealth than to any tax system, and even if the view of the Physiocrats therefore seems excessive, it could be justified by the very bad fiscal organisation and by the type of relations between social classes typical of the *Ancien Régime* (Gide and Rist 1922, 47). From their point of view, verifying the effectiveness of the proposed economic policies was quite simple: if the *impôt unique* produced expansionary effects on economic activity, it was to be considered useful; if it led to a contraction, it was to be considered inappropriate and had to be replaced (Meek 1977, 47–48).

Since "the corner-stone of [the Physiocratic] policy was obedience to Nature" (Marshall [1890] 2013, 625), every kind of economic policy measure had to be undertaken in full respect of the "natural laws" of economics (Meek [1962] 2003, 370 ff.; Zangheri 1966, xx ff.), in order to determine a rational allocation of resources that would increase national wealth (Hoselitz 1968, 655 ff; Candela and Palazzi 1979, ix). As Gianni Vaggi pointed out in his *The Economics of François Quesnay* (1987), the Physiocrats explain the origin of surplus and wealth through the theory of exclusive productivity of agriculture (Vaggi 1987, 94).

In turn, the *impôt unique* on the landowners' rent derives from this theory and is directly connected to the Physiocrats' conception of the "never closed and always new [circuit] of production and consumption" (Einaudi 1941, I, 334), based on a precise dynamic of the relations between the three identified social classes:

1 the *landowning* class includes the categories of nobles, clergy, civil servants, and the sovereign. All these categories are entitled to enjoy the fruits of the land, since "they contributed their landed property to the productive process" (Hoselitz 1968, 647). *After deducting production expenses*, landowners receive rent, which dispenses them from working, and which they use to purchase agricultural and craft goods from the other two classes. It is decisive that the landowning class—also referred to as the "distributive class"—spend on essential goods, because "if their incomes were not distributed to the lucrative professions, the state would become depopulated" (Quesnay [1757–1758b] 2005, 218; *my translation*). What is desirable, however, does not automatically translate into reality: "The landlords' usual pattern of expenditure was very different from that advocated by the Physiocrats; the nobles purchased large amounts of manufactured commodities, *luxe de decoration*, and of foreign-made products" (Vaggi 1987)[7];
2 the *artisan* class includes all workers employed in sectors other than agriculture and is defined as *sterile*, as it merely transforms raw materials into consumer goods for the community, without, however, generating additional wealth and economic growth;
3 these last two results are the exclusive prerogative of the *productive* class, which includes—by extension—all the workers in the primary sector and finds its key figure in the farmer (*fermier*). The simple "worker who personally works the land"—as well as that of industry—produces just the value necessary for his maintenance. Only "an entrepreneur who administers and conducts his enterprise with… intelligence and with his wealth" (Quesnay [1757] 2005, 185; *my translation*), an entrepreneur who, in other words, *rationally* organises agricultural activity, is able to derive a surplus from the "land" factor. This surplus, called *produit net* by the Physiocrats, is what remains, at the end of the production cycle, *after deducting production expenses.*

As can be seen, the expression 'deducting production expenses' is used for both landowners and farmers. This should not be misleading: in both cases, the reference is to the *same* production costs, necessary to carry on the productive activities and to produce a quantity of foodstuffs sufficient to feed "those who produce them […], those who process them, […] those who circulate them", respectively, employed in agriculture, industry, and commerce (Mirabeau 1760, 424; *my translation*).

The rent of landowners obviously does not coincide perfectly with the *produit net*. They, in fact, must give up a part of the total wealth produced in a year (the duration of the periods in which the Physiocrats divide the production process), making it available to the farmers. Only in this way can the latter reinvest the profit in *avances primitives*, which serve to renew the fixed capital of the farm (fences, ploughs, draught animals, and cattle to fertilise the land, etc.) and in *avances annuelles*,[8] which serve to annually supply themselves with raw materials (seeds, fertilisers, etc.) and paid workers. To the *avances primitives* and *avances annuelles* must be added the *avances souveraines*, that is, the investments by the sovereign to improve infrastructure (roads, canals, etc.) and administer laws which make property safe and balance the economy. In short, the sovereign creates the conditions for the social order to be as close as possible to the natural order of things. For this service, the sovereign is entitled to rent (Hoselitz 1968, 647).

Farmers also provide for the *annual costs of cultivation* in the following year (Quesnay [1756] 2005, 129; Quesnay [1760] 2005, 452; see also Dupont [1768] 1910, 12), leading to a progressive modernisation of cultivation methods (Vaggi 1987, 21).

Given the *produit net*, the proposal of the *impôt unique* arises from two different needs (Klotz, Minard, and Orain 2017, 13):

1 cutting the cost of collecting taxes,[9] characterising the *impôt unique* as "a form of tax that is less burdensome to the nation" (Quesnay [1757–1758b] 2005, 225; *my translation*);
2 "freeing" capital, without affecting the portion of wealth reinvested by farmers and burdening only the portion of *produit net* due to landowners (*rente*).

Otherwise, the negative consequences would have spilled over onto the entire production system:

> taxation which takes resources away from investments, is a devastation which ruins the peasants, which annihilates the income of the landlords and the sovereign, and which extinguishes the remuneration with which the other classes of men subsist
>
> (Mirabeau 1760, 477–478; *my translation*).

A well-functioning economic system based on free competition would ensure the effectiveness of the single tax. According to Quesnay, a more competitive system guarantees advantageous and profitable current prices for the producer because, since the demand for agricultural goods always exceeds supply, they are always higher than the unit costs of production. Therefore, the *bon prix* is a *proper price,* not necessarily high, but "both higher than the existing one and less subject to violent fluctuations in years of extreme plenty and scarcity" (Meek [1962] 2003, 389). Quesnay does not ignore the fact that most of the population can barely afford to consume the necessary goods (Vaggi 1987, 103–104) and, in his article on *Impôts*, he mentions the problem of rising prices in relation to the purchasing power of wage earners.

If the general level of prices rises, subsistence wages need to be adjusted to the new level, resulting in lower profits for business owners and a "very mediocre gain [for] the prince" (Quesnay [1757–1758b] 2005, 228; *my translation*).[10] On the other hand, if wages are not adjusted to the average price level, demand contraction inevitably occurs: consumers can no longer afford to spend to the same extent and producers are forced to keep prices stable (or even to sell at lower prices), with the risk of not being able to fully cover production costs.

Even more interesting is Quesnay's reflection on the damage that taxes on wages would cause to the whole society, hindering the development of innovative processes that are usually performed by workers with satisfactory wages and employment conditions. If the peasant is gripped by the

> uncertainty in which the arbitrary tax keeps him, [...] he cannot hope for anything from his work: he does not even dare to work, for fear that the gain, which he believes he has obtained from his work, will attract increases in taxes. Moreover, he cannot deceive himself into deriving any advantage from it; he is not sure that he will preserve a bed or other effects; he surrenders himself to misery and laziness; this indolence is a great evil [...] and [the] loss to the state is huge.
>
> (Quesnay [1757–1758b] 2005, 243; *my translation*)

Also, Mercier de la Rivière takes a stand on the direct relationship between labour costs and production costs. He excludes the levying of taxes directly on peasants' wages because the workers cannot survive the tax burden unless the entrepreneurs increase the wage level *in return for the same amount of work* (Mercier (de) la Rivière, [1767] 1910, II, 113; *my translation* and *my italics*). Ultimately, entrepreneurs would be charged taxes, causing negative effects on the profitability of production, and forcing many farmers to give up investments. The abandonment of the less productive lands would cause "a first and considerable diminution in the total mass of subsistence, of the affluence of the people, and immediately of the population" (Dupont [1768] 1910, 22; *my translation*). The first demographic decline occurred within the ranks of workers, resulting in a drop in effective demand and—in the long run—in supply, due to a lack of farm workers.

Subsequently, this vicious circle would also affect investment in the most fertile lands. An entire generation of agricultural entrepreneurs would disappear, because the sons would prefer to abandon their fathers' business to seek their fortunes in the cities, ending up being "not very productive and even useless or at the expense of other citizens" (Quesnay [1757–1758a] 2005, 311; *my translation*).

In short, the Physiocrats present the *impôt unique* on the *produit net* of landowners as the only policy capable of preventing the unfolding of such negative effects. On the one hand, agricultural entrepreneurs, unburdened by taxes, can continue to invest their capital in technological innovations useful to reduce production expenses (Schumpeter [1954] 2006, 227). They can therefore obtain a higher net product, for the same gross product (Cartelier 1976, 70–77). On the other hand, by spending their income appropriately (on agricultural goods, more than on luxury goods), the nobles contribute to determining a balanced price level, "securing the re-creation of surplus value in agriculture" (Vaggi 1987, 109).

Now, one might ask: why should landowners agree to give up part of their rents? For the Physiocrats, the answer is obvious: any "deterioration" of the national wealth "so terrible for the population, would fall… necessarily in the end on the landowners" (Dupont [1768] 1910, 23; *my translation*).

The linkage between causes and effects deriving from a composite tax system[11] is effectively summarised by Dupont in *De l'origine et des progress d'une science nouvelle*: "indirect taxation →poor peasants; poor peasants→poor realm; poor realm→poor sovereign" (Dupont [1768] 1910, 23; *my translation*).

Theoretical and Practical Limits of the *impôt unique*

Considering the era in which it was put forward, the Physiocrats' analysis (and the proposal of economic policy that derives from it) cannot but arouse positive, if not enthusiastic, judgements: the insight that the material progress of France (or of any other nation) should necessarily pass through a capitalist reorganisation of the economy was called "revolutionary" by several authors and analysts, both in their era and in the following centuries (Zangheri 1966, x–xxi; Vaggi 1987, 100–101; Meek [1962] 2003, 34; Carvalho 2020, 35).

Marx, beyond his strong criticisms of the Physiocrats, recognises two indubitable merits:

1 they placed the origin of value (and of national wealth) in the system of production, not in the system of circulation of goods, like the mercantilists (Marx [1861–1863] 1969, 45, 50);
2 they analysed "the various *material components* in which capital exists and into which it resolves itself in the course of the labour-process" (Marx [1861–1863] 1969, 44).

Marx, however, reproached the Physiocrats for conceiving "the material law of a definite historical social stage […] as an abstract law governing equally all forms of society" (Marx [1861–1863] 1969, 44). The mistake of the Physiocrats lies not in generalising their view only from a temporal standpoint, but also from a spatial point of view (Delmas, Demals and Steiner 1995, 18–19). They considered abstract laws valid not only in France but also in England, Holland, and Italy—as Galiani had critically noted, in his *Dialogo sul commercio dei grani*, 1770—(Higgs 2001 [1897], 65) or anywhere else—as the antiphysiocrat Cameralist Johann Friedrich von Pfeiffer pointed out (Frambach 2011, 104).[12] In short, their naturalistic approach, i.e. the idea that the social order must simply follow the laws of the natural order to work perfectly (Cartelier

2008, 13), led them to consider the *agricultural sector* as the *only* one with a propensity for capitalist development. In this theoretical framework, they ended up confusing "the ethical principle of conformity to Nature, which is expressed in the imperative mood, and prescribes certain laws of action, with those causal laws which science discovers by interrogating Nature, and which are expressed in the indicative mood" (Marshall [1890] 2013, 626).

For this and other reasons, despite their innovative character, the Physiocratic economic analyses and policies provoked strong resistance from both the intellectuals (Hoselitz 1968, 637, 662) and public opinion (Ingram 1888, 67) of their time. The landowning class was concerned about a single tax replacing all the numerous indirect ones, even though the Physiocrats had shown that the latter would still burden land rent with higher costs. Why were landowners worried? Again, the answer seems obvious. They feared that the intention of the Physiocrats was to strip the nobles of their privileges and, therefore, of their property. This fear had no reason to exist. As Marx pointed out, Quesnay imagined a kind of capitalism far from the type that Adam Smith envisaged in England. The Physiocratic analysis considered only some fundamental components of capitalism, leaving out others: the agricultural entrepreneurs—who played an important role in the Physiocratic scheme—were not considered an independent and powerful social class like the capitalist bourgeoisie that, elsewhere, were already investing in the industrial sector.

Proof of this is the fact that the Physiocrats never clearly defined the profit due to agricultural entrepreneurs, "*primum mobile* of a capitalist economy" (Meek [1962] 2003, 385), even though they recognised in the "separation of landed property from labour" the only possible way for the accumulation of capital and the introduction of capitalist methods of production (*large crops*, crop rotation system, introduction of innovations in agriculture, etc.) (Marx [1861–1863] 1969, 50).

This "shortcoming" is no small thing, especially when one considers that the Physiocrats had developed an unprecedented technical language, with new categories such as *avances*, *productive class*, and *despote légale* (Carvalho 2020, 44). Among these, the main one is that of the *produit net*, which is made to coincide with the income due to landowners, without clearly explaining the profit. Smith, in defining the "natural price", and Marx, in defining the "price of production", did not show the same hesitancy as the Physiocrats, who, while claiming that the *prix fondamental* is determined by profit and production costs, never clearly distinguished the former from the latter (Zangheri 1966, xxx).

Therefore, are we faced with a theoretical weakness on the part of the Physiocrats or, rather, with the precise desire to use a vocabulary capable of expressing certain political (and ideological) convictions regarding the "nature" of the "social order" at the basis of their thought? I tend towards the second hypothesis. Quesnay mentions the "above-average profits" of large-scale agriculture, guaranteed by the rising prices of end products and the reduction of costs. The differential between the part of the rent due to the landlords and that due to the farmers can only be determined if the rental periods are long enough. On a theoretical level, the Physiocrats identify the part of *produit net* that goes to the farmers, who convert it into investments, as the key factor of economic growth.

Nevertheless, on the level of political theory, it appeared rather difficult to accept the idea that, from then on, the preservation of the social order in which they lived depended on profit (a variable not attributable to the ruling class). The landowners felt endangered by the outcomes of the Physiocratic definition of capitalism: the source of profit was identified only in the agricultural sector,[13] preventing "their system from being fully 'capitalist'" (Meek [1962] 2003, 391).

On the other hand, Quesnay and his disciples were not wrong, since—at the time they published their first works—about 65–70% of French gross income came from investments in the agricultural sector, while the amount of capital employed in sectors other than primary production was rather small overall (Marczewski 1960–1961, 371). Such data justified the Physiocrats' proposal that the *impôt unique* could be levied only on the rent of landowners (Meek 1977, 52).

Edgar Salin argued that, in contrast to the conservative attitude typical of the Physiocrats, the implementation of the *impôt unique* "would have presupposed the subversion of existing conditions" (Salin 1973, 91), thus justifying the fears of the landowning class. Actually, even the proposal of the single tax was an expression of the Physiocrats' desire to keep the privileges of the landowners unaltered, consciously pursuing a process of bourgeois reproduction of the feudal system (Marx [1861–1863] 1969, 49–50; Weulersse 1910, II, 710; Vaggi 1987, 180–181; Cartelier 2008, 20; Llombart 2009, 133; Argemí d'Abadal 2012, 153). The aristocratic class could remain an integral part of the new "ruling class", transforming itself into a "landed bourgeoisie" (Meek 1977, 61, footnote n. 28, and 55), but this is possible only if it accepts the levy of the *impôt unique* on rent, which would ensure the annual reproduction of the *produit net*. This process absolutely does not threaten the property rights of the aristocrats, guaranteed by the sovereign, co-owner of all the lands of the kingdom (Hoselitz 1968, 647):

> landowners, who appear to pay the tax on their rent, pay it on the contrary *on an increase in available wealth or net product*, which would not exist without the institution of the tax. Only the security that the tax gives to property can support and encourage enterprises and work, through which a considerable product can be obtained.
>
> (Dupont [1768] 1910, 27; *my translation* and *my italics*)

Mercier de la Rivière also developed the legal aspect of the sovereign's land co-ownership. The portion of the *produit net* due to the sovereign represented "a kind of shared wealth, intended for the common use of the whole nation". The interests of the sovereign and those of the rest of the population converged and were opposed only "to the eyes of ignorance" (Mercier (de) la Rivière [1767] 1910, II, 26; *my translation*). By attempting to reduce the aristocrats' prejudices against tax reform, the author of *L'Ordre naturel et essentiel des sociétés politiques* (1767) proposed to replace the term *impôt*—"which announces itself as a serious burden to be respected"—with the expression *revenu public*, whose usefulness is easier to understand (Mercier (de) la Rivière [1767] 1910, II, 40; *my translation*).

Yet, as much as the Physiocrats tried to explain the collective utility (aimed at safeguarding the existing social order) of a radical tax reform, they met not only the resistance of the nobles and the sovereign (who feared to antagonise those living at court), but also the criticism of other intellectuals of the time, both French and foreign.[14] In contrast with Mercier de la Rivière's *Ordre naturel*, Voltaire wrongly ascribed to it the claim that all landowners should pay exactly half of their income into the sovereign's coffers, given the condition of co-ownership.[15] He reproached the Physiocrats for hitting landowners hard with an *inique* (unequal), rather than *unique*, *impôt*, while those who became rich by trading products derived directly or indirectly from the land (wheat, which they resold at a higher price; cloth, made from hemp; fabrics, woven from wool) were exempt from taxation. Voltaire ignored, or disagreed with, the propulsive role the Physiocrats attributed to the single tax in terms of capital accumulation and increased investment.

This hypothesis was, on the other hand, supported by Turgot and Condorcet who, although not explicitly adhering to the group of *Économistes*, appreciated this proposal of economic policy and tried (at least for a certain period) to implement it in the context of their governmental functions (respectively, *Contrôleur des Finances* and *Inspecteur de Monnaie*). Condorcet was so convinced (at least at an early stage) of the strength of the theory of the single tax that he undertook to defend it against the critical remarks of Adam Smith (Condorcet [1786] 1847, 45).

The author of the *Wealth of Nations* declared himself an admirer of the Physiocrats (Smith [1776] 1976, II, 678), sharing the idea of surplus as a tax base. Nevertheless, by conceiving "productivity as the capacity to give rise to net product" and therefore inherent "in work and only in work" (Napoleoni 1970, 36–37), Smith rejected the erroneous Physiocratic assumption that *produit net* derived only from land and that the *impôt unique* should be levied only on this.

Smith's position is supported by Marx:

> Surplus-value itself is wrongly conceived [by the Physiocrats], because they have a wrong idea of value and reduce it to the use-value of labour, not to labour-time, social, homogeneous labour. Nevertheless, there remains the correct definition that only the wage-labour which creates more value than it costs is productive. Adam Smith frees this definition from the wrong conception with which the Physiocrats linked it.
>
> (Marx [1861–1863] 1969, 154)

In addition to the problem of correctly defining the theoretical category of *produit net*, there was difficulty determining with certainty the amount of the tax base. For this purpose, both Turgot and Condorcet considered it indispensable to precede the tax reform with a significant reorganisation of the cadastral system, from which would derive important advantages: to establish the real quantity and extent of the landed properties present in the kingdom, and to identify which and how many of these properties were rented to agricultural entrepreneurs. In this way, it would be possible to calculate the rent actually enjoyed by the landowners, thus eliminating the risk of arbitrariness in taxation (Mercier (de) la Rivière [1767] 1910, II, 32–33; Einaudi 1941, I, 357; Ardant 1972, 72).

Carrying out such an operation, however, took time. Probably, if it had been carried out quickly, it would have emerged that the nobility represented only 1–2% of the population (Rich-Wilson 1978, v, 709; see also Delmas 2009, 95). The supporters of the *impôt unique* would have realised that the effective tax base was too narrow for the tax reform they were advocating to become anything more than a "utopian project" (Tribe 1988, 125, footnote 18). It is no coincidence that, in his last writings on the issue—*Sur l'impôt personnel* (1790) and *Sur l'impôt progressif* (1793)—Condorcet proposed to reduce the taxation on land and to tax other kinds of income (Condorcet [1790] 1847, 473). In particular, he put forward the idea that the value of buildings could serve as a new tax base. In this way, while recognising that the craft sector had the same productivity as the agricultural sector, Condorcet remained faithful to the Physiocrats' assumption that taxes should not be levied on income intended for productive investment. In any sector, the spirit of entrepreneurial initiative had to be preserved, to ensure the economic growth of the nation with an adequate level of capital accumulation.

The failure to put the *impôt unique* into effect did not only depend on the fact that the Physiocrats's contemporaries among intellectuals and politicians did not support their proposal. There were at least two other reasons for it: the vagueness of the proposal and the inability to secure the technical conditions necessary for its implementation. The "illusion of the reformers" ended up shattering against the persistent inefficiency of the French tax administration (Ardant 1972, 123) and, not less important, the serious state of indebtedness of the French monarchy. The latter was also burdened by war expenses that worsened the already worrying situation of public finances, especially when France found itself involved in the Seven Years' War (1756–1763). In this sense, replacing all indirect taxes with a single tax on rent could indeed have been a hazardous move, risking bankrupting the state (Llombart 2009, 130).

Conclusions

In this chapter, I have shown that the Physiocrats were concerned with translating their economic theories into economic policies, because of their belief that political economy had to improve society in practical terms. Among their projects, fiscal reform was of utmost importance because it could ensure that less money was wasted on collection costs, making more capital available for economic growth. Since the Physiocrats were convinced that agriculture was the sole economic activity able to produce a surplus, the *impôt unique* on land rent was the cornerstone of their fiscal reform proposal.

In theory, landowners were supposed to be in favour of the *impôt unique*, which the Physiocrats presented as a more useful tool for them than for anyone else, guaranteeing both the increase of their wealth and the preservation of their privileged position. In fact, the *impôt unique* "seduced" more intellectuals (Marion 1910, 94) than aristocrats and politicians. The aura of renewal that emanated from Quesnay's *entresol* soon faded: nothing changed significantly in the French *status quo* and the implementation of the *impôt unique* remained a "chimera" (Marion 1910, 94).

Nonetheless, many thinkers found inspiration in the Physiocratic model of economic science embodying the "concept of economic justice" (Dwyer 2014, 673) and aimed "to raise the quality of human life" (Marshall [1890] 2013, 626). It is certainly no coincidence, then, that Marx and "other German authors such as August Oncken" attached great importance to the "Physiocrats' proposals", considering them "among the milestones of the history of economic thought" (Argemí d'Abadal 2012, 157). Moreover, in the second half of the twentieth century, many contemporary economists considered Quesnay's *Tableau* a valuable "analytical reference" for growth theory (Deane 1978, 30).

Notes

1 See Mirabeau's letter to Rousseau dated 1767, quoted in Schelle 1907, 225–235. Cf. also Hect 1958, 256 and Vaggi 1987, 22.

2 Recently, Jean Cartelier returned to the cooperation between Quesnay and Mirabeau, clearing Mirabeau's name of an alleged "intellectual submission" to the author of the *Tableau économique* (Cartelier 2008, 13ff., esp. 14).

3 Quesnay defined natural laws as "physical or moral laws" and positive laws as "authentic rules established by a sovereign authority" (Quesnay 1765 [2005], 121–122).

4 For Quesnay, see *Fermier* (1756), *Grains* (1757), *Hommes* and *Impôts* (1757–8), *Tableau économique* (1758), chapter vii of *Philosophie rurale ou économie générale et politique de l'agriculture* (1767), *Maximes générales du gouvernement économique d'un royaume agricole* (1763). For Mirabeau: *Théorie de l'impôt* (1760) and *Supplément à la théorie de l'impôt* (1776), memoir addressed to the King of Sweden.

Bear in mind that Quesnay and Mirabeau were not the first to advance the idea of a single tax. On Vauban's influence on the Physiocrats regarding this issue, see Vaggi 2018, 10297.

5 Cf. Mercier de la Rivière, *Ordre naturel et essentiel des Sociétés politiques* (1767); Dupont de Nemours, *Physiocratie, ou constitution naturelle du gouvernement le plus avantageux au genre humain* (1767) and *De l'origine et des progrès d'une science nouvelle* (1768); Guillaume François Le Trosne, *De l'administration provinciale, et de la réforme de l'impôt* (1778).

6 On the limits of such positive effects resulting automatically from the transition from *petite* to *grande culture*, see Llombart 2009, 127–129.

7 The landowners, however, can also play another important role, which is linked to the definition of the *available class*: "the only [class] which, not being confined by a want of support to a particular species of labour, may be employed in the general service of society, as for war, and the administration of justice, either by a personal service, or by the payment of a part of their revenue, with which the state may hire others to fill these employments. The appellation which suits the best with this division, for this reason, is that of the *disposable* class" (Turgot 1774, § 15).

8 For a definition of *avances annuelles*, composed of "annual production expenditure" and "sterile production", see Quesnay [1760] 2005, 448–449.

9 Often, the costs of tax collection by the *Ferme générale* (the financial company set up in 1726 for this specific purpose) are so high that there is a considerable discrepancy between what taxpayers pay and what the State coffers actually receive. Among other things, Quesnay notes, all these "agents employed in the collection of taxes [...] do not produce by their work any wealth for the State; so, the expenditure and the men are at a pure loss to the kingdom" (Quesnay, [1757–1758b] 2005, 230; *my translation*).

10 Here, Quesnay is quoting the *Testament politique du Cardinal de Richelieu*, attributed to Paul Hay, Marquis de Chastelet.

11 For more information on the multiplicity of taxes (*taille, dime, gabelle, aides, capitation*, and other lesser-known taxes) see Vaggi 1987, 21; McLain, 1977, 18; Beer, 1939, 42–44.

12 For an alternative view, which holds that the Physiocrats were concerned with the practical problems of the country and society of their time, see Rossi 1843, I, 21.

13 The question was so thorny that it represented a controversial point during the drafting of the *Philosophie rurale* (1762). According to Gianni Vaggi, Mirabeau would not have hesitated to make an explicit distinction between profit (attributed to agricultural entrepreneurs) and net product (attributed to landowners). Quesnay, on the other hand, would have been more prudent, so as not to arouse concern and opposition on the part of the sovereign and the noble class (Vaggi 1987, 146–148). The lack of total overlap between the opinions of the two co-founders of the Physiocratic school has also been noted with reference to other issues (Vardi 2013, 165–166).

14 On the opposition to the Physiocrats by well-known publicists of the time (Grimm, Linguet, Abbé de Mably, Forbonnais, Necker, etc.), see Hoselitz 1968, 637–638. On other distinguished critics of Physiocratic ideas, see Klot-Minard-Orain 2017, 18, f 25 and Bernard Delmas's chapter (pp. 79–104) on Charles-Étienne Pesselier's (1712–1763) opposition to the *impôt unique* proposal (Delmas 2017). Pesselier belongs to one of the categories that would have been most harmed by the implementation of the tax policy of the Physiocrats, that of *fermiers généraux* (tax collectors).

15 Condorcet retorts that what is demanded is only "the portion required to defend and govern the State well" (Condorcet-Beaumarchais [1768] 1879, 315; note no. 2; *my translation*).

Bibliography

Ardant, Gabriel. 1972. *Historie de l'impôt. Livre II. XVIIIe et XXIe siècles*. Paris: Fayard.

Argemí d'Abadal, Lluís. 2012. The Physiocrats. In Jürgen Georg Backhaus (ed.), *Handbook of the History of Economic Thought Insights on the Founders of Modern Economics*. New York, Dordrecht, Heidelberg, London: Springer, 137–159.

Beer, Max. 1939. *An Inquiry into Physiocracy*. London: Allen & Unwin.

Candela, Guido, Maura Palazzi (eds.). 1979. Presentazione. In Id. *Dibattito sulla fisiocrazia*. Florence: La Nuova Italia, vii–lxi.

Cartelier, Jean. 1976. *Surproduit et Reproduction. La formation de l'économie politique classique*. Grenoble: Press Universitaires de Grenoble François Maspero.

Cartelier, Jean. 2008. *L'économie politique de François Quesnay ou l'Utopie du Royaume agricole*. Paris: Flammarion.

Carvalho, Thérence. 2020. *La physiocratie dans l'Europe des Lumières*. Le Kremlin-Bicêtre: Éditions mare&martin.

Condorcet, Marie-Jean-Antoine-Nicolas. [1786] 1847. Vie de M. Turgot. In O'Connor & F. Arago (eds.), Œuvres de Condorcet, t. v. Paris: Firmin Didot Frères, 5–233.

Condorcet, Marie-Jean-Antoine-Nicolas. [1790] 1847. Sur l'impôt personnel. In O'Connor & F. Arago (eds.), Œuvres de Condorcet, t. xi. Paris: Firmin Didot Frères, 473–483.

Condorcet, Marie-Jean-Antoine-Nicolas, Pierre Augustin Caron Beaumarchais. [1768] 1879. Avertissement des éditeurs de l'édition de Kehl. In A.J.Q. Beuchot (ed.), Œuvres complètes de Voltaire. Paris: Garnier Frères, 305–368.

Deane, Phyllis. 1978. *The Evolution of Economic Ideas*. Cambridge: Cambridge University Press.

Delmas, Bernard. 2009. Les physiocrates, Turgot et 'le grand secret de la science fiscale'. *Revue d'histoire moderne et contemporaine*, 2/2009, 56-2: 79–103.

Delmas, Bernard. 2017. L'anti-physiocratie des financiers: les *Doutes* de Charles-Étienne Pesselier sur la *Théorie de l'impôt* du marquis de Mirabeau et l'instruction générale. In G. Klotz, P. Minard, A. Orain (eds.). *Les Voies De La Richesse?: La Physiocratie en Question (1760–1850)*. Rennes: Presses Universitaires de Rennes, 79–104.

Delmas, Bernard, Thierry Demals, and Philippe Steiner. 1995. Présentation: les physiocrates, la science de l'économie politique et l'Europe. In Id., *La diffusion internationale de la Physiocracy (XVIIIe-XIXe)*. Grenoble: Presse Universitaires de Grenoble, 7–29.

Dupont de Nemours, Pierre-Samuel. [1768] 1910. *De l'origine et des progrès d'une science nouvelle*. Paris: Librairie Paul Geuthner.

Dupont de Nemours, Pierre-Samuel. [1815] 1848. *Lettre à J.B. Say*, 22 avril 1815,. In J.B. Say, *Œuvres diverses*. Paris: S.I., 366–387.

Dwyer, Terence M. 2014. Taxation: The lost history. *The American Journal of Economics and Sociology*, 73, 4: 664–988.

Einaudi, Luigi. 1941. Contributi fisiocratici alla teoria dell'ottima imposta. In Id., *Saggi sul risparmio e l'imposta* (331–361). Torino: Einaudi.

Frambach, Hans. 2011. Cameralism and physiocracy as the two sides of a coin: Example of the economic policy of Johann Friedrich von Pfeiffer. In Jürgen Georg Backhaus (ed.), *Physiocracy, Antiphysiocracy and Pfeiffer* (97–113). New York, Dordrecht, Heidelberg, London: Springer.

Gide, Charles, and Charl Rist. 1922. *Histoire des doctrines économiques depuis les physiocrates jusqu'à nos jours*. Paris: Librairie de la Société du Recueil Sirey.

Hect, Jacqueline. 1958. *La vie de François Quesnay*. In I.N.E.D., *François Quesnay et la Physiocratie*, I. Paris: Presses Universitaires de France, 211–294.

Higgs, Henri. [1897] 2001. *The Physiocrats Six Lectures on the French Économistes of the 18th Century*. Kitchener: Batoche Books.

Hoselitz, Bert F. 1968. Agrarian capitalism, the natural order of things: François Quesnay. *Kiklos. International Review for Social Sciences*, 21, 637–664.

Ingram, John Kells. 1888. *A History of Political Economy*. New York: August M. Kelley (Reprints of Economic Classics).

Klotz, Gérard, Philippe Minard, and Arnaud Orain. 2017. La physiocratie vouée aux gémonies? Introduction. In Id. (eds.), *Les voies de la richesse?: La Physiocratie en Question (1760–1850)* (7–39). Rennes: Presses Universitaires de Rennes.

Le Trosne, Guillaume-François. 1778. *De l'administration provinciale, et de la réforme de l'impôt*. Paris: A Basle.

Llombart, Vicent. 2009. El valor de la Fisiocracia en su propio tiempo: un análisis crítico. *Investigaciones de Historia económica*, otoño 2009: 109–136.

Marczewski, Jan. 1960–1961. Some aspects of the economic growth of France 1660–1958. *Economic Development and Cultural Change*, IX, 3: 369–386.

Marion, Marcel. 1910. *Les impôts directs sous l'ancien régime*. Paris: Édouard Cornély et Cie Éditeurs.

Marshall, Alfred. [1890] 2013. *Principles of Economics*. London: Palgrave Macmillan.

Marx, Karl. [1861–1863] 1969. *Theories of Surplus-Value (Volume IV of Capital. Part I)*. Moscow: Progress Publishers.

McLain, James J. 1977. *The Economic Writings of Du Pont de Nemours*. London: Associated University Presses.

Meek, Ronald L. [1962] 2003. *The Economics of Physiocracy*. London: Allen & Unwin.

Meek, Ronald L. 1977. Ideas, facts, environment: The case of French Physiocrats. In Robert V. Eagly (ed.), *Events, Ideology and Economic Theory* (42–61). Milan: Franco Angeli.

Mercier (de) La Rivière, Pierre-Paul. [1767] 1910. *L'ordre naturel et essentiel des sociétés politiques*, Paris: Libraire Paul Geuthner.

Mirabeau (de), Victor Riqueti. 1760. *Théorie de l'impôt*. Paris: S.I.

Napoleoni, Claudio [1970] 1973. *Smith, Ricardo, Marx*. New York: Halsted Press Book John Wiley & Sons.

Orain, Arnaud and Philippe Steiner. 2016. François Quesnay (1694–1774) and Physiocracy. In Gilbert Faccarello and Heinz D. Kurz (eds.). *Handbook on the History of Economic Analysis. Volume I. Great Economists since Petty and Boisguilbert* (28–39). Cheltenham, Northampton, MA: Edward Elgar Publishing.

Quesnay, François. [1756] 2005. Fermiers. In Christine Théré, Loïc Charles and Jean-Claude Perrot (eds.). *Œuvres économiques complètes et autres textes* (vol. I; 127–159). Paris: Ined.

Quesnay, François. [1757] 2005. Grains. In Christine Théré, Loïc Charles and Jean-Claude Perrot (eds.). *Œuvres économiques complètes et autres textes* (vol. I; 161–212). Paris: Ined.

Quesnay, François. [1757–1758a] 2005. Hommes. In Christine Théré, Loïc Charles and Jean-Claude Perrot (eds.). *Œuvres économiques complètes et autres textes* (vol. I; 257–319). Paris: Ined.

Quesnay, François. [1757–1758b] 2005. Impôts. In Christine Théré, Loïc Charles and Jean-Claude Perrot (eds.). *Œuvres économiques complètes et autres textes* (vol. I; 213–256). Paris: Ined.

Quesnay, François. [1760] 2005. Tableau œconomique avec ses explications. In Christine Théré, Loïc Charles and Jean-Claude Perrot (eds.). *Œuvres économiques complètes et autres textes* (vol. I; 439–525). Paris: Ined.

Quesnay, François. [1765] 2005. Le droit naturel (2e édition). In Christine Théré, Loïc Charles and Jean-Claude Perrot (eds.). *Œuvres économiques complètes et autres textes* (vol. I; 111–123). Paris: Ined.

Rich, Edwin Ernest and Charles Henry Wilson (eds.) (1978). Economics and society in Europe in the modern age. In *Cambridge Economic History*, vol. v. Turin: Giulio Einaudi Editore.

Ridolfi, Mauro. 1973. *Introduzione* a François Quesnay, *Il "Tableau économique" e altri scritti di economia* (ix–lxxxi), ed. M. Ridolfi. Milano: Isedi.

Rossi, Pellegrino. 1843. *Cours d'économie politique*, I. Paris: chez Thorel et Joubert.

Salin, Edgar. 1973. *Political economy. History of ideas from Plato to the present day.* Milan: Editrice Vita e Pensiero.

Schelle, Gustave. 1907. *Le Docteur Quesnay.* Paris: Felix Alcan Editeur.

Schumpeter, Joseph Alois. [1954] 2006. *History of Economic Analysis.* London: Taylor & Francis e-Library.

Smith, Adam. [1776] 1976. *An Inquiry into the Nature and Causes of the Wealth of Nations.* Oxford: Oxford University Press.

Tribe, Keith. 1988. *Governing Economy: The Reformation of German Economic Discourse, 1750–1840.* Cambridge: Cambridge University Press.

Turgot, Anne Robert Jacques. 1774. *Réflexions sur la formation et la distribution des richesses.* Paris: S.I.

Vaggi, Gianni. 1987. *The Economics of François Quesnay.* Basingstoke and London: The Macmillan Press Ltd.

Vaggi, Gianni. 2018. *Physiocracy*, entry in *The New Palgrave Dictionary of Economics.* London: Palgrave-MacMillan.

Vardi, Liana. 2013. *The Physiocrats and the World of the Enlightenment.* New York: Cambridge University Press.

Weulersse, Georges. 1910. *Le mouvement physiocratique en France (de 1756 à 1770)* (2 vols). Paris: Alcan.

Zagari, Eugenio. 1972. *Una reinterpretazione della teoria fisiocratica.* Napoli: Jovene editore.

Zangheri, Renato. 1966. *Introduzione* a F. Quesnay, *Scritti economici* (v–xxxi), R. Zangheri (ed.). Bologna: Arnaldo Forni Editore.

5 Post-Smithian Views on Poverty and Poor Relief

Cosma Orsi

Introduction

The aim of this essay is to inquiry into the attitude towards poverty and its remedies as an emerging problem in the sphere of political economy from late eighteenth century to the mid-1830s. In doing so, it deals with two issues often considered peripheral by historians of economic thought. First, though voluntary associations have been thoroughly analysed by leading economic and social historians (Hobsbawm 1957; Gosden 1974; Gorsky 1998; Ismay 2018), the economic arguments underpinning their establishment and diffusion have received scanty attention by professional historians of economic thought (Cowherd 1977; Henderson 1997; Gerke 2020). Second, by putting into perspective an array of statements eulogising *self-betterment* and *self-help*, this essay helps identify interesting connections between economic theorising and social policy and offers a broader perspective of the historical and cultural context leading to the 1834 round of reforms.

During the last quarter of the eighteenth century, England went through unprecedented social and economic changes. Among the challenges the English ruling class had to deal with, one can list the acceleration of the process of enclosure; the consequent abandonment of common lands by thousands of agricultural workers; and the difficult process of their urbanisation. From the mid-1790s onwards, the fear induced by the French Revolution, the subsequent Napoleonic wars (1793–1815), and a series of economic crises, further aggravated the situation.

In the attempt to address the above-mentioned problems which threatened to destroy its social fabric, enlightened southern local magistrates carved out a comprehensive social policy financed by the parish rates designed to reduce poverty and prevent social distress for the working poor, i.e., the *Speenhamland system*. Although it never became a law of Parliament nor it was adopted nationwide, the *Speenhamland system* radically altered the English social legislation for the following 40 years. From 1795 to 1834, poor relief was no longer an aid granted to specific segments of the population, but an entitlement to assistance that could be enjoyed by all workers either unemployed or employed at below-subsistence wages.

DOI: 10.4324/9781003228097-5

Inspired by Adam Smith and Thomas Paine's[1] perspective to favour the inclusion of the labouring poor within the newly established social system,[2] broad-minded legislators directed their efforts to secure a decent standard of living for the working poor.[3] On the assumption that ignorance, aversion to work, intemperance, and prodigality were the consequence of social and economic circumstances, they pointed at two objectives; on the one hand, they wanted 'to lift the lower classes to a new life of industry, frugality, honesty and temperance' and, on the other, 'to bring to the upper classes a new sense of social responsibility commensurate with their wealth and privilege' (Cowherd 1977: 2).

Not surprisingly, since its adoption, the *Speenhamland system* brought about mixed feelings. If the poor may claim an albeit partial victory, the same could not be said for the upper classes, who welcomed the newly established social legislation with a deep sense of alarm. On the one side, they were concerned by the potential demands for further social and economic claims (trade unionism, factory legislation, redistribution of land, etc.); on the other, they fear that offering thousands of hitherto self-supporting working families nearly free access to public relief might have brought about additional 'inflationary pressure on the *Poor Rates*' (Bahmueller 1981: 34).[4] Intercepting the anxieties of the riches, a radically different perspective concerning poverty and its remedy began to emerge.

Such a shift owes much to notable post-Smithian statisticians and economic writers who, by the end of the eighteenth century, began to conceptualise economic issues at the abstract level of macroeconomic processes. Differently from late-Enlightenment and Republican thinkers who saw poverty as the result of disadvantageous institutional and economic circumstances, writers like Frederick Morton Eden, Robert Thomas Malthus, and David Ricardo put forward the idea that poverty stems from temperamental faults (e.g., individual imprudence, indolence, and/or licentious behaviours). Accordingly, they endorsed the view that individual motivation was the only drive for the poor to escape their condition.

These authors assumed, first, that 'the requisite willpower and desire for economic independence could be found in any man, however humble' and, second, 'that it was possible for poor people to support themselves by "independent labour" alone' (Baugh in Baxter 1983: 66). On these grounds, they argued that any successful strategy meant to alleviate poverty should be designed with a unique intent, namely to 'cure' the poor's character. Following this train of thought, they suggested removing any undue financial support. On the whole, Classical-post-Smithian economic writers identified *self-betterment* as the driving principle around which anti-poverty strategies should dwell.

In doing so, they provided a theoretical map that guided the legislator in the forging of consistent legislative programmes and practices meant to alleviate poverty (Cowherd 1977; Ismay 2018). Nonetheless, their contributions in the field of political economy were useful not only as a map for the legislator who designed and implemented the social legislation of 1834 but also for advancing policy recommendations grappling with the issue of collective responsibility including the establishment of a nationwide network of provident institutions (*Friendly Societies* and/or *Savings Banks*). In the eyes of these authors, provident institutions were presented as socially useful because they would assist the poor in helping themselves in hard times while keeping relief costs under control.

The essay is structured as follows: the 'Post-Smithian Economic Writers and the *Speenhamland System*' section offers an account of the main arguments utilised by post-Smithian authors against the current social legislation; the 'Post-Smithian Self-Help Policies: Friendly Societies and Saving Banks' section deals with Eden, Malthus, and Ricardo's policy suggestions meant to establish a nationwide network of provident institutions; the 'Conclusion' section pulls together some conclusions.

Post-Smithian Economic Writers and the *Speenhamland System*

Throughout the 1790s, crop failures and consequent rising prices brought about hunger-related diseases and near-famine conditions. This led to an unprecedented period of food riots (see Patriquin 2007; 117; see also Wrigley and Schonfield 1989: 215–219, 228–528–529; Stern 1964: 168–187). The pressure reached a point of no return in 1795 when, on his way to Parliament, King George III was mobbed by a ferocious crowd shouting at him 'No Pitt – No War – Peace, Peace – Bread, Bread' (quoted in Baugh 2014: 166). Facing the 'double panic of famine and revolution' (Pretyman 1878: 27), legislators realised that more proactive measures than those incorporated in the *Gilbert Act* (1782) were needed.

Acknowledging that 'the present state of the poor requires further assistance than has been done previously' (Oxford Gazette: 1795), the Berkshire *Justices of Pace* ruled that every worker was entitled to a minimum subsistence, and that 'if they earned only part of it, then society owed them the difference'.[5] On this ground, they unanimously decided that, from that moment onwards, the *Poor Rates* would be used to finance an income supplement for the working poor distributed 'according to the price of bread, so that a minimum income would be provided for the poor regardless of how much they earned' (Oxford Gazette: 1795). In the field of social policy, the *Speenhamland system* represented a watershed. Since its introduction, in fact, the means-tested sliding scale of wage supplement became a reference point for future thought about income support policies. It undermined earlier 'commonplaces about the place of the poor in the social hierarchy', inaugurating an understanding of 'social security as a basis of citizenship' (Stedman Jones 2004: 13).

Even if the *Speenhamland system* was not devised to eradicate poverty, its establishment not only ensured subsistence in times of famine for the weakest sections of society and a modest additional purchasing power when circumstances improved but also raised the level of mobility of the labour force in search of employment throughout the country (BLAUG 1964: 229–245). Just because of its positive effect, it generated anxiety among the ruling classes. Certainly, they were worried that the lower orders might ask for more.[6] However, what scared them most was that after the establishment of the *Speenhamland system*, the poor, once regarded as mere handmaidens at their service, became a 'constituent element of the civil order' (BAUGH in BAXTER 1983: 93) enjoying proper rights.

The first blow to the *Speenhamland system* came from Sir Frederick Morton Eden, a social investigator 'with considerable practical knowledge of Poor Law administration' (WINCH 1998: 9). Truly concerned with the living conditions of the less fortunate, he believed that the destitute condition of the lower classes, how despicable a problem it might be, was, nonetheless a manageable one. Like Malthus and Ricardo after him, Eden's criterion for 'detecting appropriate policies with respect to the complex problem confronting society' (LEVIN 1964: 226) was grounded in simple economic principles. Although he acknowledged the poor's 'moral potentialities', his adherence to the natural laws of market(s) and competition along with his abstract conception of the common good urged him to search for an alternative to any form of economic redistribution in favour of the lowest ranks of society.

On the assumption that only individual motivation could help the poor to escape their condition, he argued that *Speenhamland*'s type of response to poverty had to be considered as a misconceived intervention, certainly too burdening on the taxpayer[7] and ineffective in achieving its declared objectives. In contrast to the view upheld by late-Enlightenment and Republican supporters of the poor's right to subsistence, he advanced the idea that this latter had to take on greater self-responsibility for their life conditions (EDEN 1797: 587).

Penned from a perspective that reveals Eden's general adherence to Smith's system of natural liberty, his impressive three volumes book *The State of the Poor* (1797) was meant to provide a quantitative assessment of poverty (ISMAY 2018: 67).[8] Building upon a wide-ranging statistical knowledge, he criticised the existing social legislation on the ground that it betrayed the fundamental principles of political economy. For Eden, the established practice of providing work (and/or occasional allowances) to the poor

> Proceeded from the supposed existence of facts in political economy, which was doubtful at the time, but which experience has since proved to be mistaken. It is most satisfying circumstance [...] to show that the capital stock of the public cannot enter into competition with the capital and well-exerted industry of individual.
>
> (EDEN 1797: 586)

On the assumption that only market mechanisms could secure the rising of labour productivity and the increase of national wealth, he argued that the advent of a society based on manufactures and commerce brought about 'many beneficial alterations in the condition of the labouring classes' (IBID: 29). Only the unbounded forces of market and free enterprise, Eden argued, could enhance 'the predominant principle that animates the world, and which, when expanded into action, gives birth to every social virtue' (IBID: 56), namely people's desire to better her/his conditions. Thanks to the spirit of emulation, even the *villain* would 'quit his livery for the independence of trade' (IBID: 586).

Invoking Smith's wage-fund theory, he argued that any amount of money compulsory paid to the poor 'came from employers' fund available for the payment of wages and for additional workers' (COWHERD 1977: 17). From this perspective, means-tested wage supplements helped the labouring poor in the worst possible manner.[9] By granting subsistence to the poor, they obliterated their willingness to work while protecting the vicious, idle, and lazy who would never starve. On the premise that the best relief the poor can obtain 'must come from themselves' (EDEN 1797: 587), Eden called for 'a vigorous reform in the Poor laws' (IBID: XXV).

Though Eden's analysis was exceptionally well-informed, it did not provide solid criteria for distinguishing among the poor those industrious, but unable to find employment, and those simply unwilling to work. Like many of his contemporaries discussing poverty issues, in fact, he considered poverty as an abstract social condition (HIMMELFARB 1984: 77). To debase the argument in favour of the right to subsistence, natural law advocates had to push their argument a step ahead: the affirmation of *self-betterment* as the base for a sound anti-poverty strategy called for a positive proof that poverty was a phenomenon indissolubly linked to over-population. Only in this way, they could blame the poor for market failure. Although the interlinkage between the rate of population growth and living standards was an argument already discussed by contemporary authors like Joseph Townsend (1786) and Edmund Burke (1795), it was Malthus who give it new significance.[10]

The year after the publication of Eden's *The State of the Poor*, Malthus published the *Essay on the Principle of Population*, a book that set 'the terms of discourse on the subject of poverty for half a century' (IBID: 44). Written as a rebuff of any form of radicalism (SOWELL 1962; HIMMELFARB 1984), the intention of Malthus' *Essay* was to revive old *Whig* principles. The weapon he employed to this end was the principle of population: in a nutshell, it postulated that agricultural production rises in arithmetic progression while population tends to rise geometrically.[11] Malthus' principle rested on three main propositions, namely 'that population cannot increase without the means of subsistence'; 'that population does invariably increase, where there are the means of subsistence'; and 'that the superior power of population cannot be checked, without producing misery or vice' (MALTHUS 1798: 77).

More than a vitriolic critique to contemporary radical thinkers, Malthus' target was Adam Smith's theory of economic progress. Concerning the issue of the lower classes' 'happiness and comfort', Malthus agreed with Smith that a society based on the division of labour was a harbinger of greater productivity; however, he disputed that the increase in national wealth could be translated into a better living condition for the poor. For, while it was true that increased productivity would bring about higher wages, this would not occur without a proportional increase in the foodstuffs obtainable from the already fully exploited fertile land. Hence, even in Smith's envisaged commercial society 'the lower classes would remain in the same condition, if not worse' (IBID: 109).

Although the argument that population should 'always correspond to the level of the available means of subsistence' had already been discussed, the novelty of the *Essay* resided in its focusing on 'the means by which this level is effected' (IBID: 11). By linking demographic reasoning (grounded in arithmetical calculations) to a dismissal of institutionalised aid on the behalf of the poor, Malthus succeeded in altering the general perception concerning poverty issues. Let aside abstract economic principles, he preferred contextualising poor relief within a school of thought built upon certain natural laws presiding over the economic sphere. In doing so, he was able to reframe the ongoing debate concerning the *Poor Law*'s drawbacks. While acknowledging that the current social legislation had been formulated with the sincerest intentions, Malthus disagreed with the possibility that it might achieve its purposes,[12] and urged his readers to accept 'that misery and vice were attributable to a fundamental law of human nature that was impervious to institutional change and legislative contrivance' (WINCH 1998: VIII).

In a melancholic tone, Malthus maintained that poverty was unavoidable because it stems from the tendency of the poor to be idle. Hence, nothing could be done to help them from escaping their condition.

> A man who is born in an already possessed world, if he cannot get subsistence from his parents, on whom he has a just demand, (he) has no claim of right to the smallest portion of food, and, in fact, has no business to be where he is.
>
> (MALTHUS 1803: 531)[13]

Like Eden, on several occasions, Malthus reiterated the idea that, as free and responsible individuals, the poor must recognise that 'they are themselves the cause of their poverty' (MALTHUS 1798: 498) and that 'nothing perhaps would tend so strongly to excite a spirit of industry and economy among the poor, as a thorough knowledge that their happiness must always depend principally upon themselves' (IBID: 232). If so, the *Speenhamland system* represented one of the main obstacles to the development of society. By depriving the most productive and worthy members of society of the resources aimed at financing the *Poor rate*, Malthus admonished, the entire economic system would lose its economic dynamism. Wage supplements, in fact, interfered with the incentives needed to get the poor to adopt the discipline and commitment required by the new types of work. Getting rid of the fear of misery and hunger is tantamount to removing the most powerful incentive to work and save. The *Poor Law*

> may [...] be said to diminish both the power and the will to save, among the common people, and thus to weaken one of the strongest incentives to sobriety and industry, and consequently to happiness.
>
> (MALTHUS 1798: 87)

Grounded in a rigorous market approach, Malthus' abolitionist position rested on the idea that only the dismissal of institutionalised safety net for the able-bodied would induce these latter to take care of themselves. Cases of 'extreme distress', he reasoned, could be successfully treated as they were dealt with prior to 1782, namely through the establishment of a nationwide workhouse system financed by general taxation. Within workhouses 'the fare should be hard, and those that were able to work' obliged to do so for a market wage (IBID: 97). This was quite the same argument as Jeremy Bentham's, except for the fact that the father of Utilitarianism emphasised the potentiality of workhouses to offsetting the cost attached to poor relief, while Malthus stressed upon the motivational properties of *self-help*. According to Malthus, the possibility of escaping poverty only resided in the poor's desire for *self-betterment*. For Malthus, in fact, 'it is the hope of bettering our condition, and the fear of want, rather than want in itself that is the best stimulus to industry' (MALTHUS 1817: 43).

As we shall see briefly, Malthus' ideas on poverty were further elaborated by one of his closest friends, David Ricardo. As an economic thinker speaking on the behalf of the triumphant bourgeoisie class, he believed in the natural (and impersonal) character of *laissez-faire*. Building upon this assumption, he carved out an 'objective' analysis of poverty. In the *Principles of Political Economy and Taxation* (1817), he maintained that only a well-functioning market mechanism could bring about an income distribution conducive to economic growth and capital accumulation. Within a competitive economic system, changes in the levels of supply and demand lead to a periodic restructuring of the labour market. Momentary unemployment, due to a changing sectoral structure of labour demand, is the natural consequence of the workings of the market.

Confronted by the laws of the economy, labourers must prepare themselves for misfortune caused by fluctuations in the level of economic activity and structural changes in the modes of production and consumption. Nonetheless, labour does not suffer any permanent damage: the market is well-equipped for allowing the re-absorption of the victims of technological unemployment into the labour market within a reasonable period. As a firm adherent to Say's law, Ricardo argued that subsistence could only be ensured by an increasing supply of labour on the market, provided that 'if the demand for labour is great, the number of people employed will be proportional to that demand' (RICARDO 1823 [1951]: 303).

Thus, whenever the level of wages fell below the subsistence level, capitalists found it convenient to increase investment (thus demanding more labour), bringing aggregate wages back towards the subsistence level. Because wages should 'be left to the determination of the fair and free competition of the market', Ricardo claimed that they 'should never be controlled by the interference of the legislature' (RICARDO 1817: 101–102). Ricardo's problem was no longer how to determine the just remuneration of labour; but how to secure that free competition on the labour market can restore and maintain subsistence wages over time, adjusting any variation in production, technology, and demand for goods.

Ricardo's central assumption regarding the existing social legislation was that: 'Great harm results from the idea inculcated by the *Poor Law* that the poor can enjoy the right to subsistence' (RICARDO 1819 [1952]: 248). He believed that income subsidies had a twofold disadvantage: on the one hand, they acted against the existing economic order based on the principle of free competition, with the risk of distorting its natural evolution; on the other hand, by allocating resources to the poor, they favoured a substantial increase of population. On this point, Ricardo's and Malthus' theories were very similar. By 'offering it a portion of the wages of prudence and industry' the *Poor Law* 'rendered restraint superfluous' (RICARDO 1817: 103). By benefiting from State aid, the poor would obtain the means to enlarge their families, thus increasing the number of mouths to feed. Such a course of action, only increased the costs of maintaining the poor and the demand for subsistence goods, thus shrinking the accumulation of capital necessary for sustaining England's industrial development.

> whilst the present laws are in force, it is quite in the natural order of things that the fund for the maintenance of the poor should progressively increase, till it has absorbed all the net revenue of the country, or at least so much of it as the state shall leave to us, after satisfying its own never-failing demands for the public expenditure.
>
> (RICARDO 1817: 102)

What should be done to halt the process, Ricardo suggested, was a retrenchment of State activity meant to reduce poverty

> The nature of the evil points out the remedy. By gradually contracting the sphere of the poor laws; by impressing on the poor the value of independence, by teaching them that they must look not to systematic or casual charity, but to their own exertions for support, that prudence and forethought are neither unnecessary nor unprofitable virtues, we shall by degrees approach a sounder and more healthful state.
>
> (IBID: 104)

Post-Smithian Self-Help Policies: Friendly Societies and Saving Banks

A common belief among natural law economic writers was that the poor could better their life conditions only if they become fully responsible for their conduct. For these authors, it was the poor's improvidence that intensified the immiserating effects of low wages, amplifying the attitude of dissipating their meagre savings. Who best captured this understanding was David Davies when he said that the poor, 'commonly misspend those earnings, which, if used with frugality, would render their condition comfortable and themselves happy' (Davies 1795: 55). Following this train of thought, post-Smithian economic writers came to perceive self-responsibility as an aspirational principle to be actively encouraged. In their eyes, *Friendly Societies* and *Saving Banks* would serve the purpose of instilling attitudes like thrift, frugality, and independence. In fact, these voluntary organisations would do well 'instructing (the poor) how to secure and improve [...] savings as they might make out of their pay' (Davies 1795: 55). This set the scene for *self-help* as a sound social policy leading to the poor's *self-betterment.*

Eden's policy suggestions to help the poor while lessening the financial burden of poor relief ranged from the reduction of assistance to the restitution of the enclosed land to the poor (Eden 1797: xx–xxiii). However, his fundamental recommendation was the establishment of a nationwide network of *Friendly Societies.* Eden's idea was not a novelty. Existent within the English social landscape since the time of Daniel Defoe, *Friendly Societies* played an essential role in Britain's process of transformation from an agrarian to an industrial society (Ismay 2018: 2). However, it was only by the mid-1790s that Parliament ratified the first *Act* designed to grant several privileges to *Friendly Societies'* members in return for registration. In the attempt to find an alternative to the *Poor Laws*, the *Rose Act* (1793) facilitated fundraising activities for the support and maintenance of sick, old, and infirm members when they needed it. It also extended the area of tax exemption for all club members and allowed them not to be subject to any regulations concerning their residence, as the membership status was a guarantee of their industriousness and discipline. Its relevance resided in that it regarded the encouragement of *self-help* as an integral part of *Poor Laws* reforms (Gorsky 1998: 491).

In *The State of the Poor,* Eden discussed at length the *Rose Act.* Although he criticised the fact that it did not conform to *Friendly Societies'* fundamental rule, namely that they must be 'governed by rules of their own devising to which the members had individually consented' (Gosden 1974: 8), Eden appreciated that it allowed club's members to choose the stewards (Eden 1797: xxiv–v). More important, Eden considered *Friendly Societies* 'useful institutions' both at individual and collective levels. By establishing among members an unprecedent spirit of independence, disposition towards solvency, industry, and frugality, *Friendly Societies* had become the privileged *loci* for bringing about individual *self-betterment;* by preventing many thousands of their members from becoming burthensome they were beneficial also to the whole nation (IBID: XXIV).

> Rejecting, as it were, a provision graciously held out to them by the public, and which was to cost them nothing (the Poor Law), they chose to be indebted for relief, if they should want it, to their own industry and their own frugality.
>
> (IBID: XXIV–V)

In addition, Eden believed that *Friendly Societies*' members were 'in general, comparatively cleanly, orderly, and sober, and consequently happy and good members of society' (EDEN 1801: 10). *Friendly Societies* established a 'fundamental truth, of infinite national importance', namely their members 'with very few exceptions, are perfectly competent to their own maintenance' (IBID). He further argued that while those 'who are contended to rely on the parish relief are living in filth, and wretchedness, and are often, from the pressure of a casual sickness, or accident, which incapacitates them from working, tempted to the commission of improper acts, [...] against which the sure resource of a *Benefit Club* would have been best preservative' (EDEN 1797: 615).

Eden's advocacy of voluntary associations did not prevent him from objecting to all compulsory schemes for *Friendly Societies*. Whatever benefit was intended for the poor, to oblige them to correspond on a regular basis 'a twenty-fourth, or a thirty-sixth, of a man's daily earnings', is tantamount to imposing 'a direct tax' (IBID: 603). Why use force, Eden asked, 'when mutual convenience will probably make that palatable which legislative direction may render nauseous?' (IBID). The above reflections led Eden to suggest that *Friendly Societies* should be rendered 'general and universal throughout the kingdom' (IBID: XXVI).

By the early nineteenth century, the interest in *Friendly Societies* moved from vague speculations about their usefulness to engagement in making them a 'universal reality' (ISMAY 2018: 72). Eden's approach and proposals entered the agenda of natural law reformers, providing legislators with a map for carving out alternative proposals to the *Old Poor Law*.

In the second edition of the *Essay* (1803), Malthus put aside the idea of abolishing at once the *Old Poor Law*, proposing instead a transition period during which he suggested helping the poor through the practice of public works and the establishment of voluntary organisations whose management would be carried out with the help of private charity associations. However, Malthus did not share Eden's optimistic prospect of *Friendly Societies*.[14] Malthus' uneasiness towards *Friendly Societies* was due to the fact that many of them required a compulsory amount of money to be paid on a regular basis in exchange of membership. For Malthus, this mechanism

> would add to the cost of labor and would borne eventually by the consumer; the funds would be unsound if the idle and dissolute were

> included, so there could be no guarantee of right of benefit; the cost of membership would increase indefinitely with the inclusion of bad risk who would seek unlimited benefits.
>
> (Mencher 1967: 116)

On these grounds, Malthus concluded that a universal compulsory system would be 'merely a different mode of collecting parish rates' (Malthus 1803: 569).

To encourage thrift and self-sacrifice among the poor, Malthus shared Bentham's preference for *Saving Banks*. In his grandiose scheme for *Pauper Management* (1796), Bentham proposed the institution by the National Charity Company of a chain of 250 workhouses, financed by private investors. Each workhouse would host nearly 2,000 inmates put to profitable work and fed on a spartan diet. Although Bentham's workhouses were to be managed on a strongly coercive basis, according to his creator the inmates should benefit from the institution of *Frugality-Banks* (Bentham 1796 [1843] VII: 413). Possibly for its harshness, Bentham's punitive scheme was not taken into consideration. Yet the ball had been set rolling.

To help the poor to develop habits like frugality, thrift, and independence Malthus carved out the proposal of instituting a nationwide network of *Saving Banks*. Within Malthus' scheme, these institutions would be more successful than *Friendly Societies* in inducing the poor to better their material lot

> Of all plans which have yet been proposed for the assistance of the labouring classes, the saving-banks [...] appear to me much the best, and the most likely, if they should become general, to effect a permanent improvement in the condition of the lower classes of society. By giving to each individual the full and entire benefits of his own industry and prudence, they are calculated to strengthen the lessons of Nature and Providence.
>
> (Malthus 1803: 309)

Advantages would be many. The establishment of such a network 'would (be) gradually reducing and fixing the amount of the poor's rates' (Ibid: 310), induce the poor to defer marriage *vis-à-vis* unfavourable financial conditions and, consequently, have fewer children. However, since the attitude of saving goes along with 'prudence and foresight', Malthus thought the most important result would be

> To prevent want and dependence by enabling the poor to provide against contingencies themselves. And in a natural state of society, such institutions, with the aid of private charity well directed, would probably be all the means necessary to produce the best practicable effects.
>
> (Ibid)

A clause Malthus envisaged as essential to the success of any plan of this kind, namely 'that the laborer should be able to draw out his money whenever he wanted it and have the most perfect liberty of disposing of it in every respect as he pleased' (Malthus 1807: 474–475).

Around 1815 and 1817, there occurred a general shift away from *Friendly Societies*. If in Eden's time the upper classes had few objections towards voluntary associations because they perceived them as a sound alternative to the *Speenhamland system*, 20 years later, that feeling temporarily faded away.[15] The well-to-do now denied support to *Friendly Societies* on the ground that they were organisation allowing the labouring population to meet without infringing the anti-combination law. One of the most refined observers of the time, William Cobbett, noted that the ruling class wanted 'to avoid their congregational evil' (Cobbett 1816: 617).[16] Around that time, the upper classes' desire was to replace *Friendly Societies* with the institution 'predicated on the individual accumulation of wealth' (Ismay 2018: 89). The MP George Rose intercepted these feelings, when, in 1816, submitted to Parliament a new *Bill*, this time on *Saving Banks*.[17]

Ricardo's comments on *Saving Banks* are contained in an exchange of letters with his friend Hutches Trower, in which the two discussed in-depth the imminent ratification of the *Rose Bill*. In Ricardo's envisaged society, *Saving Banks* had a fundamental role to play[18] because they inculcate in the mind of the poor prudence and forethought. Like Malthus, Ricardo believed that provident institutions could prevent excessive population growth, which he regarded as a major cause of distress among the lower classes. The general diffusion of these institutions

> In all parts of the kingdom will be of great services, if the rich and well informed will continue to bestow some attention on them. They will tend to introduce economy and forethought amongst the poor, which may in time check the propensity to a too abundant population, the great source from whence all the miseries of the poor flow in so profuse a stream.
>
> (Ricardo to Trower 9 march 1816 in Coll. Works VII 1952: 26)

Even if voluntary institutions were excellent in improving the material conditions and morals of the low-rank society, Ricardo's analysis pointed out aspects that might be ameliorated. He believed that *Saving Banks* might be set up by merchants willing to speculate and to profit personally. This led him to recommend that the poor holding a deposit must have control over the management of the money deposited.

> My fear is that though they will at first be established by gentlemen of great respectability and fortune, as they spread, they will at last be undertaken by speculative tradesmen, as a business from which to derive profit. The poor should have some check on the employment of the funds, or

> some evils will arise as from the indefinite multiplication of Country Banks. This check should be afforded by the legislature, or there will be no security against the failure of the undertakers.
> (Ricardo to Trower 4 February 1816 in Coll. Works 1952 VII: 16)

The Rose *Bill* included specific clauses. The non-exclusion clause stipulates that public relief should not be refused to those who had a deposit worth more than £30. The *Bill* further stipulated the guarantee of a fixed rate of interest and the possibility to withdraw the sum of money deposited at any time. In the first clause, Ricardo was crystal-clear:

> If the poor rates are to be resorted not only by those who have no other means of subsisting, but by those who are possessed of property, instead of limiting their (of the Poor Laws) application you would extend it; instead of repressing population you would still further encourage it, and would place at a greater distance the ultimate effect which we have in view.
> (Ricardo to Trower 27 January 1817, in Sraffa VII: 125)

If the clause were maintained, Ricardo reasoned, labourers would introject neither the habits of independence nor prudence. If so, any attempt to reform the *Poor Laws* would become more burdensome, the real rate of wages will remain depressed, and the standard of living of the poor would not increase.[19] In the eyes of an economist whose primary concern was that *Saving Banks* served the purpose to help the poor to introject prudence and independence, the second clause was a risky one. In his opinion, if deposit were worth less than £50 pound, then the clause would be worth the risk. However, if the deposits exceeded that limit, and if the fixed rate of interest guaranteed would exceed the market rate of interest, the State should pay a large sum for the difference between those interest rates (Ricardo to Trower 9 May 1817, in Sraffa VII: 154).

Thanks to the pre-eminence of these economic writers in the social and political spheres, *laissez-faire* and *self-help* policies quickly spread, becoming the norm. However, it took few more years and a decisive strengthening of the bourgeoisie classes' political power before the replacement of the *Speenhamland system* could effectively occur (Mandler 1987: 146). What prompted the shift from social legislation associated with provident institutions to the one based on repression and discipline was the blow-up of the *Swing Riots*, a bitter popular uprising that broke out in the south and east of the country between 1830 and 1831. That episode allowed the application of a much more radical approach to the fields of social policy. It was prompted by a powerful middle industrial class that, miles away from the Smithian wisdom, recognised disciplining measures as the best cure for combating poverty.

The task to pen the 1834 *Report from His Majesty's Commissioners for Inquiring into the Administration and Practical Operations of the Poor Law* principally fell upon William Nassau-Senior, a liberal economic thinker. Since the beginning of his intellectual career, the working poor's living conditions had attracted much of Senior's attention. Before 1830, reading Malthus and Ricardo's works he felt uncomfortable because, in the long run, both seemed to imply keeping the working classes at a subsistence level. After the *Swing Riots*, he abandoned any benevolent feelings towards the working poor and began to brand them as violent and capable only of resorting to strikes. In a Ricardian fashion he said that an arrogant mass of poor with no control would have led the country to ruin: 'rent, tithes, profit, and capital, are all eaten up, and pauperism produces what may be called its natural effects (…) famine, pestilence, and civil war' (Senior 1830: xiv).

His attack on the *Speenhamland system* was heavily influenced by both Bentham's social thinking as well as by the natural law approach to economic and social problems:

> The poor-laws, as administered in the southern districts of England, are an attempt to unite the irreconcilable advantages of freedom and servitude. The labourer is to be a free agent, but without the hazards of free agency; to be free from the coercion, but to enjoy the assured subsistence of the slave. He is expected to be diligent, though he has no fear of want; provident, though his pay rises as his family increases; attached to a master who employs him in pursuance of a vestry resolution; and grateful for the allowance which the magistrates order him as a right.
>
> (Senior 1830: ix–x)

The time was ripe for drastic changes. The *Swing Riots*, along with the political crisis which led to the defeat of the Tory government and the Great Reform Act of 1832, 'created a space for innovatory policies', supported by a rising industrial middle class (Mandler 1987: 148–149). Under these circumstances, there was the political will necessary for an architectonic reform of the English social legislation. If the poor were to lead England to ruin because of their ill-character, and if only the poor could save themselves by improving their thrift, independence, and self-reliance, then social policies should be designed in a more disciplinarian fashion. By introducing Bentham's principle of less eligibility for entering the revived workhouses the *New Poor Law* shifted 'the burden of responsibility for the pauper's maintenance […] from the community to the paupers' (Mandler 1987: 157). In doing so, Victorian liberal law legislators redefined the very concept of 'individual responsibility', shifting the notion of *self-betterment* from being an aspirational principle to one entailing greater discipline and control of the poor.

However, the 1834 reform did not dismiss either *Friendly Society* or *Saving Banks*.

> The course of proceeding which we recommend for adoption, is in principle that which the legislature adopted for the management of the

> savings' banks, the friendly societies, and the annuity societies throughout the country. Having prescribed the outline and general principles on which those institutions should be conducted, a special agency [...] was appointed to see that their rules and detailed regulations confirmed the intention of the law.
>
> (REPORT FROM HIS MAJESTY ... 1834: 297)

Despite the usual connotation of Eden, Malthus, and Ricardo as anti-poor economic writers *tout-court*, their approach to the social question betrayed social ethics able to grapple with both individual and collective responsibility during the delicate transition from the first to the second industrial revolution. The attempt to offer solutions to the social question by these strenuous enemies of the *Old Poor Law* did not prevent them to carved out policy suggestions supporting a legislative framework combining *laissez-faire* and public planning.

Conclusion

Since the *Speenhamland system* was established in many southern rural districts and manufacturing centres, a vigorous debate on poverty and its remedy took place. Established in 1795 because of a sudden rise in the price of wheat, it was a measure which extended the rate in aid of wages via a double graduated scale linked both upon the price of bread and the size of the family. It was in this context that influential economic thinkers like Eden, Malthus, and Ricardo exposed an alternative approach to poor relief. To their eyes, the notion of social responsibility embodied by the *Old Poor Law* was soaked into a mediaeval understanding of benevolence and humanitarianism unsound for an industrial society based on the principle of *laissez-faire*. Bring back into the economic discourse the argument that poverty was the result not of social and economic circumstances but of personal misconduct (an idea that both Smith and Paine's analyses had already proved false), they presented *self-betterment* as the organising principle around which the English social legislation ought to be geared around.

It took from the mid-1790s to the mid-1830s for this mind-setting to become the prevalent 'language of politics deployed to legitimate political action' (NORVAL 2000: 320). Building upon Bentham's harsher reflections on *self-betterment*, Nassau Senior and his Assistants, the most prominent of whom was Edwin Chadwick (Bentham's literary secretary), succeeded in replacing the *Old Poor Law* – still anchored to the traditional community-level responses to scarcity – a with more punitive and disciplinarian social legislation meant to render the lower ranks of a society fully responsible for their condition.

Although the 1834 reform much owes to Bentham's repressive principles, it also incorporated Eden, Malthus, and Ricardo's idea that a *laissez-faire* society called for a mix of individual *and* collective responsibility. Following this train of thought, the 1834 Commissioners recognised *Friendly Societies* and *Saving Banks* for the working class as crucial institutions for the welfare of hundreds of thousand working poor. They intended this course of action as a sound economic strategy for both reducing poverty and social dislocation and establishing renewed national moral identity.

A social legislation supporting the establishment of provident institutions not only epitomised the Victorian ideals of thrift and respectability but also helped to reinforce concepts like neighbourliness, cooperation, and mutual aid both within the borders of English local communities and nationwide. *Friendly Societies* and *Saving Banks* offered the lower classes financial support in hard times and safe possibilities of saving part of their meagre income, allowing the working poor to become relevant economic and political actors.

Notes

1 Interesting is Ailsa McKay's comments according to which Paine's proposal of state provision for a minimum income based on general taxation closely resembles the rationale supporting the *Speenhamland system* (McKay 2005: 112).

2 As Edward Palmer Thompson pointed out '*The Right of Men* and the *Wealth of Nations* should supplement and nourish each other' (Thompson 1963: 96). Both Smith and Paine refused the eighteenth-century 'natural law theory of labour'. According to its advocates, 'poverty was essential to the progress of civilization, for only under the spur of hunger would man bear the heavy burdens of progress and do all those irksome tasks which society needed done. The natural law theorists deduced their labour theory from certain self-evident proposition which they deemed to be laws of nature. These theorists thought all the able-bodied poor should be set to work, and those refusing to work should be punished' (Cowherd 1977: 2).

3 By people living in poverty in this chapter we shall intend not merely the paupers but all working people.

4 It is worth noticing that the cost of poor relief has always been a major problem hunting the upper class since the establishment of the Elizabethan *Poor Law* in 1601. The situation exacerbated starting from 1782 when Parliament passed the *Gilbert Act*. By the later eighteenth century, Samantha Williams reported, the 'poor law expenditure rocketed, as did the numbers being relieved. In 1776, the total poor relief expenditure in England and Wales was £1.5 million (£0,21 *per capita*), by 1803 it had reached just over £4 million (£0,44 *per capita*), in 1813 it was £6.3 million (£0,63 *per capita*) and thereafter fluctuated between £5 million and £7 million' (Williams 2011: 8).

5 That the *Speenhamland system* was an income support policy, rather than a simple wage subsidy has been underlined by Donald McCloskey when he said that it was the first guaranteed minimum income indexed to the cost of living distributed in the form of a negative income tax 'with a marginal taxation of 100 per cent on any additional form of income earned below the minimum' (McCloskey 1973: 434).

6 For the propertied classes, any concession to the poor entailed an increase of the tax burden.

7 Apropos, he believed that wage supplements were nothing more than an undisguised form of charity, extorted from the richest members of the community.

8 His analysis can be conceived of as a criticism to inaccurate writers who 'making bricks without straw' raised 'specious systems without well authenticated facts to support them' (Eden 1797 I: xxix).

9 Had not been for this intrusion in the natural working of the labour market, Eden believed, the demand for labour would have increased wages far beyond merely meeting the needs of the poor (EDEN 1797: 582–583).

10 For earlier discussions, see Botero G. (1588 [2012)]; Petty W. (1686); Cantillon R. (1755); Marquis de Mirabeau (1756 [1883]); Steuart J. (1756); Ortes G. (1790).

11 If so, 'the contrast between the two rates guaranteed that there must be a tendency of population to outturn food production' (WRIGLEY AND SMITH 2020: 33).

12 Malthus' position on this point was extremely clear:

> But there is one right which man has generally been thought to possess, which I am confident he neither does nor can possess- a right to subsistence when his labour will not fairly purchase it. Our laws indeed say that he has this right, and bind the society to furnish employment and food to those who cannot get them in the regular market; but in so doing they attempt to reverse the laws of nature; and it is in consequence to be expected, not only that they should fail in their object, but rather that the poor, who were intended to be benefitted, should suffer most cruelly from the inhuman deceit thus practiced upon them. (Malthus 1803: 531)

13 This phrase was deleted from successive editions.

14 Malthus was closer to Jeremy Bentham's negative outlook on *Friendly Societies.* According to the father of English Utilitarianism, these voluntary associations often risked either to over- or under-estimate the contributions needed to cover the benefits; in the latter case the risk was bankruptcy. Furthermore, he believed that *Friendly Societies* tended to generate disagreements and provoke dissolution. The labouring poor gathered at public houses, which often required the members to spend in alcoholics. Caustically, Bentham penned a vitriolic statement 'choosing a tippling-house for a school of frugality, would be like choosing a brothel for a school of continence' (*BENTHAM* (1796 [1843]): 423).

15 *Friendly Societies* regained central stage by the end of 1818 as it could be evinced in official document and books by politicians like the Esquire of Somersetshire William Hanning (HANNING 1818: 34), and James Scarlett, MP for Peterborough (HOUSE OF COMMONS THE DERBY MERCURY 1821: JUNE 27).

16 Around that time there was a clear understanding about the relevance of *Saving Banks* in the process of inclusion of the lower class into the social and political arena. The drafter of an official *Report* published in 1818, clearly stated that a *Saving Bank* 'connects, by a new link the different orders of society. It tends to cement those ties between the government and the people, which are equally essential to the prosperity of both' (HERTFORDSHIRE SAVING BANK REPORT 1818).

17 Rose was not alone in his attempt to turn the self-betterment principle into action. Although several of the clauses entailed by the Sturges Bone *Act* (1818) 'encouraged the use of workhouses as part of newly restricted regime', it displayed hope for *Savings Banks* (SHAVE 2013: 412). The same year, in the *Quarterly Review* appeared an article where the author portrayed *Saving-Banks* as 'a true sinking fund for the extinction of pauperism' (ANONYM 1818: 300).

18 Despite his uneasiness with bankers (HENDERSON 1997: 391), Ricardo was actively engaged in the management of two *Saving Banks*, the Westminster *Saving Banks,* and the *Saving Bank* in Tetbury where he became a trustee.

19 In the 1817 edition of the *Essay*, Malthus agreed with Ricardo on this point. He said that the non-exclusion clause was a

> short-sighted policy that sacrificed the end with the means. It is sacrificing the principle for which *Saving-Banks* are established, to obtain an advantage which, on this very account, will be comparatively of little value. We wish to teach the labouring classes to rely more upon their own exertions and resources, as the only way of really improving their condition; yet we reward

their saving by making them still dependent upon that very species of assistance which it is our object that they should avoid.
(Malthus 1817: 283–284)

Bibliography

Anonym (1818) On the Poor Law, in *Quarterly Review*, XVIII, 250–307.
Bahmueller C.F. (1981) *The National Charity Company Jeremy Bentham's Silent Revolution*, University of California Press, Berkeley.
Baugh D.A. (1975) The Cost of Poor Relief in South-East England, 1790–1834, in *Economic History Review*, 2nd Series, 28, 50–68.
Baugh P. (1983) Poverty, Protestantism, and Political Economy: English Attitudes Toward the Poor, 1660–1800, in Baxter S.B. (ed.), *England's Rise to Greatness, 1660–1763*, University of California Press, Berkeley-Los Angeles-London.
Baugh D.A. (2014) John Patrick William Ehrman 1920–2011, in *Biographical Memoirs of Fellows of the British Academy*, XIII, The British Academy, London, 145–175.
Bentham J. (1796 [1843]) Pauper Management, in Bowring J. (ed.) *The Works of Jeremy Bentham*, VIII, William Tait, Edinburg.
Blaug M. (1963) The Myth of the Old Poor Law and the Making of the New, in *The Journal of Economic History*, 23, 2, 151–184.
Blaug M. (1964) The Poor Law Report Reexamined, in *The Journal of Economic History*, 24, 2, 229–245.
Botero G. (1588 [2012)] *On the Causes of the Greatness and Magnificence of Cities*, Toronto University Press Toronto.
Cantillon R. (1755) *Essai sur la nature du commerce en général*, Fletcher Gyles, Londres.
Cobbett W. (1816) To the People of the United States of America, Letter XIII, in *Cobbett's Weekly Political Register*, XXX, May 18.
Cowherd R. (1977) *Political Economists and the English Poor Laws: A Historical Study of the Influence of Classical Economics on the Formation of Social Welfare Policy*, Ohio University Press, Athen.
Davies D. (1795) *The Case of Labourers in Husbandry Stated and Considered,* G.G. and J. Robinson, London.
Eden F.M. (1797) *The State of the Poor*, J. Davis, London.
Eden F.M. (1801) *Observations on Friendly Societies: For the Maintenance of the Industrious Classes, During Sickness, Infirmity, Old Age,* White&Wright, London.
Gerke C. (2020) Ricardo on Poverty, in Lundahl M., Rauhut D., Hatti N. (eds.) *Poverty in the History of Economic Thought. From Mercantilism to Neoclassical Economics*, Routledge, London, 56–75.
Gorsky M. (1998) The Growth and Distribution of English Friendly Societies in the Early Nineteenth Century, in *The Economic History Review*, New Series, 51, 3, 489–511.
Gosden P.H. (1974) *Self-Help Voluntary Associations in Nineteenth-Century Britain*, Barnes&Noble, New York.
Hanning W. (1818) *A Letter to the Members of the Selected Committees of the Two Houses of Parliament, Appointed to Examine and Report on the Poor Laws*, Taunton, London
Henderson J.P. (1997) Provident Institution, in Henderson J.P., Davies J.P. (1997) *The Life and Economics of David Ricardo*, Kluver Academic Publisher, Boston, MA, 388–397.

HERTFORDSHIRE SAVING BANK REPORT (1818 [2013]), in BURDETT F. *Annal of Books for Saving; Containing an Account of Their Rise and Progress*, Cambridge University Press, London.

HIMMELFARB G. (1984) *The Idea of Poverty. England in the Early Industrial Age*, Faber and Faber, London.

HOBSBAWM E. (1957) Friendly Societies, in *Amateur Historian*, 3, 3, 81–101.

HOUSE OF COMMONS (1817) *Report on the Selected Committee on the Poor Law*, C. Clement, London.

HOUSE OF COMMONS THE DERBY MERCURY (1821) June 27.

HOUSE OF COMMONS (1843) *Report from His Majesty's Commissioners for Inquiry into the Administration and Practical Operation of the Poor Laws with Evidence and Appendices*, B. Fellowes, London.

ISMAY P. (2018) *Trust Among Strangers. Friendly Societies in Modern Britain*, Cambridge University Press, Cambridge.

LEVIN S.M. (1964) Thomas Robert Malthus. Philosopher of Education, in *History of Education Quarterly*, 4, 4, 224–231.

MALTHUS R.T. (1798) *An Essay on the Principle of Population; as It Affects the Future Improvement of Society. With Remarks on the Speculations of Mr. Godwin, M. Condorcet and Other Writers*, J. Johnson, London.

MALTHUS R.T. (1803, 1807, 1817) *An Essay on the Principle of Population; or, a View of Its Past and Present Effects on Human Happiness*, J. Johnson, London.

MANDLER P. (1987) The Making of the New Poor Law Redivivus, in *Past & Present*, 117, 1, 131–157.

MARQUIS DE MIRABEAU (1756 [1883]) *L'Ami des hommes ou traité de la population*, Paris.

MCCLOSKEY D. (1973) New Perspectives on the Old Poor Law, in *Explorations in Economic History*, 10, 4, 419–436.

MCKAY A. (2005) *The Future of Social Security Policy: Women, Work and a Citizen's Basic Income*, London, Routledge.

MENCHER S. (1967) *Poor Law to Poverty Program: Economic Security Policy in Britain and the Unites States*, University of Pittsburgh, Pittsburgh.

NORVAL A.J. (2000) Review Article: The Things We Do with Words: Contemporary Approaches to the Analysis of Ideology, in *British Journal of Political Science*, 30, 2, 313–346.

Oxford Gazette, The Reading Mercury (1795) 11th May.

ORTES G. (1790) *Riflessioni sulla popolazione delle nazioni per rapporto all'economia nazionale*, Firenze.

PATRIQUIN L. (2007) *Agrarian Capitalism and Poor Relief in England, 1500–1860: Rethinking the Origins of the Welfare State*, Palgrave, Basingstoke.

PETTY W. (1686) *An Extract of Two Essays in Political Arithmetick Concerning the Comparative Magnitude, People and Wealth of the Cities of London and Paris*, in Philosophical Transaction, 16, 183.

PRETYMAN H.R. (1878) *Dispauperization: A Popular Treatise on Poor-Law Evils and Their Remedies*, Longmans, Green&Co., London.

Report from His Majesty's Commissioners for Inquiring Into the Administration and PracticalOoperation of the Poor Laws, Published by Authority, B. Fellowes, London.

RICARDO D. (1817) *Principles of Political Economy and Taxation*, John Murray. London.

RICARDO D. (1819 [1952]), Poor Rates Misapplication Bill, in SRAFFA P., DOBB M. (eds.), *The Works and the Correspondence of David Ricardo*, V, Speeches and Evidence 1815–1823, Cambridge University Press, Cambridge.

Ricardo D. (1823 [1951]), Wages of Manufactures – Use of Machinery, in Sraffa P., Dobb M. (eds.), *The Works and the Correspondence of David Ricardo*, V, Speeches and Evidence 1815–1823, Cambridge University Press, Cambridge, 303.

Ricardo D. (1816–1817 [1952]), Letters to Trower, in Sraffa P., Dobb M. (eds.), *The Works and the Correspondence of David Ricardo*, VII, Letters 1816–1818, Cambridge University Press, Cambridge.

Senior N. (1830) *Three Lectures on the Rate of Wages,* Jhon Murray, London.

Shave S.A. (2013) The Impact of Sturges Bourne's Poor Law Reforms in Rural England, in *The Historical Journal*, 56, 2, 399–429.

Solar P.M. (1995) Poor Relief and English Economic Development Before the Industrial Revolution, in *The Economic History Review*, New Series, 48, 1, 1–22.

Sowell T. (1962) Malthus and the Utilitarians, in *Canadian Journal of Economics and Political Science*, 28, 2, 268–274.

Stedman Jones G. (2004) *An end to Poverty? A Historical Debate*, Columbia University Press, New York.

Stern W.M. (1964) The Bread Crisis in Britain, 1795–96, in *Economica*, 31, 168–187.

Steuart J. (1756) *An Inquiry into the Principles of Political Economy*, A. Millar and T. Cadell, London.

Thompson E.P. (1963) *The Making of the English Working Class*, Harmondsworth, Penguin, London.

Watarai K. (2009) Ricardo on Poverty: His Vision of a Market Society, in *Economic Thought on Market Economy and Welfare*, 50, 2, 1–20.

Williams S. (2011) *Poverty, Gender and Lifecycle Under the English Poor Law 1760–1834*, Cambridge University Press, Cambridge.

Winch D. (1998) Poverty and Pauperism: From Smith to Malthus, in *Kumamoto Journal of Economics*, 3, 4, 1–15.

Wrigley E.A., Schonfield R.S. (1989) *The Population History of England 1541–1871: A Reconstruction*, Cambridge University Press, Cambridge.

Wrigley E.A., Smith R. (2020) Malthus and the Poor Law, in *Historical Journal,* 1, 63, 33–62.

6 Karl Marx

A Critical View on Economic Policy

Charalampos Konstantinidis and Andriana Vlachou

Introduction

Famously, Karl Marx intended to complete *Capital* in six volumes, one of which would be entirely devoted to the state and another to labor (Heinrich, 2012, 202; Lebowitz, 2003, 27–50). Given that this plan did not materialize, future scholars have been left with remarks on the relationship between the state and the economy that are "heterogeneous, fragmented, ambiguous, and inconsistent" (Jessop, 2020, 267). Moreover, as Lebowitz (2003) argued, in the first three volumes of *Capital*, Marx focused more on capital and paid limited attention to the working class as an active economic and political subject. This well-taken reflection also extends to issues of state policy. As a result, the work of Marx and Engels gives rise to subsequent diverse Marxist views of the state (see Gramsci, 1971; Holloway and Picciotto, 1978; Jessop, 1982; Lenin, 1964; Miliband, 1969; O'Connor, 1973; Poulantzas, 1978). These include accounts of the state: (a) as an instrument (even a passive one) of class rule; (b) as an autonomous authority "that can win significant freedom for manoeuver when an unstable balance of forces threatened disorder" (Jessop, 2020, 269); and (c) a synthesis of the previous two versions which regards the state "as an alienated form of political organization that is based on the separation of rulers and ruled" but also asserts the role of state power for the maintenance of social order (Jessop, 2020, 270).[1]

Many contemporary Marxists agree that, in capitalism, the state secures conditions for the successful completion and renewal of the circuits of capital (see, for instance, Fine and Harris, 1979, 94–95; Resnick and Wolff, 1987, 253–258; Vlachou and Maniatis, 1999, 150–151). These conditions can be generally classified into three major categories: (a) general infrastructural, economic, technological, and material conditions for smooth and efficient surplus value extraction; (b) conditions securing the reproduction of labor force in the necessary quantity and quality (provision of education, skills, health and work safety regulation, and so forth) along with the maintenance of the reserve army of labor; and (c) political, legal and cultural conditions that allow the extraction of surplus value and secure the valorization of capital. To engage in these processes, the state receives a share of

DOI: 10.4324/9781003228097-6

surplus value which has been produced by workers and extracted by industrial capitalists.

In this chapter, we revisit Karl Marx's economic texts, particularly his discussion of original accumulation and of legislation limiting the length of the workday in *Capital*, to establish a distinct understanding of the state and economic policy. We argue that Marx conceptualizes economic policy as the outcome of class struggles – that is struggle between and among classes over the production, appropriation, and distribution of surplus – and as the result of a conjectural coincidence of interests among competing classes or class segments, or as an incident of class dominance. The state thus tends to mediate social demands and conflicts waged by class forces. In this sense, the need for and the extent of state involvement in the provision of certain conditions or services/goods cannot be derived from a general theory. It is rather contingent upon the struggle for dominance between competing class processes (such as capitalist against feudal ones) as well as upon the class struggle between labor and capital and the intra-capitalist rivalry, all taking place outside and inside the state.[2] Moreover, a close reading of the text reveals that economic policy in capitalism intervenes in class struggle and the process of capital valorization by expanding conditions for capitalist exploitation, altering the rate of exploitation, and bringing changes to processes of concentration and centralization of capital.

The structure of this chapter is as follows. The second section briefly presents Marx's theory of exploitation. We show that class struggle, i.e. the struggle over the production, appropriation, and distribution of surplus, is at the center of Marx's theoretical apparatus. The state, we argue, mediates this struggle via economic policy. The third section highlights the specific ways in which Marx argues that state policy is crucial for the making of capitalism. State intervention restricts mobility, wages, and worker combinations, and thus generates conditions for the favorable extraction of surplus. Furthermore, siding with feudal aristocracy and in the interest of maintaining the stability of the old order, the state attempts to block enclosures of land during the Tudor period (1485–1603). However, under the rising power of commercial and capitalist interests, the state eventually legislates enclosure acts which accelerate in the eighteenth century. The fourth section turns to Marx's presentation of the Factory Acts, legislation that limits the length of the workday for young persons and women in the nineteenth century. Our reading of Marx again underlines that Marx understands economic policy as an outcome of class struggle within the existing economic, political and ideological framework of the time. The rise of the working class, in the context of the split between capitalists and landlords over the repeal of the Corn Laws (1846), generated conditions which allowed for the legislative shortening of the workday. In turn, the newly adopted legislation changed the coordinates of surplus value extraction, thereby intervening in the class struggle between workers and capitalists. Furthermore, since economic policy asymmetrically affects different sectors of capital, as well as capitals of different sizes, economic policy intervenes in intra-capitalist competition, generating opportunities for the realization of superprofit by favored capitalists. The fifth section presents the relevance of these insights on economic policy for two contemporary examples, the transition to capitalism after the fall of the USSR and environmental regulation, and the sixth section concludes.

Marx's Theory of Surplus Value and the State

In Marx's theoretical scheme, wage labor is a condition of capitalist exploitation and, consequently, of capital valorization. Industrial capitalists use money as capital to purchase means of production (spending on what Marx calls constant capital) as well as the capacity of workers to perform labor, i.e. labor power (variable capital) and mobilize these two elements in the production of commodities (Marx, 1975, 317). Following the labor theory of value, Marx argues that the value of means of production, like any other commodity, is determined "by the labour-time socially necessary to produce" them (Marx, 1975, 293). Similarly, the value of labor power reflects the value of the commodities that are necessary for the production and reproduction of the worker and his/her family (Marx, 1975, 274–275). Marx further assumes that commodities are sold at their value: "In its pure form, the exchange of commodities is an exchange of equivalents, and thus it is not a method of increasing value" (Marx, 1975, 261).

Labor power, however, constitutes a special commodity, i.e. "a commodity whose use-value possesses the peculiar property of being a source of value, whose actual consumption is therefore itself an objectification of labour, hence a creation of value" (Marx, 1975, 270). Assuming that commodities are sold at their value, workers' wages reflect the value of labor power. However, when workers perform labor, they not only transfer the value of labor power to the final commodity but also generate new value. From the perspective of the capitalist, the final value embodied in the newly produced commodities, i.e. the value appropriated by the industrial capitalist expressed in money terms, (M') surpasses the original value they used to purchase constant and variable capital (M). The difference between these two elements constitutes surplus value, the origin of capitalist profit. From the perspective of the workers, the disparity between their remuneration and the work they perform constitutes the exploitative relation in the capitalist process of production.

The establishment of capitalist relations does not generate stasis. Workers and capitalists are in a constant struggle over the production, appropriation, and distribution of surplus value (see also Resnick and Wolff, 1987). On the one side, capitalists seek to extract as much surplus value as possible. Since surplus value depends on the difference between the hours of labor workers perform and their remuneration, capitalists have two major options. The most straightforward, and historically prior, way to do so is to lengthen the workday, extracting what Marx calls absolute surplus value (Marx, 1975, 432). After paying for the workers' labor power, the capitalist seeks to pump as much labor as possible out of the workers, either by trying to snatch minutes of work here and there (e.g. by cutting lunch or bathroom breaks)[3] or by outright extending the workday. The working day presents physical and social limits, associated with workers' need to rest and feed themselves, or workers' need to meet intellectual and social needs. However, Marx writes,

> ...these limiting conditions are of a very elastic nature, and allow a tremendous amount of latitude. So we find working days of many different lengths, of 8, 10, 12, 14, 16 and 18 hours.
>
> (Marx, 1975, 341)

The second option is to suppress the value of labor power, through methods such as productivity increases in wage-goods sectors, while keeping the length of the workday constant. Marx associates this strategy with the extraction of relative surplus value.

On the other side, workers resist their exploitation and seek to minimize the hours of unpaid labor they perform. They resist the extension of the workday and fight for limits to the duration of the workday. Furthermore, workers fight for better working conditions and for wages that would be higher than the value of their labor power (or resist the suppression of wages to levels below their value of labor power that jeopardize social reproduction).

Capitalists also compete over the production and the realization of surplus value, a battle which Marx argues, "is fought by the cheapening of commodities" (Marx, 1975, 777). For Marx, competition forces capitalists to increase productivity by adopting improved methods of production, which Marx associates with a higher level of mechanization, as expressed via the ratio of constant to variable capital (the organic composition of capital) (Marx, 1975, 762). More mechanized capitalist firms in a sector are able to produce their product in less than the average socially necessary labor time, i.e. less than the (social) value of the commodity. Hence, mechanized firms realize extra surplus value than what was produced by their own workers (see also Semmler, 1982; Wolff, 1978). On the other hand, firms that produce their product in above-average time are not able to realize normal profits and may even experience losses, even though they have exploited their workers. Hence, competition provides a powerful incentive to firms to mechanize, and decrease the labor time in which they produce their commodities (Marx, 1975, 772–781).

Marx writes,

> the law of the determination of value by labour-time makes itself felt to the individual capitalist who applies the new method of production by compelling him to sell his goods under the social value; this same law, acting as a coercive method of competition, forces his competitors to adopt the new method.
>
> (Marx, 1975, 436)

Furthermore, as illustrated in Volume 3 of Capital, class conflict extends to the distribution of surplus value. Competition among capitals functioning in different sectors of the economy leads to the equalization of the profit rate across all sectors of the economy in the long run, via capital mobility, and the formation of the prices of production (see also Semmler, 1982). The deviation of prices of production from values affects a redistribution of surplus value among capitals working in different sectors so that all capitals tend to enjoy the same profit rate despite differences in their organic composition necessitated by their production process (Marx, 1981, 273–301).

Moreover, capitalists are not the sole recipients of surplus value (Marx, 1981). Surplus value, once produced, is distributed to actors and classes that enable its extraction by industrial capital. Merchant capital, for example, plays a crucial function in enabling the sale of commodities (Marx, 1981, 395–407). Interest-bearing (or financial) capital provides industrial capitalists with credit and loans (Marx, 1981, 493–505). For these functions, merchant and interest-bearing capital are compensated with merchant profit and interest respectively, both payments that come out of the surplus value industrial capitalists directly appropriate from productive workers. Furthermore, access to land is "a condition of production competed for by all possible branches of business, including non-agricultural ones" (Marx, 1981, 775). However, "landed property presupposes that certain persons enjoy the monopoly of disposing of particular portions of the global as exclusive spheres of their private will to the exclusion of all others" (Marx, 1981, 752). Hence, industrial capitalists pay rent to landlords for the permission to use their land for their production process. Like merchant profit and interest, rent is a portion of surplus value in capitalism. Marx writes, "all ground-rent is surplus-value, the product of surplus labour" (Marx, 1981, 772–773). These groups of actors (industrial capitalists, merchant capitalists, financial capitalists, landlords) stand in conflict over the distribution of surplus value.

What is the role of economic policy in the production, appropriation, and distribution of surplus value? For Marx, rather than being a passive outcome of economic relations, the state – a political entity – plays a crucial role in the establishment and maintenance of capitalist labor relations. Hence, in capitalism, the state provides conditions of existence for social and economic reproduction, and as such for the valorization of capital and the production of surplus value (see also Fine and Harris, 1979, 94–95; Resnick and Wolff, 1987, 253–258; Vlachou and Maniatis, 1999, 150–151). Furthermore, opposing classes (or class segments) and social movements call upon the state to mediate their demands. In particular, the state interferes in the struggle between capitalists and workers by regulating the conditions of surplus value extraction: it regulates the length of the workday, other working conditions, and wages. Dobb (1946, 23–24) in particular, argues that in class societies the state plays a vital role in securing an ample labor supply and low wages when the labor reserve is depleted while moving in the opposite direction when the opposite is true. The balance of power between different classes and class segments in different historical periods shapes state policy (Fine and Harris, 1979, 96; Resnick and Wolff, 1987, 252–253). In turn, state policy interferes in the struggle among different segments of capital, i.e. the struggle between industrial, financial, and merchant capital, as well as the struggle between capitalists and landlords over the distribution of surplus value.

Engels's assessment of his joint work with Marx also shows an awareness of the complex role of state, contrary to the economic determinist view that political processes are simply derivative of economic ones (see Cohen, 1978; Resnick and Wolff, 1987). Engels argues that political processes have a trenchant effect on economic aspects. In an 1890 letter to Conrad Schmidt, Engels writes:

> Hence if Barth alleges that we altogether deny that the political, etc., reflections of the economic movement in their turn exert any effect upon the movement itself, he is simply tilting at windmills. He should only look at Marx's *Eighteenth Brumaire*, which deals almost exclusively with the *particular* part played by political struggles and events, of course within their *general* dependence upon economic conditions. Or *Kapital*, the section on the working day, for instance, where legislation, which is surely a political act, has such a drastic effect.
>
> (Marx and Engels, 1975, 398–401, emphasis in the original)

The following two sections turn to the writings of Marx to show the specific interventions of the state via economic policy in the emergence of capitalism and the regulation of the workday, respectively.

Original Accumulation and the Making of Capitalism

As explained above, industrial capital mobilizes constant (means of production) and variable capital (labor power) to extract surplus value. However, this does not explain how industrial capitalists amass wealth that allows them to procure means of production. It also doesn't explain why workers would enter – freely – into a relationship which does not remunerate them according to their contribution to production.

For Marx, nature does not create a group of people with nothing to sell but their ability to perform labor and another group that owns money or means of production (Marx, 1975, 273). Hence, in the last section of the first volume of *Capital*, Marx examines the establishment of wage workers and capitalists as the product of a historical development which spanned centuries and was marked by violence. On the one hand, enclosures, expropriation through legal and illegal means, colonialism, and previously valorized merchant or interest-bearing capital generated a mass of money that could be mobilized as productive capital. On the other hand, the separation of direct producers from the means of production, primarily agricultural land, through enclosures, and the parallel establishment of anti-vagrancy laws forced the former peasants to sell their labor power in exchange for a wage, as feudal restrictions on production were fading (Dobb, 1946; Marx, 1975).

Enclosures are a key feature of the "so-called" original (or primitive) accumulation in England. In the fourteenth century, and even prior to the Black Death epidemic, the feudal economy went into a deep crisis whose causes have been heavily debated, with Dobb arguing that they lie in the inefficiency of feudalism and intensified pressure from feudal lords for revenue, and Sweezy attributing to pull factors from trade and the rise of towns (Dobb, 1946, 44–49; Sweezy, 1976, 39–46). Nevertheless, the outcome of the feudal crisis was that "[i]n England, serfdom had disappeared in practice by the end of the fourteenth century" (Marx, 1975, 877). A transitional period of two centuries ensued. In the fifteenth and sixteenth centuries, incentivized by the rise of the wool trade in Europe, certain commercially oriented landlords turned arable land into pasture land and enclosed the commons, driving tenants off the land, in their attempt to profit either via hiring wage labor themselves or more commonly via renting out the newly created large farmers to rent-paying capitalist tenants (see also Brenner, 1976, 63; Marx, 1981, 755–756).[4] Reformation and the dissolution of the monasteries in the sixteenth century further enabled the creation of large-scale farms by giving away the land to "rapacious royal favorites, or [selling it] at a nominal price to speculating farmers and townsmen, who drove out the old-established hereditary sub-tenants in great numbers and threw their holdings together" (Marx, 1975, 881–882).

Marx notes the shifting stance of the state vis-à-vis enclosures over the centuries, as the balance of power also changed over the transition from feudalism to capitalism. During the Tudor period (1485–1603), the state, which had been associated primarily with feudal elements, attempted to halt enclosure with the ultimate objective of maintaining social order (see also Brenner, 1976, 72; Dobb, 1946, 162). "Legislation shrunk back in the face of this immense change" (Marx, 1975, 879). Marx catalogs how state legislation attempted to prevent changes in agricultural practices and the use of land for commercial purposes. The state maintained that peasant houses should have at least four acres of arable land (Marx, 1975, 877, 881), imposed limits on the number of sheep one could own and attempted to regulate the ratio of arable to pasture land. Peasants also revolted – especially in the sixteenth century – seeking to establish tenant security (see also Brenner, 1976, 61–62). To no avail: "The cries of the people and the legislation directed, for 150 years after Henry VII, against the expropriation of the small farmers and peasants, were both equally fruitless" (Marx, 1975, 880).

In the seventeenth century, and particularly after the Stuart Restoration in 1660 and the Glorious Revolution in 1688, Marx notes a transition in state attitudes toward enclosures. Not only did the state stop posing obstacles to enclosures, but it also began to ratify enclosures via Acts of Parliament, a practice that accelerated in the eighteenth century. Marx writes that "the law itself now becomes the instrument by which the people's land is stolen"

(Marx, 1975, 885). Marx interprets this policy shift as an outcome of novel class alliances between the landed aristocracy, emerging financial capital, and large manufacturers, as these classes sought to commodify land and expand commercial agricultural production.

Large estates do not suffice for the establishment of capitalist farming. Wage labor on a mass scale was also necessary for the establishment of capitalist relations in agriculture. Enclosures separated small tenant farmers from the means of production (land), forcing them to turn to wage labor to make ends meet. Marx also notes that enclosures came with new demands on the supply of labor, and describes the "bloody legislation against the expropriated" in detail. Since the reign of Henry VII in the late fifteenth century, and throughout the sixteenth and seventeenth centuries, refusal to work and vagabondage were criminalized in England. Marx describes the punishment:

> By 27 Henry VIII [1536]... [f]or the second arrest for vagabondage the whipping is to be repeated and half the ear sliced off; but for the third relapse the offender is to be executed as a hardened criminal and enemy of the common weal.
>
> Edward VI: A statute of the first year of his reign, 1547, ordains that if anyone refuses to work, he shall be condemned as a slave to the person who has denounced him as an idler.... If it happens that a vagabond has been idling about for three days, he is to be taken to his birthplace, branded with a red hot iron with the letter V on the breast, and set to work, in chains, on the roads or at some other labour....
>
> Elizabeth, 1572: Unlicensed beggars above 14 years of age are to be severely flogged and branded on the left ear unless someone will take them into service for two years; in case of a repetition of the offence, if they are over 18, they are to be executed, unless someone takes them into service for two years; but for the third offence they are to be executed without mercy as felons.
>
> (Marx, 1975, 896–898)

Marx concludes,

> Thus were the agricultural folk first forcibly expropriated from the soil, driven from their homes, turned into vagabonds, and then whipped, branded and tortured by grotesquely terroristic laws into accepting the discipline necessary for the system of wage-labor.
>
> (Marx, 1975, 899)

Marx notes that state policy goes beyond its extraordinary criminalization of vagabondage in setting the conditions of surplus extraction. Marx highlights the passage of the first Statute of Labourers in 1349, which sought to address labor shortages and rising wages due to the Black Death epidemic by restricting labor mobility and setting maximum wages for those workers who were engaged in wage labor. Moreover, starting in the fourteenth century and until the nineteenth century, state policy in England criminalized combinations of workers, again siding with employers. Marx also observes the asymmetric treatment of employers and workers by the legal system. Workers receiving wages above the maximum set by law faced harsher punishment than employers paying such wages. Furthermore, workers breaking contracts faced criminal actions, while employers only faced civil actions (Marx, 1975, 900–903).

These actions show that the state intervenes to secure the extraction of surplus value under terms that would generate profitability. It aims to reduce wages, both by directly setting maximum wages and by interfering to throw more workers into the labor force, thus first creating the proletariat and alleviating labor shortages. It also objects – for a long historical period – to combinations of workers which could allow workers to bargain more effectively for higher wages, thus jeopardizing the conditions of surplus value extraction and capitalist profitability. Hence, Marx observes that "reasonable terms" are those that leave "employers a reasonable quantity of surplus labour" (Marx, 1975, 383). Marx writes:

> [D]uring the historical genesis of capitalist production... [t]he rising bourgeoisie needs the power of the state and uses it to 'regulate' wages, i.e. to force them into the limits suitable for making a profit, to lengthen the working day, and to keep the worker himself at his normal level of dependence. This is an essential aspect of so-called primitive accumulation.
>
> (Marx, 1975, 899–900)

Finally, Marx identifies colonialism, protectionism, national debt, and the modern tax system, as crucial factors for the emergence of the capitalist system, by employing:

> the power of the state, the concentrated and organized force of society, to hasten, as in a hothouse, the process of transformation of the feudal mode of production into the capitalist mode, and to shorten the transition.
>
> (Marx, 1975, 915–916)

It is clear why colonialism hinges upon the power of the state to amass, through violence, wealth that can be used as capital. Protectionism also confers benefits to merchant capital, either at the expense of industry or, in the case of international trade, of other countries (again, assisted by colonialism). Furthermore, Marx also argues that public debt is

> one of the most powerful levers of primitive accumulation. As with the stroke of an enchanter's wand, it endows unproductive money with the power of creation and thus turns it into capital, without forcing it to

> expose itself to the troubles and risks inseparable from its employment in industry or even in usury.
>
> (Marx, 1975, 919)

Perhaps the most insightful element in this list is Marx's argument that the modern tax system makes debt repayment fall on workers. For Marx, eventually, debt will have to be backed by state revenue. To raise such revenue, the state resorts to heavy taxation of the more essential means of subsistence, making wage workers "submissive, frugal, industrious... and overburdened with work... Over-taxation is not an accidental occurrence, but rather a principle" (Marx, 1975, 921). Marx highlights that debt is the only institution in England that is not "royal" but "national", a semantic choice which implies that debt burdens shall be distributed across the nation (Marx, 1975, 919). Thus, beyond affecting the rate of exploitation, the state intervenes in the process of the production and distribution of surplus value. Taxation of wage commodities to raise state revenue (instead of, say, tax revenue coming from surplus value) jeopardizes workers' ability to reproduce themselves and their families. Workers could react by working longer hours, thus contributing to additional production of value and surplus value.

To sum up, Marx argues that the state provides conditions for capitalist production. Through enclosures, colonial policies, and protectionism, it enabled the amassment of wealth in private hands. Furthermore, it forced the expropriated to sell their labor power for a wage, generating a second condition for the valorization of industrial capital (beyond the amassment of an original M). Marx argues that the state continued to intervene in the process of surplus value extraction, even after its role in the original establishment of capitalist relations of production. It regulated maximum wages and criminalized worker associations, making it more difficult for workers to negotiate effectively against their employers. Furthermore, it shifted the burden of raising state revenue onto workers, placing additional pressure on the latter to produce surplus value to meet their subsistence needs. Thus, again, the state intervened in the struggle between collective labor and capital, taking the side of capitalists.

Factory Acts

In the first volume of *Capital*, Marx devotes a lengthy chapter (Chapter 10) to a specific instance of legislation to show the "first conscious and methodical reaction of society" (Marx, 1975, 610) against the unlimited exploitation of workers by capital. In the nineteenth century, and against the imperative of lengthening the workday, the British Parliament passed the Factory Acts, a series of laws which limited the length of the working day for children and women and restricted labor and night labor for children under a certain age.[5] Marx focuses on the laws enacted between 1833 and 1864. In Marx's description, the Factory Act of 1833 restricted the working day in textile factories to the period between 5:30 AM to 8:30 PM for people under 18, with the provision that young persons (13–18 years old) could not work for more than 12 hours and children between 9–13 years could not work for more than eight hours, while also banning employment of children under nine years old (Marx, 1975, 390–391). The Factory Act of 1844 further limited the work hours of children to 6.5 hours, added women to the same category as young persons, and specified uniform starting times as a mechanism against the undermining of implementation by the relay system (to be discussed below). As a concession toward capitalists, it also reduced the working age for children from nine to eight years (Marx, 1975, 393–394). The Factory Act of 1847 (also known as the Ten Hour Act) gradually introduced the ten-hour day for young persons and women (Marx, 1975, 395). Industrialist backlash led to the compromise Factory Act of 1850, which increased the length of the workday to 10.5 hours for young persons and women, but also specified that all work had to take place between 6 AM and 6 PM, ending the relay system. The subsequent Factory Act of 1853 extended the same provisions to children aged 8–13, who had been excluded from the 1850 Factory Act (Marx, 1975, 407–408). Furthermore, workers and their allies succeeded in extending the scope of the Factory Acts between 1850 and 1863 beyond textiles to include dye-works, bleach-works, lace and stocking factories, open-air bleaching and baking (Marx, 1975, 408–410).

How are we to explain the passage of legislation that *prima facie* goes against capitalist interests, by limiting the exploitation of workers? In various passages in *Capital*, Marx ascribes the emergence of the Factory Acts, at least partly, to class struggle and the "daily more threatening advance of the working-class movement" (Marx, 1975, 348). For Marx, the passage of the Factory Acts is connected to a working-class movement, which, after an initial period of being "stunned by the noise and turmoil of the new system of production, had recovered its senses to some extent, [and] began to offer resistance" (Marx, 1975, 390). The working-class movement managed to extract some labor regulation (but no implementation) starting in 1803 (ibid.). Beginning in 1825, it started undoing the legislation prohibiting worker combinations (Marx, 1975, 903). The working-class movement also benefitted from the rise of Chartism and the call for the expansion of the vote.

> The factory workers, especially since 1838, had made the Ten Hours Bill their economic, as they had made the Charter their political, election cry. (Marx, 1975, 393)

Marx writes:

> It has been seen that these highly detailed specifications, which regulate, with military uniformity, the times, the limits and the pauses of work by the stroke of the clock, were by no means a product of the fantasy of Members of Parliament. They developed gradually out of circumstances

> as natural laws of the modern mode of production. Their formulation, official recognition and proclamation by the state were the result of a long class struggle.
>
> (Marx, 1975, 394–395)

Marx also points out the significance of shifting class alliances in the context of antagonism between capitalists and landlords and their role in the extraction of concessions. For example, Marx argues that in the 1840s, the capitalist class switched its attitude toward the restriction of the working day as part of the strategy to generate worker support for the repeal of the Corn Laws.

> Moreover, however much the individual manufacturer might like to give free rein to his old lust for gain, the spokesmen and political leaders of the manufacturing class ordered a change in attitude and in language towards the workers. They had started their campaign to repeal the Corn Laws, and the needed the workers to help them to victory. They promised, therefore, not only that the loaf of bread would be twice its size, but also that the Ten Hours' Bill would be enacted in the free trade millennium.
>
> (Marx, 1975, 393)

Hence, the restriction of the working day was viewed sympathetically among certain factory owners. On the other hand, landlords and their political representative, the Tories, "threatened in their most sacred interest, the rent of land, thundered with philanthropic indignation against the 'nefarious practices' of their foes" (Marx, 1975, 393). Later, the repeal of the Corn Laws in 1846 gave landlords an opportunity to take revenge on industrialists, by their supporting the passage of the Ten Hours Bill in 1847 (Marx, 1975, 395). The adjective "threatening" stands out when reading Marx's description of the working-class movement. For Marx, it is a class struggle rather than the ideas of economists that engenders economic policy.[6]

For Marx, the implementation of economic policy is as crucial as the passage of legislation. Marx points out that the English Parliament passed five Factory Acts between 1802 and 1833 but did not fund their implementation (Marx, 1975, 390). Furthermore, the passage of laws often leads to the adoption of novel evasion strategies: Marx notes that capital responded to the passage of the 1833 Factory Act by intensifying the relay system. Capitalists moved children from one workstation to another during the workday and specified different start times for different workers, making it impossible for factory inspectors to determine compliance with limits to the workday (Marx, 1975, 393). Furthermore, the failure of the 1848 revolutions and the simultaneous decline of Chartism gave capital the opportunity to revolt against pro-worker legislation (Marx, 1975, 398). Capitalists reintroduced night work for male workers and designed work hours in ways to evade mandatory meal breaks for children. Capital also pushed hard against factory inspectors who were charged with detecting violations of legislation (Marx, 1975, 401). When factory inspectors were able to proceed with charges against industrialists, they turned to courts that were friendly to their interpretation of the Factory Acts (Marx, 1975, 401–404).

On the other hand, workers did not stand idle watching capital's revolt. Marx writes that workers moved from relatively passive forms of resistance to protesting "in threatening meetings" (Marx, 1975, 405), much as they had done a few decades earlier to force the removal of legislation banning combinations of workers (Marx, 1975, 905). The rise of workers turned the regulation of the workday into a fait accompli.

Marx writes that

> after the factory magnates had resigned themselves and submitted to the inevitable, capital's power of resistance gradually weakened, while at the same time the working class's power of attack grew with the number of its allies in those social layers not directly interested in the question.
>
> (Marx, 1975, 409)

Hence,

> The establishment of a normal working day is therefore the product of a protracted and more or less concealed civil war between the capitalist class and the working class.
>
> (Marx, 1975, 412–413)

Did capitalists enact policy against their own interests? Marx understands capitalist class interests as complex. The Factory Acts went against the immediate class interests of the capitalist class by limiting the degree of exploitation. However, Marx also argues that the voracious appetite for profits generates a necessity for limiting the workday, much in the same way as the necessity "as forced the manuring of English fields with guano" (Marx, 1975, 348). Long workdays and the exploitation of children enabled short-run profits but jeopardized the existence of a healthy, educated, and productive labor force, a condition for the future valorization of capital. Being in competition with each other, individual capitalists are not concerned with the reproduction of the labor force. One could argue that the state has to step in to ensure the condition of capitalist production and exploitation.[7] According to Fine and Harris (1979, 115), "no such stimulus to state intervention from capitalists could develop until the advent of machinery. For then the lengthening of the working day forms an object of competition between capitalists [small- and large-scale ones] as well as between classes."[8] They properly argue that Factory Acts legislation "developed and was implemented according to the conjuncture of class forces that support the working class's struggle for limitation of working hours" (ibid.).

An important issue is how the Factory Acts set new conditions for surplus value extraction and interfered in the class struggle. Restricting the length of the working day reduces the rate of exploitation. Hence, the immediate effect of the shorter workday is to restrict the absolute surplus value extracted by capitalists. However, one could argue that the shorter workday created a healthier workforce, hence benefitting capital in the longer term through the higher productivity of workers. Marx writes:

> If then the unnatural extension of the working-day, that capital necessarily strives after in its unmeasured passion for self-expansion, shortens the length of life of the individual labourer, and therefore the duration of his labour-power, the forces used up have to be replaced at a more rapid rate and the sum of the expenses for the reproduction of labour-power will be greater... It would seem therefore that the interest of capital itself points in the direction of a normal working-day.
>
> (Marx, 1975, 377)

Moreover, the Factory Acts did not affect all capitalists uniformly. Not all industries were regulated at the same time; hence, economic policy affected the profitability of different sectors disproportionately. Furthermore, Marx argues that the incomplete implementation of the Factory Acts led some manufacturers to complain about their competitors' unfair advantage (Marx, 1975, 393). Furthermore, Marx argues that the Factory Acts intervene in intra-capitalist competition. Capitalists rejected the introduction of the Factory Acts, arguing that restrictions to the working day would hurt profitability. However, Marx argues that the Factory Acts spurred rapid technical change which reduced the cost of production and protected profitability. Marx cites an industrialist who states:

> The inconveniences we expected to arise from the introduction of the Factory Acts into our branch of manufacture, I am happy to say, have not arisen. We do not find the production at all interfered with; in short we produce more in the same time.
>
> (Marx, 1975, 606)

> Not all capitalists, however, are able to respond to changing regulation by adopting new capital-intensive processes. Hence, the cheapening of commodities, when confronted with a decrease in absolute surplus value, is possible only for capitalists who are able to command significant sums of capital. Hence, state regulation alters the playing field. The extension of factory legislation hastens the generous conversion of isolated small industries into a few combined ones - concentration of capital – and because of the concentration of workers in large-scale industries also intensifies worker-capitalist struggle.
>
> (Marx, 1975, 635)

Marx writes:

> The Factory Acts artificially ripen the material elements necessary for the conversion of the manufacturing system into the factory system, yet at the same time, because they make it necessary to lay out a greater amount of capital, they hasten the decline of the small masters, and the concentration of capital.
>
> (Marx, 1975, 606)

In conclusion, the enactment and implementation of the Factory Acts, as a historical process, reveals that state policy was shaped by the pulls and pushes of contending classes and class segments (working class, capitalists, and landlords). Their concrete forms inscribed the balance of power among the struggling agents at different time periods. In due course, the Factory Acts gave rise to new conditions for surplus value extraction, without challenging capitalist class relations directly.

Marx's Relevance: Two Modern Examples

Marx's perception of economic policy and regulation, as shown in his treatment of the role of the state for initial capital accumulation and the Factory Acts, is of more than historical interest. It is also valuable in understanding, among other things, the transition to capitalism in post-Soviet Russia and the shaping of contemporary environmental policy.

Since the demise of the Soviet Union (USSR) at the end of 1991, a capitalist transition was initiated in Russia by the involvement of the post-Soviet state under the influence of favoring forces ingrained in the former Soviet economic and political system and with a strong support from abroad (Hanson, 1997; Kagarlitsky, 1997).[9] As Menshikov (1999, 2) argues,

> its immediate predecessor [of capitalism] was the underground, or shadow, economy...[it] was not only a group of speculators and underground producers outside the official state sector; it also included a network of state managers functioning as private entrepreneurs from inside the official system, as well as people placed strategically in high government agencies... Market reforms came as the logical reflection of the interests of this new class in search of an open and legalized capitalist identity.

Menshikov also argues that a considerable number of the new Russian capitalists were versed in criminal and corrupt practices and continued to apply them on the road toward a new system. This reiterates Marx's argument that violence has always been a method of initial accumulation.

Extensive privatization of public property (eventually depriving direct producers, i.e. workers, of access to the national means of production) and appropriation of public funds on a huge scale stand out as actions engendered by state legislation of the pro-capitalist government. State-owned assets were transferred to emerging capitalists at a fraction of their actual value. For instance, voucher privatization in the early 1990s, instead of giving rise to employee-managed firms as proclaimed, resulted in vouchers being bought in many cases by former managers of state enterprises at low prices. During the later 'loans for shares' stage, banks acquired ownership of previously state-owned enterprises in strategic sectors of the economy, after the indebted Russian government had borrowed from them using enterprises shares as collateral. As Menshikov argues, this turned bank owners – who were also benefitting from high commissions and interest rates from their dealings with the government – into oligarchs. Finally, politically connected firms became special exporters of oil and metals on terms that took advantage of the domestic-foreign price differentials and were also able to avoid taxes and repatriation of hard-currency revenues (Menshikov, 1999). Such modern processes bring to mind Marx's analysis of the role of the state in propelling capitalism in England through facilitating sales of valuable assets to political favorites, public debt, and monopoly privileges.[10]

Besides curtailing access of the working people to the means of production, the pro-capitalist state, during the transition, abandoned previous full employment policies, facilitated the decline in the real standard of living (for instance, by being unable to control inflation), and reduced social guarantees for working people. These conditions strengthened the formation and the workings of a labor market under terms which weaken labor and facilitate surplus value extraction, recalling Marx's analysis of the anti-labor legislation that accompanied the emergence of capitalism.

Marx's analysis of work-time legislation has inspired and guided eco-socialist critiques of capitalism in deriving environmental regulation as an outcome of struggles over the appropriation of nature in capitalism (Vlachou, 2008). From a Marxist perspective, environmental degradation is the outcome of many diverse and interacting processes in capitalism. The production of commodities under the profit motive plays a substantial role in this degradation (O'Connor, 1998). Simultaneously, pollution and natural resource exhaustion have serious negative effects on capital and labor in capitalist societies, potentially triggering economic and political reactions to contain or eliminate such ramifications. The state may be called upon to regulate access to nature. The establishment and the concrete shaping of environmental regulation then becomes an arena in which various classes or class segments and social movements struggle to secure their access to nature (Vlachou, 2002, 2004, 2005).

Marx acknowledges that work-time legislation emerged as the outcome of working-class struggles and of a conjectural coincidence of interests among competing classes or class segments. Following this line of reasoning, capitalists suffering from pollution and capitalists that stand to profit from pollution abatement, resource conservation, and substitution, and recycling, engage in intra-capitalist struggles, which shape environmental regulation and change (Vlachou, 2004). Polluting and resource-depleting capitalists tend to resist (often vehemently) the establishment and enforcement of regulation, especially policies affecting them on an individual or local basis, fearing competitive disadvantage (Beder, 2002; Kovel, 1999; O'Connor, 1998). Nevertheless, there is an emerging tendency among several polluting and resource-depleting capitalist firms (most of them large and transnational) to view environmental regulation as an opportunity for restructuring and capitalist growth (Vlachou, 2004).

Insofar as deteriorating natural environments affect the living conditions (biological, psychological, aesthetic, and other social ones) of working people, they can increase people's cost of living and/or worsen their standards of living. These consequences tend to instigate environmental, economic, and social struggles. As in the case of labor market regulation, workers-citizens engage in struggles over access to nature, while also searching for policies conducive to their own individual and collective safety and human development.

Conlcuding Remarks

In this chapter, we show that Marx's analysis of two sets of legislation in *Capital* illustrates a nuanced understanding of the role of the state in economic outcomes. Opposing classes and class segments put pressure on the state to fulfill its economic and political demands. In turn, economic policy and legislation enacted and implemented by the state propels different class interests and has significant implications for capitalism. Following Marx, we trace these arguments by examining, first, the state's stance vis-à-vis enclosures during the transition to capitalism and, second, the passage of legislation regulating the supply and conditions of labor, including anti-vagabondage laws and legislation restricting wages and worker combinations. Moreover, we substantiate how the rise of the working class contributed to the passage of laws restricting the length of the workday in the nineteenth century and how this set of laws favored one set of capitalists over another. We further argue that Marx's insights on the role of the state have modern relevance, as they illuminate that the state, under pressure from specific social subjectivities, enables or restricts modern forms of enclosure, and implements or resists legislation which protects working and living conditions. We use the cases of post-Soviet Russia and environmental policy to exemplify these arguments.

What lessons should working people derive from this analysis? Should working people, for example, abandon struggles for systemic transformation and focus their energies on corrective transformations within capitalism? It may be tempting, for instance, to consider the success of nineteenth-century labor-time legislation restricting the working day as a blueprint for modern labor and environmental struggles. However, as Marx wrote to Engels in 1868, the regulation of the working day is one of "the starting points of any 'serious' working-class movement" (Marx and Engels, 1975, 198). As long as struggles for shorter hours are not the ultimate goal of trade unions, Marx and Engels celebrated these daily struggles against capital as a valuable tool of political training and organization (Marx and Engels, 1975, 275). Work-time regulation may be far from materializing a socialist transformation; the same is the case with environmental regulation. However, Marx's analysis points to struggles that defend worker living conditions in capitalism as a way toward empowering and organizing workers toward achieving a far-reaching social transformation.

Notes

1 This account relates to Marx's view that, contrary to Hegel's account, "the state could represent only an 'illusory' community of interest beneath which would lie the continuing antagonisms ...of a society based on private property and wage labour" (Jessop, 2020, 268–271).

2 Clarke points to the specific historical context of these struggles:

> the outcome of such [social and political] struggles would not be determined by the will and the determination of the forces in play but would also be circumscribed by the economic, political and ideological framework within which they were fought out.
>
> (Clarke, 1991, 2)

3 Marx writes about the "small thefts of capital", concluding that "[m]oments are the elements of profit" (Marx, 1975, 352).

4 Marx differentiates between the old and the new nobility: "The new nobility was the child of its time, for which money was the power of all powers" (Marx, 1975, 889).

5 Since the introduction of machinery in production resulted in transferring many of the qualitative characteristics of labour, previously performed by the dexterity of workers, to machines, factories made extensive use of the unskilled labour of children and women. Moreover, beyond the logic of absolute surplus value, the lengthening of working day was used as a way of reducing physical depreciation of fixed capital due to wear and tear and also of "moral depreciation" due to technical change (Marx, 1975, 528).

6 Booth argues that political pressure from two sides helped the passage of the Factory Acts: on the one hand, Tories and factory owners, such as Robert Owen, who were guided by philanthropic sentiments and, on the other hand, landlords, as well as commercial and financial capitalists who sought to deliver a blow to industrial capital (Booth, 1978, 152). Contrary to Booth, we maintain that Marx highlights workers and their threatening attitude as a key source of political pressure.

7 Moos (2021) employs a social coordination framework and argues that capitalists and workers faced two different coordination problems. Individual capitalists' quest for immediate profits led them to extend the workday, hence undermining collective profitability. Workers' attempt to meet their needs, given low wages, forced them to supply child labor power to industrial capital further reducing adult wages. For Moos, the Factory Acts limited the workday and restricted child labor, hence solving two coordination problems.

8 They argue that the limitation of working day can at times act against the interests of small-scale backward capitalists, who continue to rely upon the extensive exploitation of their workers through long hours and low wages; in this sense, large-scale capital can support the working day limitation to drive out of business small capitalists. On the other hand, small capitalists may support a limitation of the working day to render large-scale fixed capital idle and thus uncompetitive (Fine and Harris, 1979, 115).

9 The argument for a transition to capitalism in Russia assumes that, irrespective of its particular character, the former Soviet system was not a capitalist system.
10 According to David Kotz, all these efforts in post-Soviet Russia have produced "not a process of primitive accumulation, but the emergence of a non- capitalist predatory/extractive system from the former state socialist system" and the explanation "for this unexpected development is found in the Western-inspired neoliberal transition strategy" (Kotz, 2001, 157). For a debate, see Kotz (2002) and Laibman (2002).

Bibliography

Booth, Douglas E. 1978. Karl Marx on State Regulation of the Labor Process: The English Factory Acts. *Review of Social Economy*. 36 (2): 137–157.

Brenner, Robert. 1976. Agrarian Class Structure and Economic Development in Pre-Industrial Europe. *Past & Present*. 70: 30–75.

Clarke, Simon (ed.) 1991. *The State Debate*, Basingtoke: Palgrave-Macmillan.

Cohen, G.A. 1978. *Karl Marx's Theory of History: A Defense*, Princeton, NJ: Princeton University Press.

Dobb, Maurice. 1946. *Studies in the Development of Capitalism*, London: George Routledge & Sons.

Fine, Ben and Laurence Harris. 1979. *Rereading Capital*, London: The MacMillan Press.

Gramsci, Antonio. 1971. *Selection from Prison Notebooks*, London: Lawrence & Wishart.

Hanson, Philip. 1997. What Sort of Capitalism Is Developing in Russia? *Communist Economies and Economic Transformation*. 9 (1): 27–42.

Heinrich, Michael. 2012. *An Introduction to the Three Volumes of Karl Marx's Capital*, New York: Monthly Review Press.

Holloway, John and Sol Picciotto (eds.) 1978. *State and Capital: A Marxist Debate*, London: Edward Arnold.

Jessop, Bob. 1982. *The Capitalist State: Marxist Theories and Methods*, Oxford: Martin Robertson.

Jessop, Bob. 2020. State. In *The Marx Revival: Key Concepts and New Interpretations*, Marcelo Musto (ed.) pp. 266–284. Cambridge: Cambridge University Press.

Kagarlitsky, Boris. 1997. The Unfinished Revolution. *New Left Review*. 226 (1): 155–159.

Kotz, David. 2001. Is Russia Becoming Capitalist? *Science & Society*. 65 (2): 157–181.

Kotz, David. 2002. Is Russia Becoming Capitalist? Reply. *Science & Society*. 66 (3): 388–393.

Laibman, David. 2002. Is Russia Becoming Capitalist? Comment. *Science & Society*. 66 (3): 381–388.

Lebowitz, Michael A. 2003. *Beyond Capital: Marx's Political Economy of the Working Class*, Basingtoke: Palgrave-Macmillan.

Lenin, Vladimir Illich. 1964. The State and Revolution. In *Lenin: Collected Works, Volume 25*, pp. 381–492. Moscow: Progress Publishers.

Marx, Karl. 1975. *Capital. Volume I*, New York: Penguin Books.

Marx, Karl. 1981. *Capital. Volume III*, New York: Penguin Books.

Marx, Karl and Friedrich Engels. 1975. *Selected Correspondence*, Moscow: Progress Publishers.

Marx, Karl and Friedrich Engels. 1987. *Marx & Engels Collected Works. Volume 25: Engels*, London: Lawrence & Wishart.

Menshikov, Stanislav. 1999. Russian Capitalism Today. *Monthly Review*. 51 (3): 81–99.
Miliband, Ralph. 1969. *The State in Capitalist Society*, New York: Basic Books.
Moos, Katherine A. 2021. The Political Economy of State Regulation: The Case of the British Factory Acts. *Cambridge Journal of Economics*. 45 (1): 61–84.
O'Connor James. 1973. *The Fiscal Crisis of the State*, New York: St. Martin's Press.
Postan, M. 1937. The Chronology of Labour Services. *Transactions of the Royal Historical Society*. 20: 169–193.
Poulantzas, Nicos. 1978. *Political Power and Social Classes*, London: Verso.
Resnick, Stephen A. and Richard D. Wolff. 1987. *Knowledge and Class: A Marxian Critique of Political Economy*, Chicago, IL: University of Chicago Press.
Semmler, Willi. 1982. Theories of Competition and Monopoly. *Capital & Class*. 6: 91–116.
Sweezy, Paul. 1976. A Critique. In *The Transition from Feudalism to Capitalism*, Rodney Hilton (ed.) pp. 33–56. London: NLB.
Vlachou, Andriana. 2002. Nature and Value Theory. *Science & Society*. 66 (2): 169–201.
Vlachou, Andriana. 2004. Capitalism and Ecological Sustainability: The Shaping of Environmental Policies. *Review of International Political Economy*. 11 (5): 926–952.
Vlachou, Andriana. 2005. Environmental Regulation: A Value-Theoretic and Class-Based Approach. *Cambridge Journal of Economics*. 29 (4): 577–599.
Vlachou, Andriana. 2008. Capital, Labor and the Environment. *New School Review*. 3 (1): 46–51.
Vlachou, Andriana and Thanasis Maniatis. 1999. Paving the Road to Privatization: The Case of the Public Power Corporation in Greece. In *Rethinking Democracy and the Welfare State*, John Milios, Louka Katseli, and Theodore Pelagidis (eds.) pp. 146–175. Athens: Ellinika Grammata.
Wolff, Richard. D. 1978. Marxian Crisis Theory: Structure and Implications. *Review of Radical Political Economics*. 10 (1): 47–57.

7 Economic Policy in Marginalist and Early Neoclassical Economics 1871–1920s

Michel S. Zouboulakis

Introduction

Economics after 1871 made a significant epistemological turn due to the so-called "Marginal Revolution" which is usually associated with the simultaneous discovery of the concept of marginal utility and the application of differential calculus in various fields of economic theory. Both innovations have been possible thanks to the relocation of the scope of economic analysis, from the social conditions of production, distribution and accumulation of wealth, to the subjective factors of exchange and production, which is from Political Economy to Economics. As the discipline became more formal and more individualistic, it became narrower in scope. As Heilbroner (1953, 173) observed, "it became the special province of professors, whose investigations threw out pinpoint beams rather than wide-searching beacons of the earlier economists".

The period 1873–1896 is marked by the Long Depression, during which the world economy faced constantly falling prices, falling interest and profit rates, generating massive business failures and rising unemployment.[1] Increased economic growth returned slowly after the substantial re-organization of labor and capital, the rise of protectionism and the push of imperialistic expansion to its limits. How the turn to formal theorizing has affected the economist's view on burning economic policy issues? This chapter concisely considers the views on the economic policy of some exceptional economic minds such as W.S. Jevons, L. Walras, A. Marshall, F.Y. Edgeworth, J.B. Clark, V. Pareto, K. Wicksell, I. Fisher and A.C. Pigou (to name the most influential), covering almost 60 years from 1871 to 1929, in three major policy issues: international trade, monetary policy and public finance. It will be shown that mainstream economists of that period were not less involved with social and political considerations than their classical predecessors and not less heterogeneous as to their policy prescriptions.

Free Trade Policy from the Great Depression to the 'Roaring Twenties'

The greatest part of the period under study was called by Hobsbawm (1987) the "Age of Empire, 1875–1914" for a reason: it corresponds to the age of the

DOI: 10.4324/9781003228097-7

greatest colonial expansion of Europe overseas and the escalation of nationalism worldwide.[2] The rise of protectionism was only a consequence of the growing antagonism between nations. As Hobsbawm remarked, in 1914 the world of liberal bourgeois society was irreversibly gone (Hobsbawm 1987). It is therefore in that particularly anti-liberal climate that marginalist and early neoclassical economists developed their policy recommendations on international trade.

Reading the manuals of Political Economy of the 1870s and the early 1880s in Britain (i.e. Mill, Cairnes, Fawcett and Sidgwick), one understands that the academia still fully endorsed the classical theory of international trade. In few words, Mill improved the Ricardian theory of comparative advantage explaining that international exchange depends on the terms of trade between the comparative cost ratios of the two countries. The reciprocal demand, or "the quantity of home produce which must be given to the foreign country in exchange for it", determines the price of the imported commodity (Mill 1848, 584). In Britain and in France, economists and politicians, like Mill and Gladstone, celebrated the success of the Cobden-Chevalier Treaty of 1860 which ended tariffs on the main items of trade between the two economic superpowers. Britain signed also commercial treaties with Belgium (1862), the Zollverein (1862), Italy (1863), Switzerland (1864), Spain and Holland (1865). Jevons (1835–1882) in his *Coal Question* (1865) asserted that keeping low prices of imported coal was crucial for a growing industrial nation to maintain its competitiveness and prosperity (Mosselmans 2007, 14). But, as industrialization advanced and the economic position of Germany grew after the Unification of 1871 and the US economy revealed its strength after the Civil War, the protectionist policy agenda became popular again by the mid-1880s in the worst days of the Great Depression.[3] One can see the evolution in the spirit of the age through Henry Fawcett's six consecutive editions of his *Free Trade and Protection*, aiming to give "full and careful consideration to the arguments that are advanced by protectionists" (1872, 12), especially those related to the movement of "fair trade". Bounties on exports, protective subsidies and various restraints on imports are advantageous for a country only if this country wishes "to hinder the prosperity of neighbouring countries", thus starting a perpetual economic war (1872, 73). As Fawcett concludes (192), one should not consider only the interests of the manufacturers, ignoring thus "the interest of the people, as consumers". Similar arguments were advanced in America by Henry George in his *Protection or Free Trade* published in 1886: tariffs only keep prices high for consumers, they fail to produce any increase in wages, and at the end of the day they increase the power of monopolistic companies. In the very same year John Bates Clark (1847–1938), in his *Philosophy of Wealth*, made the strongest analytical defense of free market and the limits of government intervention. Clark (1886, 1901) championed large competition against predatory pricing practices both domestically and internationally and contributed significantly to the propagation of the anti-trust legislation in the USA (cf. Pressman 2014, 105).

Alfred Marshall (1842–1924) is the first major mainstream economist who actually gave some credit to the new protectionist mood. In his *Principles of*

Economics (1890, 633) he recognizes that free trade was more advantageous to Britain than to Germany or the USA, along with the old Millian argument on the need for temporary protection of a young industrial country or sector. But whereas he understands the patriotic meaning of the protectionist measures suggested by the German Historical School, he does not approve their views. Marshall's position will evolve during the tariff reform controversy in 1903 when he "allowed his name to be included in the manifesto of fourteen Professors published in *The Times*" in favor of protective tariffs (Backhouse, in Raffaelli et al. 2006, 478). After the end of WWI, his *Industry and Trade* sound more comprehensive to "economic nationalism" recognizing the efficiency of protecting tariffs for the infant industry in developing countries: English economists "overlooked the fact that many of those indirect effects of Protection which aggravated then, and would aggravate now, its direct evils in England, worked in the opposite direction in America" (Marshall 1919, 476). After a thorough historical account of the economic history of France, Germany, the USA and other countries like Japan, Marshall recognizes that "leadership in industry and trade has been obtained in the past by cities or by nations, which have thrown energy into the use of their own 'native commodities'" (1919, 76).

In a nutshell, on both sides of the Atlantic, the popular tune was protectionist as we approached WWI and Marshall's ambivalence reflects the pressure of public opinion. Nevertheless, he never abandoned the canon of free trade, believing that state protection becomes harmful to trade as it often becomes an instrument of preferential treatment and political corruption (Marshall 1923). Despite the peak of imperialism and nationalism, neoclassical economists remained free traders in principle and in theory.[4] As Heilbroner (1953, 193) brilliantly concluded, "the officialdom of economics stood to one side, watching the process of imperial growth with equanimity, and confining its remarks to the effect that new possessions might have on the course of trade".

Monetary Policy and the Origins of Monetarism

The second most important policy issue concerned money and the gold standard. In the UK, after the *Bank Charter Act* of 1844, the ideas of the Currency School prevailed despite Thomas Tooke's monumental *History of Prices* demonstrating the independence of the movement of prices from the circulating quantity of money.[5] Classical Political Economy was devoted to the so-called quantity theory of money and actually conceded this bicentennial idea (since Petty and Locke) – that commodity prices depend on the amount of the circulating medium – to the next generation. Along with Mill and Jevons, Marshall retained this position from his first "Essay on Money" in 1871 until his last book of 1923 and claimed that

> if everything else remains the same, there is this direct relation between the volume of currency and the level of prices, that if one is increased by ten per cent, the other will also be increased by ten per cent.
>
> (Marshall 1923, 45; Cf. Mill 1848, 495)

Together with equiproportionality, Marshall exposes all the elements of the Classical quantity theory such as neutrality of money, exogeneity, absolute price/relative price dichotomy and indirect money to price causality (Humphrey, in Raffaelli et al. 2006, 421–433). Marshall did write, "Money is not desired for its own sake" (1923, 38), but at the same time, he also did recognize that cash may be not entirely spent but held for "future expenditure" (1890, 189), creating thus a link between the growth of money and its circulation.

In matters of monetary policy, one notices this striking theoretical continuity from Mill to Jevons and Marshall: the regulation of money supply was the full responsibility of the state. The norm was a commodity-based monetary system with full convertibility into a precious metal (gold and/or silver). Notwithstanding the general agreement for a competitive free banking system, Walter Bagehot (1826–1877) in his illustrious *Lombard Street* (1873) described the obligation of the central bank to hold the adequate reserves of the commercial banks, but also to maintain the nation's solvency and to preserve the viability of the whole financial system. Bagehot wanted the Bank of England (BoE) "to recognize its special position at the base of the economy's credit pyramid" (Laidler 1991, 42) and claimed that the BoE had a duty to lend freely the commercial bankers at high rates, when no other lenders would, long before Keynes.[6] Still, Bagehot distinguished himself from monetary orthodoxy of the Currency School questioning the causality between money supply and price fluctuations believing that the quantity of money was a passive variable that followed price fluctuations rather than causing them.

And yet, British Monetary Orthodoxy was not monetarist! Monetarism came later with Irving Fisher (1867–1947) and the definite formal exposition of the quantity theory of money in *The purchasing power of money* (1911). Directly inspired from Boyle's Law of Perfect Gases (cf. Zouboulakis 2003), and following numerous historical and empirical studies on US monetary history, Fisher rewrites Simon Newcomb's equation willing to explain the purchasing power of money.[7] Going further than the then-existing literature, Fisher wishes to establish a causal relation between the price level (P) and the quantity of money in circulation (M). In doing so, he considers that the velocity of circulation of money (V) is determined by institutions and habits and changes imperceptibly through time and that in the short "transitional period" the amount of goods (T) bought by M "within a year" is given. His equation of exchange $MV = PT$ meant not to express an equilibrium condition (like Walras), but to explain the one-way causality from the exogenous increase of money supply to the nominal prices.[8] As he wrote, "the price level is normally the one absolutely passive element in the equation of exchange" (Fisher 1911, 172). Although Fisher offered a detailed statistical verification of the transitional adjustments between the different elements of the equation (1911, ch. XI–XII. Cf. Laidler 1991, 81–82), his principal aim was to proclaim his monetarist program loud and clear considering V and T as stable and M as exogenous and independent. Schumpeter (1954, 1103) has rightly conjectured that Fisher has sacrificed scientific adequacy for practical utility: the quantity theory was "conceived as a scaffolding for statistical work that in turn was to serve a piece of social engineering". His "compensated dollar plan" aimed to restrain the issue of new money from commercial banks to 100% of their gold reserves. Fisher's theory was merely the theoretical backup of his crusade to stabilize the value of the dollar (Tobin 1985, 35). In that sense it diverged not only from the old British quantitativist tradition but also from the new alternative approach, the Cambridge Cash-Balance theory (see Blaug 1985, ch. 15).

The quantity theory central to the monetarist policies of Fisher, and later of Friedman, focuses on the supply of money considering it as the primary driver of economic growth and in the long run, as the main cause of inflation if unduly expanded. Therefore, money supply should be the main concern of economic policy decision-makers. On the contrary, Mill, Bagehot and Marshall consider also the demand for money and the motives for holding money, opening the road for Keynes' concept of "liquidity preference" (Mill 1848, 496; Bagehot 1873; Marshall 1890, 189. Cf. Raffaelli 2003, 134). Cambridge economists after Marshall, especially Pigou and Keynes expressed the demand for cash balances depending on the proportion of income that people wish to hold in the form of cash (k), the price level (p) and the level of real income (Y): $\boldsymbol{M = k \cdot p \cdot Y}$. In that sense, people may not desire to use money as cash immediately and store it for later use, reducing thus its quantity in circulation. The crucial factor is the rate of interest which remunerates the abstinence from immediate consumption.

Knut Wicksell (1851–1926) was the economist who developed completely the theory of interest and secured the link between monetary, banking and stabilization policies. He distinguishes "market interest", the remuneration for saving, from the "natural interest", the return (or marginal efficiency) of new invested capital (Wicksell 1898).[9] The marge between the two interests determines the decision to save or to invest. Since the banks have the possibility to extend credit beyond their cash deposits, maintaining the gap between the two interests they can feed consumer demand for goods above its natural rate and raise prices. Wicksell thus defies the classical quantitative theory of money long before Keynes' *General Theory*, demonstrating theoretically that the aggregate demand may be artificially sustained by banking interests lower than the normal rate, creating a cumulative effect on prices (Wicksell 1898, 95, 1907). From the point of view of the aggregate supply, banking interest may cause economic depression, by maintaining the market rate of interest above the natural rate. In that case, investment becomes too expensive and production falls. Wicksell offers by the same token a substantial explanation for economic fluctuations, the divergence between the natural and the market rates of interest, as against Fisher's monetarist explanation of business cycles caused by "money illusion", or the divergence between nominal and real interest. Wicksell's hint was further developed by Ludwig von Mises in his first work *The Theory of Money and Credit* (1912), before becoming the cornerstone of the Stockholm School of Economics in the 1930s.

Public Finance and the Role of the State Until 1929

Concerning internal economic policy and the role of the state, early neoclassical economists believed that "the function of Government is to govern as little as possible, but not to do as little as possible" (Pigou 1925). Inspired by the last Classical political economists such as Mill, Cairnes and Sidgwick, the Marginalists broadened the traditional functions of the state (internal and external security, justice, compulsory education, infrastructures) using different tools and from a distinct methodological starting point. After Marshall, most of the neoclassical economists opposed the distinction between the science and the art of economics, which was the trade mark of the classical school after Ricardo and even in Walras (1874, 39). For Marshall, there was no pure science and all economics was art, defying his spiritual parents' opinion, Henry Sidgwick.[10] Accordingly, Marshall's successor in Cambridge, Arthur Cecil Pigou (1877–1959) stated that he was interested in fruit-bearing science, not light-bearing science (1920, 3). Pure economics separated from policy, as Walras dreamed of, had no meaning as economics is conceived as "the basis of an art" aiming to increase social welfare. For that purpose, the state plays a significant role in reallocating resources through taxes and subsidies in order to cure the failures of the market that hinder the boost of the "national dividend" and decrease the well-being of a nation. Among his systematic analysis of state intervention, Pigou's mostly known contribution refers to the mechanisms of the reduction of social cost through the internalization of externalities.

The concept of externality was first discussed by Sidgwick as a result of the observation that individual actors fail to be aware of the full social impact of their activities (Sidgwick 1883, 412–413. Cf. Medema 2009, 43). Next, Marshall referred to positive externalities (without using the term) as a corollary to the idea of external economies produced by the concentration of specialized industries in particular localities (1890, Book IV, ch. x–xi; 1919, 287). Marshall grasped altogether the idea of boosting positive externalities and suggested a "fresh air rate", a special moderate tax on urban land with "special site value" to be spent by local authorities "on breaking out small green spots in the midst of dense industrial districts" (Marshall 1890, 662; Cf. Caldari and Masini 2011, 723). Yet, it was Pigou who formulated externality as a problem of market inefficiency and suggested as a remedy the reallocation of resources from the state or some public authority, and "put Sidgwick's ideas into Marshallian theoretical framework" (Medema, in Raffaelli et al. 2006, 640). Pigou (1920, 174) conceived productive externalities pretty much like mainstream textbooks do nowadays, as a divergence between the values of "the marginal private net product and marginal social net product". In order to avoid a third party being charged with extra "disservices" diminishing thus the "social net product", the government can remedy negative externalities via taxes, unless an arrangement is concluded between the parties involved. Pigou's most famous contribution to economics, the "Pigouvian tax" was not a panacea, but only one effective cure, when direct compensation or legal remedies were ineffective to improve economic welfare (cf. Collard, in Raffaelli et al. 2006, 594; Pressman 2014, 136). Briefly, Pigou argued that because the industrial firm has no incentive to internalize the cost of the marginal social cost it produces, the state should impose a tax on that firm that would correct the inefficient market outcome. From the point of view of the market, in the presence of externalities, prices do not express the total cost of production and the firm overproduces misusing thus rare resources.

Vilfredo Pareto (1848–1923) as well, aimed to offer the tools to evaluate economic welfare in an objective way. In contrast to Pigou's welfarism, Pareto (1909) introduced ordinal measures to estimate the optimal allocation of resources, bypassing thus the deadlock of measurement of utility and interpersonal utility comparisons (cf. Drakopoulos 1989, 40). Departing from his initial marginalist positions and the legacy of Walras, Pareto focused not on the map of individual tastes, like Edgeworth did, but rather on the observable actions to acquire goods. His celebrated optimality criterion helps to decide whether a policy measure is good or bad: good, if it benefits at least someone without harming anyone; bad, if it harms at least one without benefiting anyone. Nonetheless, Pareto's optimality too rests on assumptions that are definitely value-laden, such as the idea that social welfare is defined as the sum of the welfare of individuals as they perceive it (Blaug 1985, 591–592).

Backhouse et al. (2021, 1) have recently argued that "when economists have tackled practical problems they have adopted a much broader range of ethical judgments beyond welfarism", meaning an approach to social decisions that claims individual welfare to be the main criterion of social welfare. Unexpectedly, this applies also to the case of the early Neoclassicals. Marshall declared that "Wealth exists only for the benefit of mankind. It cannot be measured adequately in yards, nor even as equivalent to so many ounces of gold; its true measure lies only in the contribution it makes to human well-being" (Pigou 1925, 366). Analogously, Pigou (1920, 11) stated that economic welfare is "that part of social welfare that can be brought directly or indirectly into relation with the measuring-rod of money". Despite this statement, Pigou himself recognized that individual tastes depend also on social conditions making thus their choices on imprecise criteria of comparison. Hence, social dividends could be used only as a rough guide for evaluating redistribution policies from the rich to the poor. Pareto (1897) frankly recognized the limits of economic analysis and not only urged economists to consider "other models of man closer to reality" when it comes to applying their theories to practice but also reduced the field of economic analysis only to "logical actions". The greater part of social behavior – the domain of Non-logical actions – became the subject matter of Sociology, and the economists had to take account of its conclusions in order to make policy suggestions (Pareto 1909, 41, 1916).[11]

In many specific fields of economic policy, the Marginalists and early Neoclassicals espoused divergent views as they shared different political ideologies. Marshall's case is very instructive. Groenewegen (1995, ch. 16) describes his "tendency to socialism" as always of the mild variety, supporting state regulation and intervention to achieve "equality of opportunity" but hostile to the undue extension of public property and bureaucratic methods. Marshall's role as a member of the Labour Commission from 1891 to 1895 reveals an economist particularly involved with social policy measures aiming at poor's relief and health (Jensen 1987). His attitude evolved in the subsequent editions of his *Principles*, as shown by his proposals to promote "the wellbeing of the poorer working class" through state regulation "that no row of high buildings be erected without adequate free space in front and behind" (Marshall 1890, 597–598).[12]

Similarly remarkable was the case of Leon Walras (1834–1910). His outstanding model of General Equilibrium described the economy as a single giant market comprising all goods, factors of production and services in a united trade operation. This abstract model had the quality – among other things – to divulge the idea that different sectors of an economy are interrelated. But when it comes to speaking about the application of this model to policy issues, Walras abandons the hypothetical regime of perfect competition and becomes quite critical of "laissez-faire" policies: "Obviously! It should be proven that free competition does indeed maximize utility" (1898, 418). The main reason for this lies in his triple division between "économie pure", "économie sociale" and "économie appliquée". The last two sub-disciplines do not depend on the laws of nature like pure economics, but on "human will which is a free and insightful force" (Walras 1874, 39).[13] As human creations, applied and social economic phenomena draw their principles not exclusively from science but also from Morals. A policy principle, like "laissez-faire" should be evaluated according to its practical efficiency and impact on social welfare. Equally state intervention has the responsibility to provide goods and services of public interest and to use its authority to reduce social inequality and promote individual liberty (Walras 1896, 162. Cf. Dockès 1996). On the contrary, the idea of social equality was totally strange to his successor in Lausanne (Pareto 1900. Cf. Legris 2000). Pareto suggested a reformulation of the process of natural selection in order to explain social inequality as a phase of the social order. What is more, the presence of the elite at the top of social hierarchy is an indication of an effective social selection (Pareto 1909, §97–115). On that basis, any state intervention to protect a particular social group would disturb social equilibrium and produce the opposite effect, in the long run, favoring the stronger members of society (Pareto 1909, §2216–2217. Cf. Steiner 1995).

Disagreements are also manifested concerning the eternal problem of optimum taxation: how to levy a level of taxes so as to maximize public earnings with the least harm to both production and consumption, following the four maxims of Adam Smith.[14] In a sense, every tax contains some injustice as it deducts part of personal income obtained through work, investment or enterprise. Thus, Mill (1848, 808) accepted the redistributive role of direct taxation up to a certain limit: "not so as to relieve the prodigal at the expense of the prudent". Marshall agreed on that as a starting point and supported the progressive income tax, exactly because it decreases excessive social inequality, although he recognized its negative effects on consumer's surplus (Marshall 1890, 661. Cf. Reisman in Raffaelli et al. 2006, 497). Walras and Pareto on the contrary were absolutely against any progressive income tax for different reasons. Walras believed that income tax defies the principle of natural liberty and accepts only property taxes (Walras 1896, 413. cf. Potier 2019). Pareto, directly inspired from Frederic Bastiat, considered that taxes consists of a form of "spoliation" of riches by the state and therefore should be reduced to a minimum (Pareto 1909, §26–27).

The most radical idea on taxation came from an American self-educated political economist and activist, Henry George (1839–1897). Believing that he had discovered the main cause of poverty, which was also the principal impediment to social progress, George suggested a single massive tax on the fortune from the land property that would replace other taxes and would provide social services and also finance public utilities. Although *Progress and Poverty* lacked the analytical qualities of the Political Economy textbooks of that era, it was sold in thousands and became the best seller for almost half a century (Heilbroner 1953, 188–190). Both the ideas of a single tax and the negative impact of rents were not new. Since 1760, Quesnay and then Turgot had defended the necessity of the *impôt unique* on land property, and Ricardo since his 1815 essay and definitely in his *Principles* of 1817 had demonstrated the dramatic impact of rents on capitalist accumulation and the dark future of the stationary economy. Yet, George initiated a social reform movement – Georgism – that influenced many people from the Fabians to the Original Institutionalists, such as J.R. Commons.

To contextualize the above debate, it should be mentioned that up to WWI, public revenues in developed Western countries, from any source of taxation, represented less than 10% of their GDP (Piketty 2013, graph 13.1). A large part of these revenues continued to arrive from tariffs on imported goods that grew rapidly in Europe after 1880. Except for Britain, Holland and Denmark, all European nations increased their tariffs and duties on grain, coal, steel and other materials by up to 30% between 1880 and 1913 (Graff et al. 2014, 75). Liberal economists such as F.Y. Edgeworth (1845–1926), tried to "restate" as he claimed, the classical theory of taxation as it was left by Mill. Using once more his famous two-persons barter model, Edgeworth tried to determinate the incidence of taxes levied upon imported goods in an exchange between two nations to conclude that "the tax inflicts more loss on either party, the less the elasticity of that party's demand or supply" (Edgeworth 1897, 48).[15]

To sum up, Marginalists and early neoclassical economists were favorable to state intervention as complementary to the forces of the market. To accept "the violation of the general principle that the individual knows what is better for him", as Jevons (1882) has stated, there must be no other way to elevate collective utility. In social matters, neoclassical economists being keen observers of their social environment, were particularly attentive to the improvement of the conditions of the working classes and the eradication of pauperism. Jevons recognized the problem as an institutional failure and suggested more education as the unique way to "raise the intelligence and provident habits of the people" (1883, 186; Sekerler and Sigot 2013). Likewise, he suggested public libraries as an efficient means to increase people's education (Mossselmans 2007, 81). Marshall also underlined the need for better education of the poor (1890, 562. Cf. Jensen 1987). In his turn, Pigou (1920, 29–30) combined the lack of education of the poor with their low capacity to foresee the future and therefore with their low savings, neglecting thus the unfortunate level of their salaries. Analogous treatment of pauperism and low wages is nowhere to be found in Walker (1876) and Clark (1886) who believed that workers were fairly remunerated according to the marginal productivity of their work.

Conclusion

In matters of economic policy, marginalists and early neoclassical economists demonstrated a notable continuity with Classical economists and showed similar heterogeneity in their political recommendations. To start with the latter, between Ricardo's and Say's pure liberalism and Mill's philosophical radicalism, there were Conservatives like Malthus and Whigs like Senior who more or less agreed on the fundamental principles of political economy and yet endorsed distinct political agendas. Analogous was the political differentiation of their successors. On the one side, there were Pareto's ultra-liberal positions in line with Clark and Fisher. Jevons, Edgeworth and later Pigou were less negative on state intervention in case the market fails to be efficient, marking milder liberalism. In contrast, Marshall and Walras, the two greatest economists of this era, although adopting separate theoretical models, shared in common many ideas of the socialist utopian plans of their age. Proposals like the regulation of profits (Marshall) or the nationalization of land (Walras) would simply enrage Pareto or Fisher, despite their many theoretical kinships. So, the first conclusion from our concise outlook of the economic policy suggestions of the mainstream until the 1920s is that they were very heterogeneous despite their unquestionable membership to the school of Marginalist and Early Neoclassical economic thought.

As to the former characteristic, continuity in the policy agendas between the Classical and the early Neoclassicals, regardless of the relocation of the scope of economic analysis to microeconomic issues of exchange and production, was in fact a transmissive phenomenon. In matters of competition (both internal and external), the most significant shift came from the appearance of big firms that pushed some economists like Marshall and Clark to support anti-trust policies and state regulation. Monetary policy remained quantitativist and shifted to monetarism only with Fisher. Finally, the role of the state in domestic public policy continued to be a disputable matter, in the same manner as in the previous epoch.

Notes

1 Despite the established view, there was no real Depression after 1873, but only a deceleration. Thus, for the leading world manufacturer the annual growth rate of the British industrial production fell from 2.7 in 1853–1873, to 2.1 in 1873–1899 and the growth rate of total GDP from 1.95 to 1.85 respectively (Lewis 1978, 112–113).

2 In 1913, European colonial powers dominated over 550 mn people, which is 2.7 times the European population (Bairoch 1997, vol.II, 557), although they will expand after 1918 to the ex-Ottoman territories of the Middle East.

3 Karl Knies, Gustav Schmoller in Germany, and Henry Carey, R.T. Ely in the US, spread protectionist ideas.

4 Beyond the liberal dogma, F. Y. Edgeworth (1894) will use offer curves and community indifference curves to endeavor the issue of optimal tariffication.

5 Thomas Tooke published his six volumes of his *History of Prices* from 1838 to 1857 – the last two co-authored with William Newmarch – to demonstrate empirically that prices varied through time mainly because of good harvests, foreign exchange variations, obstructions to free trade, high prices of raw materials, technological innovations etc. See Schumpeter (1954, 708–713).

6 Thus, Keynes wrote about it as "the one book in the whole library of economic literature which every economic student, however humble, will have read, though he may read nothing else" (EJ, 1915, 371). *Lombard Street* was a huge success (21 editions from 1873 to 1933), making Bagehot the greatest authority on central banking. High rates are suggested to prevent bankers borrowing money without requiring it.

7 Fisher refers to the works of Simon Newcomb (1885), Alexander Del Mar (1885), Charles Dunbar (1901), Charles Laughlin (1903), Wesley Mitchell (1903) and mostly Edwin Kemmerer (1909). See Tobin (1985) and Laidler (1991).

8 Fisher first expressed it as $MV = \Sigma pQ$, i.e the sum of prices multiplied by the quantities bought (1911, 26) and then as $MV + M'V' = \Sigma pQ$, to include the quantity of checking deposits and their separate velocity (1911, 149).

9 The distinction between 'market rate' and 'natural rate' was already present in Mill (1848, 639–640), within a classical theoretical frame.

10 In his *Principles of Political Economy*, Henry Sidgwick (1883, 13, 395–396) still subscribes to the classical idea of the distinction between the science and the art of political economy established by Senior and Mill, half a century before. The two branches differ on their scope and the method of reasoning, the science being positive and hypothetical and the art being practical aiming to obtain "some desirable result not for an individual but for a political community". It was Ronald Coase who described Sidgwick as Marshall's "spiritual mother and father".

11 Non-logical actions were not necessarily irrational but only actions following a non-logical process of deliberation (Cf. Steiner 1995; Zouboulakis 2014, 40).

12 Marshall endorsed Mill's pro-Unionist views as against Edgeworth's idea that Unions create indeterminacy to wage bargaining. See Creedy (1990). Similarly, Clark suggested that labour unions are hindering competition (Pressman 2014, 104).

13 Walras recognised that J.S. Mill (1848, 200) and his distinction between laws of production and laws of distribution, was the source of his inspiration.

14 In his Chapter 2 of the last Book of *The Wealth of Nations*, Adam Smith formulated four maxims regarding taxes: equity, certainty, convenience of payment and economy of collection.

15 As Edgeworth explained when there are monopolistic circumstances the price of the taxed good will actually fall. This result was later called "the Edgeworth paradox".

Bibliography

Backhouse, R.E. (2006), "Sidgwick, Marshall and the Cambridge School of Economics", *History of Political Economy*, 38 (1): 15–44.

Backhouse, R.E., Baujard A. and Nishizawa, T. (2021), *Welfare Theory, Public Action and Ethical Values*, Cambridge: Cambridge University Press.

Bagehot, W. (1873), "Lombard Street: A Description of the Money Market," in N. St John-Stevas (ed.) *The Collected Works of Walter Bagehot*, London: The Economist, 1978 vol. IX, pp. 45–233.

Bairoch, P. (1997), *Victoires et déboires. Histoire économique et sociale du monde du XVI s. à nos jours,* Paris: Gallimard, 3 vols.

Blaug, M. (1985), *Economic Theory in Retrospect*, Cambridge: Cambridge University Press, 4th ed.

Bruni, L. (2002), *Vilfredo Pareto and the Birth of Modern Microeconomics*, Cheltenham: E. Elgar.

Caldari, K. and Masini, F. (2011), "Pigouvian versus Marshallian Tax: Market Failure, Public Intervention and the Problem of Externalities", *European Journal of the History of Economic Thought*, 18 (5): 715–732.

Clark, J.B. (1886), *The Philosophy of Wealth: Economic Principles Newly Formulated*, New York: Macmillan.

Clark, J.B. and Clark, J.M. (1901), *The Control of Trusts*, Charleston, SC: Nabu Press 2010.

Creedy, J. (1986), *Edgeworth and the Development of Neoclassical Economics*, Oxford: Blackwell.

Creedy, J. (1990), "Marshall and Edgeworth", *Scottish Journal of Political Economy*, 37 (1): 18–39.

Dockès, P. (1996), *La société n'est pas un pique-nique. Léon Walras et l'économie sociale*, Paris: Economica.

Drakopoulos, S. (1989), "The Historical Perspective of the Problem of Interpersonal Comparisons of Utility", *Journal of Economic Studies*, 16 (5): 35–51.

Edgeworth, F.Y. (1894), "Theory of International Values", *The Economic Journal*, 4 (16): 606–638.

Edgeworth, F.Y. (1897), "The Pure Theory of Taxation", *The Economic Journal*, 7 (25): 46–70.

Fawcett, H. (1872), *Free Trade and Protection*, London: MacMillan, 6th ed. 1885.

Fisher, I. (1911), *The Purchasing Power of Money* (with H. Brown), New York: MacMillan, 1926.

George, H. (1879), *Progress and Poverty*, Dodo Press 2009.

George, H. (1886), *Protection or Free Trade*, London: Kegan Paul, Tresch and Co.

Graff, M., Kenwood, A.G. and Lougheed, A.L. (2014), *Growth of the International Economy, 1820–2015*, London: Routledge, 5th ed.

Groenewegen, P. (1995), *A Soaring Eagle: Alfred Marshall, 1842–1924*, Aldershot: E. Elgar.

Groenewegen, P. (2003), "English Marginalism: Jevons, Marshall, and Pigou", in W.J. Samuels, J.E. Biddle and J.B. Davis (eds.) *A Companion to the History of Economic Thought*, Oxford: Blackwell, pp. 246–261.

Heilbroner, R. (1953), *The Worldly Philosophers*, New York: Simon and Schuster, 6th ed. 1992.

Hobsbawm, E. (1987), *The Age of Empire, 1875–1914*, London: Weidenfeld and Nicolson.

Jensen, H.E. (1987), "Alfred Marshall as a Social Economist", *Review of Social Economy*, 45 (1): 14–36.

Jevons, W.S. (1865), *The Coal Question*, New York: Kelley 1965.

Jevons, W.S. (1871), *The Theory of Political Economy*, London: MacMillan 1879, 2nd ed.

Jevons, W.S. (1882), *The State in Relation to Labour*, London: MacMillan 1968.

Jevons, W.S. (1883), *Methods of Social Reform*, New York: Kelley reprints 1965.

Keynes, J. M. (1924), "Alfred Marshall 1842–1924", *Economic Journal*, 34 (135): 311–372.

Laidler, D. (1991), *The Golden Age of the Quantity Theory. The Development of Neoclassical Monetary Economics, 1870–1914*, New York: Allan.

Legris, A. (2000), "La distribution des revenus chez Walras et Pareto : une analyse Comparative", in P. Dockès et al. (eds.) *Les Traditions économiques françaises*, Paris: CNRS éditions, pp. 503–518.

Lewis, A.W. (1978), *Growth and Fluctuations 1870–1913*, London: Allen & Unwin.

Marshall, A. (1890), *Principles of Economics*, London: MacMillan Press 1985, 8th ed. 1920.

Marshall, A. (1919), *Industry and Trade*, London: MacMillan Press, 3d ed. 1920.

Marshall, A. (1923), *Money, Credit and Commerce*, London: MacMillan Press.

Medema, S. (2009), *The Hesitant Hand: Taming Self-Interest in the History of Economic Ideas*, Princeton, NJ: Princeton University Press.

Mill, J.S. (1848), *Principles of Political Economy with Some of Their Applications to Social Philosophy*, New York: A. Kelley, 1973.

Mosselmans, B. (2007), *William Stanley Jevons and the Cutting Edge of Economics*, London: Routledge.

Pareto, V. (1897), "The New Theories of Economics", *Journal of Political Economy*, 5: 485–502.

Pareto, V. (1900), *Libre-échangisme, protectionnisme et socialisme*, in G. Busino (ed.) Œuvres Complètes vol. 4 Genève: Librairie Droz 1965.

Pareto, V. (1909), *Manuel d'Economie Politique*, in G. Busino (ed.) Œuvres Complètes vol.7, Genève: Librairie Droz 1966.

Pareto, V. (1916), *Traité de Sociologie générale*, in G. Busino (ed.) Œuvres Complètes vol. 12, Genève: Librairie Droz 1968.

Peart, S. (1996), *The Economics of William Stanley Jevons*, London: Routledge.

Pigou, A.C. (1906), *Protective & Preferential Import Duties*, London: MacMillan.

Pigou, A.C. (1920), *The Economics of Welfare*, London: MacMillan, 3d ed. 1929.

Pigou, A.C. (1921), *The Political Economy of War*, London: MacMillan.

Pigou, A.C. (1925), *Memorials of Alfred Marshall*, London: MacMillan.

Piketty, T. (2013), *Le Capital au XIX siècle*, Paris: Seul.

Potier, J.-P. (2011), "Marché du travail et législation sociale dans la pensée de Léon Walras", Œconomia, 1–3: 437–458.

Potier, J.-P. (2019), *Léon Walras, économiste et socialiste libéral*, Paris: Classiques Garnier.

Pressman, S. (2014), *Fifty Major Economists*, London: Routledge, 3d ed.

Raffaelli, T. (2003), *Marshall's Evolutionary Economics*, London: Routledge.

Raffaelli, T., Becattini, G. and Dardi, M. (2006), *The Elgar Companion to Alfred Marshall*, London: Routledge.

Robbins, L. (1973), *The Evolution of Modern Economic Theory*, London: MacMillan Press.

Schumpeter, J.A. (1954), *History of Economic Analysis*, London: Allen & Unwin.

Sekerler, P. and Sigot, N. (2013), "William Stanley Jevons et la « réforme sociale »: Une théorie du bien-être sans postérité", *Cahiers d'économie Politique*, 64: 221–251.

Sidgwick, H. (1883), *The Principles of Political Economy*, London: MacMillan and Co., 3d. ed. 1901.

Steiner, P. (1995), "Vilfredo Pareto et le protectionnisme : l'économie politique appliquée, la sociologie générale et quelques paradoxes", *Revue Economique*, 46 (5): 1241–1262.

Tobin, J. (1985), "Neoclassical Theory in America: J.B. Clark and Fisher", *American Economic Review*, 75 (6): 28–38.

Walker, F.A. (1876), *The Wages Question. A Treatise on Wages and the Wages Class*, New York: H. Holt & Co.

Walker, F.A. (1884), *Political Economy*, New York: H. Holt & Co.

Walker, D.A. (2003), "Early General Equilibrium Economics: Walras, Pareto, and Cassel", in W.J. Samuels, J.E. Biddle and J.B. Davis (eds.) *A Companion to the History of Economic Thought*, Oxford: Blackwell, pp. 278–293.

Walras, L. (1874/1877), *Eléments d'économie politique pure ou Théorie de la richesse sociale*, in Auguste et Léon Walras Œuvres économiques complètes, vol. VIII, Paris: Economica 1988.

Walras, L. (1896), *Etudes d'économie sociale: Théorie de la répartition de la richesse sociale*, in Auguste et Léon Walras Œuvres économiques complètes, vol. IX, Paris: Economica 1990.

Walras, L. (1898), *Etudes d'économie appliquée: Théorie de la production de la richesse sociale*, in Auguste et Léon Walras Œuvres économiques complètes, vol. X, Paris: Economica 1992.

Wicksell, K. (1898), *Interest and Prices: A study of the Causes Regulating the Value of Money*, London: Macmillan 1936.

Wicksell, K. (1906), *Lectures on Political Economy*, 2 vols, London: Routledge 1938.

Wicksell, K. (1907), "The Influence of the Rate of Interest on Prices", *The Economic Journal* 17 (6): 213–220.

Wicksteed, P.H. (1910), *The Common Sense of Political Economy, Including a Study of the Human Basis of Economic Law*, London: MacMillan.

Winch, D. (1969), *Economics and Policy: A Historical Study*, London: Hodder and Stoughton.

Zouboulakis, M. (2003), "L'équation de l'échange de Fisher et la loi des gaz parfaits. Les limites de l'analogie physique en économie", *Economies et Sociétés*, Série PE, 33: 2191–2206.

Zouboulakis, M.S. (2014), *The Varieties of Economic Rationality: From Adam Smith to contemporary Behavioral and Evolutionary Economics*, London: Routledge.

8 The German Historical School on Economic Policy

Harald Hagemann

Introduction

Economic policy and public finances had been at the centre of the training of civil servants since the first chairs for Cameralism had been created at the Prussian universities of Frankfurt /Oder and Halle in 1727. Austria followed with a considerable delay in 1763 when Joseph von Sonnenfels was appointed to the newly founded professorship on "Police and Cameral Science" at the University of Vienna. From the late 1790s onwards, Smithian ideas increasingly diffused, and new terms such as *Nationalökonomie* (Jakob 1805) and *Volkswirthschaftslehre* (Hufeland 1807) came up. In contrast to *Staatswirthschaftslehre* (state economics), which was basically restricted to police and finance, economics was no longer restricted to state administration, but now included wealth creation and the study of economic processes in the private domain. Ludwig Heinrich von Jacob (1759–1827), who was also a philosopher and a close adherent of Kant, which is characteristic of the first generation of Smithian followers in Germany, had translated main works of David Hume and Henry Thornton as well as Jean Baptiste Say's *Traite d'économie politique* in 1807. In Jakob's own textbook we can already find the new systematization of economic theory into production, distribution, and consumption. The concept and practice of *Polizei* central to Cameralism and an active conception of government were reduced substantially. However, the perseverance of cameralistic doctrines should not be overlooked. Thus, when Karl Heinrich Rau (1792–1870), a disseminator of liberal ideas, who became the main mediator of the doctrines of Smith, Ricardo, Malthus, and Say, founded the first scholarly journal in economics in Germany in 1835, the *Archiv der politischen Oekonomie und Polizeiwissenschaft*, he had to make a compromise in choosing its title.[1]

Rau was appointed as a chair of economics at the University of Heidelberg in 1822 where he taught for almost half a century until his death.[2] There he published his *Lehrbuch der politischen Oekonomie* in three volumes (Rau 1826–1837) which became a bestseller and a standard textbook for the next decades before it was succeeded by Roscher's *System der Volkswirthschaft.*[3] With Rau's *Principles*, the tripartite division of economics into *economic theory*

DOI: 10.4324/9781003228097-8

(Volkswirthschaftslehre), *economic policy* (Volkwirthschaftspflege[4]), and *public finance* (Finanzwissenschaft) as the three main areas became the established tradition in the teaching of economics at German universities until the late twentieth century.

Roscher's *Principles*, with 26 editions between 1854 and 1922, became the most successful textbook in economics. Wilhelm Roscher (1817–1894), who taught at the University of Leipzig from 1848 until his death, basically kept Rau's tripartite division, with economic theory (Vol. 1 of his System der Volkswirthschaft), public finance (Vol. 4), and economic policy comprising three volumes on agriculture (2), commerce (3) and social policy (5). The last volume reflects the increasing importance of the social question in the last three decades of the nineteenth century.

Among the "triumvirate", Roscher, Bruno Hildebrand (1812–1878), and C(K)arl Knies (1821–1898), normally considered as the leading representatives of the "older" Historical School, Roscher (1843) laid the programmatic basis in his *Outline to Lectures on the State Economy in Accordance with the Historical Method*. There he transferred the approach of Friedrich Karl von Savigny (1779–1861) and the Historical School of Law to economics[5] and suggested an embracing historical and comparative study of economic systems to identify the stages of development and the laws of economic life.[6]

Joseph Schumpeter (1954, p. 442, my italics) stated that this belief in evolutionary sequences or stages of economic development, a common characteristic for the representatives of the German Historical School (GHS), is only "a simple expository device for impressing upon beginners (or the public) the lesson that *economic policy* has to do with changing economic structures and therefore cannot consist of a set of unchanging recipes". Friedrich List (1789–1846), an important precursor of the GHS, can be considered the founding father of the stages doctrine, which later was elaborated in various features from Roscher, Hildebrand, and Knies to Schmoller, Karl Bücher, and Werner Sombart's *Modern Capitalism*. List observed that nations pass through different stages of economic development and that at his time only Britain had fully developed the most advanced agricultural plus manufacturing plus commercial stage. He represented the forward-looking perspective of the rising industrial bourgeoisie in catching-up countries (France, the United States of America, and Germany lagging behind), one not compatible with the leading British economy at an early stage. He therefore developed the infant-industry argument and his stages theory of economic development, emphasizing productive powers and the specificity of national endowments, wants, cultures, and conditions, to be applied in the context of economic policy in catching-up nations.

In the following, I will discuss the main areas of economic policy to which members of the GHS made important contributions or which were major topics for controversial debates. This includes the social question, the debate on trade policy between free traders and protectionists, as well as fiscal and monetary policies.

The Social Question and the Verein für Sozialpolitik

It is not an easy task to define precisely what constitutes a "historical school". There even existed a historical school in England, where the social question in an industrializing economy came up first. Historism was not exclusively a German phenomenon but came up in many European countries, apart from France, in the eighteenth century as a reaction to the dominance of science and reason ensuing from the age of enlightenment and against a purely axiomatic argumentation. There never existed a German monopoly on the historical approach to economics.

What are the criteria considering the question of what constitutes a "school"? Schumpeter (1954, p. 470) has a rather strict definition when he points out, regarding the "Ricardian school", *that it had a master, a doctrine, a spirit of community, a core, zones of influence, and borderlands.* Even with a less rigid definition, there are good arguments to dismiss the term for the older GHS since the triumvirate Roscher, Hildebrand and Knies was too diverse[7] and "does not form any real unit at all". Schumpeter therefore confines "the concept, Historical School of Economics, to the age and to the group of Gustav von Schmoller" (ibid., p. 507). However, the other two outstanding figures in the period of Schmoller (1838–1917) and his followers, that is the so-called "younger GHS", Lujo Brentano (1844–1931) and Adolph Wagner (1835–1917), show that a certain variety and differences existed. This is even more reflected in the international diffusion and dissemination process of the ideas of the GHS. The multifaceted meanings made suitable to the conditions and economic and social needs of the country of adaptation are well illustrated in the 12 national case studies and the insightful Introduction of José Luís Cardoso and Michalis Psalidopoulos to *The German Historical School and European Economic Thought* (2016).[8]

The pressing poverty and social problems associated with the increasing industrialization, i.e., the "Social Question" was the main reason for the foundation of the *Verein für Sozialpolitik* shortly after German unification at the end of the French-German war.[9] The *Verein* has kept social policy in its title until today, although the focus on these problems had already started to evaporate in Imperial Germany. The founding members were opposed to both Manchester liberalism on the one side and Socialism and the revolutionary ideas of Marxism on the other side. Since this group of social reformers was dominated by university professors, critics denounced them as *Kathedersozialisten* (socialists of the chair).

The main driver of the foundation of the Verein für Sozialpolitik had been Schmoller who initiated the first major conference on the social question, which took place in Halle in July 1872. Shortly thereafter Schmoller moved from Halle to the newly established German university in Strassburg. A decade later he became a professor at the University of Berlin where he stayed until his death. Berlin was not only the capital of Germany but also of Prussia, by far the largest German state in which two-thirds of the German universities were located. Representing the University of Berlin since 1889 in the second chamber, the Prussian Upper House,[10] Schmoller also exerted a greater influence on the appointment of new professors. Although he took over chairmanship of the Verein für Sozialpolitik only in 1890 from Erwin Nasse who had been chairman in the preceding 16 years, as the initiator and leader of the centre Schmoller had been the most influential member from the beginning. Wagner was a leading member of the right, who as a long-time enemy of Brentano often aligned himself with the industrialists.

Brentano, on the other hand, was the undisputed leader of the liberal left who retained the democratic tradition of his family. In contrast to Schmoller and particularly Wagner he was alienated by any demonstration of power by the Prussian monarchy. When a generational conflict escalated at the Mannheim conference in 1905, and Schmoller and his historical-ethical approach were attacked by Max Weber, Werner Sombart, and the other radical democrats, it was Brentano, who had a good personal relationship with Schmoller but was also highly appreciated by Weber, who settled the conflict.

Brentano was the most anglophile member of the younger GHS. Over many decades he had been in close contact with Alfred Marshall and contributed a Preface to the German edition of Marshall's *Principles of Economics*. Ever since he made a long visit to Britain together with the leading statistician Ernst Engel in the late 1860s, Brentano turned out to be a strong supporter in establishing and strengthening trade unions, which provided the adequate means to improve the working conditions. He was deeply convinced that the organized coalition of workers was the decisive means to solve the labour question, which became the central topic of his life. Workers should receive a fair share in the general increase of wealth and productivity which would contribute to better living conditions of working-class families and overcome poverty in the long run.

It is no accident that Heinrich Herkner (1863–1932), who was a former PhD student of Brentano, wrote the book which became the standard textbook on the labour question. Herkner also succeeded Schmoller in his professorship at the University of Berlin and as chairman of the Verein für Sozialpolitik in 1917. Herkner's main work *Die Arbeiterfrage* dealt with the social history of France, England, and Germany, ethical considerations of the labour question, liberalism and communism, and finally social reforms. It grew substantially over time from 298 pages in 1894 to two volumes comprising more than 1300 pages in its eighth and final edition in 1922. Herkner's book on the labour question was also well received internationally and translated into Russian (1899), Finnish (1902), Polish (1905), Spanish (1915) and Greek (1919/1920).

In contrast to Brentano and the young Herkner, Schmoller advocated a paternalistic social policy. As a social conservative, Schmoller believed in an improvement of the living conditions of working-class families through social reforms by the Prussian state. Schmoller and Wagner are two famous cases of economists who indicate the socializing power of the Prussian state in the period between 1871 and 1914. Schmoller in a limited sense remained a liberal, convinced that the civil service – whose leading members got a greater part of their education from the chair socialists (!) – was best suited to overcome the class struggle. Wagner, although coming from Freiburg in liberal Baden (after professorships in Vienna and Dorpat), when he was appointed professor at the University of Berlin in 1870, was a strong conservative not immune to anti-Semitism. He held strong state-socialist beliefs so that the term "socialist of the chair" is most appropriate for him. In 1910 he was nominated directly by the King as a member of the Prussian Upper House where in a speech in 1913 he stated: "I have been annexed and owe it to Bismarck that I have become Prussian, and that fact I always have thought to be the greatest."[11] Long before he had already dubbed Bismarck and Emperor Wilhelm I "State socialists".

The year 1878/1879 was a great political turning point. Bismarck increasingly attacked the Liberals and in October 1878 launched the *Sozialistengesetze* to contain the rising influence of social democracy. It was, however, Bismarck's reorientation of trade policy towards protective tariffs which caused a great crisis in the Verein für Sozialpolitik. The 1879 meeting was characterized by heavy controversies between free traders and protectionists. The turbulent meeting ended with the decision to shy away from controversial issues and to abstain from final votes on sensitive policy issues in all future meetings. A prolonged period of social conservative dominance began. It also had the consequence that the Verein, whose founding rationale had been the social question, had only little influence on Bismarck's great projects of social legislation, with which he tried to pacify the workers in the period of the anti-socialist laws.

Bismarck recognized the importance of the social question. On the other hand, Bismarck, and the State executive in Prussia increasingly tended to suppress all socialist activities by police and judicial power, which was strongly executed in the period of socialist laws between 1878 and 1890. He chose a policy of carrots and sticks. Health insurance for workers was introduced in 1883, accident insurance a year later, and, finally old-age insurance in 1889. However, the major motive to alienate the workers from social democracy failed. After the abolition of the socialist laws, the Social Democrats were much stronger than before. Shortly after Bismarck's dismissal as Chancellor a limitation of child work and Sunday rest were introduced, and the working day was restricted to a maximum of 11 hours. It took until the end of World War I, and the foundation of the Weimar Republic that trade unions were fully recognized and that the eight-hour working day was introduced.

Trade Policy: Between Free Trade and Protectionism

The free trade versus protectionism debate was a controversy that took place in many European countries during the nineteenth century.[12] It is a myth and an overly simplified view that the members of the GHS were all hostile to classical economics and free trade. The overall picture is much more differentiated and complex, as can already be seen by taking a closer look at the work of Friedrich List as an important precursor. Undoubtedly, List was a political liberal fighting for human rights and civil liberties, which caused him severe problems with his lifelong enemy Metternich. In his positions List consequently represented the interests of a country which is a late-comer in economic development. This made his argument attractive and appealing for all subsequent catching-up economies until China in the more recent past (Mei Junjie 2019).

List was a theorizing practitioner. As a young man he had observed in his home region Wuerttemberg, in France, and in some other countries the flourishing of new industries during the Continental blockade and their following collapse after the end of the Napoleonic period when cheaper exports from the dominant British industries, exploiting an economies-of-scale effect, were flooding the market. Some years later he experienced in Pennsylvania the levying of high import tariffs for the protection of young industries. The infant-industry argument, which originated with Alexander Hamilton, certainly belonged to List's American heritage.

As a liberal, List always considered economic freedom and free trade as highly desirable, but a valuable ideal only appropriate for a group of nations with some degree of equality in their stage of development. He made a strong plea for the abolition of barriers to trade and for the generation of free trade within Germany (at that time still divided into 39 medium and small states with customs barriers and different currencies) in his memorandum to the newly founded German Association for Trade and Commerce in April 1819. He considered the abolition of internal tariffs as a precondition for German (economic) unification. There can be no doubt that he would have expressed a similar position for economic unification in Western Europe after World War II.

In case the condition of an approximate stage of development was not met, List regarded some form of protectionism as necessary aiming at the optimal development of national productive forces. List approved temporary but not permanent protective tariffs, and he explicitly excluded agriculture from protection. For him, it was not a departure from liberal principles but a tool to shape society by fostering its development potential in areas of comparative advantage. He underestimated the problem that tariffs once introduced as temporary protection tend to become permanent due to vested interests acting in the political sphere.

List did not witness the final abolition of the corn duties in Britain in the year of his death in 1846. Two years later, in the Frankfurt National Assembly, the trade debate was one of the most controversial in the brief period from May to September 1848.[13] The elected members also included Bruno Hildebrand,[14] who soon became the chairman of the important seventh subcommittee on general working conditions, and Friedrich Benedict Wilhelm von Hermann (1795–1868). Hermann, a Professor at the University of Munich since he had made his reputation with *Staatswirthschaftliche Untersuchungen* in

1832, was the most outstanding theoretician in the Paulskirchen parliament. He was heading the third subcommittee on Trade, Sea Traffic, and Customs Regulation in which the trade controversy mainly took place. The main controversy between a "greater" (including Austria) and a "smaller" Germany (with Prussia in the leading role), which dominated the political debates, also affected the trade controversy. The *Zollverein*, the customs union which had been established under Prussian leadership in 1834, initially favoured free trade ideas. The followers of List, mainly from Southern Germany, finally got the majority for the levying of tariffs to protect the domestic economy. However, even deputies who favoured protective tariffs, like the leader of the "Greater Germans" Hermann, favoured the customs union with Austria.

Furthermore, there had been a strong current supporting free trade. The leading figure was Wilhelm-Adolf Lette (1799–1868), a member of the liberal right, the Casino group, which was the largest group in the National Assembly. Lette was an activist in the German free trade movement, ever since the raising of the first protective tariff on pig iron in 1844 had caused major controversies in the Zollverein and generated opposition. Lette later became the first chairman of the permanent delegation of the *Congress* of German economists from its foundation in 1858 until his death.[15] Whereas at its beginnings the free trade movement in Germany had been influenced by the ideas of Adam Smith and David Ricardo, the movement took a more radical twist under the influence of Frédéric Bastiat, who had constituted an Association of Free Trade in Paris in 1846. Shortly afterwards, in March 1847, John Prince-Smith (1809–1874), a naturalized Prussian citizen who had come from England, established a German Free Trade Union in Berlin. He soon became the dominant figure in the free trade movement. Prince-Smith was also instrumental in the foundation of the Congress in 1858. From the beginning, the Congress attracted many practitioners and industrialists and became the mouthpiece of Manchester liberalism in Germany. It had a stronger influence in Prussia than in the south of Germany. The ignorance towards the poverty problems and the social question associated with the growing industrialization process, which characterized many members and the debates in the Congress, caused increasing opposition among the ranks of academic economists and thereby contributed decisively to the foundation of the Verein für Sozialpolitik in 1872/1873. Some years after Bismarck's reorientation of trade policy towards protective tariffs, the Congress was dissolved in 1885.

Bismarck and the higher civil servants in Prussia had favoured free trade over decades. The successful Prussian policy in the customs union had been free trade policy. In alliance with the National Liberals, this policy was continued in the first years after German unification. In 1873 the Reichstag decided that the last remaining tariffs on pig iron should be abolished by 1877. However, shortly after the decision was made, a longer and major economic crisis started, and the iron industry became one of the main protagonists in the introduction of protective tariffs. Outside Prussia, in the south of

Germany, the textile industry had a long tradition supporting protectionism. In the northeast of Germany, in Prussia, the big producers in agriculture historically were favouring free trade, particularly due to their interest in exporting wheat to England. In the 1870s, agriculture had to face increasing competition from the importation of cheap corn from overseas. As a result, the protectionist movement got stronger and gained influence due to a new coalition of industrial and agricultural protectionists. The crisis implied that the government increasingly suffered from insufficient tax income in the late 1870s. The resulting financial problems were the main motive for Bismarck's drastic change in trade policy, combined with his anti-liberal turn in the political sphere and his break with the Liberals who were the leading champions of free trade.

In this situation, Schmoller showed his "flexibility". In 1862, the young Schmoller, after the signing of the new French – Prussian trade agreement, even had written an anonymous pamphlet *Der französische Handelsvertrag und seine Gegner* (The French trade treaty and its enemies), in which he made a strong plea for a liberal trade policy. There he argued against protective tariffs as well as too much considerateness for Austrian interests, positions which had been quite common in the south of Germany for a long time. At the 1879 conference of the Verein für Sozialpolitik in Frankfurt Schmoller, in a complete reversal of his earlier view, emphasized that protective tariffs were an adequate policy. In a synthesizing historical speech, Schmoller put the free trade and protectionist policies of the large nations in comparative perspective, pointing out that the character of trade policy is not a matter of principle but a matter of practical value in the main political or economical upswings and downswings of nations. Thus, a rationale and legitimization of Bismarck's drastic change in trade policy was given by the most influential member of the Verein.

Schmoller's main opponent at the 1879 conference was Erwin Nasse (1829–1890), Professor of economics at the University of Bonn since 1860 and long-time chairman of the Verein from 1874 until his death. Nasse, who was also a member of the Prussian parliament from 1869 to 1879 for the Liberal-Conservative Party, stood firm in his free trade views but was left in a minority position. In the general assembly finally, only 63 members voted for free trade and 82 members for Bismarck's protectionist course. Nasse personally felt offended and considered his resignation as chairman. Due to strong personal support from many members (including Schmoller!), second thoughts led Nasse to stay.

The vote for protectionist policies was mainly due to two reasons: an unusually high number of industrialists attending the 1879 Frankfurt conference, and the absence of Brentano who was suffering from typhus fever. Brentano always argued that Germany's development into an industrial economy implied the necessity to supply cheap food for the workers and the rapidly growing population and to generate export markets for industrial products. In analogy to the strong increase of wealth in Britain after the final abolition of the Corn Laws, he concluded that "[t]he German economy requires free trade", as this important social reformer still argued in retrospect in his autobiography *My Life as a Fight for the Social Development of Germany* (Brentano 1931, p. 172). It is an open question whether the appearance of this charismatic speaker would have changed the majority at the conference which left the chairman Nasse defeated.

Finanzwissenschaft and Fiscal Policy

Finanzwissenschaft traditionally enjoyed a high reputation in the German language area and a preferred role among the subareas of economics, as indicated in Rau's tripartite scheme. A characteristic of Cameralism was an organic view of the state. The German tradition of *Finanzwissenschaft* had a broader perspective, including institutional, historical, legal, and sociological aspects than the Anglo-Saxon tradition of *public finance*, which had developed as part of economic theory and shared the rigour of its analysis.[16] In the latter, the focus was on taxation whereas in the German tradition the expenditure side of the budget was also in the focus, which offered the possibility of a more positive view of the public sector. This holds, for example, for the contribution of public infrastructure to the economic growth of a nation, the financing of human capital – from an elaborate system of apprenticeship to the foundation of technical and economic universities particularly in the second half of the nineteenth century – and the redistribution of income and wealth to solve the social question.

Given the above, the work of an early pioneer of modern fiscal policy is highly interesting. Carl Dietzel (1829–1884) was Professor of Economics at the University of Marburg since 1867 and a member of the Prussian Parliament from 1868 to 1873. As a cosmopolitan and convinced liberal, he was politically active in the National Liberal Party. His scholarly masterpiece is his Heidelberg habilitation thesis *The System of Government Loans in the Context of the Economy* (Dietzel 1855). In his work, Dietzel pointed out the discrepancy between the orthodox view that public debt is detrimental to economic growth and the empirical fact that the leading economic nations England and France had made the most extensive use of government loans. As well as taxes do not only constitute costs for the private sector but can also create benefits by properly spending the money, this also holds for public debt. Following a macroeconomic perspective, Dietzel emphasized that public capital formation is important for economic growth. He argued particularly that long-run investment should be financed by long-term government loans as a necessary condition for higher growth of production, productivity, and national income.

Dietzel pointed out that public investment would exert a crowding-in effect for the private sector. He thus can be considered as a precursor of the Aschauer hypothesis. David Aschauer gave reasons in support of the importance of investment in core public infrastructure as a relevant complementary factor for macroeconomic growth in various articles since the late 1980s. Investment in public infrastructure can increase the productivity of the private capital stock and therefore induce additional private investment.[17]

Dietzel did not only emphasize the macroeconomic interaction between the public and the private sector and the productivity of debt-financed public capital formation, but he also put an early focus on intangible assets. He extended the investment/capital concept and considered the state as the most important immaterial capital. The government therefore should not only provide vital physical infrastructure but is also responsible for human resource development including education, research, and health. This shows that Dietzel, although a firm economic liberal, fits well into the German tradition with its emphasis on the tasks of the state.

Richard Musgrave (1997, p. 70) has emphasized that in contrast to "Dietzel's analysis of public debt, macro concerns had entered the mainstream of British fiscal thinking only with the Keynesian revolution, but then with a vengeance". It is therefore not surprising that Walter Stettner (1914–1998), who was an assistant in the Fiscal Policy Seminar of Alvin Hansen at Harvard, had rediscovered this neglected German economist.[18] Stettner's (1948) contribution "Carl Dietzel, public expenditures and the public debt" to the Festschrift for Hansen is an outcome of his unpublished Harvard dissertation *Nineteenth Century Public Debt Theories in Great Britain and Germany* (1944), in which Stettner also took a closer look at the British outsiders James Steuart and Thomas Robert Malthus on the subject of public borrowing from a Keynesian perspective. He appraises Dietzel's work as "the most penetrating and original theory of the public debt of his century" (Stettner 1948, p. 278).

It is generally recognized that German public finance was at its height from the 1860s to the 1890s. Characteristically, in this period a new specialized journal, the *Finanzarchiv*, was founded by Georg von Schanz (Professor at the University of Würzburg) in 1884 focusing on all issues of public finance. However, over the first decades finance statistics with emphasis on budgetary questions, finance legislation, and archive material dominated. In contrast to the glorious Italian school of public finance, economic theory was rather neglected although important contributions were written in German by Emil Sax (1887), and Knut Wicksell's *Finanztheoretische Untersuchungen* (1896) later had a stronger impact on such diverse authors as Erik Lindahl, Richard Musgrave, and James Buchanan.

Lorenz von Stein (1815–1890), Albert Schäffle (1831–1903), and Adolph Wagner formed the triumvirate of German *Finanzwissenschaft* in the late nineteenth century. They all held a positive view of the economic role of the state. The fiscal system had to satisfy communal wants as in Lorenz von Stein's Hegelian approach, who defined public finance as an integral part of state sciences. "Schäffle and Wagner recognized the individual as the basic beneficiary of public services but did not view their provision as a function of private preferences" (Musgrave 1997, p. 74).

Wagner's textbook on public finance, which initially had grown out of a revision of the third volume of Rau's Principles, remained the dominant one until World War I. Politically Wagner was a reactionary but theoretically, he steered a middle course between the historical and a more theoretical approach in the classical tradition, which distinguished him from Schmoller. Wagner was the incarnation of a state socialist reflecting a characteristic type of social conservatism in Imperial Germany, based on the rejection of liberalism and an organic concept of the state. Today he is remembered for his historical law of increasing expansion of public activities and government spending, which he first observed for Germany and then for other countries. *Wagner's law* suggests that progressive industrialization in advanced economies causes increasing political pressure for social services which results in a rising share of the public sector in national income. The law implies an increasing expansion of fiscal requirements. Wagner, in his teachings and writings, favoured progressive income taxation, taxes on wealth and inheritance, and taxes on luxury goods and capital gains. He exerted a considerable influence on his students who later acquired higher positions in public administration or became politicians. In the *Miquelsche Finanzreform* of 1891/1893 Prussia, which for a long time had relied on indirect taxes, for the first time introduced a progressive income tax, supplemented by a tax on wealth. Wagner also strongly influenced foreign students such as Gustav Cassel and other Swedes.[19] Edwin R.A. Seligman (1861–1939), who had studied in Berlin with Wagner and Schmoller, and in Heidelberg with Knies, from 1879 to 1881, as an influential professor at Columbia University in New York later became a leading proponent of progressive income taxation in the USA (Seligman 1911).[20]

Monetary Economics

For a long time, monetary economics in Germany was lagging and echoing the developments in Great Britain such as the Bullion Controversy and the controversy between the Currency and the Banking School. An outstanding case was Adolph Wagner who at the age of 22 wrote his Göttingen dissertation on money and banking, and five years later became widely known with his *Theory of Money and Credit behind Peel's Bank Act* (Wagner 1862). Wagner's hero was Thomas Tooke and he clearly sided with the Banking School. He criticized Peel's Bank Charter Act of 1844, which separated the Bank of England into a Banking and an Issuing Department, and the dominant influence of the Currency School, led by Torrens and Lord Overstone in the tradition of Ricardo's quantity theory of money, time and again, at a time when the Act had already been suspended in the crises of 1847 and 1857 (and thereafter in 1866) to avoid the collapse of the payment system. Wagner shared the view that convertibility of bank notes into gold is a necessary condition to stabilize the value of money but criticized the transfer of Ricardo's doctrine to redeemable bank notes, which are not paper money proper, let alone currency, for which they have not been conceived.[21] He shared Tooke's view that the circulation of bank notes has to adapt to the needs of the economy and that an increase in the circulation of notes would at best be the effect of price increases produced by other factors but not their cause. It is mainly due to the works of Wagner and Erwin Nasse as experts on money and banking that the doctrines of the Banking School dominated the monetary debate in Germany for decades, to the great annoyance of later authors such as Ludwig von Mises.

When Germany was politically unified in 1871, an independent and elaborated monetary theory did not exist. The main reason for this analytical deficit was the fact that due to the former separation seven different currencies circulated, with the *Taler* prevailing in Northern Germany and the *Gulden* in Southern Germany (and Austria). In the currency conventions of Munich (1837) and Dresden (1838), the ratio between Taler and Gulden had been fixed at 2:3. Germany's former political division and the lagging behind England and France in the process of industrialization was reflected in the disruption and backwardness of the German monetary system with underdeveloped financial markets and institutions. Major reforms were required.

In 1871, a very dynamic transformation period started, with the Currency Act of 1871 introducing the Mark, the Coinage Act of 1873 regulating the transition from the existing multi-currency system to the new uniform Mark system,[22] and finally the Bank Act of 1875 with the foundation of the *Reichsbank* which began operation in January 1876. The Reichsbank which grew out of the Bank of Prussia[23] became the Central Bank and lender of last resort of Imperial Germany, but in the south, the state banks of Baden, Bavaria, Saxony, and Wuerttemberg continued to co-exist and to issue notes until the end of the Wilhelminian era. Germany opted for the gold standard, thereby strengthening the British model rather than the French one of a silver standard, but it was a "limping" gold standard until 1909 when silver coins were not legal tender anymore. In contrast to modern central banks, the Reichsbank did not pursue a special monetary policy. It was following the market and interest rates instead of setting them, with procyclical consequences, in the founding boom 1871–1873 as well as in the following *Gründerkrise* 1873–1879. In the "Great Depression" from 1873 to 1896 (Rosenberg 1967), the real national income grew, but the nominal one decreased because of deflationary effects of the gold standard.

In the political sphere, Ludwig Bamberger (1823–1899), who was one of the most important representatives of liberalism in Germany, played a decisive role. He had studied with Rau at Heidelberg and law in Göttingen and Giessen where he got his doctorate. In 1848, Bamberger had been a progressive liberal fighting for the democratic revolution. When it failed, he just could escape the Prussian military, which later sentenced him to death in absence, and emigrated via Switzerland to Paris. As an offspring of a Jewish banking family, Bamberger was among the founders of the Banque Paribas, as well as after his return to Germany in 1866, he was among the co-founders of the Deutsche Bank in 1870. As a member of the Reichstag, Bamberger was the most important advocate of the gold standard. He had a decisive influence on the Bank Act which was passed by the Reichstag with an overwhelming majority on 30 January 1875 and signed by the Emperor in March. Emphasis was placed on the Reichsbank as the lender of last resort, with currency stability guaranteed by the gold standard. Like the Bank of England, the Reichsbank was a privately owned institution which, despite the highly authoritarian system, was remarkably independent of direct political interference by the government. As a National liberal, Bamberger was a personal advisor of Bismarck until the latter's shift to a *Schutzzollpolitik* (protective tariffs) and the socialist laws caused a final split.

According to Schumpeter (1954, pp. 539 and 809), Knies was the most eminent theorist of the Older Historical School, and he was the only one who focused on issues of money and banking. Although his main work on *Money and Credit*, comprising three volumes with about 1200 pages (Knies 1873, 1876–1879), was mainly written in the turbulent years of the German monetary transition, it was much less affected by the historical events than the works of Wagner and Nasse. Knies's trilogy was an academic treatise written in an inaccessible language, which had no impact on the real course of events.

Knies demonstrated his analytical qualities in a precise elaboration of the functions of money. However, his emphasis on the outstanding importance of credit could hardly be reconciled with his rigorous metallism which was more fundamental than the one of Wagner and Nasse. The question of (non-) neutrality of credit regarding overall production is answered contradictory, and interest theory is separated from the credit, capital, and monetary theory, as pointed out by Trautwein (2005) in his critical assessment. Knies constructed a synthesis of the Currency and the Banking School defending the quantity theory in arguing that the amount of credit would also affect the value of money, while at the same time agreeing to the reverse causation argument from price increases to the monetary aggregate of the Banking School.

Schumpeter's view that Knies's theoretical writings contrast heavily with his early favouring of the historical method (Knies 1853), which he republished three decades later, must be qualified. Knies's procedure in his analysis of money and credit does not adhere to his historicist programme but attempts to discover general laws; however, not by strict theoretical analysis but by a typical German way of taxonomy and classification which resembles juridical argumentation, illuminating but tiring. This procedure is quite different from the application of the inductive method in modern empirical social sciences. Furthermore, it explains why in contrast to Knies's successes as an outstanding teacher at Heidelberg, where he had a profound influence on excellent students from Max Weber, Eugen von Böhm-Bawerk, and Friedrich von Wieser to Americans such as Richard T. Ely, John Bates Clark, and Edwin R.A. Seligman, his work on money and credit had only a limited success compared to the later works by Knapp and Helfferich.

Although Knut Wicksell's *Interest and Prices* (1898), the outstanding theoretical work which laid the foundations for modern monetary macroeconomics, was written in German and printed by a publisher with a high academic reputation, it did not make a greater impact in the next two decades. This differed from *The State Theory of Money* (1905) by Georg Friedrich Knapp (1842–1926), a close friend of Schmoller, who put emphasis on the investigation of the legal and historical aspects of money rather than on theoretical analysis. Knapp conceived money as a creature of the legal order, as an alternative to theoretical metallism. In his chartalist approach, the validity of all forms of money is decisively based on state authority. Knapp's approach therefore can be considered a legitimate child of the German Historical School. Knapp completely neglects the role of the quantity of money.

The most successful textbook, however, was *Money* by Karl Helfferich (1872–1924) which went into six editions from 1903 to 1923. Helfferich got his PhD with Knapp at the University of Strassburg in 1894 but was a loyal metallist. Like the banker Friedrich Bendixen (1864–1920), who was an enlightened chartalist and follower of Knapp, Helfferich addressed problems of money and banking more theoretically and was also looking at practical applications. As Secretary of State in the Treasury Office in World War I, Helfferich became the architect of German war financing making recourse to extreme borrowing rather than raising taxes, a method which was later rightly blamed for its inflationary consequences.

Epilogue

Although still influential, with the deaths of Schmoller and Wagner in 1917, and the end of Imperial Germany in November 1918, the Historical School lost its dominant position. On pressing practical problems in the young Weimar Republic, such as the socialization question, the reparation problem, or the disastrous hyperinflation in 1922/1923, the representatives of the Historical School had no satisfying answers.

Notes

1 In 1853, the journal was absorbed by the *Zeitschrift für die gesamte Staatswissenschaft*, which in 1844 had been founded and thereafter for a long time edited by the members of the Faculty of State Economics at the University of Tübingen, created in 1817 with Friedrich List as Professor of Administrative Practice in his short career as an academic. The journal was renamed into *Journal of Institutional and Theoretical Economics* in 1986 and is the oldest scholarly journal existing in Germany. For greater details, see Hagemann (1991).

2 His direct successors holding this prominent chair in economics were C(K)arl Knies (1821–1898) and Max Weber in January 1897 (until 1903).

3 For greater details see Hagemann (1996) as well as Hagemann and Rösch (2012). On the many facets of Rau's textbook see also Tribe (1988, ch. 9).

4 From the second edition onwards, the outdated term was replaced by Volkswirthschaftspolitik (economic policy). With the fourth edition, the second volume was split into two parts (1854–1858).

5 For greater details, see Rieter (2002).
6 Roscher's historical viewpoint does not exclude theoretical considerations. He based his analysis for a greater part on the doctrines of British classical political economics, with emphasis on historical relativism and in some eclectic way. Nevertheless, Roscher surely was closer to the ideas of classical economics than were Hildebrand and Knies, and much closer than later Schmoller. Regarding the later dispute on method, it should not be overlooked that Carl Menger dedicated his *Grundsätze* to Roscher. See also Roscher (1861).
7 See Schumpeter (1954, pp. 507–509 and 808–809).
8 On the role of the GHS in American economic thought, see Dorfman (1955) and Bateman (2011).
9 For a more detailed analysis of the history of the Verein für Sozialpolitik from its foundation until World War I, see Hagemann (2001).
10 For a more detailed analysis of German economists in Parliament in the period 1848–1914, see Hagemann and Rösch (2005).
11 See Lindenlaub (1967, Vol. 1, p. 156).
12 See the contributions in Cardoso and Psalidopoulos (2016).
13 For greater details, see Hagemann and Rösch (2005).
14 Hildebrand and Knies both were progressive liberals and stood up for the democratic revolution in 1848. In the restoration period that followed both emigrated to Switzerland. Hildebrand, who had lost his chair in Marburg, was appointed professor at the University of Zurich and founded the Swiss Statistical Office in Berne.
15 For a detailed history of the German free trade movement and the Congress, see Hentschel (1975) and Winkel (1977, pp. 38–49).
16 For an excellent comparison see Musgrave (1996–1997), whose own work benefited from a fruitful combination of these two different approaches (Musgrave 1997).
17 See, for example, Aschauer (1989).
18 For a critical re-assessment of Dietzel's pioneering work on public debt and fiscal policy see also Glaeser (2003).
19 See Carlson (2003).
20 On the transfer and diffusion of ideas within the field of public economics from Germany to America see the detailed study by Schulz (2013).
21 In contrast to England where due to the Bank Act of 1833 notes issued by the Bank of England were made legal tender, it took until 1909 that in Germany bank notes finally became legal tender.
22 The Taler which circulated in the Prussian-dominated areas was fixed 3:1 toward the Mark, the Gulden at 1,71 Mark.
23 The Preußische Bank was among the 12 out of 32 banks of issue which gave back their concessions immediately.

Bibliography

Aschauer, D. (1989), Is Public Expenditure Productive? *Journal of Monetary Economics*, 23 (2): 177–200.

Bateman, B. (2011), German Influences in the Making of American Economics, 1885–1935, in H.D. Kurz, T. Nishizawa and K. Tribe (eds.), *The Dissemination of Economic Ideas*, Cheltenham: Edward Elgar, pp. 108–124.

Brentano, L. (1931), *Mein Leben im Kampf um die soziale Entwicklung Deutschlands*, Jena: Eugen Diederichs Verlag.

Cardoso, J.L. and Psalidopoulos, M. (2016), *The German Historical School and European Economic Thought*, London and New York: Routledge.

Carlson, B. (2003), Wagner's Swedish Students: Precursors of the Middle Way?" *Journal of the History of Economic Thought*, 25 (4): 437–459.

Dietzel, C. (1855), *Das System der Staatsanleihen im Zusammenhang der Volkswirthschaft betrachtet*, Heidelberg: Akademische Verlagsbuchhandlung Mohr.

Dorfman, J. (1955), The Role of the German Historical School in American Economic Thought, *American Economic Review*, 45 (2): 17–28.

Glaeser, R. (2003), Carl Dietzel (1829–1884): A Pioneering and Unorthodox Thinker on Public Debt and Fiscal Policy, in W.J. Samuels (ed.), *European Economists of the Early 20th Century. Studies of Neglected Continental Thinkers of Germany and Italy*, Cheltenham and Northampton, MA: Edward Elgar, pp. 81–103.

Hagemann, H. (1991), Learned Journals and the Professionalization of Economics: The German Language Area, *Economic Notes*, 20 (1): 33–57.

Hagemann, H. (1996), German Economic Journals and Economic Debates in the Nineteenth Century, *History of Economic Ideas*, 4 (3): 77–101.

Hagemann, H. (2001), The Verein für Sozialpolitik from its Foundation (1872) until World War I, in M.M. Augello and M.E.L. Guidi (eds), *The Spread of Political Economy and the Professionalisation of Economists. Economic Societies in Europe, America and Japan in the Nineteenth Century*, London and New York: Routledge, pp. 152–175.

Hagemann, H. and Rösch, M. (2005), German Economists in Parliament (1848–1918), in M.M. Augello and M.E.L. Guidi (eds), *Economists in Parliament in the Liberal Age (1848–1920)*, Aldershot: Ashgate, pp. 163–189.

Hagemann, H. and Rösch, M. (2012), Economic Textbooks in the German Language Area, in M.M. Augello and M.E.L. Guidi (eds.), *The Economic Reader. Txtbooks, Manuals and the Dissemination of the Economic Sciences during the Nineteenth and Early Twentieth Centuries*, London and New York: Routledge, pp. 97–122.

Helfferich, K. (1903), *Das Geld*, 6th edn, Leipzig: Hirschfeld, 1923; English Translation, *Money*, London: Benn, 1927, and New York: Adelphi, 1927.

Hentschel, V. (1975), *Die deutschen Freihändler und der volkswirtschaftliche Kongress 1858 bis 1885*, Stuttgart: Ernst Klett.

Herkner, H. (1894), *Die Arbeiterfrage: Eine Einführung*, Berlin: J. Guttentag.

Hermann, F.B.W. von (1832), *Staatswirthschaftliche Untersuchungen*, Munich: Anton Weber.

Hufeland, G. (1807–13), *Neue Grundlegung der Staatswirthschaftskunst*, 2 vols, Gießen and Wetzlar: Tasche und Müller.

Jakob, L.H. von (1805), *Grundsätze der National-Oekonomie oder National-Wirthschaftslehre*, Halle: Ruff.

Knapp, G.F. (1905), *Staatliche Theorie des Geldes*, Munich and Leipzig: Duncker & Humblot; 2nd edn, 1918; 3rd edn, 1921; 4th edn, 1923; English Translation, *The State Theory of Money*, London 1924: Macmillan.

Knies, K.G.A. (1853), *Die politische Oekonomie vom Standpunkte der geschichtlichen Methode*, Braunschweig: Schwetschke; 2nd edn, *Die politische Oekonomie vom geschichtlichen Standpuncte*, 1883.

Knies, K.G.A. (1873), *Das Geld*, Berlin: Weidmann; 2nd edn, 1885.

Knies, K.G.A. (1876–1879), *Der Credit*, 2 vols, Berlin: Weidmann.

Lindenlaub, D. (1967), *Richtungskämpfe im Verein für Sozialpolitik. Wissenschaft und Politik im Kaiserreich vornehmlich vom Beginn des 'Neuen Kurses' bis zum Ausbruch des Ersten Weltkriegs (1890–1914)*, 2 vols., Wiesbaden: Franz Steiner Verlag.

List, F. (1841), *Das Nationale System der Politischen Ökonomie*, Stuttgart and Tübingen: Cotta; English Translation by S.S: Lloyd as *The National System of Political Economy*, London 1885: Longmans, Green and Co.

Marshall, A. (1890), *Principles of Economics*. German Translation of the 4th English edition by Hugo Ephraim and Arthur Salz, with a Preface by Lujo Brentano as *Handbuch der Volkswirtschaftslehre*, Stuttgart 1905: Cotta.

Mei Junjie (2019), Friedrich List in China's Quest for Development, in H. Hagemann, S. Seiter and E. Wendler (eds.), *The Economic Thought of Friedrich List*, London and New York 2019: Routledge, pp. 213–222.

Menger, C. (1871), *Grundsätze der Volkswirthschaftslehre*, Wien: Wilhelm Braumüller; 2nd Revised edn by his son Karl, Vienna and Leipzig 1923; English Translation; *Principles of Economics*, with an Introduction by F.A. von Hayek, New York and London 1981: New York University Press.

Musgrave, R.A. (1996–1997), Public Finance and Finanzwissenschaft Traditions Compared, *Finanzarchiv* 53 (2): 145–193.

Musgrave, R.A. (1997), Crossing Traditions, in H. Hagemann (ed.), *Zur deutschsprachigen wirtschaftswissenschaftlichen Emigration nach 1933*, Marburg: Metropolis, pp. 63–79.

Rau, K.H. (1826–37), *Lehrbuch der politischen Oekonomie*, Heidelberg: C.F. Winter, Vol. I, *Grundsätze der Volkswirthschaftslehre*, 1826; 9th edn. 1876; Vol. II, *Grundsätze der Volkswirthschaftspflege*, 1828; 5th edn, 1862; Vol. III, *Grundsätze der Finanzwissenschaft*, 1832–1837; 5th edn, 1864–1865.

Rieter, H. (2002), Historische Schulen, in O. Issing (ed.), *Geschichte der Nationalökonomie*, Munich: Franz Vahlen, pp. 130–168.

Roscher, W. (1843), *Grundriss zu Vorlesungen über die Staatswirthschaft, nach geschichtlicher Methode*, Göttingen: Dieter.

Roscher, W. (1854–1894), *System der Volkswirthschaft*, 5 vols., Stuttgart: Cotta, Vol. I, *Die Grundlagen der Nationalökonomie*, 1854; 26th edn, 1922; English Translation from the 13th edn by J.J. Lalor, *Principles of Political Economy*, 2 vols, Chicago, IL: Callaghan and Company, 1878; Vol. II, *Nationalökonomik des Ackerbaues und der verwandten Urproduktionen*, 1859; 14th edn, Revised by H. Dade, 1912; Vol. III, *Nationalökonomik des Handels und Gewerbefleißes*, 1881; 8th edn, Revised by W. Stieda, 1912–1917; Vol. IV, *System der Finanzwissenschaft*, 1886; 5th edn, Revised by O. Gerlach, 1901; Vol. V, *System der Armenpflege und Armenpolitik*, 1894; 3rd edn, 1906.

Roscher, W. (1861), *Ansichten der Volkswirthschaft aus dem geschichtlichen Standpunkte*, Leipzig and Heidelberg: C.F. Winter'sche Verlagshandlung, 3rd enlarged and corrected edition, 2 vols., 1878.

Rosenberg, H. (1967), *Grosse Depression und Bismarckzeit*, Berlin: De Gruyter.

Sax, E. (1887*), Grundlegung der theoretischen Staatswirtschaft*, Vienna: Hölder.

Schulz, J.P. (2013), *Finanzwissenschaft im deutschsprachigen Raum und in den Vereinigten Staaten, 1865–1917*, Marburg: Metropolis.

Schumpeter, J.A. (1954), *A History of Economic Analysis*, London: George Allen & Unwin.

Seligman, E.R.A. (1911), *The Income Tax. A Study of the History, Theory and Practice of Income Taxation at Home and Abroad*, New York: Macmillan.

Sombart, W. ([1902–1927], 1987), *Der moderne Kapitalismus: Historisch-systematische Darstellung des gesamteuropäischen Wirtschaftslebens von seinen Anfängen bis zur Gegenwart*, 3 vols., Munich: Deutscher Taschenbuch Verlag.

Stein, L. von (1860), *Lehrbuch der Finanzwissenschaft*, 5th Revised edn, 4 vols., Leipzig: Brockhaus, 1885–1886.

Stettner, W.F. (1948), Carl Dietzel, Public Expenditures and the Public Debt, in L.A. Metzler (ed.), *Income, Employment and Public Policy. Essays in Honor of Alvin H. Hansen*, New York: W.W. Norton, pp. 276–299.

Trautwein, H.-M. (2005), Carl Knies' Erörterungen über den Kredit, in C. Scheer (ed.), *Studien zur Entwicklung der ökonomischen Theorie*, Vol. XX, *Die Ältere Historische Schule; Wirtschaftstheoretische Beiträge und wirtschaftspolitische Vorstellungen*, Berlin: Duncker & Humblot, pp. 73–106.

Tribe, K. (1988), *Governing Economy. The Reformation of German Economic Discourse 1750–1840*, Cambridge: Cambridge University Press.

Wagner, A. (1862), *Die Geld-und Credittheorie der Peel'schen Bankacte*, Vienna: Braumüller.

Wagner, A. (1871–182), *Finanzwissenschaft*, 4 vols., Leipzig and Heidelberg: C.F. Winter; First Published as a Revision of Vol. III of Rau's *Prinicples of Political Economics*, Vol. I *Einleitung. Ordnung der Finanzwirthschaft, Finanzbedarf. Privaterwerb*, 3rd edn, 1883; Vol. II, *Gebührenlehre und Allgemeine Steuerlehre*. 1880; Vols. III and IV, *Specielle Steuerlehre*, 1889 and 1899–1901.

Wicksell, K. (1896), *Finanztheoretische Untersuchungen*, Jena: Gustav Fischer.

Wicksell, K. (1898), *Geldzins und Güterpreise*, Jena: Gustav Fischer.

Winkel, H. (1977), *Die Deutsche Nationalökonomie im 19. Jahrhundert*, Darmstadt: Wissenschaftliche Buchgesellschaft.

9 The Old Institutional School and Labour Market Functions and Policies*

Stavros Drakopoulos and Ioannis Katselidis

Introduction

Many historians of economic thought recognize the separate existence of the Old Institutional School (e.g. Rutherford, 1996; Dequech, 2002). A unique theoretical and methodological approach of the school is the main reason for this classification. More specifically, early institutional economists conceived of the economy as a nexus of institutions, highlighting the important role of non-market factors such as proprietary rights, professional and trade associations, traditions, customs, etc. in the economies' functioning. In addition, they expressed the belief that the economic concept of welfare, in addition to the criterion of effectiveness and satisfaction of consumer desires, should include issues concerning e.g. human "self-development", justice, and workers' well-being. Further, the rejection of the model of homo economicus is a key characteristic of their economic methodology (Veblen is the main figure in this respect). Some of the above features may be also regarded as reasons/factors for the differentiation of the school from the subsequent New Institutional Economics (Hodgson, 1989; Rutherford, 1996; Dequech, 2002).[1]

Their conception of the labour market functions is another example of the uniqueness of their approach. In their framework, the nature of labour markets has numerous peculiarities compared to other markets. In contrast to the standard approach, labour market functioning does not depend only on the price mechanism, but is also affected by other key factors and parameters such as social norms, several psychological factors, and various labour institutions. Old Institutional Economics has long attached great significance to the above-mentioned factors, and that was one of the main reasons for its intellectual dominance in the economic analysis of labour markets during the first decades of the twentieth century.

This chapter seeks to examine and highlight the contribution of the old institutional economics towards labour market functions and policies. Its structure is the following: the "Origins and Method of the Old Institutional School of Economics" section succinctly presents the origins, the sources of influence, and the methodological characteristics of the School, while the "Labour Market: Old Institutionalism vs. Early Neoclassical Economics"

DOI: 10.4324/9781003228097-9

section briefly compares Old Institutionalism and early Neoclassical Economics focusing on labour market issues. The next section presents the main theses and approaches of institutional labour economics. After this discussion, the "Collective Action and Labour Policy" section looks at the old institutional approach with respect to collective action and labour market policy. Through the Ross-Dunlop debate on labour unions, the "Old Institutionalists' Legacy: The Ross-Dunlop Debate on Labor Unions" section provides an example of the impact and the gradual decline of Old Institutionalism's influence. The "Old Institutional Economics and Current Labour Issues: The Case of Minimum Wages" section briefly discusses the case of minimum wage policy in order to highlight the relevance of early institutional ideas in analysing contemporary labour market issues. Finally, the concluding remarks bring together some key arguments of the chapter.

Origins and Method of the Old Institutional School of Economics

It is generally accepted that the institutional school of economics emerged in the United States by the end of the nineteenth century and flourished in the first decades of the twentieth century. The three major figures of early institutional economics were Thorstein Veblen (1857–1929), Wesley Clair Mitchell (1874–1948), and John Rogers Commons (1862–1945). The first explicit (at least prominent) reference to the term "institutional economics" seems to have appeared in an article written by Walton Hamilton in 1919, entitled "The Institutional Approach to Economic Theory", which was published in the American Economic Review. The old institutional school of economics reached its peak in the 1920s, while in the 1930s gradually began to decline, and until the end of World War II had lost much of its previous influence on economic thought (Kaufman, 2000; Rutherford, 2003; Hermann, 2018; Mayhew, 2018).

The philosophical background (Weltanschauung) of old institutional economics was shaped by both European (e.g. Hegel, Darwin, and Spencer) and American (e.g. Peirce, James, and Dewey) intellectual influences. In contrast to the mechanistic and static perception of classical and neoclassical economic tradition, institutional economists regarded the economic system as a dynamic and evolutionary process (Papageorgiou et al., 2013). Within such a system, the individual is considered a social being whose behaviour is affected by the force of habit and formed by the individual's interaction with the other members of the community. The institutional methodological approach has been characterized as holistic since institutional economists were interested in the functioning of the economy as a whole, as opposed to the methodological individualism of the neoclassical paradigm (Biddle and Samuels, 1998).

Institutionalists argued that the understanding of the institutional structure of an economy is also a basic prerequisite for finding solutions to problems of economic and labour policy. Nevertheless, institutions, should not be regarded as given, since they are human constructs and are subject to perpetual change (Witte, 1954). Furthermore, the (direct) observation of the real world – and not the construction of (abstract) models – was one of the main components of institutional economics, whose members did not regard economics as an exercise of logic, but as an endeavour to explain the behaviour of the real economies.

One of the fundamental institutionalist theses was that an economy should not be conceived only in terms of the market mechanism, but should also include all those institutions that operate through the market and interact with it (Samuels, 1987). In this context, the institutional structure and arrangements of the economy – and not the market mechanism – were the crucial factors for good economic performance and the effective allocation of productive resources; the market is nothing more than a mere, though very important, institution. Furthermore, institutions, as human constructs, are subject to continuous modification. In institutionalists' view, institutions play a significant role not only in the shaping of human behaviour, but also in the evolution of capitalism. However, this role is in fact quite intricate given that institutions are part of the contradictory powers that form instincts, conducts, and habits of thought (see e.g. Veblen, 1909).

The old Institutional school of economics composed many studies concerning the conditions of work and employment, playing also a substantial role in the formation of the US labour legislation during the first decades of the twentieth century (Katselidis, 2011). Furthermore, these reform-minded academic economists founded in 1906 the American Association for Labour Legislation (AALL), "launching a national movement for compulsory social insurance and protective labour legislation" (Moss, 1996, p. 2). Thus, they had a significant impact on the formation of the US welfare state and highly affected the making of the New Deal policy of President Roosevelt in the 1930s. Finally, institutionalists, by adopting an interdisciplinary approach in their works, extended as well their contributions to non-economic fields such as sociology, psychology, and labour history (Hermann, 2018).

Labour institutionalism had several intellectual roots, such as the "German Historical School" of economics, the progressive reform movement in America, and some dissenting British economists, including Sidney and Beatrice Webb and William Beveridge (Kaufman, 2004). In addition, some late nineteenth-century American economists, such as Richard Ely and Henry Carter Adams, who both had studied in Germany and were influenced by the historical school of economics, were the main origins of the Institutionalists' emphasis on legal institutions (Rutherford, 2003). Finally, both the interest of institutional economists in social reform and their belief that the state can significantly contribute to this end had also their roots in "historical economics" (Tribe, 2003).

All the above-mentioned sources of influence led many

> institutional economists to adopt an empiricist approach to theorizing, namely they first collect the data and the observations, involving themselves

> in the facts (Richard Ely's 'look and see' method), and then adduce from the facts and other grounded empirical work the major premises for theorizing, so as to draw conclusions about reality. This approach was opposed to the deductive, a priori method of mainstream economics.
>
> (Katselidis, 2011, pp. 988–989; see also Chasse, 2017)

However, it should be explicitly noted that the aforementioned empiricist approach mainly characterizes the Commons' and Mitchell's institutionalist tradition and not the Veblenian approach. Veblen's main contribution to labour issues, as we will see in the next section, is related to his rejection of the (neoclassical) pleasure-pain approach to labour theorizing. Though this rejection might be relied upon observation, it was not based on the kind of "go and see" approach that Commons and his fellows used.[2]

Labour Market: Old Institutionalism vs. Early Neoclassical Economics

From the beginnings of economic science, both the concept of the market and that of labour had a central role in economic thought. However, labour market analysis and the examination of industrial problems had been limited for a very long time. Accordingly, the early economic literature on labour institutions and their objectives was rather short and incomplete. In particular, "classical economic thought advocated free labour markets and considered the relationship between labour and capital to be non-competitive" (Drakopoulos and Katselidis, 2014, p. 1135). In addition, classical economists were more interested in long-term economic processes under the assumption of perfectly competitive markets, and less in the actual conditions of the (imperfect) job market. On the other hand, marginalists and early neoclassical analysts, such as Stanley Jevons and Francis Edgeworth, asserted that the existence of labour institutions, like trade unions, renders the labour market problem mathematically indeterminate (Edgeworth, 1881; Jevons, 1882). Therefore, practical issues concerning labour did not pertain to economic science (e.g. Jevons, 1882, pp. 154–155; see also Kaufman, 2004).

Consequently, early neoclassical economics under the hypothesis of perfectly competitive markets, could not shed light on fundamental labour market issues, including the role of collective bargaining, the interplay between labour unions and employers' associations, or labour legislation matters. Thus, the goal of the institutional economists was twofold:

> On the one hand, they attempted to make labour problems more widely known, emphasizing the crucial role of labour issues both in the economy and the society. On the other hand, they tried to 'prove' that the neoclassical analysis could not contribute to any solution of this kind of problems; therefore, a different scientific approach was needed.
>
> (Katselidis, 2011, p. 988)

Early neoclassical theorists conceived labour as a pure commodity or a factor of production. Hence, the payment of labour in the neoclassical system is determined by the marginal productivity theory, according to which wages are equal to the value of marginal product of labour, under the hypothesis of perfect competition both between workers and between employers (see e.g. Clark, 1899, pp. 166 and 179). Moreover, the marginal productivity condition determines also the level of the demand for labour. Nevertheless, the final magnitude of wages and employment is also influenced by the supply of labour (Marshall, [1920/1890] 1949). The neoclassical supply of labour relied upon the utilitarian hedonic principle, according to which, labour provides negative utility to the worker (for a neoclassical definition of labour, see Jevons, [1879/1871] 1965, pp. 168–169).

The neoclassical conception of labour was in full contrast to the institutional viewpoint; for instance, the institutional-Veblenian notion of the "instinct of workmanship" was diametrically opposed to the hedonistic interpretation of human behaviour and the aversion to work (Veblen, 1898, 1914). In addition, the neoclassical hypothesis of the negative utility of labour is incompatible with human biological evolution, since if humans were systematically avoided useful labour, then the human species would not have survived (Hodgson, 2004).

Furthermore, during at least the first third of the twentieth century, Arthur Pigou may be regarded as the most prominent early neoclassical author on labour market analysis. Specifically, Pigou was one of the first neoclassical economists who found a strong positive correlation between the real wage rate and unemployment level, attributing more and more importance to wage rigidities as the main cause of the unemployment problem. Additionally, in contrast to the institutional economists, he considered particular institutional factors like the trade unions' power or the minimum wages to be mainly responsible for labour market malfunctioning (Pigou, 1913, 1927; see below the "Old Institutional Economics and Current Labour Issues: The Case of Minimum Wages" section).

On the other hand, the majority of the institutional economists underlined the importance of social and institutional parameters in determining the level of wages and strongly expressed their reservations as regards the connection of the principle of marginal productivity with the real firms' conduct (see e.g. Lescohier, 1935). Moreover, institutionalists argued that the nature of labour supply is totally different from the supply of other input factors or commodities. For instance, Wisconsin institutionalism emphasized the significant role of human will in economic life and tried to construct a human theory of labour as an alternative to a mechanical/physics-type theory of mainstream/neoclassical economics (Lescohier, 1919a; Commons, 1950, 1964/1913).

In spite of the aforementioned differences – both in theory and in methods – between early neoclassical and institutional economists, it is worth noting that there were also some convergent points of view. For instance, Arthur Pigou, in his work *Unemployment* (1913), endorsed some policies and labour market institutions proposed by institutional economists, such as insurance against unemployment or a net of labour exchanges (Katselidis, 2011). Moreover, it is also noteworthy that Alfred Marshall did not piously adopt the abstract – deductive approach with respect to labour issues. Although Marshall's labour market approach was not differentiated from the competitive market reasoning, he developed some arguments which seem to bear a close resemblance to the institutional analysis. For instance, Marshall's view that "there is no such thing in modern civilization as a general rate of wages" may have a strong institutional bend (see Marshall, [1920/1890] 1949, p. 442).

Labour Market: The Institutional Approach

As already noted, the first systematic and special studies on the labour markets and their problems emerged in the last decades of the nineteenth century and the first decades of the twentieth century. During that period, the large Western economies were gradually driven to full industrialization and production concentrated in big factories where, in many cases, mainly in the United States, a scientific organization of the work process (Taylorism) was adopted. At the same time, labour was taking the form of "regular employment", and a large part of the workforce consisted of salaried employees (Wisman and Pacitti, 2004). Then, the trade union movement in Europe and America was significantly strengthened, and the first powerful factory unions, which enumerated a thousand members, were created. Within this historical context, the first generation of institutional economists provided their analyses on numerous labour issues.

The labour market, as an imperfect human-made institution, may break down due to various reasons, causing thus a host of problems. Institutional labour economists tried to resolve these "labour questions" primarily through three means/methods: a) unions, b) labour law and c) (personnel) management. Firstly, mainly during the period from 1885–1886 to 1905–1906, there were a considerable number of labour studies and books focusing on the problems of organized-unionized labour. Accordingly, that trend in the labour studies placed emphasis on the various evils connected to the use of labour in an industrial system, on trade unionism and collective bargaining (McNulty, 1980). For example, a popular work in American literature related to a great degree to the study of organized labour was the Thomas S. Adams and Helen L. Sumner's textbook *Labour Problems* (1905). However, it is here noteworthy that the analysis of all these works published during the first phase of labour institutionalism is concerned more with the impact of labour problems on individuals than on the economy.

In the first decade of the twentieth century, there was a shift as regards the ways to address the various labour issues, instigating thus the second "phase" in the study of labour problems and solutions. In particular, labour specialists and policy makers attributed more and more importance to labour law and specifically to social insurance and protective labour legislation

(Kaufman, 2003). "That shift played also a role to the gradual emphasis given to the labour market as an institution and how the employment relationship is embedded and operates within a web of institutions" (Katselidis, 2011, p. 993). In addition, as has been mentioned, the "American Association for the Labour Legislation" was founded in 1906, encouraging this kind of research, and Commons and Andrews's book entitled *Principles of Labour Legislation* (1916) was regarded as the leading work in this area down to about the mid-1930s. Labour institutionalists, by underlying the peculiar nature of the labour contract, conceived of labour and the "free access to a labour market" as an intangible property right: "It is intangible because it is merely the act of offering and yet withholding services or commodities. It is property and becomes labour in the sense that it is the power of getting value in exchange" (Commons and Andrews, 1916, p. 8). For that reason, the government should intervene both in the economy and the labour market in order to protect the aforementioned property right.

Around WWI, the field of industrial relations/personnel management emerged, commencing a third "phase" of labour institutionalism. In general, early labour institutionalists, such as John Commons, Don Lescohier, William Leiserson, and Sumner Slichter, made a substantial contribution towards the examination, development, and promotion of this new approach to labour management, stressing its positive impact both on employee relations as well as on firms' profits. For instance, Commons' book *Industrial Goodwill* (1919), strongly criticized the old personnel methods such as the so-called "drive" methods of management and the scientific management, known as Taylorism. On the other hand, he highlighted the positive consequences of more participative and collaborative practices like his "goodwill" approach (see Commons, 1919, p. 19).

It is worth pointing out here that all the above-mentioned research approaches and programmes were influenced both by the scientific progress in the labour studies field and by the real-life phenomena such as the disorganized nature of the American labour market or the pervasive dissatisfaction displayed by workers.

> Thus, the serious economic and political pressures generated by the WWI, in conjunction with the development of the institutional program of labour studies, help explain why institutional economists gave emphasis to certain subjects such as labour turnover, labour management or the organization of the labour market through an extensive system of labour Exchanges.
>
> (Katselidis, 2011, p. 993)

In general, labour institutionalists strongly criticized both the unreal character of the various neoclassical assumptions and the overreliance on abstract mathematical analysis. Institutionalists' work was focused on the "rejection of the three then-prevalent orthodox doctrines: the commodity conception of labour, a laissez-faire approach to market/employment regulation, and the monarchial or 'employer autocracy' model of work force governance" (Kaufman, 2003, p. 4).

Collective Action and Labour Policy

A fundamental theme of American institutionalism was that the employee-employer relationship, as embedded in the employment contracts, is not regarded only as a kind of market transaction, but is also formed through the interaction of legal, economic, social, and political factors. For that reason, institutional economists contended that the study of labour issues requires the adoption of a multidisciplinary approach (Kaufman, 2006). In addition, they recognized that labour, even conceived as a commodity, displays at least two important peculiarities: (a) in a free labour market, the "labour commodity" is sold for a specified time period, preserving thus the worker's personal freedom, and (b) it is a commodity that cannot be separated from its owner. Therefore, institutionalists argued that the labourer is not just an input in the production process or a tool of production. On the contrary, most emphasized the human and social aspects of work, regarding the worker as a citizen and a social being who has family, personal life, etc. (see e.g. Commons and Andrews, 1916; Lescohier, 1919b). They also considered that the monolithic perception of labour as a market commodity and a supplement to the other factors of production impedes the implementation of these policies which promote labourers' welfare, a better education system, health protection, improvement of living conditions of the working class, etc. (Commons, 1964/1913; Commons and Andrews, 1916).

Furthermore, institutional economists, by stressing the importance of collective action, rejected the neoclassical conception of society as a simple sum of individuals (Commons, 1934). Therefore, an additional essential characteristic that differentiates labour from the other factors of production is the collective behaviour of individuals that induces them to form groups and unions based on common interests and goals (Wolman, 1924; Perlman, 1928). Besides the economic purpose of unions, that is the improvement of working conditions and labourers' living standards or the redistribution of wealth, John R. Commons and other early institutional economists also attached great significance to "the more general function of unionism – responsibility for representative democracy in industry" (Perlman, 1960, p. 341; see also Kaufman, 2000). Furthermore, the first generation of institutional economists – Robert Hoxie, Selig Perlman, and George Barnett – did not try to formalize their ideas on trade unions, but instead adopted a more sociological-historical approach which clearly demonstrates the interdisciplinary character of their studies. This viewpoint was also part of their holistic methodological approach emphasizing the social nature of man, collective decision-making, and particular institutional histories (for a discussion, see Rutherford, 1989, 2009). In general, they conceived of unions as politico-economic organizations whose members were motivated by relative comparisons and were concerned with issues of equity and justice (Drakopoulos, 2011, p. 8). They also sought to place unions into different categories according to their structure, specific purpose, or social function (e.g. Hoxie, 1914). Finally, they described in detail the various duties and responsibilities of unions and explained the factors that influenced the development of unionism.

Institutional labour economists were at that time in front of a host of labour issues and questions that require investigation and resolution: first, workers were exposed to many risks, facing a variety of problems such as low wages, poor and unhealthy working conditions, frequent labour accidents, gruelling working hours, unemployment, etc. Therefore, the creation of those institutions, for example minimum wages and accident prevention statutes, that would protect employees and restrict their suffering was indispensable (Commons and Andrews, 1916). Second, cyclical as well as seasonal fluctuations were permanent in the United States economy, making both product and labour markets highly volatile. Thus, the stabilization of these markets and the reduction of casual and unstable employment were also two crucial issues (Lescohier, 1919a). Third, the relationship between workers and employers was to some degree confrontational; institutionalists were in favour of the alleviation of this struggle through institutional measures and labour laws. In a similar vein, they also supported the equality of bargaining power of employers and workers (Commons, 1919). Finally, a fourth important issue, with adverse effects on both employees and employers, was related to the workers' behaviour and attitude. Specifically, workers were often indifferent to their work and their duties; for that reason, institutionalists proposed ways of improving work climate and employee involvement in the operation and management of the companies (Slichter, 1926).

The main pillars of the institutional school's agenda with respect to labour market policy and the creation of appropriate institutions were the following: first of all, the American institutional economists strongly supported the systematic organization of the labour market through the institution of manpower employment agencies that would contribute, inter alia, to the increase of market efficiency (Leiserson, 1914, 1917; Lescohier, 1919a). Second, they suggested strengthening regular and stable employment and reducing the very high rate of labour turnover, i.e. the workers' movement rate from one job to another, which was considered to be one of the most serious evils of industrial life. Besides their attempt to find the causes and remedies of the problem, institutionalists tried to statistically analyse it so as to determine, if possible, the optimal-normal turnover rate (Slichter, 1919; Brissenden and Frankel, 1922). Third, influenced by the so-called industrial education/vocational guidance movement developed in the United States in the period under consideration, they underlined the importance of the systematic policy of vocational education and training with a view to further developing employee skills (Lescohier, 1919a). Fourth, institutional economists were the founders of personnel management and industrial relations, developing progressive ideas about how to manage employees in enterprises (Commons, 1919; Leiserson, 1959). Moreover, a fifth pillar of the early institutional labour market policy agenda is related to the institutionalists' aim to improve working conditions with an emphasis on healthy workplaces (Lescohier, 1919a). Sixth, they proposed a counter-cyclical macroeconomic policy aimed at smoothing both cyclical economic fluctuations and the destructive, as proved, rapid rises and falls in the size of the production activity and employment (Commons, 1934; for a discussion see Kaufman, 2006). Finally, institutionalists were pioneers in the issue of social security, proposing, for example, insurance against unemployment and medical insurance (Witte, 1935; Altmeyer, 1937, 1950).

Old Institutionalists' Legacy: The Ross-Dunlop Debate on Labour Unions

During the 1940s, there was a controversy among labour economists concerning the underlying incentives of the behaviour of unions. This controversy is an indicative example of the Institutionalists' legacy but also of the gradual decline of their impact. The leading figures of this debate were Arthur Ross and John Dunlop. The former was closer to the institutional-political approach, while the latter adopted a more neoclassical point of view. The "Ross-Dunlop debate" (see, for instance, Kaufman and Martinez-Vazquez, 1987) reflected the rising current of the expansion of the method of mainstream economics to the study of unions (Mitchell, 1972).

Dunlop discarded the idea that wage determination under collective bargaining is a political process. Thus, he asserted that the institutional methodological approach to the study of labour unions should be rejected. More specifically, Dunlop (1944), by conceiving unions as analogous to business firms, developed a formal analytical model of trade union behaviour based on the microeconomic theory of the firm. He held that a union is a "decision-making unit" which attempts to maximize some objective, considering "wage bill for the total membership" to be the most appropriate union's goal, subject to various constraints such as the firm's labour demand curve (Dunlop, 1944, pp. 4–5, 44; see also Kaufman, 2002). However, besides wage-bill maximization, Dunlop also referred to other union objectives, such as the guarantee of the largest possible union employment or the maximization of the "collective wage 'rents' of those employed" (Dunlop, 1944, p. 41). Moreover, he maintained that wages and employment levels are also influenced by the different positions of the membership function (Kaufman, 2002).

On the other hand, mainly through his works *The Trade Union as a Wage-Fixing Institution* (1947) and *Trade Union Wage Policy* (1948), Ross strongly criticized Dunlop's "economic" union model, placing emphasis on the nature of the union as a political agency (see e.g. Ross, 1947, p. 587). In particular, Ross rebutted Dunlop's contention that wages are determined by impersonal market forces since the "union is not a seller of labour and is not mechanically concerned with the quantity sold" (Ross, 1948, p. 4). Furthermore, Ross conceived of trade unions as a "collectivity," which implies that the influence of group behaviour is stronger than individual behaviour. Thus, in order to understand unions' behaviour, one should not limit the analysis to a narrow economic context by using a mechanical application of the maximization principle but should place it in a broader framework, taking into consideration psychological, sociological, and (mainly) political aspects. Moreover, he contended that union, as a political entity, not only strengthens democracy but also plays a significant role in issues like social justice and equity. By contrast, Dunlop's microeconomic framework could not deal with such themes, thus expelling from trade union analysis some important non-economic parameters that have a strong influence on unions' behaviour.

It should also be noted, however, that Ross recognized that trade unions and business firms do have some particular aspects in common. Nevertheless, not only did he reject the existence of the close analogy between the firm and the union (a necessary assumption in order to implicate the mathematical framework of microeconomics), but he also turned against Dunlop's thesis of a well-defined microeconomic-based union objective function. First of all, although both institutions have a formal purpose or rationale, he asserted that unions aim to maximize a non-measurable variable, viz. the economic welfare (wages, hours, and conditions of work, etc.) of their members, in contrast to firms' goal of maximizing their stockholders' profits. In addition, trade unions' feature of the heterogeneity of their members implies that individual union members often have conflicting preferences and interests due to differences in age, seniority, wages, and other related factors. These features render the aggregation of the individual preferences of union members an extremely difficult task. Significant differences also exist between union leaders and the rank and file as long as the former behave according to their personal ambitions, having in mind also as the main purpose of the survival and growth of the organization. Hence, the trade union wage policy is not actually formed through the rank and file decisions, but it is a function of leadership (for the above points, see Ross, 1947, pp. 569–573, 582, and 584).

Despite the fact that the approaches of Dunlop and Ross emphasized different aspects of union behaviour, there were also some converging points of view. First, both writers advocated, though to a different degree, an "interdisciplinary 'industrial relations' approach to studying unions" (Kaufman, 2002, p. 118). Even Dunlop, who was engaged in theory-building and strongly criticizes institutional and historical methodological approaches, rebutted the neoclassical contention that economic theory can explain all aspects of human behaviour related to markets. It is very interesting to note that Dunlop's concerns about the methodological "imperialism" of economics were preceding the literature on the issue which grew in the 1960s, stimulated mainly by Gary Becker's works (see Fine, 2000; Rothschild, 2008).

In the following decades, however, Dunlop's reservations concerning the complete abandonment of the political aspects of union behaviour and the excessive reliance on the equilibrium techniques were downplayed. The differences between Dunlop and Ross's perspectives became more and more profound, thus establishing the dichotomy between analytical labour economics and institutional labour economics, as these two approaches are often called (see also Rees, 1976). In spite of this, however, Ross's impact on the analysis of unions is still discernible: the conception of unions in terms of power and collective entity can also be found in parts of modern standard labour economics. For example, current managerial or political models of trade unions acknowledge their debt to Ross's arguments (e.g. Pemberton, 1988; see also Mitchell, 1972; Kaufman, 2002)

Old Institutional Economics and Current Labour Issues: The Case of Minimum Wages

For neoclassical/mainstream economics, in general, the enforcement of a minimum wage is considered to be foreign to the laws of political economy, diminishes the size of employment – especially the employment of low-wage workers – and discourages capital and firms to expand. For instance, A. C. Pigou, though accepted a broad Minimum Conditions programme with respect to several aspects of life (*e.g.* education, consumption, medical care, and housing), argued that a minimum wage was a deficient measure due to its possible negative impact on employment level and its failure to take into account individual variations (Pigou, 1913; see also Katselidis, 2016).

Nowadays, although there is no consensus among economists on the effect of minimum wages on the unemployment level, it is argued that the imposition of minimum wages mainly has an adverse impact on the employment of young people and low-skilled workers (see e.g. Nickell and Layard, 1999; Neumark and Wascher, 2008; Ehrenberg and Smith, 2017). The opponents of minimum wages hold that though those workers who remain in the labour market have higher wages, this is in fact at the expense of both lower firms' profits and lower employment. However, this analysis assumes that firms operate in competitive markets with little or no economic rent that can be extracted in the form of higher wages. But what happens if the labour market does not function in a competitive framework? After the publication of Card and Krueger's influential book *Myth and Measurement* (1995), there have been many mainstream economists who assert that imposing a minimum wage may have a positive effect on employment (increase in employment) (only) when the business firm has some form of monopsony power in the labour market due to e.g. labour immobility (Card and Krueger, 1995). In this case, a monopsonistic firm pays a wage significantly lower than both the competitive one and the marginal product of labour, employing also fewer workers than it would if it were in a competitive labour market. The introduction here of a minimum wage will be expected to increase employment up to the point where the minimum wage level is equal to the competitive equilibrium wage (Polachek and Siebert, 1993). Even then, nevertheless, neoclassical practitioners are likely to contend that monopsony conditions do not characterize the real markets where minimum wages apply.

On the other hand, for institutionalists, as already noted, this is the wrong way to conceive of markets. Therefore, as Kaufman (2010) points out, institutional theory tells a more convincing story and presents a more positive case for minimum wages, broadening also the relevant theory and policy debate. Specifically, from the early institutional economics' viewpoint, the implementation of a statutory minimum wage may affect positively both workers and employers, promoting also long-term economic efficiency and productivity. For instance, "high road" employers, who face an increased production cost due to the existence of a minimum wage, will be forced to improve their production methods, investing in new technologies, R&D, and human capital (Kaufman, 2010). In addition, the enforcement of a minimum wage higher than the competitive one will lead to a revision of firms' hiring policy; firms will mainly turn to hiring permanent and capable employees, reducing thus the number of low-quality casual workers. This may also have a positive impact on workers, provided that they will try to improve their technical dexterities and qualitative characteristics with a view to becoming more competitive (Commons, 1921). Consequently, in the long run, the most effective and advanced enterprises survive in the markets, since they gradually displace those firms which follow old and obsolete management and production methods.

Early institutional economists also held that minimum wages legislation is one of the instruments against the exacerbation of labour standards caused by adverse economic circumstances like unemployment, which gives employers the power to exploit the labourers' need to work, leading also to more elastic employment conditions (lower wages, worse working conditions, illegal labour with close to zero salaries, etc.). Additionally, workers have no power to react since they are easily replaceable and have a strong need to work at any labour price. In other words, this power structure violates any equality in the negotiations between employers and workers, giving the comparative advantage to the stronger part. Therefore, the minimum wage measure can also contribute towards the reduction of inequality of bargaining power (Commons and Andrews, 1916). Finally, early institutionalists, in a "proto-Keynesians" vein, connected minimum wages to macroeconomic stability and aggregate demand's boost (Kaufman, 2010).

Concluding Remarks

The early institutional economists helped shape labour market policy in the United States during the first decades of the twentieth century, aiming both at the improvement of working conditions and at the rise in the labourers' standard of living. The observed labour market inequalities and malfunctions rendered imperative the creation of mechanisms for the redistribution and readjustment of power between employees and employers. The majority of the old institutional economists attached great significance and attention to real-life economic phenomena and empirical facts, stressing that not only should an economic theory of labour markets be relied on realistic assumptions, but it should also be tested empirically.

Institutional economists, in contrast to neoclassical economists, regarded economy as a nexus of institutions, underlying, therefore, the important role of institutional and non-market factors (e.g. property rights, professional and trade associations, tradition, social norms, and customs) in the functioning of an economic system. They also criticized those who define (economic) welfare only in terms of efficiency and satisfaction of consumer wants; institutionalists instead focus on issues related to justice, human self-development, and labourers' welfare.

The classical and early neoclassical economists did not pay much attention to the economic analysis of labour market institutions since they contend that such an issue was outside the standard domain of economic analysis (e.g. Jevons, 1882), and that the institutional presence hampers the application of formalism to economics (e.g. Edgeworth, 1881). By contrast, early institutionalists had paid considerable attention to the examination of the institutional framework of the labour market. In particular, the first generation of institutional economists highlighted the importance of institutions and other non-market factors in determining the level of wages and employment (e.g. the role of the bargaining power of workers and employers). Furthermore, they made substantial contributions towards the field of labour policy and they were pioneers in the formulation of economic and social policy. Specifically, after the recommendation of the institutional labour economists, various modern institutions and labour market policies, such as unemployment benefits, industrial training, and active employment policies, were implemented in the United States during the period under consideration. Hence, judging by the number of their published papers in leading scientific economic journals and by their participation in various committees and councils, it seems that institutionalists were very influential both in the scientific circles and in the government officials. Therefore, their ideas, besides being interesting from a historical point of view, may also be useful in today's analysis of workers' problems and the functioning of modern labour markets.

Notes

* This chapter is based on Katselidis (2019). Parts of the "Labour Market: Old Institutionalism vs. Early Neoclassical Economics" and "Labour Market: The Institutional Approach" sections have also drawn from Katselidis (2011). A preliminary version of this work was presented at the 3rd International Conference in Economic and Social History, 24–27 May 2017, organized by the Greek Economic History Association and the Faculty of History and Archaeology, University of Ioannina, Ioannina, Greece. The authors thank Michel Zouboulakis and Michael Chletsos for their useful comments. Many thanks also to Anne Mayhew, Arturo Hermann, Sebastian Thieme for their constructive comments on earlier versions of the chapter. The usual disclaimer applies.

1 For a recent discussion about the similarities and dissimilarities between Original and New Institutional Economics, see Spithoven (2019).
2 Many thanks to Anne Mayhew for this argument.

Bibliography

Adams, T. S. and Sumner H. L. (1905). *Labour Problems: A Textbook*. New York: Macmillan.
Altmeyer, A. J. (1937). The Scope of Departmental Personnel Activities. *Annals of the American Academy of Political and Social Science*. 189, Improved Personnel in Government Service, January, 188–191.
Altmeyer, A. J. (1950). Government and Individual Security. *Proceedings of the Academy of Political Science*. 24, 1, Freedom and the Expanding State, May, 93–99.
Biddle, J. E., and Samuels, W. J. (1998). John R. Commons and the Compatibility of Neoclassical and Institutional Economics. In R. P. F. Holt and S. Pressman (Eds.). *Economics and Its Discontents: Twentieth Century Dissenting Economists*. Aldershot and Lyme, NH: Edward Elgar, 40–55.
Brissenden, P. and Frankel, E. (1922). *Labour Turnover in Industry: A Statistical Analysis*. New York: Macmillan.
Card, D. and Krueger, A. (1995). *Myth and Measurement: The New Economics of the Minimum Wage*. Princeton, NJ: Princeton University Press.
Chasse, J. D. (2017). *A Worker's Economist: John R. Commons and His Legacy from Progressivism to the War on Poverty*. London and New York: Routledge.
Clark, J. B. (1899). *The Distribution of Wealth: A Theory of Wages, Interests and Profits*. New York: Macmillan.
Commons, J. R. (1964/1913). *Labor and Administration*. New York: Augustus M. Kelley.
Commons, J. R. (1919). *Industrial Goodwill*. New York: McGraw-Hill.
Commons, J. R. (1921). *Industrial Government*. New York: Macmillan.
Commons, J. R. (1934). *Institutional Economics: Its Place in Political Economy*. New York: Macmillan.
Commons, J. R. (1950). *The Economics of Collective Action*. New York: Macmillan.
Commons, J. R. and Andrews J. B. (1916). *Principles of Labour Legislation*. New York and London: Harper & Brothers.
Commons, J. R., Saposs, D. J., Sumner, H. L., Mittleman, E. B., Hoagland, H. E., Andrews, J. B. and Perlman, S. (1918). *History of Labor in the United States*. 2 Volumes, New York: Macmillan.
Dequech, D. (2002). The Demarcation between the "Old" and the "New" Institutional Economics: Recent Complications. *Journal of Economic Issues*. 36, 2, 565–572.
Drakopoulos, S. (2011). The Neglect of Comparison Income: An Historical Perspective. *European Journal of the History of Economic Thought*. 18, 3, 441–464.
Drakopoulos, S. and Katselidis I. (2014). The Development of Trade Union Theory and Mainstream Economic Methodology. *Journal of Economic Issues*. 48, 4, December, 1133–1149. DOI 10.2753/JEI0021-3624480413
Dunlop, J. (1944). *Wage Determination under Trade Unions*. New York: Macmillan.
Edgeworth, F. Y. (1881). *Mathematical Psychics*. London: E. Kegan Paul.
Ehrenberg, R. G. and Smith, R. S. (2017). *Modern Labor Economics: Theory and Public Policy*. New York: Routledge.
Fine, B. (2000). Economics Imperialism and Intellectual Progress: The Present as History of Economic Thought? *History of Economics Review*. 32, 10–36.

Hamilton, W. H. (1919). The Institutional Approach to Economic Theory. *American Economic Review.* 9, 1, Supplement, Papers and Proceedings of the Thirty-First Annual Meeting of the American Economic Association, March, 309–318.

Hermann, A. (2018). The Decline of the "Original Institutional Economics" in the Post-World War II Period and the Perspectives of Today. *Economic Thought.* 7, 1, 63–86.

Hodgson, G. M. (1989). Institutional Economic Theory: The Old Versus the New. *Review of Political Economy.* 1, 3, 249–269.

Hodgson, G. M. (2004). *The Evolution of Institutional Economics: Agency, Structure, and Darwinism in American Institutionalism.* London: Routledge.

Hoxie, R. F. (1914). Trade Unionism in the United States: The Essence of Unionism and the Interpretation of Union Types. *Journal of Political Economy.* 22, 5, 464–481.

Jevons, S. W. (1879/1871). *The Theory of Political Economy.* New York: Augustus M. Kelley (1965).

Jevons, S. W. (1882). *The State in Relation to Labour.* London: Macmillan.

Katselidis, I. A. (2011). Don Lescohier on Labour Market Policy: The Case of the United States after the First World War. *Journal of Economic Issues.* 45, 4, 985–1009. DOI 10.2753/JEI0021-3624450412

Katselidis, I. A. (2016). Unemployment and Labour Market Policy in British Economic Thought during the Late Victorian and Edwardian Era (1885–1914). *History of Economic Ideas.* 24, 1, 57–82.

Katselidis, I. A. (2019). Institutions, Policy and the Labour Market: The Contribution of the Old Institutional Economics, *Economic Thought.* 8, 2, 13–30.

Kaufman, B. E. (2000). The Early Institutionalists on Industrial Democracy and Union Democracy. *Journal of Labour Research.* 21, 2, 189–209.

Kaufman, B. E. (2002). Models of Union Wage Determination: What Have We Learned Since Dunlop and Ross? *Industrial Relations.* 41, 1, 110–158.

Kaufman, B. E. (2003). John R. Commons and the Wisconsin School on Industrial Relations Strategy and Policy. *Industrial and Labour Relations Review.* 57, 1, 3–30.

Kaufman, B. E. (2004). The Institutional and Neoclassical Schools in Labour Economics. In D. P. Champlin and J. T. Knoedler. (Eds.). *The Institutionalist Tradition in Labour Economics.* Armonk, NY: M. E. Sharpe, 13–38.

Kaufman, B. E. (2006). Industrial Relations and Labour Institutionalism: A Century of Boom and Bust. *Labour History.* 47, 3, 295–318.

Kaufman, B. E. (2010). Institutional Economics and the Minimum Wage: Broadening the Theoretical and Policy Debate. *Industrial and Labor Relations Review.* 63, 3, 427–453.

Kaufman, B. E. and Martinez-Vazquez (1987). The Ross-Dunlop Debate and Union Wage Concessions: A Median Voter Analysis. *Journal of Labor Research.* 8, 3, Summer, 291–305.

Leiserson, W. M. (1914). The Theory of Public Employment Offices and the Principles of their Practical Administration. *Political Science Quarterly.* 29, 1, 28–46.

Leiserson, W. M. (1917). A Federal Labour Reserve Board for the Unemployed. Outlines of a Plan for Administering the Remedies for Unemployment. *Annals of the American Academy of Political and Social Science.* 69, The Present Labour Situation. Compulsory Investigation and Arbitration, January, 103–117.

Leiserson, W. M. (1959). *American Trade Union Democracy.* New York: Columbia University Press.

Lescohier, D. D. (1919a). *The Labour Market*. New York: Macmillan.

Lescohier, D. D. (1919b). Immigration and the Labour-Supply. *The Atlantic Monthly*. 123, 4, 483–490.

Lescohier, D. D. (1935). The Theory of Wages. *Political Science Quarterly*. 50, 2, 272–277.

Lescohier, D. D. (1960). *My Story for the First Seventy-Seven Years*. Madison, WI: Art Brush Creation.

Marshall, A. (1920/1890). *Principles of Economics*. London: Macmillan & Co, Ltd (1949).

Mayhew, A. (2018). Comments on Arturo Hermann's Paper, "The Decline of the Original Institutional Economics". *Economic Thought*. 7, 1, 87–91.

McNulty, P. J. (1980). *The Origins and Development of Labour Economics: A Chapter in the History of Social Thought*. Cambridge, MA: MIT Press.

Mitchell, D. (1972). Union Wage Policies: The Ross-Dunlop Debate Reopened. *Industrial Relations*. 11, Winter, 46–61.

Moss, D. A. (1996). *Socializing Security: Progressive-Era Economists and the Origins of American Social Policy*. Cambridge, MA: Harvard University Press.

Neumark, D. and Wascher W. (2008). *Minimum Wages*. Cambridge, MA: MIT Press.

Nickell, S. and Layard R. (1999). Labour Market Institutions and Economic Performance. In O. Ashenfelter and D. Card (Eds.) *Handbook of Labor Economics*, Vol. 3. Amsterdam: North Holland, 3029–3084.

Papageorgiou, T., Katselidis, I. and Michaelides, P. (2013). Schumpeter, Commons, and Veblen on Institutions. *American Journal of Economics and Sociology*. 72, 5, 1232–1254.

Pemberton, J. (1988). A 'Managerial' Model of the Trade Union. *The Economic Journal*. 98, 392, 755–771.

Perlman, S. (1928). *A Theory of the Labour Movement*. New York: Macmillan.

Perlman, M. (1960). Labor Movement Theories: Past, Present, and Future. *Industrial and Labor Relations Review*. 13, 338–348.

Pigou, A. C. (1913). *Unemployment*. London: Henry Hold and Company.

Pigou, A. C. (1927). Wage Policy and Unemployment. *Economic Journal*. 37, 355–368.

Polachek, S. W. and Siebert W. S. (1993). *The Economics of Earnings*. Cambridge: Cambridge University Press.

Rees, A. (1976). H. Gregg Lewis and the Development of Analytical Labor Economics. *The Journal of Political Economy*. 84, 4, Part 2: Essays in Labor Economics in Honor of H. Gregg Lewis (August): S3–S8.

Ross, A. (1947). The Trade Union as a Wage-fixing Institution. *The American Economic Review*. 37, 4, 566–588.

Ross, A. (1948). *Trade Union Wage Policy*. Berkeley: University of California Press.

Rothschild, K. W. (2008). Economic Imperialism. *Analyse & Kritik*. 30, 2, 723–733.

Rutherford, M. (1989). What Is Wrong with the New Institutional Economics (and What Is Still Wrong with the Old)? *Review of Political Economy*. 1, 3, 299–318.

Rutherford, M. (1996). *Institutions in Economics: The Old and the New Institutionalism. Cambridge*. New York, and Melbourne: Cambridge University Press.

Rutherford, M. (2003). American Institutional Economics in the Interwar Period. In W. J. Samuels, J. E. Biddle, and J. B. Davis (Eds.). *A Companion to the History of Economic Thought*. Oxford: Blackwell Publishing, 360–376.

Rutherford, M. (2009). Towards a History of American Institutional Economics. *Journal of Economic Issues*. 43, 2, 308–318.

Samuels, W. J. (1987). Institutional Economics. In Eatwell, J., Milgate M. and Newman P. (Eds.). *The New Palgrave: A Dictionary of Economics*. London: Macmillan. Volume 2, 864–866.

Slichter, S. H. (1919). *The Turnover of Factory Labour.* New York: D. Appleton.

Slichter, S. H. (1926). The Worker in Modern Economic Society. *Journal of Political Economy*. 34, 1, 100–124.

Spithoven, A. (2019). Similarities and Dissimilarities between Original Institutional Economics and New Institutional Economics. *Journal of Economic Issues*. 53, 2, 440–447.

Tribe, K. (2003). Historical Schools of Economics: German and English. In W. J. Samuels, J. E. Biddle, and J. B. Davis (Eds.). *A Companion to the History of Economic Thought*. Oxford: Blackwell Publishing, 215–230.

Veblen, T. (1898). The Instinct of Workmanship and the Irksomeness of Labour. *American Journal of Sociology*. 4, 187–201.

Veblen, T. (1909). The Limitations of Marginal Utility. *Journal of Political Economy*. 17, 9, 620–636.

Veblen, T. (1914). *The Instinct of Workmanship and the State of the Industrial Arts*. New York: Macmillan.

Wisman, J. D. and Pacitti A. (2004). U.S. Labour Reexamined, 1880–1930: Success, Ideology, and Reversal. In D. P. Champlin and J. T. Knoedler. (Eds.). *The Institutionalist Tradition in Labour Economics*. Armonk, NY: M. E. Sharpe, 88–102.

Witte, E. E. (1935). Features of the Economic Security Program. *Annals of the American Academy of Political and Social Science*. 178, Increasing Government Control in Economic Life, March, 88–94.

Witte, E. E. (1954). Institutional Economics as Seen by an Institutional Economist. *Southern Economic Journal*. 21, 2, 131–140.

Wolman, L. (1924). *The Growth of American Trade Unions, 1880–1923*. New York: National Bureau of Economic Research.

10 Austrian Economics and Economic Policy*

Peter T. Leeson and Louis Rouanet

Introduction

What became the Austrian School of Economics began in 1871 with the publication of Carl Menger's *Grundsätze der Volkswirtschaftslehre* (*Principles of Economics*). By the end of the 1870s, Eugen von Böhm-Bawerk and Friedrich von Wieser had extended what they learned from Menger to other areas. Böhm-Bawerk made contributions to capital theory. Wieser refined Menger's theory of value and introduced the concept of opportunity cost. Reference to an "Austrian School" emerged only in the 1880s amid debates between the German historicists and Menger. Although policy played an indirect role in those debates, their direct subject was methodology. Menger, moreover, maintained that economic theory should be kept distinct from "Economic policy, the science of the basic principles for suitable advancement...of 'national economy' on the part of the public authorities" (1886, p. 211).

In other words, the "main and only concern" of the early Austrian economists "was to contribute to the advancement of economics" (Mises 1969, p. 149). It is therefore surprising that later Austrian economists, in particular Ludwig von Mises and Friedrich Hayek, were actively engaged in debates about economic policy and are perhaps best known for their defense of "free-market" policies. This chapter argues that only after the socialist calculation debate of the 1920s and 1930s did Mises and Hayek progressively develop a more distinctive approach to economic policy. That approach considers policies and institutions in light of their (in)congruity with broad principles, most notably the idea that knowledge is dispersed and incomplete. In the 1960s and 1970s, several insights of the later Austrian School were integrated into other "schools," such as Public Choice and New Institutional Economics. The integration, however, was not total, and an emphasis on "knowledge problems" in the context of economic policies and institutions remains a distinctive feature of the contemporary Austrian School.

DOI: 10.4324/9781003228097-10

Early Austrians

As Wieser observed,

> The modern theory of utility arose aside from the problems of national-economic policy, as the outgrowth of the mere need, the urgency of scientific quest. It aspires to be an empirical theory, pure and simple, not aiming at any definite, practical application.
>
> (1914, p. 41)

It makes sense, then, that what distinguished early marginalists—Menger, William Stanley Jevons, Leon Walras, and later Alfred Marshall—were not policy differences but theoretical ones. Walras, for example, was mainly concerned with the conditions ensuring general equilibrium, but marginalism occupied his framework only secondarily (Jaffé 1976). Menger, in contrast, developed a theory of value imputation, but he was not concerned with the conditions under which general equilibrium exists. Or consider Marshall and his followers, for whom the law of diminishing "marginal utility plays a minor part in the main body of equilibrium theory" (Robbins 1933, p. xvii) and for whom costs were objective quantities. For Menger and his followers, in contrast, the law of diminishing marginal utility was a tool for equilibrium analysis, and costs were foregone alternatives traceable back to the subjective value judgments of individuals.

These theoretical differences would end up playing an important role in defining the Austrian School. The distinction, however, was largely "one of emphasis and conception of theory rather than in the substance of theory itself" (Robbins 1933, p. xvi). And it would be wrong to think that the early Austrians offered an alternative to neoclassical economics. They did not. Austrian economics is a branch of neoclassical economics, and that is how the most prominent later Austrian economists understood their school. According to Mises, for instance,

> the Austrian and the Anglo-American schools and School of Lausanne… differ only in their mode of expressing the same fundamental idea and that they are divided more by their terminology and by peculiarities of presentation than by the substance of their teachings.
>
> (1933, p. 228)

Or as Hayek observed,

> A school has its greatest success when it ceases as such to exist because its leading ideals have become a part of the general dominant teaching. The Vienna school has to a great extent come to enjoy such a success.
>
> (1968, p. 52)

The focus of the early Austrian economists on economic theory does not mean they had no interest in or influence on economic policy. Menger, Wieser, and Böhm-Bawerk each served in the Austrian Cabinet. And the cabinet that Menger served in was "composed of members of the Liberal Party that stood for civil liberties, representative government, equality of all citizens under the law, sound money, and free trade" (Mises 1969, p. 128). Even so, economic policy featured little in the academic works of the early Austrians, whose general policy outlook was similar to that of other early marginalists: pro-market, tempered by government intervention.

Marshall, for example, was "willing to have a great extension of public control over private and semi-public undertakings" to "preserve what is essential in the benefits of free competition" (1925, p. 290). And Wieser, for instance, was sympathetic to progressive taxation, espoused Friedrich List's infant-industry argument for tariffs, favored social insurance (Ekelund 1970), and countenanced the importance of what would later be dubbed "market failures":

> Even if we ourselves should not have succeeded in finding the precise theoretical expression for the conditions of the capitalistic domination, there can be no doubt that this aim may be attained from the basis of the utility-theory. Nor can there be any doubt that, once this expression has been found, a sound modern economic policy will find in such a completed utility theory the fundamental substructure which it requires. For a sound modern economic policy, the safeguarding of the highest possible social benefit in the face of the capitalistic despotism must be the paramount law. A completed theory of utility will be able to demonstrate to that policy under what conditions the law will meet with compliance, under what conditions it will miscarry.
>
> (Wieser 1914, p. 412)

Some early Austrians were more critical of government intervention than others. But so were some Anglo-American marginalists and some members of the Lausanne School. Vilfredo Pareto, for example, "became known as an ultraliberal in the nineteenth-century sense of uncompromising advocate of laissez-faire" (Schumpeter 1949, p. 152). What is notable is that policy views did vary systematically across early marginalists by "school," and the early Austrians' theoretical differences from other schools did not manifest in a distinctive Austrian approach to economic policy.

Later Austrians

In 1920, Ludwig von Mises levied a challenge to the proponents of socialism. Socialist economy, he averred, is oxymoronic; for there can be no economy in the sense of rational resource allocation absent private ownership of the means of production. Mises' argument was simple. Absent private ownership of the means of production, there is no market for the means of production. Absent a market for the means of production, there are no money prices for the means of production. And absent money prices reflecting the relative scarcities of the means of production, the opportunity cost of resource use cannot be assessed. Under socialism, therefore, economic calculation—computation of profits and losses—is impossible, hence so is rational resource allocation.

Perhaps the most famous response to Mises' challenge came from Oskar Lange (1936), who suggested that socialists should be grateful to the Austrian. "For it was his powerful challenge that forced the socialists to recognise the importance of an adequate system of economic accounting to guide the allocation of resources in a socialist economy." Then, Lange added wryly,

> Both as an expression of recognition for the great service rendered by him and as a memento of the prime importance of sound economic accounting, a statue of Professor Mises ought to occupy an honourable place in the great hail of the Ministry of Socialisation or of the Central Planning Board of the socialist state.
>
> (1936, p. 53)

There was indeed a solution to the calculation problem that Mises identified, Lange argued: central planners could use the formal conditions of economic efficiency identified by marginalist principles to allocate resources rationally. Socialist firm managers should be instructed to price output equal to marginal cost and to produce that level of output which minimized average cost.

Mises rejected Lange's answer to his challenge on the grounds that it was no answer at all. Lange assumed a solution to the socialist calculation problem rather than deriving one. Supposing that planners or socialist firm managers know the marginal cost of output is equivalent to assuming that they know the opportunity costs of resources. The question that Mises had asked, however, was how, in a system without private ownership and thus without exchange, the opportunity costs of resources could ever be known. Omniscience, Mises insisted, was not an answer (Mises 1949, p. 706). Yet omniscience seemed to lie at the core of Lange's "solution."

Hayek built on Mises' argument by articulating the role of market prices as communicators and generators of economically useful knowledge (Kirzner 2018). Because much of the knowledge that individuals have is "knowledge of particular circumstances of time and place," our focus, Hayek maintained, should be on "the method by which such knowledge can be made as widely available as possible" (1945, p. 521, 522). Markets provided that method. An entrepreneur needn't concern himself with whether the price of tin, for instance, increased because of a fall in tin supply or because of a rise in demand for tin in other sectors. What matters is that tin has become relatively scarcer, and that knowledge is communicated to the entrepreneur through the increased price of tin.

Neither Mises nor Hayek, it should be recognized, saw the knowledge problem confronted by central planners as suggesting that state involvement in the economy was always unworkable or undesirable. Hayek (1944, p. 86), for example, endorsed government intervention "to limit working hours," "to require certain sanitary arrangements," and to provide welfare, health insurance, and accident insurance. Nor did Mises and Hayek see in the ability of markets to cope with knowledge problems a flawless system of private order. Mises, for instance, observed that in the presence of externalities the economic calculations of private firms are "manifestly defective and their results deceptive" (1949, p. 653), that "monetary calculation has its...serious defects" (1920, p. 22). The confidence in markets expressed by the most prominent later Austrians was relative, not absolute. Economic calculation made possible by markets and private ownership is desirable not because of its perfection but because "we have certainly nothing better to put in its place" (Mises 1920, p. 22).

The socialist calculation debate had far-reaching consequences for the Austrian School. For it revealed a distinction between members of that school, whose central debate concern revolved around how dispersed and incomplete knowledge may (or may not) be organized into what Mises called "the intellectual division of labor" (1927, p. 75), and other neoclassical economists, whose central debate concern revolved around the welfare properties of competitive equilibrium. The Austrians, it turned out, had a rather different view of what constituted the important economic questions, which for them were "who makes the decision, under what constraints, and subject to what feedback mechanism" (Sowell 1980, p. 17). Those questions both suggested and underlaid a rather different view of the market.

Other neoclassical economists conceived of the market as a set of optimality conditions. Mises and Hayek, in contrast, conceived of it as a set of *institutions*, whose sin qua non was private property. The former seemed to see the market as furnishing instructions that, if followed, would assure economic efficiency. The latter, however, saw the market as a method of generating economically useable information, a means of coping with "knowledge problems" that would otherwise stand in the way of economic coordination.

The distinctiveness of the later Austrians' perspective is perhaps easier to make out against the backdrop of broader economic thinking in the 1930s and 1940s. During that period, economists often were quick to recommend major government interventions or outright public ownership of firms as remedies for market "imperfections." Arthur Lewis (1949), for instance, favored the nationalization of land, mineral deposits, insurance, automobile factories, and telecommunications on the grounds of monopoly power. Gunnar Myrdal (1956) argued that national economic planning was the only viable option for economic development. James Meade (1948) favored "socialization" of chemical industries as well as nationalization of iron and steel. Maurice Allais (1947) went further yet: he urged nationalizing a few firms in every industry.[1]

The perspective according to which governments should—and could—achieve perfectly competitive prices through regulation or nationalization was so widely accepted that even avowedly liberal economists like Henry Simons embraced it: "The state should" own and manage "directly...all industries in which it is impossible to maintain effectively competitive conditions" (1934, p. 51). The contrary perspective of Austrian economists was therefore exceptional during this period—as was their dim view of what was actually achieved by policies implemented to mimic perfectly competitive outcomes. "The outcome of the municipalization and nationalization policies of the last decades," Mises judged, "was almost without exception financial failure, poor service, and political corruption" (1949, p. 373).[2]

The emphasis of economists in the 1930s and 1940s on trying to secure prices that would have prevailed under perfect competition left little room for attention to the institutions under which the coordination of economic activity is made possible. As late as 1965, Armen Alchian observed that "if we look at the 'fields' of economics, say as presented by the American Economic Association's classification of the areas of interest or specialization, we find no mention of the word 'property'" (1965, p. 817). In contrast, if one looked at Mises' 1949 treatise *Human Action*, she would find that word 97 times and the word "ownership" 75 times—an indicator of the centrality of institutions to the economics of the later Austrians and of just how unusual their emphasis on institutions was.

In the 1940s, Mises and Hayek extended their economic analyses of institutions to new domains. Mises (1944), for example, pioneered the economics of bureaucracy. Echoing logic he developed in the socialist calculation debate, Mises argued that bureaucracies cannot engage in meaningful profit and loss accounting, precluding bureaucrats from making decisions in a "businesslike" manner. He further argued that bureaucracies can become interest groups weighing on government policies. He highlighted what would decades later be called principal-agent problems related to bureaucratic delegation. He noted the importance of what would decades later be dubbed soft constraints. And he was among the first to consider conditions under which bureaucratic management is efficient.

Hayek (1944), meanwhile, made a contribution to what would eventually become the economics of politics in his *Road to Serfdom*. There, he pointed to a tradeoff between democratic rule and national economic planning. As governmental planning becomes more encompassing in an economy, the details associated with carrying out the plan become overwhelming. Democratically elected bodies thus delegate more power to bureaucratic decision-makers, reducing the former's influence. In addition, Hayek argued, as the scope of governmental planning expands, so does the number of decisions that must be deliberated politically. The cost of democratic deliberation therefore rises, encouraging substitution with less democratic rule. Nearly 20 years later the founders of Public Choice, James Buchanan and Gordon Tullock (1962), would put it in these terms: when the costs of political decision-making rise, optimal decision-making arrangements move further from unanimity rules and majoritarian politics.[3]

Critics of *The Road to Serfdom* often interpret Hayek as claiming that policy deviations from laissez-faire lead inevitably to totalitarianism. But in a letter to Paul Samuelson, Hayek explicitly rejected that claim and, quoting from his *Law, Legislation and Liberty* (1973), clarified that the intended targets of his analysis were not particular policies but rather the principles guiding policy-making, which he thought ill-conceived:

> What I meant to argue in *The Road to Serfdom* was certainly not that whenever we depart, however slightly, from what I regard as the principles of a free society, we shall ineluctably be driven to go the whole way to a totalitarian system. It was rather what in more homely language is expressed when we say: "if you do not mend your principles you will go to the devil." That this has often been understood to describe a necessary process over which we have no power once we have embarked upon it, is merely an indication of how little the importance of principles for the determination of policy is understood, and particularly how completely overlooked is the fundamental fact that by our political actions we unintentionally produce the acceptance of principles which will make further action necessary.
>
> (Quoted in Farrant and McPhail 2010, p. 92)

As should be plain from the foregoing examples, Mises' and Hayek's contributions anticipated subsequent developments in economic scholarship outside the narrowly construed Austrian School. Foremost among such scholarship is that associated with Public Choice and New Institutional Economics.[4] The former challenged the public-finance economics of post-WWII welfare economists by arguing that externalities plague "political markets" no less, and perhaps more, than "economic markets" and thus must be accounted for when considering economic policies. That argument, however, only assimilated and elaborated arguments that Austrian economists had been making for decades.[5] Mises' (1929) critique of interventionism, for instance, was that government interventions in markets, especially using price controls, cannot be considered in isolation because they predictably change the incentives of political decision-makers.

Similarly, the New Institutional Economics revolution, which began in the 1960s, largely restated and elaborated insights developed by Austrian economists during and after the socialist calculation debate.[6] As noted above, agency problems, for example, were central to Mises' (1944) analysis of bureaucracy. And incomplete contracting was part of Hayek's analysis of market competition. To wit:

> in a complex society like ours no contract can explicitly provide against all contingencies and because jurisdiction and legislation evolve standard

> types of contracts for many purposes which not only tend to become exclusively practicable and intelligible but which determine the interpretation of, and are used to fill the lacunae in, all contracts which can actually be made...Here, as much as in the realm of property, the precise content of the permanent legal framework, the rules of civil law, are of the greatest importance for the way in which a competitive market will operate.
>
> (Hayek 1948, p. 115)

Incorporation of "Austrian" insights into Public Choice and New Institutional Economics, however, was not total. In particular, an emphasis on "knowledge problems," first brought to the fore by Mises and Hayek during the socialist calculation debate, remains a distinctive feature of the Austrian School. "Knowledge problems" refer broadly to the obstacles that economic and political actors face in achieving their goals when relevant information does not exist "in concentrated or integrated form, but solely as the dispersed bits of incomplete and frequently contradictory knowledge which all the separate individuals possess" (Hayek 1945, p. 519). To be robust, modern Austrian economists contend, economic policies and institutions must be able to handle those obstacles (Boettke and Leeson 2004; Leeson and Subrick 2006).

Much recent Austrian scholarship that addresses policy therefore does so, at least in part, in terms of the knowledge problems that policymakers confront (see, for instance, Sobel and Leeson 2007; Skarbek and Leeson 2009; Coyne 2013; Boettke et al. 2021; Candela and Geloso 2021; Fegley 2021; Jacobsen and Rouanet 2022). This scholarship evaluates actual or potential policy (in)effectiveness given and with respect to the policy's ostensible goals in light of knowledge problems. A common theme is that public policies tend to be overly optimistic about the extent of relevant information that is accessible by policymakers and tend to be overly pessimistic about the ability of private arrangements to achieve the goals that policymakers seek given those arrangements' capacity to handle dispersed and incomplete information.

Even in scholarship produced by Austrians that has a more normative bent, however, the (in)congruence of policies with dispersed and incomplete knowledge often plays a central role. Consider, for example, the third part of Hayek's (1960) *Constitution of Liberty*, which takes stances on a variety of policies from urban planning to labor laws to progressive taxation. The selection of policies that Hayek considers reflects his view that in certain areas, policies have been adopted that conflict with respect for rule generality. And Hayek's advocacy for (against) policies that are (in)consistent with rule generality reflects his view that general rules are best able to accommodate knowledge problems: they "allow each individual to make the fullest use of his knowledge, especially of his concrete and often unique knowledge of the particular circumstances of time and place" (1960, p. 156).

The Role of Economists in Economic Policymaking

Given their special concern for knowledge problems, modern Austrian economists tend to be more skeptical than many other economists of the idea that "economist experts" can play a productive role in economic policymaking. After all, while economist experts may be experts in their discipline, they are nevertheless limited by dispersed and incomplete information like everyone else. Indeed, on at least one crucial dimension, economist experts are more limited: they generally do not formulate and update what they "know" subject to market incentives and feedback mechanisms.

Consider, for example, a grocer who "knows" that an additional grocery store in his town would create value for consumers and so builds one. He will soon find out whether he is right or wrong since the store will either turn a profit or make losses. And the grocer has a strong incentive to inform what he knows as best he can since if he is right, he enjoys the fruits, and if he is wrong, he pays the price. Contrast that with, for instance, an economist expert who "knows" that more schools in Tanzania would improve that country's economic development and whose policy advice is heeded. It will be exceptionally hard for her to find out whether she is right or wrong, for perhaps development did not improve, or maybe it did, but so many other factors were at play, who can say for sure whether the additional schools were the cause in either case? Moreover, the economist expert has little incentive to inform what she knows as best she can since if she is right, she does not profit personally, and if she is wrong, she does not personally pay any price.

The example of the economist expert advising development policy is salient because in no other policy realm is the difference between how modern Austrians and how many other economists conceive of the economist's policymaking role easier to see. Perhaps the most influential vision of the economist's role in development policy currently is that of the economist as "plumber" (Duflo 2017). Economist-plumbers "try to predict as well as possible what may work in the real world, mindful that tinkering and adjusting will be necessary since our models give us very little theoretical guidance on what (and how) details will matter" (Duflo 2017, p. 1). The plumbing approach is predicated on the notion that local policymakers in developing countries "tend to design schemes based on the ideology of the time, in complete ignorance of the reality of the field, and once these policies are in place, they just stay in place" (Duflo 2017, p. 13). In contrast, the economist-plumber, viewing the situation from the outside, can clearly see all the "leaky pipes" and, with her expert tools—most notably the randomized controlled trial (RCT)—fix them.

From the Austrian perspective, the plumbing approach to development policy is problematic on two primary fronts. First, while that approach is correct to point out that "those who implement policies … are humans too!" (Duflo 2017, p. 16), it seems not to understand that so are economist-plumbers. Humans—whether local policymakers or economist-plumbers—are limited by dispersed and incomplete information. They thus require feedback mechanisms to inform them about when their knowledge is correct and when it is mistaken and to incentivize them to improve their knowledge. Local policymakers and economist-plumbers alike do not face such feedback mechanisms when their policymaking or advising services are supplied outside of markets. And RCTs are not substitutes for market feedback mechanisms: they do not furnish profit/loss information, and they do not reward/punish correct/incorrect knowledge.

Second, by focusing on "leaky pipes" the plumbing approach to development policy sidesteps the central "economic problem of society," which "is mainly one of rapid adaptation to changes in the particular circumstances of time and place" (Hayek 1948, p. 83). A solution to that problem must be institutional; it requires a system of secure private property rights. In the least-developed world, where institutions of secure private property rights do not prevail, the policy approach of economist-plumbers thus amounts to tinkering with the house's leaky pipes while the house is on fire. In this there is a regrettable irony. One of the few things that "economist experts" can and do know, according to Austrians, is that private property institutions are necessary for development. Much beyond that, including how to establish such institutions where they do not exist, is beyond the informational limitations of economist experts. Yet economist-plumbers, who presume to know, or—despite the lack of proper feedback mechanisms—presume to be able to learn, far more than that nevertheless seem to pay little attention to institutions of private property rights.

What, then, is the development policy role of the economist expert in the modern Austrian view? Hardly any at all. Modern Austrians, as noted above, emphasize the necessity of private property institutions for development, but they do not pretend to know more than that. The economist expert's role is accordingly limited to highlighting the importance of private property institutions and articulating their role in coping with knowledge problems. The Austrian approach to development policy, like the Austrian approach to other economic policies, is thus one whose loudest plea is for policymaker humility.

As intimated above, that plea for humility extends to designing or attempting to externally implement private property rights institutions in developing countries. For such design and implementation also presupposes access to much local information to which economist experts are not in fact privy. It is one thing to know in broad strokes what is necessary to enable economy-wide coordination, but it is another thing to know that in detail, and still another thing to know how to get to what is necessary from the present position. Boettke et al. (2008), for example, suggest that the path to private property institutions must ultimately be an indigenous one because only in that case can we be confident that such institutions as emerge comport with local knowledge and practices, which is required for those institutions to "stick." Leeson and Harris (2018) go a step further. They argue that attempts to externally create private property rights institutions in developing counties may in some cases destroy existing wealth, retarding development. Hence, even the exceptionally limited role that Austrians see for "economist experts" in development policy—that of emphasizing the importance of private property institutions—is attended by the caveat that this does not imply that economist experts should attempt to or can successfully design private property institutions in developing countries.

Conclusion

Ludwig von Mises was once asked, "let us suppose you were the dictator of these United States. What would you do?" Mises replied: "I would abdicate" (Read 1971, p. 299). That, in a nutshell, characterizes the approach of Austrian economists to economic policymaking.

Broad principles relevant to economic policy are knowable and known by economic theory—most important, the dispersed and incomplete nature of economically relevant information; the necessity of coping with consequent knowledge problems; the ability of markets to do that; and the indispensability of private property institutions for markets. Economic policies and institutions that are congruent with these broad principles will tend to promote economic coordination. Economic policies and institutions that are incongruent with them will tend to do the opposite. The claims of "economist experts" to know more than this are—like economic policies and institutions that ignore knowledge problems—a conceit. Austrian economists, therefore, do not offer a list of detailed economic policies for improving economic outcomes. Rather, they offer a warning about persons who would make such lists:

> economics as such is a challenge to the conceit of those in power. An economist can never be a favorite of autocrats and demagogues. With them he is always the mischief-maker, and the more they are inwardly convinced that his objections are well-founded, the more they hate him.
> (Mises 1949, p. 67)

Austrian economists' distinctive approach to economic policy was not part of their tradition at its inception. The early Austrian economists focused their scholarly attention on matters of economic theory, and the theoretical differences between them and other early marginalists neither led nor corresponded to systematically different policy views, let alone to an identifiable Austrian approach to economic policy. The latter emerged only gradually and pursuant to an unfolding policy-oriented debate engaged by second-generation Austrian economists Ludwig von Mises and Friedrich Hayek in the 1920s and 1930s—albeit a debate that turned out to hinge very much on different approaches to economic theory: the socialist calculation debate.

Consequent to that debate it became clear to Mises and Hayek that their conception of the market differed substantially from that of other neoclassical economists. Whereas the latter saw the market as a set of optimality conditions that could be followed like a recipe for economic efficiency independent of private economic activity, Mises and Hayek saw the market as a set of institutions whose sin qua non was private property, which copes with "knowledge problems" that otherwise stand in the way of economic coordination.

This emphasis on knowledge problems became a defining feature of Austrian economics and the "Austrian approach" to economic policy. That approach considers economic policies and institutions in light of their (in) congruity with broad principles, most notably the idea that knowledge is dispersed and incomplete. In the 1960s and 1970s, several insights of the later Austrians were integrated into other "schools," such as Public Choice and New Institutional Economics. The integration, however, was not total, and an emphasis on knowledge problems in the context of economic policies and institutions remains a distinctive feature of the contemporary Austrian School.

Notes

* We dedicate this chapter to the memory of Austrian economist Steven G. Horwitz (1964–2021).

1 Somewhat paradoxically, Allais (1947) believed that Mises and Hayek had decisively won the socialist calculation debate and that the "solutions" provided by Lerner, Lange, and Durbin were unsatisfactory.

2 Modern evidence supports Mises' judgment against the view that dominated in the 1930s and 1940s. See Shleifer (1998).

3 On Hayek's *Road to Serfdom* as a precursor to Public Choice economics, see Boettke (1995).

4 On the similarities between "property rights economics" and Austrian economics, see Piano and Rouanet (2020).

5 On the relationship between Public Choice and Austrian economics, see Boettke and Leeson (2003).

6 Cheung (1998) rightfully recognizes Hayek as a pioneer of "transaction cost economics."

Bibliography

Alchian, A. A. (1965). Some economics of property rights. *Il Politico*, 30(4), 816–829.

Allais, M. (1947). Le problème de la planification dans une économie collectiviste. *Kyklos*, 1(3), 254–280.

Boettke, P. J. (1995). Hayek's *The Road to Serfdom* revisited: Government failure in the argument against socialism. *Eastern Economic Journal*, 21(1), 7–26.

Boettke, P. J., & Leeson, P. T. (2003). An Austrian perspective on public choice. In Rowley, C. and F. Schneider (eds.). *Encyclopedia of Public Choice*. Boston, MA: Kluwer Academic Publishing, 351–356.

Boettke, P. J., & Leeson, P. T. (2004). Liberalism, socialism, and robust political economy. *Journal of Markets and Morality*, 7(1), 99–111.

Boettke, P. J., Coyne, C. J., & Leeson, P. T. (2008). Institutional stickiness and the new development economics. *American Journal of Economics and Sociology*, 67(2), 331–358.

Boettke, P. J., Salter, A. W., & Smith, D. J. (2021). *Money and the Rule of Law: Generality and Predictability in Monetary Institutions*. Cambridge: Cambridge University Press.

Buchanan, J. M., & Tullock, G. (1962). *The Calculus of Consent: Logical Foundations of Constitutional Democracy*. Ann Arbor: University of Michigan Press.

Candela, R. A., & Geloso, V. (2021). Economic freedom, pandemics, and robust political economy. *Southern Economic Journal*, 87(4), 1250–1266.

Cheung, S. N. (1998). The transaction costs paradigm: 1998 presidential address Western Economic Association. *Economic Inquiry*, 36(4), 514–521.

Coyne, C. J. (2013). *Doing Bad by Doing Good: Why Humanitarian Action Fails*. Stanford: Stanford University Press.

Duflo, E. (2017). The economist as plumber. *American Economic Review*, 107(5), 1–26.

Ekelund, R. B. Jr. (1970). Power and utility: The normative economics of Friedrich von Wieser. *Review of Social Economy*, 28(2), 179–196.

Farrant, A., & McPhail, E. (2010). No good deed goes unpunished? Revisiting the Hayek-Samuelson exchange over Hayek's alleged inevitability thesis. *History of Economic Ideas*, 18(3), 87–103.

Fegley, T. (2021). Institutional incentives and community policing. *Journal of Institutional Economics*, 17(4), 701–715.

Hayek, F. A. (1944). *The Road to Serfdom*. Chicago, IL: University of Chicago Press.

Hayek, F. A. (1945). The use of knowledge in society. *American Economic Review*, 35(4), 519–530.

Hayek, F. A. (1948). *Individualism and Economic Order*. Chicago, IL: University of Chicago Press.

Hayek, F. A. (1960). *The Constitution of Liberty*. Chicago, IL: University of Chicago Press.

Hayek, F. A. (1968). Economic thought VI: The Austrian School of economics. In Sills, D. M. & R. K. Merton (eds.). *International Encyclopedia of the Social Sciences*. New York: Macmillan, 458–462.

Hayek, F. A. (1973). *Law, Legislation and Liberty, Volume 1: Rules and Order*. Chicago, IL: University of Chicago Press.

Jacobsen, P., & Rouanet, L. (2022). Economists versus engineers: Two approaches to environmental problems. *Review of Austrian Economics*, 35(3), 359–381.

Jaffé, W. (1976). Menger, Jevons and Walras de-homogenized. *Economic Inquiry*, 14(4), 511–524.

Kirzner, I. M. (2018). *Competition, Economic Planning, and the Knowledge Problem*. Indianapolis, IN: Liberty Fund.

Lange, O. (1936). On the economic theory of socialism: Part one. *Review of Economic Studies*, 4(1), 53–71.

Leeson, P. T., & Harris, C. (2018). Wealth-destroying private property rights. *World Development*, 107, 1–9.

Leeson, P. T., & Subrick, J. R. (2006). Robust political economy. *Review of Austrian Economics*, 19(2), 107–111.

Lewis, W. A. (1949). *The Principles of Economic Planning*. London: George Allen & Unwin Ltd.

Marshall, A. (1925). *Memorials*. London: Macmillan and Co.
Meade, J. E. (1948). *Planning and the Price Mechanism: The Liberal-Socialist Solution*. London: George Allen & Unwin Ltd.
Menger, C. (1871) [1976]. *Principles of Economics*. Menlo Park, CA: Institute for Humane Studies.
Menger, C. (1886) [1985]. *Investigations into the Method of the Social Sciences*. New York: New York University Press.
Mises, L. von. (1920) [1990]. *Economic Calculation in the Socialist Commonwealth*. Auburn, AL: Ludwig von Mises Institute.
Mises, L. von. (1927) [1985]. *Liberalism: In the Classical Tradition*. Irvington-on-Hudson: Foundation for Economic Education.
Mises, L. von. (1929) [1996]. *A Critique of Interventionism*. Irvington-on-Hudson: Foundation for Economic Education.
Mises, L. von. (1933) [2003]. *Epistemological Problems of Economics*. Auburn, AL: Ludwig von Mises Institute.
Mises, L. von. (1944). *Bureaucracy*. New Haven, CT: Yale University Press.
Mises, L. von. (1949). *Human Action*. New Haven, CT: Yale University Press.
Mises, L. von. (1969) [2013]. *Notes and Recollections: With the Historical Setting of the Austrian School of Economics*. Indianapolis, IN: Liberty Fund.
Myrdal, G. (1956). *Development and Under-Development: A Note on the Mechanism of National and International Economic Inequality*. Cairo: National Bank of Egypt.
Piano, E. E., & Rouanet, L. (2020). Economic calculation and the organization of markets. *Review of Austrian Economics*, 33(3), 331–348.
Read, L. E. (1971). To abdicate or not. In Hayek, F. A., H. Hazlitt, L. E. Read, G. R. Velasco, & F. A. Harper (eds.). *Toward Liberty, Volume II: Essays in Honor of Ludwig von Mises on the Occasion of his 90th Birthday, September 29, 1971*. Menlo Park, CA: Institute for Humane Studies, 299–302.
Robbins, L. (ed.) (1933). Introduction. In Wicksteed, P. H. *The Common Sense of Political Economy, and Selected Papers and Reviews on Economic Theory*. London: Routledge & Kegan Paul Limited, v–xxiii.
Schumpeter, J. A. (1949). Vilfredo Pareto (1848–1923). *Quarterly Journal of Economics*, 63(2), 147–173.
Shleifer, A. (1998). State versus private ownership. *Journal of Economic Perspectives*, 12(4), 133–150.
Simons, H. C. (1934). *A Positive Program for Laissez-Faire: Some Proposals for a Liberal Economic Policy*. Chicago, IL: University of Chicago Press.
Skarbek, D. B., & Leeson, P. T. (2009). What can aid do? *Cato Journal*, 29(1), 391.
Sobel, R. S., & Leeson, P. T. (2007). The use of knowledge in natural-disaster relief management. *Independent Review*, 11(4), 519–532.
Sowell, T. (1980). *Knowledge and Decisions*. New York: Basic Books.
Wieser, F. von. (1914) [1927]. *Social Economics*. New York: Adelphi Company.

11 Keynes on Theorising for Policy

Sheila Dow

Introduction

For many economists 'Keynesian policy' simply means short-run demand management through fiscal policy. Recent events have revived attention to such a policy stance, but just as a necessary crisis response; within a mainstream framework, 'Keynesian policy' only addresses what are regarded as temporary aberrations from the self-equilibrating norm. Yet the primary expression of Keynes's theory of macroeconomic policy (Keynes 1936) was offered as a *general* theory, of which the mainstream approach was a special case. Indeed, the generality of Keynes's theorising refers to Keynes's understanding of economics as 'a method rather than a doctrine':

> [T]he theory of economics does not furnish a body of settled conclusions immediately applicable to policy. It is a method rather than a doctrine, an apparatus of the mind, a technique of thinking, which helps its possessor to draw correct conclusions.
>
> (Keynes 1983, p. 856)

The focus here will therefore be more on Keynes's approach to theorising with a view to designing policy than on the content of his policy conclusions.

There is a vast literature on Keynes's approach to economic policy and the context in which his ideas were formed. An important aspect of that context was that, as well as being an academic, Keynes was actively engaged in government, with increasing influence on the policy-making process. For example, his early work in the India Office led to membership in the Royal Commission on Indian Currency; his wartime appointment to the Treasury led to his involvement in a range of critical policy debates and international negotiations. This active role continued until his central involvement in the 1944 Bretton Woods conference. While Keynes maintained his academic connections with Cambridge and his drive to pursue academic questions, his main focus was consistently on pressing policy issues (Skidelsky 1992, p. 425).

But perhaps the most important development in Keynes's scholarship has been the increasing prominence given to his early work on probability

DOI: 10.4324/9781003228097-11

(Keynes 1921). The reissue of this book by Macmillan in 1973 spurred on the pioneering work of Carabelli (1988) and O'Donnell (1989), as well as Lawson and Pesaran (eds, 1985), which in turn propagated substantial literature on Keynes's philosophy. As a result, it is now conventional among Keynes scholars to see the influence of Keynes's philosophy running through the body of his work in economics. Accordingly, such a perspective is important for understanding the meaning and significance of Keynes's writing on economic theory and policy.

We start therefore with a brief account of Keynes's philosophy. Given his focus on practical reason, we move directly to considering the implications for Keynes's views on the process of policy-making. Keynes's philosophy clearly had important consequences also for the content of his theory and its policy implications, but more particularly for the distinctions between theory and policy. The analysis to follow sets out an interpretation of Keynes drawing on an immensely rich body of material where controversy over interpretation is still very much alive. Following a discussion of Keynes's political philosophy, we take domestic and international monetary reform as case studies of how Keynes understood the relationship between economic theory and the theory and practice of economic policy. We conclude with a discussion of the unintended consequences of Keynes's macroeconomics for the way in which the relationship between theory, policy-making and its governance actually evolved.

Keynes's Philosophy: Ethics, Ontology and Epistemology

A key early influence on Keynes's philosophical development was G E Moore's ethics, with his injunction to 'be good' alongside the moral injunction to 'do good'. The latter was to be promoted by following rules based on expectations of the consequences of actions. This early period of philosophical development under Moore's influence was to prove critical for Keynes's economics and in particular his approach to economic policy (Davis 1994). While Keynes's adoption of Moore's focus on ethics underpinned his approach to economic policy, it was the ways in which he diverged from Moore that forged the distinctiveness of Keynes's philosophy and economics.

First, rather than focusing on the potential conflict between 'being good' and 'doing good', Keynes developed a framework which integrated them. Keynes's economic policy focus on long-term socio-economic improvement (his 'doing good') was addressed to facilitating the pursuit by individuals of the good life: 'being good'. This motivation for policy has been an increasing focus in the Keynes literature, highlighting and explaining this moral and ethical driver of Keynes's thinking on economic policy for the long run (see for example O'Donnell 1999, Skidelsky and Skidelsky 2012, Guizzo Archela 2016, Chick and Freeman 2018).

Second, Keynes was dissatisfied with the way in which Moore derived the rules for 'doing good' from expectations as to the likely consequences of action based on a frequentist notion of probability. For Keynes, the necessary comprehensive evidence was not generally available.[1] Keynes rather pursued an alternative, logical approach to probability to provide a moral justification for action which was reasonable even if not demonstrably true. This approach was set out in his *Treatise on Probability* which was eventually published in 1921. The epistemology that Keynes developed there was to prove fundamental to his economic theory and consequent policy analysis.

Where Moore's frequentist approach to probability provided a moral justification for action based on certain knowledge, Keynes explored the absence of certainty as the general case. This was due to the absence of the conditions for certainty.[2] The *Treatise on Probability* is focused on the epistemological level. But Keynes's critique of the frequentist approach to probability refers to ontology, pointing to the organic interdependence of the subject matter, rather than its atomic unity. Particularly when Keynes discussed economic relations in these terms we see an increasingly explicit position which we would now understand as an open-system ontology. Thus, for example, he criticises reliance on mathematical models as precluding attention to the 'complexities and interdependencies of the real world' (Keynes 1936, p. 298).

The classical logic of deductive mathematical systems requires certainty as to the truth of premises. But Keynes argued that such truth could not be demonstrated with respect to a subject matter where organic interdependence prevailed. The problem of induction with respect to the truth value of the premises created a problem with deduction from those premises. In the absence of demonstrative logic, therefore, some other basis was required for reasoned belief as the justification for action. Keynes therefore developed an alternative logic – 'ordinary' or 'human' logic – as the basis for belief. In order to consider how decisions are made, in philosophy, science and in everyday life, without demonstrable proof as to their consequences, Keynes developed a form of rationality – reasonableness – based on argument which was of necessity inconclusive.

Probability was a logical relation, but one which could rarely be quantified (Carabelli 1988, 2021). The *Treatise on Probability* sets out procedures by which reasonable beliefs can be established in the absence of quantifiable probabilities. Different conditions give rise to different capacities for judgement about unquantifiable probability, e.g. as to whether probabilities are nevertheless comparable, i.e. capable of ordinal ranking. Probability is a logical relation with respect to evidence and is in that sense positive. But, since judgement with respect to that relation depends on the evidence and analytical framework available to the subject, probability is subjective.[3]

Separate from the probability judgement itself is the confidence held in it, which depends on the weight of argument. Weight increases with the extent of relevant evidence relative to relevant ignorance. Ideas of relevance depend on evolving non-demonstrative knowledge with respect to an evolving subject matter. Thus, not only may the availability of evidence change but also the notion of what is relevant may change. As Runde (1990) argues, new evidence may reveal ignorance which had gone unrecognised, reducing the weight of argument: more evidence need not increase weight.

Since a unified deductive basis for probability judgement is generally unavailable, ordinary logic draws on a plurality of strands of argument to which judgement can be applied. These strands apply different methods, including reasoned analysis of evidence alongside conventional judgement. But, while the rationality of classical logic provides motivation for positive action, the uncertainty of non-demonstrative logic does not.[4] Keynes thus emphasised the role of intuition, conventional judgement and animal spirits as contributors to belief and motivation for action in spite of uncertainty.

As Carabelli and Cedrini (2015) explain, Keynes developed his theoretical logic separately from his logic of action, where it is the latter which is relevant to policy-making. For Keynes, theorising was an exercise in abstraction in order to arrive at general propositions. The abstraction might involve mathematical modelling as an aid to thought:

> It is the essence of a model that one does *not* fill in real values for the variable functions. To do so would make it useless as a model. For as soon as this is done, the model loses its generality and its value as a mode of thought.
>
> (Keynes 1938, p. 296)

Theorising, which may include models, seeks to illuminate logical causation, i.e. causation in terms of the abstract structure of the theory. Theory in turn acts as a guide to thinking about causation in the real world: ontological causation, which refers to specific circumstances in the real world (Carabelli 1988, ch. 6; Carabelli and Cedrini 2015).

Keynes thus made a clear distinction between theory and policy, between his 'apparatus of thought' and his 'apparatus of action'. In *The General Theory*, Keynes (p. 297) emphasised the need to keep in mind what had been abstracted from in theorising so that it could be brought back into analysis for the purposes of application. It is uncontroversial that policy implementation in a specific context requires consideration of institutional and (possibly non-numerical) empirical detail. But for Keynes, the modifications to provisional theory in order to design policy were a matter of logic prior to considering the specifics of implementation. Any theory was just the starting point for application, not a universal prescription. The next necessary step was to take into account interdependencies between variables which had been classified as either endogenous or exogenous (independent) for the purposes of the abstract model. A key focus of Keynes's (1936, p. 257) critique of the (neo-)classical approach was therefore that theoretical assumptions as to independence were retained, without acknowledgement, when theory was applied with a view to policy (Carabelli and Cedrini 2014b; Carabelli 2021, p. 91).

Keynes's 'two-stage' approach to the logic of economic policy design thus required abstraction first and then relaxation of abstraction:

> [A]fter we have reached a provisional conclusion by isolating the complicating factors one by one, we then have to go back on ourselves and allow, as well as we can, for the probable interactions of the factors amongst themselves.
>
> (Keynes 1936, p. 297)

We turn now to consider more widely Keynes's views on policy-making, drawing on his two-stage approach.

Keynes on the Policy-Making Process

The account here started with Keynes's ethics, not just because of the chronology of his philosophical development, but also because it was foundational to his economics. A distinction between positive, normative and applied economics had been a notable contribution of Keynes's father's work on economic methodology. But he regarded the interrelationships between the three as being linear. According to J N Keynes (1981, p. 21) theorising was positive, establishing economic laws: 'matters of fact'; values would then be applied in order to guide policy; finally, policy implementation required arts, including drawing in factors (often non-economic factors) from which economic theorising had abstracted.

Whether positive economics is even possible is an issue in itself; normative notions of market freedom, social welfare, etc., imbue mainstream theory even though it purports to be value-free. Indeed, for J M Keynes, economics was, in the Classical tradition, a moral science and his stance on social justice was a moral one which imbued his economic analysis. The ultimate motivation for pursuing knowledge of the economy was ethical – the promotion of the good. But in any case, as far as J M Keynes was concerned, the distinctions between theory, ethics and application took on a different character from the apparently separable and sequential distinctions drawn by his father:

> It would be a mistake to presuppose a somehow linear relation from theory to policy in Keynes's economics, with the corollary that external events—the real world, or even experience—would de facto dictate shifts in theoretical approaches and therefore in policy suggestions.
>
> (Carabelli and Cedrini 2015, p. 510)

The theoretical stage in pursuing ethical goals involved abstraction designed to tease out logical causation relevant to the pursuit of these goals. O'Donnell (1989, p. 331) distinguished between Keynes's theorising and his economic policy as follows: 'The ultimate goal of theoretical reason was truth (whether of primary or secondary propositions), while that of practical reason was the attainment of greater goodness'. This truth is relative to the abstract theoretical structure, referring to correct logic. But theorising is not independent of the logic of application since the abstractions which allow derivation of theoretical statements need to be capable of relaxation. For Keynes, theory is constructed with a view to application and is provisional with respect to the relaxation of abstractions, where the abstractions are selected for their relevance to the problem at hand. Models are designed

> to segregate the semi-permanent or relatively constant factors from those which are transitory or fluctuating so as to develop a logical way of thinking about the latter, and of understanding the time sequences to which they give rise in particular cases.
>
> (Keynes 1938, pp. 296–297)

The positivist approach to theorising purports to be general by abstracting from particularities. But Keynes objected that (neo)classical theory was a special case, particular to the panoply of assumptions on which it rested without these all being laid out. Keynes accordingly challenged the direct application of theory to policy without attention to the nature and implications of the assumed abstractions.

The intrinsic interconnectedness of theory and policy for Keynes is evident in his list of attributes required of an economist. He set these out in his memoir of Alfred Marshall in terms which could well be applied to himself:

> [T]he master-economist must possess a rare *combination* of gifts. ... He must be mathematician, historian, statesman, philosopher—in some degree. He must understand symbols and speak in words. He must contemplate the particular in terms of the general, and touch abstract and concrete in the same flight of thought. He must study the present in the light of the past for the purposes of the future. No part of man's nature or his institutions must lie entirely outside his regard. He must be purposeful and disinterested in a simultaneous mood; as aloof and incorruptible as an artist, yet sometimes as near to earth as a politician.
>
> (Keynes 1924a, pp. 321–322, emphasis in original)

The focus of Keynes's thinking was grounds for belief as a justification for action, where beliefs had particular applicability to policy circumstances. He saw his role as an economic adviser, building such knowledge, sharing it with policy-makers ('inner opinion') and persuading as to its worth. But then there was a duty to share with, and persuade, the general population ('outer opinion').

Keynes's Political Philosophy

Keynes brought to his thinking on economic policy a particular political philosophy. He was influenced by Edmund Burke to consider the implications of policy design based on limited, because undemonstrable, knowledge. But while the resulting uncertainty encouraged Burke to be cautious about policy action, Keynes did not hold back, seeing it as a moral duty to apply such knowledge as there was for the social good.

There is debate about how to classify Keynes's political philosophy, particularly with respect to socialism (O'Donnell 1989, 322ff, 1999; Dow 2017; Fuller 2019). Keynes (1932, p. 500) himself specified his political principles as follows (see also Keynes 1925a):

> liberal socialism, by which I mean a system where we can act as an organised community for common purposes and to promote social and economic justice, whilst respecting and protecting the individual – his freedom of choice, his faith, his mind and its expression, his enterprise and his property.

Keynes's advocacy of liberal socialism rather than state socialism exemplifies his epistemology in that it referred to contemporary circumstances and what they allowed (O'Donnell 1989, ch. 14). For Keynes, assigning functions to the state was a matter of judgement. 'True socialism' for him involved deciding where the individual and where the social spheres apply (Keynes 1924b, p. 222).

> I have said that it is of the essence of state planning to do those things which in the nature of the case lie outside the scope of the individual. It differs from Socialism and from Communism in that it does not seek to aggrandise the province of the state for its own sake. ... Its object is to take hold of the central controls and to govern them with deliberate foresight and thus modify and condition the environment within which the individual freely operates with and against other individuals.
>
> (Keynes 1932, p. 88)

With state planning assigned to those areas outside the scope of the individual, the benefits of individualism could still be enjoyed: efficiency, safeguarding of personal liberty and variety of life.

> The political problem of mankind is to combine three things: *economic efficiency, social justice, and individual liberty.* The first needs criticism, precaution, and technical knowledge; the second, an unselfish and enthusiastic spirit, which loves the ordinary man; the third, tolerance, breadth, appreciation of the excellencies of variety and independence, which

> prefers, above everything, to give unhindered opportunity to the exceptional and to the aspiring.
>
> (Keynes 1926, p. 311, emphasis added)

From a positivist perspective, economic efficiency is separable from social and political goals. Keynes rather emphasised their interdependencies: efficiency takes its meaning from the goals to which it is applied, goals to be traced back to ethics. Further, for Keynes, the interdependencies arise from the central economic roles of institutions and conventions.

Keynes's economic policy stance arose from his theorising about the nature of finance capitalism, with its prioritisation of financial accumulation over well-being. In particular, such a system was unable to generate a full-employment level of investment. While 'Keynesian policy' is popularly identified with his advocacy of particular short-run fiscal policy measures, his long-run focus was on establishing institutions to contribute to the state's necessary involvement in the economy, especially with respect to capital investment and income distribution (Davis 1994, ch. 6). These were semi-governmental institutions, like the Bank of England and the universities, which were state-owned, run by state appointees and answerable to parliament but otherwise independent (O'Donnell 1989, ch. 14). These institutions would extend the role of expertise and 'inner opinion'.

In addition to formal institutional arrangements, Keynes saw the role of conventions as central to the promotion of economic efficiency, social justice, and individual liberty. Conventions had both a positive and a negative role to play. On the positive side, socio-economic systems function by means of formal institutional arrangements but also by conventional practices. Thus, in the absence of 'true' risk measures and thus 'true' market pricing, economic stability is promoted by habitual behaviours. One such is price and wage stickiness on the part of companies. Another is trust, notably in the expertise and good intentions of government and semi-governmental institutions.

But conventions, particularly with respect to knowledge in financial markets, could be highly damaging. Keynes was particularly concerned with the scope for conventional judgement in aggregate to be precarious and thus to destabilise economic activity. In particular, he was concerned that conventional judgement would discourage investment finance and thus consign the economy to habitual slumps (Carabelli 2021, ch. 2). In the absence of reliable knowledge, recourse is made to conventional opinion as a basis for action (Keynes 1937). In financial markets, the outcome may be a cost of finance for real economic activity which exceeds the level required for full employment.

The policy implication was for greater state involvement in promoting capital investment. This could be implemented directly, or indirectly by improving confidence in expectations. Rivot (2021) argues that fiscal policy is directed at the first, aiming to enhance expectations as to investment prospects. Monetary policy, on the other hand, strengthens the weight of argument in favour of such assessments in relation to the prospect of the long-term interest rate. Keynes advocated the maintenance of a low and steady long-term interest rate which would underpin capital investment planning in the private sector. By sustaining expectations of such a rate, monetary policy would defuse the liquidity preference fostered by financial instability, thus reducing the liquidity premium, making it easier to maintain a low rate.

Domestic and International Monetary Reform: A Case Study

We have seen that Keynes's approach to economic policy was not to treat it as separable from theory, but rather to *theorise with a view to devising policy*. In particular, this required the abstractions of theory to be such that they could be relaxed, including any assumptions of independence between variables. Carabelli and Cedrini (2015) show how Keynes implemented his two-stage approach to policy in the way he structured his work: separating theory from application in the two volumes of the *Treatise on Money*, and in the division between Chapters 1–17 and Chapters 19–21 of *The General Theory* with respect to theory and application respectively (Chapter 18 being transitional). They also illustrate the approach in terms of specific areas of policy discourse, such as Keynes's assessment of Lerner's functional finance proposal. Keynes would assess theoretical propositions in terms of whether they were workable in particular real circumstances. Workability would depend substantially on the ability to incorporate interdependencies that had been assumed away in theoretical abstraction.

Keynes's ideas on monetary reform provide a good case study of the application of his two-stage approach to policy-making. Carabelli and Cedrini (2010, 2014a) demonstrate the consistency of Keynes's methodological approach to analysing monetary reform, from *Indian Currency and Finance* to the *Tract on Monetary Reform*, to the *Treatise on Money*, to his plans for an International Clearing Union.[5] Yet this consistent approach could lead in different directions in different circumstances, as is evident from his treatment of domestic monetary reform in *The General Theory* compared to his plans for international monetary reform at Bretton Woods (Dow 2017, 2018). Considering this difference serves to illuminate his two-stage approach.

Keynes (1936, pp. 353–358) gave detailed consideration to Silvio Gesell's (1916) proposal for domestic monetary reform. Their political philosophy had much in common and, like Keynes, Gesell was concerned about the effect on effective demand of hoarding money. Since Gesell identified the absence of carrying costs as the cause of hoarding he proposed that a cost be imposed by government – effectively a negative interest rate. A stamp would periodically be required to be attached to government-issued notes as long as they were held (Dow 2016). Keynes took Gesell's proposal seriously, appreciating Gesell's emphasis on effective demand and the monetary nature of the rate of interest. But, while Keynes (1936, p. 357, emphasis added) thought that '[t]he *idea* behind stamped money is sound', nevertheless he rejected it as a workable policy.

This difference of opinion stemmed partly from the fact that Keynes was concerned primarily with the short run and the need to stabilise the economy at full employment, while Gesell had a long-term focus. Keynes looked to fiscal measures to stabilise economic conditions, which would address high liquidity preference more effectively than monetary reform.

Their differences as to whether monetary reform could be effective stemmed more fundamentally from a difference in approach. Gesell's approach accords with the (neo)classical approach to which Keynes objected. He believed his argument to be demonstrably true and universally applicable. He extrapolated from the apparent success of a range of small-scale experiments to predict success for a general application. Further, money was whatever it was declared to be by the state; it was independent of any other variables that might change as a result of his policy.

Keynes's (1936, pp. 357–358) critique referred to the unwarranted preservation by Gesell of independencies.[6] First Keynes pointed to the way in which liquidity preference responded to uncertainty. Without attention to the need for short-run stabilisation a negative interest rate might not deter hoarding if liquidity preference is very high. Second the asset(s) which are regarded as money are not fixed but rather reflect how far they have the characteristics of money (as set out in Chapter 17 of *The General Theory*). It is not only state money that has a liquidity premium. A negative rate of interest on government-issued cash therefore would divert demand to other liquid assets which did not have a negative return. The issue of hoarding would then transfer to what became the safest asset. Further, such a shift would occur within the context of financial innovation, specifically the emergence of new liquid assets, which itself can be prompted by actions by the authorities.

Finally, while Gesell favoured a radical approach to introducing reform, Keynes (1936, p. 378) favoured a gradual approach: 'the necessary measures of socialisation can be introduced gradually and without a break in the general traditions of society'. Keynes was acutely aware that dramatic policy change can set in train a series of unintended consequences due to the interdependence between variables endogenous to an abstract theory and those from which theory temporarily abstracted. Accordingly, Keynes's approach to monetary arrangements was pragmatic rather than dogmatic.

Keynes's motivation was the same when it came to international monetary reform: to consider monetary arrangements that would promote economic stability at full employment along with international equity. He was concerned consistently, dating from his work on India (Keynes 1913) and continuing in his *Tract on Monetary Reform* (Keynes 1923), with the propensity to hoard international liquidity in the form of precious metals at the domestic and national levels. Whether this propensity could actually be exercised depended on relative economic power, further exacerbating imbalances of power. Keynes was thus critical (at least as far as the context of the early part of the twentieth century was concerned) of the abstract gold standard model which portrayed international flows of precious metals as an equilibrating mechanism. That model fit the neoclassical pattern of establishing a universal principle whereby any independencies were preserved in its application. Rather, understanding the gold standard in terms of the key interdependency of power relations, Keynes argued that it was both economically inefficient and violated principles of social justice (Dow 2018).

For Keynes what was required was a new international currency administered at the international level to take the place of precious metals. While this would mitigate to some extent the force of international imbalances of power, a mechanism was required to discourage hoarding. Keynes's (1942) plan was therefore to set up an International Clearing Union (ICU) which would issue and centrally manage an international money called bancor. The ICU would discourage the need to hoard on the part of countries prone to payments deficits by providing credit to tide them over temporary imbalances. At the same time, it would impose charges on credit balances above a given level held by surplus countries, thus discouraging hoarding on their part too. Given the mutuality of surplus and deficit positions, the ICU would encourage simultaneous adjustment on both sides of the balance sheet.

By advocating a charge on credit balances at the ICU Keynes seems to be offering a Gesellian solution. Why would he reject this solution at the domestic level and then advocate it at the international level? The answer lies in his philosophy of deriving policy from theory. As we have seen this involves drawing into the analysis the interdependencies from which theory has abstracted. In the case of domestic reform, this included the scope for increasing liquidity preference to outweigh a negative interest rate and for financial innovation to change the relative attractiveness of existing and new financial assets as money.

The international monetary system in the post-war period was very different, not least because of the legacy of currency inconvertibility and capital controls. These circumstances allowed the kind of fresh start which Gesell had tried to impose on a pre-existing open financial system. Indeed, it was not until the 1970s, with the burgeoning power of international financial markets, that it was accepted that the international monetary system was not international-state-run. In the 1940s, virtually all international transactions were routed through central banks, within what was effectively a closed monetary system. Some of these transactions might be speculative capital flows, but Keynes advocated controls on such flows as part of his plan (De Cecco 1979). Such a measure would reinforce efforts to discourage hoarding for protection against speculative attacks. Keynes was proposing a new international money for which there would be no credible substitutes. He argued for an ICU as an economically-efficient system which also addressed the social injustice of international imbalances of power. His plan reflected his focus on building up semi-governmental institutions in order to pursue policy goals. It also reflected his confidence that these institutional arrangements would prevent the interdependencies arising that he saw as making the Gesell plan unworkable.

Concluding Remarks: Some Unintended Consequences

This chapter started with a reference to the popular (mis)understanding of Keynes's contributions to macroeconomic policy which has persisted in large part due to inattention (outside the specialist Keynes literature) to Keynes's philosophy, with consequences that Keynes had not intended.

First, when Keynes is seen through the mainstream methodological lens it is assumed that the atomic hypothesis applies. The policy of deficit finance to bolster aggregate demand and ward off recession, popularly regarded as the core principle of Keynesian macroeconomics, is thus popularly understood to have universal application. The principle of effective demand is indeed central to Keynes's macroeconomics, but how that is to be applied in particular circumstances requires that attention be paid to the relevant interdependent factors at work. The principle is just the (provisional) start – an aid to thought. Chick (1983, 2018) demonstrates how Keynes's macroeconomics can be adapted to guide policy relevant to two very different subsequent contexts.

Further, the mainstream economics version of Keynes ignores his ethical motivation and political philosophy. Macroeconomic goals are conventionally couched in neoclassical terms of social welfare, presented as if value-free. Economic efficiency is pursued with respect to optimising social welfare in this sense rather than in Keynes's sense of the 'good life'. The mainstream approach associates individual liberty with the free-market activities of atomistic economic agents, while any consideration of social justice is treated as the object of separable enquiry. Yet these ethical concerns underpinned Keynes's critique of financial capitalism.

Keynes is also popularly identified with an increased role for the state, but we have seen that Keynes had a well-developed political philosophy drawing on his ethics whereby economic activity was a means of action with a view to enjoying the good life, rather than as an end itself. Guizzo Archela (2016) argues that this activity is therefore a form of self-governance facilitated by governance by the state. Yet she argues that Keynes's economic policy has been translated into an exercise solely of government by the state. This involves a form of independence, or separation, characteristic of mainstream economics, of the state from the private sector. For Keynes, there was a fundamental interdependence.

Keynes's views on the role of the economist have tended to reinforce the independence position, seeming to support the role of economist as expert. Skidelsky (1992) explains Keynes's self-confidence in championing the role of reason in economic policy-making, tellingly subtitling this volume of his Keynes biography 'The Economist as Saviour'. As a product of his times, Keynes sought 'to restore the expectation of stability and progress in a world cut adrift from its nineteenth-century moorings' (ibid., p. xv). 'The simple message of Keynes's economics seems to be that, when a society's self-governing mechanisms break down, it needs more governing from the centre' (ibid., p. xxviii).

Expertise takes its form from epistemology, and here again, we see the importance of disregarding Keynes's philosophy. For Keynes, propositions relevant to policy-making were in general non-demonstrable, given the nature of the subject matter and the ensuing uncertainty. Theories were aids to thought, but, as abstractions, they required fleshing out with analysis of the interdependencies from which the theories had abstracted. This was an exercise in logic prior to an exploration of the material particularities relevant to policy implementation. From a mainstream perspective, the aim is for theory to be universal, with the institutional and empirical detail for implementation separable from the theory itself. For Keynes theorising was one stage but the second stage of using the theory as an aid to analysing the interdependencies relevant to the context demonstrated that the two were not separable.

It is well known that Keynes was particularly critical of theory being regarded as universal on account of its mathematical formulation. He was also critical of spurious quantification; his theory of probability specified the limited scope for quantifiable probability. Yet he understood the rhetorical power of quantification: '[t]he statistical result is so attractive in its definiteness that it leads us to forget the more vague, though more important considerations which may be, in a given particular case, within our knowledge' (Keynes 1921, p. 356). For Keynes, reliable knowledge under uncertainty is built up using an incommensurate range of methods and strands of reasoning, put together with judgement. But where there is a pervasive lack of confidence in judgement, economic experts can be encouraged to narrow their focus to the apparent safety of quantifiable measures. Keynes was not at all averse to statistical evidence, nor to building models. But the importance of his approach to policy-making is that much of importance is unquantifiable and models by their nature exclude the 'complexities and interdependencies of the real world' (Keynes 1936, p. 298). Thus, while data and models can be useful they are subject to serious limitations.

Notes

1 Keynes's concerns with inductivism mirror those of Hume, whose work was a significant influence (Meeks 2003).

2 There is debate about the basis of Keynes's epistemological stance, in particular how far it is grounded in a particular ontology, i.e. in a particular understanding of the nature of the subject matter. See Lawson (2003, Chapter 7) for the argument that Keynes's epistemology is ontologically grounded and Carabelli (2021) for the counterargument.

3 There is debate as to whether or not Keynes was a subjectivist, but drawing sharp distinctions between subjectivism and objectivism is typical of the dualism of the deductivist approach. As with so many of these dualities, both duals are evident in Keynes's thought (Carabelli 1988).

4 Keynes discussed the investment decision in the former terms in Chapter 11 of *The General Theory* and in the latter terms in Chapter 12.
5 Keynes's motivation to address monetary reform stemmed from his moral critique of a monetary system which rewarded financial accumulation: the 'love of money' was the 'moral problem of our age' (Keynes 1925b).
6 Arguably these interdependencies were less significant for the small rural communities where experiments with a Gesellian system appeared to have been successful, compared to a national context dominated by a more advanced financial system.

Bibliography

Carabelli, A M (1988) *On Keynes's Method*. London: Macmillan.

Carabelli, A M (2021) *Keynes on Uncertainty and Tragic Happiness: Complexity and Expectations*. London: Palgrave Macmillan.

Carabelli, A M and M A Cedrini (2010) 'Indian currency and beyond: the legacy of the early economics of Keynes in the times of Bretton Woods II', *Journal of Post Keynesian Economics*, 33 (2): 255–280.

Carabelli, A M and M A Cedrini (2014a) 'Keynes's *General Theory, Treatise on Money* and *Tract on Monetary Reform*: different theories, same methodological approach', *European Journal of the History of Economic Thought*, 21 (6): 1060–1084.

Carabelli, A M and M A Cedrini (2014b) 'Chapter 18 of *The General Theory* "further analysed": economics as a way of thinking', *Cambridge Journal of Economics*, 38 (1): 23–47.

Carabelli, A M and Cedrini M A (2015) 'From theory to policy? Keynes's distinction between "apparatus of thought" and "apparatus of action", with an eye to the European debt crisis', *Challenge*, 58 (6): 509–531.

Chick, V (1983) *Macroeconomics after Keynes*. Cambridge, MA: MIT Press.

Chick, V (2018) 'On the relevance of *The General Theory* at 80: economic change and economic theory', in S Dow, J Jespersen and G Tily (eds), *The General Theory and Keynes for the 21st Century*. Cheltenham: Edward Elgar, pp. 1–15.

Chick, V and Freeman, A (2018) 'The economics of enough: a future for capitalism or a new beginning?' in S Dow, J Jespersen and G Tily (eds), *Money, Method and Contemporary Post-Keynesian Economics*. Cheltenham: Edward Elgar, pp. 148–159.

Davis, J B (1994) *Keynes's Philosophical Development*. Cambridge: Cambridge University Press.

De Cecco, M (1979) 'The origins of the post-war payments system', *Cambridge Journal of Economics*, 3 (1): 49–61.

Dow, S (2016) 'The political economy of monetary reform', *Cambridge Journal of Economics,* 40 (5): 1363–1376.

Dow, S (2017) 'Keynes and Gesell: political and social philosophy, epistemology and monetary reform', *Annals of the Fondazione Luigi Einaudi*, 1 (1): 77–92.

Dow, S (2018) 'Keynes on domestic and international monetary reform', in S Dow, J Jespersen and G Tily (eds), *The General Theory and Keynes for the 21st Century*. Cheltenham: Edward Elgar, pp. 132–144.

Fuller, E W (2019) 'Was Keynes a socialist?', *Cambridge Journal of Economics*, 43: 1653–1682.

Gesell, S (1916) *Die natürliche Wirtschaftsordnung durch Freiland und Freigeld*, Les Hauts Geneveys: Selbstverlag, published in English as *The Natural Economic Order* (trans. P. Pye), 1929.

Guizzo Archela, D C (2016) *Keynes, Keynesian Economics and the Political Economy of Power of the Postwar World*. Federal University of Parana PhD thesis. https://acervodigital.ufpr.br/bitstream/handle/1884/43650/R%20-%20T%20-%20DANIELLE%20CRISTINA%20GUIZZO%20ARCHELA.pdf?sequence=3&isAllowed=y

Keynes, J M (1913 [1978]) *Indian Currency and Finance, Collected Writings*, vol. I. London: Macmillan for the Royal Economic Society.

Keynes, J M (1921) *A Treatise on Probability*. London: Macmillan for the Royal Economic Society.

Keynes, J M (1923 [1971]) *A Tract on Monetary Reform, Collected Writings*, vol. IV. London: Macmillan for the Royal Economic Society.

Keynes, J M (1924a) 'Alfred Marshall, 1842–1924', *Economic Journal*, 34 (135): 311–372.

Keynes, J M (1924b [1981]) 'Does employment need a drastic remedy?' *The Nation and Atheneum* 24 May, in *Activities 1922–1929: The Return to Gold and Industrial Policy. Collected Writings*, vol. XIX. London, Macmillan for the Royal Economic Society, pp. 219–223.

Keynes, J M (1925a [1973]) 'Am I a liberal?' *Nation and Atheneum*, 8 and 15 August, in *Essays in Persuasion, Collected Writings*, vol. IX. London: Macmillan for the Royal Economic Society, pp. 295–306.

Keynes, J M (1925b [1973]) 'A short view of Russia', *Nation and Atheneum* 10, 17 and 25 October, in *Essays in Persuasion, Collected Writings*, vol. IX. London: Macmillan for the Royal Economic Society, pp. 253–271.

Keynes, J M (1926 [1973]) 'Liberalism and labour', in *Essays in Persuasion. Collected Writings*, vol. IX. London: Macmillan for the Royal Economic Society, pp. 307–311.

Keynes, J M (1930) *A Treatise on Money*, vols. 1 and 2. London: Macmillan.

Keynes, J M (1932 [1982]) 'Broadcast on state planning', 14 March, in *Activities 1931–1939. Collected Writings*, vol. XXI. London: Macmillan for the Royal Economic Society, pp. 84–92.

Keynes, J M (1936) *The General Theory of Employment, Interest and Money*. London: Macmillan.

Keynes, J M (1937) 'The general theory of employment', *Quarterly Journal of Economics*, 51: 209–223.

Keynes, J M ([1938] 1973) 'Letter to Harrod', in *The General Theory and After: Part II Defence and Development. Collected Writings*, vol. XIV. London: Macmillan for the Royal Economic Society, pp. 295–297.

Keynes, J M (1942 [1980]) 'Plan for an international currency (or clearing) union', in *Activities 1940–1944: Shaping the Post-War World: The Clearing Union, Collected Writings*, vol. XXV. London: Macmillan for the Royal Economic Society, pp. 108–139.

Keynes, J M (1983) *Economic Articles and Correspondence: Investment and Editorial, Collected Writings*, vol. XII. London: Macmillan for the Royal Economic Society.

Keynes, J N (1891) *The Scope and Method of Political Economy*. New York: Kelley and Millman.

Lawson, T (2003) *Reorienting Economics*. London: Routledge.

Lawson, T and H Pesaran (eds) (1985) *Keynes' Economics: Methodological Issues*. London: Croom Helm.

Meeks, G T (2003) 'Keynes on the rationality of decision procedures under uncertainty: the investment decision', in J Runde and S Mizuhara (eds), *The Philosophy of Keynes's Economics*. London: Routledge, pp. 19–36.

O'Donnell, R M (1989) *Keynes: Philosophy, Economics and Politics*. London: Macmillan.

O'Donnell, R M (1999) 'Keynes's socialism: conception, strategy, and espousal', in P Kriesler and C Sardoni (eds), *Keynes, Post-Keynesianism and Political Economy: Essays in Honour of Geoff Harcourt*, vol. 3. London: Routledge, pp. 149–175.

Rivot, S (2021) 'Reading Keynes's policy papers through the prism of his *Treatise on Probability*: information, expectations, and revision of probabilities in economic policy', *Journal of the History of Economic Thought*, 43 (4): 604–618.

Runde, J (1990) 'Keynesian uncertainty and the weight of arguments', *Economics and Philosophy*, 6: 275–292.

Skidelsky, R (1992) *John Maynard Keynes: The Economist as Saviour 1920–1937.* London: Macmillan.

Skidelsky, R and E Skidelsky (2012) *How Much Is Enough? Money and the Good Life.* New York: Other Press.

12 The Unfinished Revolution in Policy

The Visionary Legacy of Lord Keynes

Atsushi Komine

Introduction: Modern Issues of Economic Policies

Economic policies in the twenty-first century are becoming increasingly complicated, and we are faced with three difficulties that have become more apparent since the late twentieth century. The task of this chapter is to examine relevant answers or lessons by way of wisdom in the history of economic thought: "Can we find out a vision in Lord Keynes that will overcome these difficulties? And, can it be embodied in economic policies?"

The first difficulty is that the rapid pace of financialization and globalization has led to unprecedented inequality not only between the employed and the unemployed but also in asset and income holdings. The second difficulty is the inability to cope with qualitative aspects that emerge on the sides of growing military (or waste) demand and drastic climate change. The third difficulty is related to the potential change in economic structure (i.e., de-industrialization or softening) that may nullify the race to expand GDP.

Until now, "Keynesian policies" and "Keynesianism", as it is commonly understood, have meant supporting economic growth by stimulating countercyclical aggregate demand. With such a common notion, it is almost impossible to solve the aforementioned difficulties. This is because (1) the problem of inequality is not a priority in terms of Keynesian concerns, for example, it can be tackled only when the stimulation of aggregate demand is completed. (2) Keynesian policies that aim to stimulate aggregate demand do not question the content of effective demand and limiting or controlling economic growth. (3) Keynesian economics, which assumes a production structure centred on manufacturing, cannot cope with softening.

This chapter challenges the above notions and suggests the possibility of medium- and long-term economic policies based on Keynes's original vision, even in the difficult circumstances of the twenty-first century.

There are two main areas of novelty in this chapter. First, by dividing Keynes's vision of economic policy into three parts according to time segments, the modernity of his legacy is made clearer. Second, by adopting the perspective of an optimum organization (semi-autonomous bodies) best suited to his vision, we have bridged Keynes's vision with twenty-first-century debates that are oriented towards public purpose and economic efficiency.

DOI: 10.4324/9781003228097-12

A Vision of the Short Run

The first criticism of Keynesian policies is that we still cannot solve the two classical contradictions of capitalism[1] (unemployment and inequality, CW vol. 7: 372). Let us find a clue to the solution to this criticism, mainly by examining Keynes's short-term vision.

Keynes's short-term vision has been most accepted in current economic theory and policy as common knowledge. As numerous papers have pointed out, Keynes's enthusiastic advocacy, though poorly reasoned (Harrod 1951: 350), of public investment can be traced back to May 1924 (CW vol. 19: 219). Over the long period that followed, even after the publication of *The General Theory*, Keynes continued to search for a relevant theory justifying his intuition that aggregate demand was the key to sustaining the economy. On the one hand, this intuition, accompanied by the construction of macroeconomics and Keynesian policies, seemed to dominate the world after World War II. However, this dominance inevitably led to a simplification of his visions and the formation of a conventional notion: that Keynesian economics is nothing more than a model for the discretionary quantitative stimulation of aggregate demand.

For such naïve Keynesianism to still be useful, at least two conditions would need to be met. The first is the historical conditions under which aggregate demand growth and less income inequality are compatible. Second, there are regional and timing conditions that still make quantitative expansion necessary to a considerable extent.

First, as Kuznets (1955: 4) pointed out and Piketty (2014) reassessed from a long-term perspective, growth and equality were compatible (only) in the golden age of capitalism. Figure 12.1 shows the share of the top 10% of income earners in four countries from 1920 to 2020. This figure depicts that with the outbreak of World War II, equalization of incomes progressed rapidly and stably both in Britain and the United States, for about 30 years after the war. However, since the 1980s, inequality has increased in the UK, the United States, and Japan, while Greece is the only country with a different trend. After the Lehman shock in around 2007, two countries (the United States and Japan) are stable at a high level while the other two (the UK and Greece) are in an up-and-down motion. Considering the data, it is necessary to determine what conditions have been necessary over the past 30 years or so for quantitative expansion to have a virtuous cycle consequence. One of the conditions was that Keynes's economic policy should be supported by a broader social policy, the formation of a welfare state.

Historically, J. M. Keynes and W. H. Beveridge both realized that their approaches in theory and policy were compatible with each other: the policy of full employment and the system of social security. Moreover, Keynes recognized that the two pillars were synergistic, as he put it in 1943:

> Nothing but a major reversal of fortune which would upset a great deal more than the Beveridge Plan can prevent our national income from increasing several times as fast as our obligations under the Plan.
>
> (CW vol. 27: 259–260)

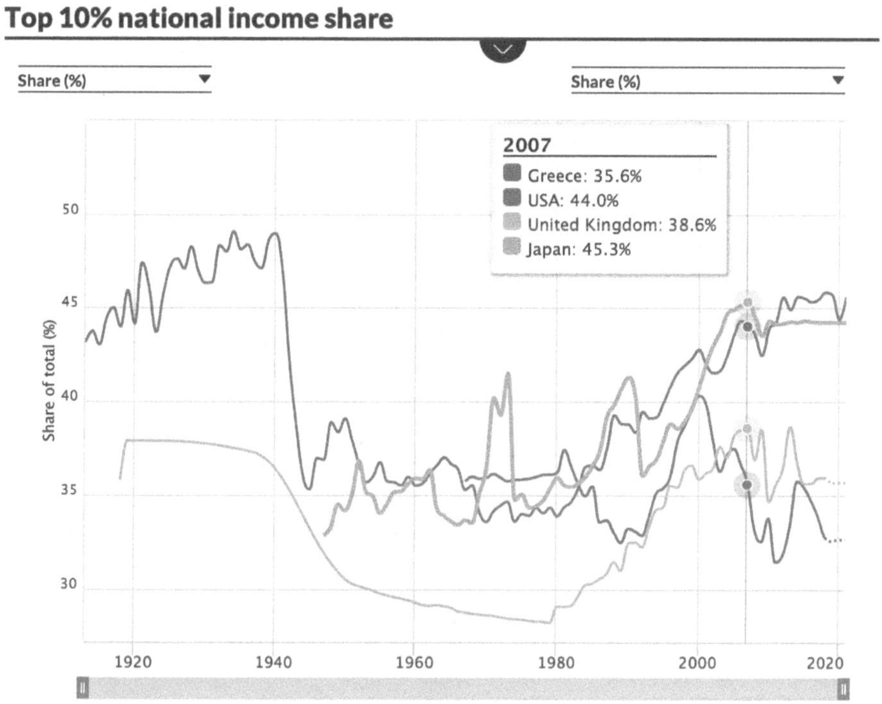

Figure 12.1 Top 10% National Income Share.[2]

He therefore praised the Beveridge scheme in March 1942 as follows:

> Meanwhile, let me say that I have read your Memoranda, which leave me in a state of wild enthusiasm for your general scheme. I think it a vast constructive reform of real importance and relieved to find that it is so financially possible.
>
> (CW vol. 27: 204)

He commented in October 1942 as follows:

> From what I have seen, it looks to me that the document is a very fine one and will impress public opinion as at the same time moderate and far-reaching and argued in the most convincing and striking manner.
>
> (CW vol. 27: 252)

Beveridge's social security scheme, based on a universal social insurance, guarantees that all citizens have a national minimum, which is translated into a certain amount of income. Then, the national minimum sustains the aggregate demand. In a context where infrastructure—electricity, gas, sewerage, railways, and airports, among others—was scarce and many workers were needed to build it, the policy of full employment and the social security system created a virtuous circle of growth and equality.

Second, fiscal stimulus can be expected to increase employment in a classic way in both developing and advanced countries. In many areas such as Africa, Asia, and Latin America, where manufacturing is underdeveloped, social infrastructure is still necessary. Therefore, we should fully consider the above-mentioned historical conditions. Moreover, regardless of regions including G20 countries, in situations such as the Lehman and Corona shocks, emergency measures to expand aggregate demand are still effective. Figure 12.2 shows that advanced countries *did* in general *respond* to the COVID-19 crisis by implementing fiscal expansions of approximately 11%, on average, of each country's GDP. This fact reveals that many leaders of the world came to re-recognize the necessity of Keynesian policy. Skidelsky (2021) calls this change "the silent revolution in economic policy" and claims that "any post-pandemic recovery policy should aim to secure the economy's sustainability, not just its cyclical stability".

In short, Keynes's short-term vision is still relevant[4] to emergency or developing areas if we deliberate on the historical conditions that made desirable growth possible after WWII. Considering the historical lessons, there is little

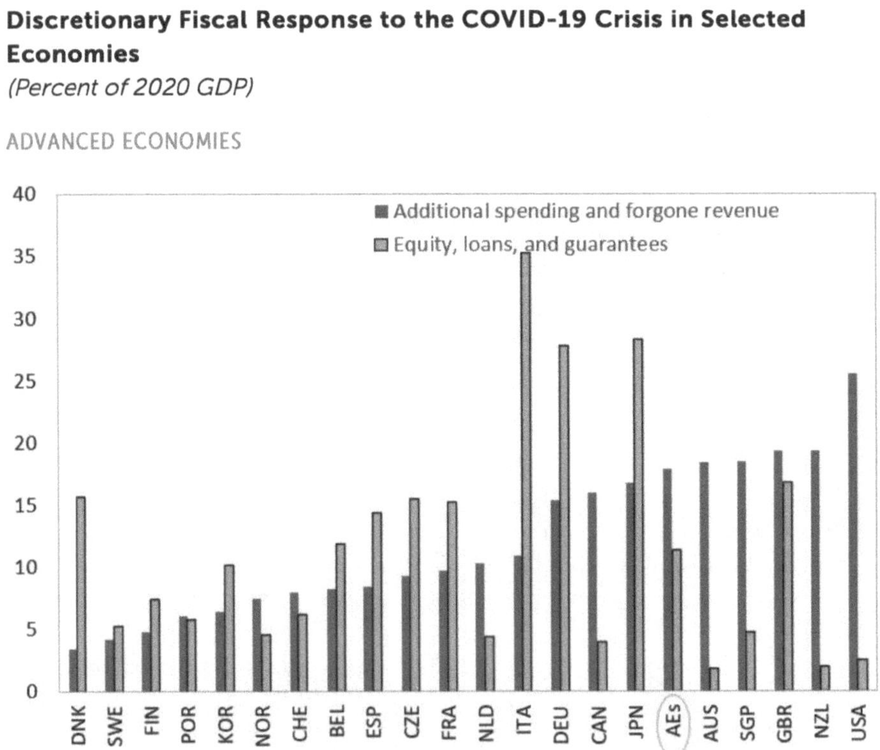

Figure 12.2 Fiscal Response to the COVID-19 Crisis.[3]

need to change peoples' recognition or brand-new institutions; a mere decision to expand public spending is needed.

A Vision of the Middle Run

The second criticism of the so-called Keynesian policy is that we can rarely cope with the limitation of naïve quantitative expansionism, which can be divided into two groups. One is a qualitative aspect of the content in aggregate demand. The other is the destructive aspect of economic growth.

Indeed, Keynes surely admits that wholly wasteful expenditure is sometimes effective, such as pyramid-building, reconstruction after earthquakes, even wars, and burying bottles with banknotes and digging the notes up again. However, it should be merely rhetoric and wasteful forms "would be better than nothing" (CW vol. 7: 129). The most conspicuous example of waste expenditure is the military one. In reality, as Atesoglu (2002: 58) concludes, a 4% rise in real military spending would lead to no less than a 2% rise in aggregate real output in the United States. Although, for measurement reasons, Atesoglu (2009: 26) reserves a definitive conclusion about the effect of military spending on GDP, Cypher (2015: 473) judges that "military Keynesianism can be understood as a particularistic attribute of U.S. Capitalism over a sustained time period".

Following Keynes's discourse to judge whether he really accepted wasteful expenditure, especially in the military after the announcement of the rearmament programme in March 1935, Britain ran headlong into rearmament. Two of Keynes's essays (*Economic Journal* and *Listener*), just before the outbreak of WWII, are important to note here:

> If only we could tackle the problems of peace with the same energy and whole-heartedness as we tackle those of war! … Nevertheless, we are at this moment allowing war expenditure for defence to help solve our problem of unemployment as a by-product of such spending, whereas if disarmament had prevailed we might have allowed a serious recession to have developed by now before introducing loan expenditure on a comparable scale for the productive works of peace.
>
> (CW vol. 21: 463)

> … measures useful for defence may eventually evolve into measures of permanent usefulness in peace.
>
> (CW vol. 21: 470)

Keynes estimated that £150 million of arms spending would create 300,000 jobs directly and 500,000 jobs indirectly in all. The conclusions are as follows.

> … the end of abnormal unemployment is in sight. … if expenditure on armaments really does cure unemployment, I predict that we shall never go back all the way to the old state of affairs. If we can cure

> unemployment for the *wasted* purposes of armaments, we can cure it for the *productive* purposes of peace. Good may come out of evil.
>
> (CW vol. 21: 532; emphasis added)

This clarifies Keynes's position. Even the worst form of waste, namely armaments, can be a measure against unemployment. However, fiscal spending for peaceful purposes is far more desirable because it provides constructive and durable materials. Nothing is the worst, waste spending is better, and peaceful spending is the best. Clearly, Keynes is deeply concerned about the qualitative aspects of fiscal expenditure. Following Keynes's suggestion, what is our beneficial public investment?

This question brings us to the second group of the matter, the 'Limits to Growth' question. Historically, there have been three booms of this issue. First, J. S. Mill[5] and W. S. Jevons[6] argued for the stationary state and coal exhaustion, respectively, in the second half of the nineteenth century. Second, the Report of the Club of Rome became well known even to scholars and politicians, who attempted to struggle to find out the right way under the oil shock in the early 1970s. The report concludes that "the limits to growth on this planet will be reached sometime within the next one hundred years", with "a rather sudden and uncontrollable decline in both population and industrial capacity" (Meadows *et al.* 1972: 23). Third, IPCC (The Intergovernmental Panel on Climate Change) concludes in 2021 that "[g]lobal warming of 1.5°C and 2°C will be exceeded during the 21st century unless deep reductions in carbon dioxide (CO2) and other greenhouse gas emissions occur in the coming decades".[7]

If we stay true to Keynes's philosophy of qualitative improvement, the Green New Deal can be one of the answers. In contrast to previous pessimistic views, as typical of the Report of the Club of Rome, that the environment and the economy were not compatible, recent optimistic views claim that economic growth is possible while reducing the use of natural resources and greenhouse gas emissions (Mastini *et al.* 2021: 1). This view, called Green New Deal, is based on the following three suppositions: the government would enact appropriate institutions and laws so that social costs[8] can be properly measured; the private sector can internalize those costs with little negotiation costs (as A. C. Pigou and R. Coase argued); and the environment and growth can be decoupled as human ingenuity can "overcome all potential limitations to economic growth" (Haberl *et al.* 2020: 31).

After the COVID-19 crisis began, not only compatibility between the economy and the environment but also an anti-inequality agenda became increasingly significant (Galvin & Healy 2020: 6). Green New Deal advocates a plan to coordinate a large-scale overhaul of the energy system, the plan which needs "transforming production, distribution and consumption across the economy" (Mazzucato 2021: 138). The government must be an entity that takes risks and supports long-term financing so that it can attract other private investors. Specifically, the following five areas should be desirable for investment, mainly because long-term multipliers of climate-positive policies are high: clean physical infrastructure investment (renewable energy and energy efficiency), building efficiency retrofits, investment in education, natural capital investment, and clean R&D investment (Hepburn *et al.* 2020: S374–S375).

In short, Keynes's middle-term vision on the quality of fiscal expenditure is also relevant, under the assumption that economic growth can overcome environmental limitations by promoting green investment. We must change our recognition dramatically, while the framework of capitalism *per se* is not so much to be changed. This is because it remains within the traditional framework of government correction of market failures. However, it takes more time than simple expansions of public spending.

A Next Capitalism and Evolved Visions

The third criticism of the simplified Keynesian policy is that we cannot catch up with the two radical changes in economic structure, i.e., deindustrialization (or softening) and degrowth (post-growth). These changes have been discussed in numerous studies.

We have three examples regarding the former change. First, Fritz Machlup defined "producing knowledge" broadly, that is, not only as discovering and inventing but also as disseminating and communicating (Machlup 1962: 7). He estimated that the number of people engaged in knowledge-producing industries had increased dramatically from 10.7% to 31.6% in about 60 years since 1900 (Machlup 1962: 386). Second, Daniel Bell examined the concept of "the post-industrial society". The economic sector has changed from a goods-producing to a service economy, and occupational distribution was of pre-eminence in the professional and technical classes (Bell 1973: 14). He also pointed out that the post-industrial society brings "the scientist or economist more directly into the political process" (Bell 1973: 43) and that knowledge and information are strategic resources of social change. The third illustration is that of Peter F. Drucker. He advocated for a "post-capitalist society", where knowledge, as a resource and a utility and a public good, becomes "the sole factor of production, sidelining both capital and labor" (Drucker 1993: 20). He also pointed out that the market superiority is derived from its organization of economic activity around information (Drucker 1993: 181). What all three of them have in common is the point that intangible services such as knowledge and information will become the core of the economy through economic softening and structural change.

More recently, Jeremy Rifkin has been discussing the impact of a digitalized society—in other words, the arrival of a society with zero marginal cost. He argues that a new regime of collaborative commons is replacing market capitalism (Rifkin 2014: 1). The former is based on collaborative interests, a deep desire to share, open-source innovation, transparency, and the search for community, while the latter is based on self-interest, material gain, property rights, caveat emptor, and the search for autonomy (Rifkin 2014: 22). The progress of digitization (easier reproduction) drastically reduces the marginal cost to almost zero, and the price of goods and services become almost free. Therefore, the source of profit, the keystone of capitalism, disappears (Rifkin 2014: 85). In such a society, not only aggregate demand policies, which emphasize the spillover effects of manufactured goods but also usual economic trends will be undermined.

Another term that indicates a new economy is "the intangible economy" by Jonathan Haskel and Stian Westlake (2018). They examine the new form of capitalism by focusing on intangible investment: "software, R&D, design, artistic originals, market research, training, and new business processes" (Haskel & Westlake 2018: 239). Figure 12.3 shows how rapidly the term "intangible" has become popular among academics in the past two decades. There are two major differences between a tangible-rich economy and an intangible-rich economy. First, these intangible assets are missing from the GDP measurement. Without a true picture of the economy, appropriate policies cannot be initiated. Second, the nature of intangible-rich capitalism differs from traditional capitalism in four ways: i.e., 4S (Haskel & Westlake 2018: 88). (i) Sunk Cost: intangible assets cannot be sold to recoup the costs incurred to date. They are difficult to resell because of the lack of second-hand markets. (ii) Spillovers: they generate high spillovers. The ideas created by R&D are non-rival. Using a piece of knowledge does not prevent the other from using it. (iii) Scalability: a new idea by someone can be used again and again by others at almost no cost. (iv) Synergy: ideas go well together with other ideas. Not by protecting individual assets, powerful companies have strong incentives to build synergistic clusters of investments. Haskel and Westlake (2018: 240) warn that an intangible-rich economy, without any proper policies, tends to bring secular stagnation, inequality, the lack of adequate financing, and firms that become more authoritarian. Policymakers must, therefore, have initiatives to facilitate knowledge infrastructure, including education, academic activities, and Internet Technology. Moreover, physical materials or tangible types of infrastructure are necessary.[9] For instance, efficient transportation, affordable housing and working spaces, and urban development are targets for public spending. Meeting and socializing in a certain area are beneficial for creating new ideas.

In the face of the above-mentioned new forms of capitalism, numerous scholars and journalists have begun calling for its radical transformation. Let us cite just three examples.[11]

First, Nathan Schneider (2018) has high hopes for the "cooperative enterprise". This idea is historically based on the traditional principles of the cooperative society, namely, democratic participation and control in particular. However, it evolves by adding a new element, a platform. A platform is a standard environment that serves as a common foundation for providing, customizing, and operating a wide range of services, systems, and software. Platforms "are multi-sided markets that connect people" (Schneider

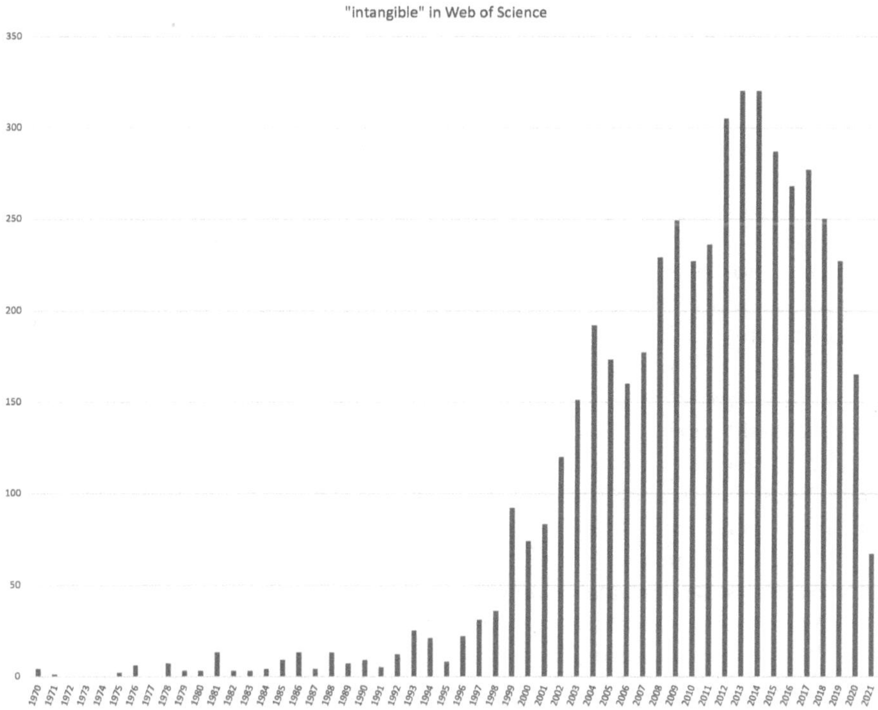

Figure 12.3 "Intangible" in Web of Science.[10]

2018: 138). As is typical of Big Tech, or the Big Five (Google, Apple, Face-Book, Amazon, and Microsoft), recent platforms, becoming dominant in the worldwide economy, appear to be neutral and blank-slate, reaping both fees from customers' transactions and indispensable information from the data of their use. Schneider (2018: 143) warns that these dominant platforms lack democratic governance and ownership, and he advocates a hybrid of democratic cooperation and transparent and innovative platforms. If capitalism is merely a system in which the priority is the pursuit of profit for fickle speculators, the future is dark. If it means "freely associating in the economy, or ingenuity and innovation, or … price-based reasoning" (Schneider 2018: 17), the future is bright, because the above-mentioned hybrid would be feasible.

Second, Mariana Mazzucato (2021) envisions a more ambitious society: a "mission-oriented" economy. In such an economy, public purpose, not financial gain, will be at the centre of policy and business activities. Public purpose is what defines the mission and guides how the public and private sectors work together to create values (Mazzucato 2021: 169). There are four flaws in capitalism (Mazzucato 2021: 15). (i) Financialization of business: most finance goes back into finance, insurance, and real estate without producing any tangible goods. This leads to economic disparities between financial and non-financial sectors. (ii) Businesses preoccupied with quarterly returns: a form of capitalism aims at maximizing returns to shareholders, not all stakeholders. (iii) Climate emergency: global warming is increasing because the industry is too carbon-dependent and fossil fuels still make up most energy resources. (iv) Slow or absent governments: governments are only fixing market failures passively, rather than actively playing a leading role in the market (Mazzucato 2021: 165). Mazzucato (2021: 192) expresses her approval of Keynes's long-term vision of investment and concludes that a mission should be set, and materialized as a concrete public purpose. The purpose should be executed by the government to create a collective value and shape the market by guaranteeing good jobs and sharing key resources, including data (Mazzucato 2021: 167).

Third, Kohei Saito (2017, 2021) provides a more radical criticism of modern capitalism from the Marxist standpoint. He named the Green New Deal as Climate Keynesianism and pointed out its impossibility. In other words, even if relative decoupling is possible in one sector, as consumption will expand in other sectors, the total effect of reducing carbon dioxide emissions will be offset. Ultimately, absolute decoupling is impossible. The Green New Deal cannot solve climate change because it remains within the framework of capitalism and cannot escape the curse of economic growth. Based on Marx's own eco-socialism (Saito 2017), he argues that capitalism is constantly developing new markets through repeated value multiplication and capital accumulation: capitalism is a device for creating artificial scarcity (Saito 2021: 94). Saito pins his hopes on the 'common' to dissipate this fundamental contradiction. The common is wealth, which should be equally shared and properly managed by people. It is "the negation of endless economic growth" (Saito 2021: 111). Instead of artificial scarcity, the "radical abundance" of the common wealth would be the final target of eco-socialism. Without waste production, a more equal redistribution would restore decent life, by way of some policies in "the common", one of which is shortening the working hours (Saito 2021: 110).

A Vision of the Long Run

To what extent can Keynes's long-term vision be helpful in contemplating these new perspectives of the world? His vision incorporates "new ideas for effecting the transition from the economic anarchy of the individualistic capitalism .... towards a regime which will deliberately aim at controlling and directing economic forces in the interest of *social justice* and *social stability*" (CW vol. 19: 439; emphasis added). This Regime should be called an "ideal social republic of the future" (CW vol. 21: 241).

Numerous papers have been published on Keynes's long-term policies,[12] the core vision of which is "the socialisation of investment" (CW vol. 7: 378). Kregel (1985: 33) argues that his priority is the stabilization of investment, by utilizing the capital budget. Davis (1992: 153) approaches it from the philosophical point of view and considers reconciling "being good", envisioning an ideal, with "doing good", reforming actual economic and social situations. Bateman (1994: 106) also argues that convention is a key to understanding Keynes's concept of the socialization of investment. Pollin (1997) points out that two concepts, the socialization of investment and euthanasia of the rentier, are essential in considering the relevance of Keynes's policy. Seccareccia (2011) advocates the return of long-term vision of Keynes after the financial crisis of 2007/2008. Crotty (2019: 6) regards Keynes as a liberal socialist judging from his long-term policy on investment, while Konzelmann *et al.* (2021: 609) oppose this label because Keynes's view of capitalism was dynamic and evolutionary, and a specific label would not be appropriate.

Based on Komine (2014: Chapter 7), Keynes's long-term vision of capitalism can be summarized as follows: his concern is to reconcile private motives (incentive, ingenuity, entrepreneurship, etc.) with public purposes (liberty, fairness, justice, stability, etc.). Joining the Liberal Party activities, Keynes began to express his notion of ideal governance of public and private sectors in the middle of the 1920s. There are four elements. (i) Optimum organizations must have "immense prestige and historical traditions" (CW vol. 19: 347), like the Bank of England and the Universities of Cambridge and Oxford. (ii) They must be "semi-independent corporation[s]" (CW vol. 19: 347), or "semi-autonomous bodies" (CW vol. 9: 288). To some limited extent, they are autonomous, but ultimately, they are democratic organizations limited by Parliament and public opinion. (iii) The board members of the organizations should be "chosen solely by their business capacity" and "adequately remunerated" (CW vol. 19: 696). (iv) "Directive intelligence" is vital; the collection and dissemination "on a great sale of data relating to the business situation" (CW vol. 9: 292) are indispensable, including audits and statistical research.

Keynes pointed out the historical phenomenon that many big businesses and large organizations have been "socialized" without people realizing it. In fact, investments by public or quasi-public organizations in 1930 were about seven times larger than those in 1914 (CW vol. 21: 135). He recognized in 1927 that "two-thirds of the typical large-scale enterprise of this country had already been removed … out of the category of pure private enterprise" (CW vol. 19: 696). The total value was equivalent to £3,500 million.[13] The semi-public areas include docks and harbours, water boards, Ecclesiastical Commissioners, colleges, schools, and universities, Charity Commissioners, building societies, cooperative societies, and railway concerns. Keynes points out that large-scale enterprises had transformed into virtually public or semi-public concerns. For him, the real problem is not a reduction of the existing principle of public concerns, but "a deliberate and persevering attempt to discover how to run the best enterprises … efficiently and to the public advantage" (CW vol. 19: 696). In other words, the key to the next economy is a semi-autonomous body that connects efficient management with public purposes.

A National Investment Board embodies the concept of a semi-autonomous body. Keynes first advocated this concept in *Britain's Industrial Future* (1928), the report of the Liberal Party's Enquiry, and again took it up in the Final Report (1931) of the Macmillan Committee. When the Labour Party dealt with this concept, in 1932 he welcomed "warmly the acceptance of the principles of setting up a National Investment Board" (CW vol. 21: 133). Later, in 1939 and 1945, he continued to be interested in this concept. A National Investment Board is an official body that matches the supply and demand for large-scale investments while stabilizing prices and exchange rates. The Board should be "self-conscious and publicly explicit" (CW vol. 27: 408), and its "task is attacked with knowledge and authority" (CW vol. 21: 136–137). However, even such an eminent organization cannot exist on its own. Sometimes they must cede authority and work "in close collaboration with" (CW vol. 21: 591) other similar (competing or conflicting) departments.

Keynes strongly indicated the fact that the "world is *not* so governed from above that private and social interest always coincide" (CW vol. 9: 287–288, emphasis in original) in modern capitalism. Although he evolved his ideas based on the above recognition in the tradition of the Cambridge School of Economics, he at some point became dissatisfied with this tradition. The point should be regarded as the beginning of the Keynesian Revolution. There are three stages of evolution and revolution, relating to his vision of influential entities that correct failures of market forces.

The first step is his careful consideration to Alfred Marshall's mission: the British industry must be led by honourable and capable industrial leaders, the "captains of industry". They should acquire a "chivalrous desire to master difficulties and obtain recognized leadership" (Pigou ed. 1925: 331). "Chivalry in business includes public spirit. ... It includes a scorn for cheap victories, and a delight in succouring those who need a helping hand" (Pigou ed. 1925: 330). Marshall envisioned competent entrepreneurs facing difficulties in capitalism. They have outstanding personal characteristics (economic chivalry). Keynes rejected this type of "master-individualist": "Yet, this one, in his turn, is becoming *a tarnished idol*" (CW vol. 9: 287; emphasis added). The modern industry grew so huge that even capable entrepreneurs could not reconcile private and public interests.

The second step is his criticism to the traditional legacy of the Cambridge School: hopes for cooperative bodies. As the master Marshall was, several members of that School, such as C. R. Fay, D. H. MacGregor, and A. C. Pigou, were all concerned with cooperative movement and actual organizations. Among others, D. H. Robertson developed the theory of an optimum organization to solve essential flaws in modern capitalism. He named the most outstanding characteristic "Capitalism's Golden Rule", which means "the proposition that where the risk lies, there the control lies also" (Robertson 1923: 89). The striking phenomenon in modern capitalism is the imbalanced distribution of risks and controls. While board members of big businesses take risks, control the company, and receive remuneration, shareholders only take risks with little control. The most serious problem is that workers bear the huge risk of wage cuts and unemployment, yet they do not participate in corporate governance in any way. One of the best solutions is "Joint Control" between employers and employees (Robertson 1923: 153). This style guarantees the balance of economic efficiency (proper incentives and burden of risks) and democratic control of industry.

Keynes, however, also rejected this type of solution and moved on to the third step. He classified three types of societies: cooperative (or real-wage), neutral, and entrepreneurial (or money-wage). In the cooperative economy, "it is easy to conceive of a community in which the factors of production are rewarded by dividing up in agreed proportions the actual output of their co-operative efforts" (CW vol. 29: 77). In this economy, Say's Law always holds true, and the gap between income earned in current production and income spent on current consumption is zero in the long run. It is calculated in real terms, and conflicts between workers and capitalists are negligible. A cooperative society automatically stabilizes prices, the volume of employment, and real wages.

Instead, Keynes introduced the leadership role of the state (which was absent in the first and second steps) and envisioned a network of multiple agents and semi-autonomous bodies, consisting of genuine entrepreneurs, statesmen with a long-term perspective, impartial civil officers, and economic advisers obtaining special knowledge and wisdom (Komine 2014: 138). This network is not merely a sum of cooperatives, but an active entity in which heterogeneous organizations develop in a zigzag fashion, keeping each other in check. Keynes once called such an entity "organic unity",[14] "discreteness", or "discontinuity" (CW vol. 10: 262). This is a phenomenon in which the whole is not the sum of its parts, in which comparisons of quantities are not useful as they are, and in which small changes can have large effects.

Here, Keynes was concerned with how public purpose-bearing organizations should be governed by evolving capitalism. Rather than the specific policies he described, his thinking style is more instructive. We should, and can, derive significant lessons from his words. In this sense, the Keynesian Revolution is not over, but a continuous event.

In short, Keynes's long-term vision is still relevant, if we interpret it as a treasury from which we extract contemporary lessons as to how to live decent lives economically, politically, and socially. The treasury is more than just a recommendation of mere expansionary public works.

Concluding Remarks

In his Moscow lecture of 1925, Keynes simplified J. R. Commons's argument and classified the development of capitalism into three stages (CW vol. 19: 438–439). First, in the age of scarcity, supply shortages were the norm, so quotas by feudal powers were the best solution. Second, in the era of abundance, supply capacity increased and, conversely, insufficient demand became the norm. In this world, private transactions became dominant and individual liberty was maximized. However, according to Keynes, even as of 1925, we are moving into the third stage, the age of stability. In this world, individual liberty is being diminished by economic coercion through secret or open collective action by associations, cooperatives, trade unions, and other collective movements of manufacturers, merchants, workers, farmers, and bankers. Individual liberty is limited by the collective action of voluntary associations.

Capitalism today should be gradually moving towards an era of stability, with a spotty mixture of abundance and stability. In an era of abundance, a carefully considered quantitative expansion will be the solution. This would correspond to Keynes's vision of the short and medium term. There will be a time when the entire world will have to decide immediately on a policy of emergency expansion of aggregate demand. Or, in the case of developing countries, there will be a need to ensure a minimum level of demand on a permanent basis. In times of stability, however, we need to start by questioning the very purpose and means of economic policy in an appropriate organization. In the modern era, we must take into account the new structural changes of softening and degrowth (which were absent in Keynes's time). Keynes's long-term vision, in which individual ingenuity is exercised in a heterogeneous organization to make a full and decent life possible, may be helpful in this regard.

Keynes expressed his straightforward feelings of an ideal society once in 1926; "The political problem of mankind is to combine three things: economic efficiency, social justice, and individual liberty" (CW vol. 9: 311). When Keynes used the term "socialised", or "socialisation of investment", he must have had the above three phases in mind. In other words, while standing on the foundation of individual liberty, all economic, social, and political aspects must be balanced for the sake of the public good. We have also a maxim from Keynes: "[Economists] must study the present in the light of the past for the purposes of the future. No part of man's nature or his institutions must lie entirely outside his regard" (CW vol. 10: 173–174).[15]

We are facing so many difficulties. Even in these times, the discipline of the history of economic thought works to settle original words of prominent thinkers and ordinary persons as well and to connect prevailing ideas in an ordinary world with specialized knowledge. Finally, we should remember the following optimistic words of Keynes: "when we are ready for reforms, opinion will be found to have hardened a good deal in this direction" (CW vol. 21: 590–591).

Notes

1 Capitalism here is defined as a highly evolved form of the market economy, multiplying capital by itself with money and labour having peculiar characteristics.
2 World Inequality Database, Top 10% national income share (URL: https://wid.world, Access: 27 September 2022).

3 IMF, Fiscal Monitor Database of Country Fiscal Measures in Response to the COVID-19 Pandemic, October 2021 (URL: https://www.project-syndicate.org/commentary/covid19-economic-recovery-plans-fiscal-policy-by-robert-skidelsky-2021-02, Access: 21 December 2021).
4 If we take into account Keynes's long-term vision of 'euthanasia of the rentier', we can also address inequality in income and assets.
5 "[E]very flowery waste or natural pasture ploughed up, all quadrupeds or birds … exterminated …, every hedgerow or superfluous tree rooted out …" (Mill 1848: Book IV, Chapter VI).
6 "[C]oal is almost the sole necessary basis of our material Power, … which gives efficiency to our moral and intellectual capabilities" (Jevons 1865: ix).
7 IPCC, the Sixth Assessment Report, 9 August 2021 (URL: https://www.ipcc.ch/report/ar6/wg1/downloads/report/IPCC_AR6_WGI_Headline_Statements.pdf, *Access*: 21 December 2021).
8 Nordhaus (2017: 1518) describes that the social cost of carbon (SCC) is the most important single economic concept in the economics of climate change. This is the economic cost caused by an additional ton of carbon dioxide emissions or its equivalent.
9 Haskel and Westlake (2018: 155) also point out infrastructure that is itself intangible, like institutions, rules, and information. Moreover, trust and social capital which means "the strength, number, and quality of the relationships among people in a society" are important.
10 Web of Science amounts of papers whose title includes 'intangible' in 5,000 scientific papers from 1911 to 2021 (URL: https://www.webofscience.com/wos/woscc/basic-search, Access: 27 December 2021).
11 A fourth example is Raghuram Rajan's theory of 'the third pillar'. He compares the state (the first pillar) to Leviathan and big business (the second pillar) to Behemoth. He argues that since "we are predisposed to be social" (Rajan 2019: 23), our solutions are "to be found in bringing dysfunctional communities [the third pillar] back to health" (Rajan 2019: 3) and in restoring the imbalance in these three pillars.
12 Fitzgibbons (1988: 174), who connected Keynes's long-term ideal with his philosophical roots, concluded that "Keynes rejected Plato's authoritarian politics, but he accepted Plato's political ideal".
13 Rifkin (2019: Chapter 5) points out that global (public and private) pension funds are the largest pool of investment capital. According to Global Pension Assets Study, pension assets in the world are 52,522 billion dollars in 2021. If we could control these assets, Keynes's vision becomes more realistic. https://www.thinkingaheadinstitute.org/research-papers/global-pension-assets-study-2021/ (Access: 14 February 2022).
14 As for this term being deeply involved in Keynes's understanding and diagnosis of capitalism, see Winslow (2021).
15 We already know that Keynes' choice of pronouns is inappropriate and that economists, or whoever, are not confined to gender.

Bibliography

The Collected Writings of John Maynard Keynes, London: Macmillan (St Martin's Press for the Royal Economic Society), 1971–1983 [CW].
vol. 7, *The General Theory of Employment Interest and Money*, 1973.
vol. 9, *Essays in Persuasion*, 1972.
vol. 10, *Essays in Biography*, 1972.
vol. 14, *The General Theory and After: Part II, Defence and Development*, 1971.

vol. 19, *Activities 1922–1929: The Return to Gold and Industrial Policy*, 1981.
vol. 21, *Activities 1931–1939: World Crises and Policies in Britain and America*, 1982.
vol. 27, *Activities 1940–1946: Shaping the Post-war World, Employment and Commodities*, 1980.
vol. 29, *The General Theory and After: A Supplement*, 1979.

Atesoglu, H. S. (2002) "Defense Spending Promotes Aggregate Output in the United States: Evidence form Cointegration Analysis", *Defense and Peace Economics*, 13(1): 55–60, DOI: 10.1080/10242690210963

Atesoglu, H. S. (2009) "Defense Spending and Aggregate Output in the United States", *Defense and Peace Economics*, 20(1): 21–26, DOI: 10.1080/10242690701775533

Bateman, R. W. (1994) "Rethinking the Keynesian Revolution", in J. B. Davis (ed.) *The State of Interpretation of Keynes*, New York: Springer Science + Business Media, 103–122.

Bell, D. (1973) *The Coming of Post-Industrial Society: A Venture in Social Forecasting*, New York: Basic Books.

Crotty, J. (2019) *Keynes against Capitalism: His Economic Case for Liberal Socialism*, London and New York: Routledge.

Cypher, J. M. (2015) "The Origins and Evolution of Military Keynesianism in the United States", *Journal of Post Keynesian Economics*, 38(3): 449–476, DOI: 10.1080/01603477.2015. 1076704

Davis, J. B. (1992) "Keynes on the Socialization of Investment", *International Journal of Social Economics*, 19(10/11/12): 150–163. DOI: 10.1108/EUM0000000000509

Drucker, P. F. (1993) *Post-Capitalist Society*, New York: HarperBusiness.

Fitzgibbons, A. (1988) *Keynes's Vision: A New Political Economy*, Oxford: Clarendon Press.

Galvin, R. and N. Healy, (2020) "The Green New Deal in the United States: What It Is and How to Pay for It", *Energy Research and Social Science*, 67: 1–9.

Haberl, H. *et al.* (2020) "A Systematic Review of the Evidence on Decoupling of GDP, Resource Use and GHG Emissions, Part II: Synthesizing the Insights", *Environmental Research Letters*, 15(6): 065003: 1–42, DOI: 10.1088/1748–9326/ab842

Harrod, R. F. (1951) *The Life of John Maynard Keynes*, London: Macmillan & Co. Ltd.

Haskel, J. and S. Westlake (2018) *Capitalism without Capital: The Rise of the Intangible Economy*, Princeton, NJ and Oxford: Princeton University Press.

Hepburn, C., B. O'Callaghan, N. Stern, J. Stiglitz, and D. Zenghelis (2020) "Will COVID-19 Fiscal Recovery Packages Accelerate or Retard Progress on Climate Change?" *Oxford Review of Economic Policy*, 36(Supplement_1): S359–S381.

Jevons, W. S. (1865) *The Coal Question: An Inquiry Concerning the Progress of the Nation, and the Probable Exhaustion of Our Coal-Mines*, London and Cambridge: Macmillan and Co.

Komine, A. (2014) *Keynes and His Contemporaries: Tradition and Enterprise in the Cambridge School of Economics*, London and New York: Routledge.

Konzelmann, S. J., V. Chick, and M. Fovargue-Davies (2021) "Keynes, Capitalism and Public Purpose", *Cambridge Journal of Economics*, 45(3): 591–612, DOI: 10.1093/cje/beab002

Kregel, J. A. (1985) "Budget Deficits, Stabilisation Policy and Liquidity Preference: Keynes's Post-War Policy Proposals", in Fausto Vicarelli (ed.) *Keynes's Relevance Today*, London: Macmillan, 28–50.

Kuznets, S. (1955) "Economic Growth and Income Inequality", *American Economic Review*, 45(1): 1–28.

Machlup, F. (1962) *The Production and Distribution of Knowledge in the United States*, Princeton, NJ: Princeton University Press.

Mastini, R., G. Kallis, and J. Hickel (2021) "A Green New Deal without Growth?" *Ecological Economics*, 179: 1–9. DOI: 10.1016/j.ecolecon.2020.106832

Mazzucato, M. (2021) *Mission Economy: A Moonshot Guide to Changing Capitalism*, with an Afterword, London: Penguin Books.

Meadows, D. H., D. L. Meadows, J. Randers, and W. W. Behrens III (1972) *The Limits to Growth: A Report for THE CLUB OF ROME's Project on the Predicament of Mankind*, New York: Universe Books.

Mill, J. S. (1848) *Principles of Political Economy with Some of Their Applications to Social Philosophy*, London: John W. Parker.

Nordhaus, W. D. (2017) "Revisiting the Social Cost of Carbon", *Proceedings of the National Academy of Sciences of the United States of America*, 114(7): 1518–1523, DOI: 10.1073/ pnas.1609244114.

Pigou, A. C. ed. (1925) *Memorials of Alfred Marshall*, London: Macmillan.

Piketty, T. (2014) *Capital in the Twenty-first Century*, translated by A. Goldhammer, Cambridge, MA: Belknap Press of Harvard University Press.

Pollin, R. (1997) "'Socialization of Investment' and 'Euthanasia of the Rentier': The Relevance of Keynesian Policy Ideas for the Contemporary US Economy", in Arestis, P. and Sawyer, M. (eds.) *The Relevance of Keynesian Economic Policies Today*, London: Macmillan: 57–77.

Rajan, R. (2019) *The Third Pillar: How Markets and the State Leave the Community Behind*, New York: Penguin Press.

Rifkin, J. (2014) *The Zero Marginal Cost Society: The Internet of Things, the Collaborative Commons, and the Eclipse of Capitalism*, New York: Palgrave Macmillan.

Rifkin, J. (2019) *The Green New Deal: Why the Fossil Fuel Civilization Will Collapse by 2028, and the Bold Economic Plan to Save Life on Earth*, New York: St. Martin's Press.

Robertson, D. H. (1923) *The Control of Industry*, Nisbet: Cambridge University Press.

Saito, K. (2017) *Karl Marx's Ecosocialism: Capitalism, Nature, and the Unfinished Critique of Political Economy*, New York: Monthly Review Press.

Saito, K. (2021) "Primitive Accumulation as the Cause of Economic and Ecological Disaster", in M. Musto (ed.) *Rethinking Alternatives with Marx: Economy, Ecology and Migration*, Cham: Palgrave Macmillan, 93–112.

Schneider, N. (2018) *Everything for Everyone: The Radical Tradition That Is Shaping the Next Economy*, New York: Bold Type Books.

Seccareccia, M (2011) "The Role of Public Investment as Principal Macroeconomic Tool to Promote Long-Term Growth: Keynes's Legacy", *International Journal of Political Economy*, 40(4): 62–82; DOI: 10.2753/IJP0891–1916400403

Skidelsky, R. (2021) "The Silent Revolution in Economic Policy", *Project Syndicate*, February 16, 2021. (URL: https://www.project-syndicate.org/commentary/covid19-economic-recovery-plans-fiscal-policy-by-robert-skidelsky-2021–02; access: 21 December 2021).

Winslow, T. (2021) "The Role of Keynes's Idea of 'Organic Unity' in His 'General Theory' of Capitalism", in B. Gabor (ed.) *Humanity and Nature in Economic Thought*, London and New York: Routledge, 133–162.

13 Post-War Heterodox Approaches and Economic Policy

Robert McMaster

Introduction

As Jamie Galbraith (2021: 67) observes, "Economics is a policy discipline". Indeed, Galbraith argues that the discipline evolves with the economy. Just as there are varieties of an economy, there are different ideas and theories about the workings of an economy and ways to address its problems. Yet, in the late 1990s and early 2000s, many economists prided themselves on how they had apparently solved the perennial issue of capitalism: how to ensure sustained prosperity and eliminate inflation (for example, Greenspan, 1998). They coalesced around the idea that the economy was fundamentally stable, and that government should only be concerned with addressing "frictions", while enabling markets to allocate resources to their best use. The basis of this cozy consensus was severely challenged by the Great Financial Crisis (GFC) in 2007. Most economists were, at best astonished by the turn of events (Galbraith, 2009; Mirowski, 2010). After all, how could such chaos emerge from stability? (Minsky, 1982) There were dissenting groups, confined to the margins of or expunged from the main corpus of the discipline, who argued about the inevitability of a crisis but could not predict its timing (Galbraith, 2009). The fault line between the "mainstream" and "heterodoxy" was exposed beyond the malcontents' academic gatherings.

The "Heterodox Economics" terminology is subject to some debate. "Heterodox" necessarily contrasts with "orthodox" in a rather binary division and can be defined in terms of its opposition, or at least its contrast to the mainstream, or standard approach (for recent contributions, see Hodgson, 2019; Lawson, 2006; Morgan and Embery, 2017). Mainstream economics is frequently defined in terms of its method (for example, Lawson, 2006). Indeed, in many standard textbooks on the subject, students are introduced to the "economic way of thinking", or "thinking like an economist" (for example, Mearman and McMaster, 2019; Sloman *et al.*, 2015; Taylor and Mankiw, 2017). I follow Sheila Dow *et al.* (2018), in delineating the mainstream in economics as broadly possessing six notable traits: (1) equilibrium reasoning, which discounts uncertainty in the Keynesian/Knightian meaning of the term; (2) assumes *homo economicus* – "Max U" (Hodgson, 2019; McCloskey,

DOI: 10.4324/9781003228097-13

2016); (3) assumes ahistoricism in that real time has, at best a limited influence; (4) the ontological privileging of the individual; (5) power only manifests as market power in the ability to influence prices; and (6) belief in the Humean dichotomy between positive and normative, such that economic analysis is value-free. Geoff Hodgson (2019) and Deirdre McCloskey (2016) argue that the defining feature of the mainstream is utility maximisation: "Max U". These features lead to a strong preference for the application of mathematical reasoning, which echoes the Samuelsonian dictum that all economic problems are essentially reducible to constrained optimisation (for example, Hodgson, 2019; Skidelsky, 2020). By contrast, heterodoxy may be viewed as a rejection of all or, at least some of those properties. Austrianism, for example, has affinities with the mainstream privileging of the individual, but emphatically rejects mathematical techniques in the study of the economy. Other heterodox traditions emphasise, for example, historical contingencies and evolutionary processes (Institutionalism); class and power (Marxism); uncertainty, class, and the non-neutrality of money (Post Keynesianism); and social provisioning, power, and gender (Feminist economics).

The methodological and theoretical distinctions between the mainstream and heterodoxy have to some extent spilled over to the policy domain. Arguably, since the decline of Keynesianism, the mainstream has been associated with an inclination to *laissez faire*. Indeed, one might argue that the emergence of the Monetarist counter-revolution in the 1970s and New Keynesianism in the 1990s shared common policy positions in favouring inflation-targeting over unemployment and the abandonment of Keynesian demand management, reflected in the Washington consensus endorsed and implemented by the International Monetary Fund, the World Bank, and US Treasury. Was this Say's Law Redux? Of course, it wasn't always like this: some form of Keynesianism was mainstream in the 1960s and the socialist calculation debate of the 1920s–1940s involved the application of general equilibrium theorising to demonstrate the superiority of socialist central planning by the likes of Oskar Lange and Abba Lerner (Hodgson, 2001). Arguably, one of the contributory factors in the mainstream turn to increasing its market orientation and willingness to embrace facets of neoliberalism lay in the Cold War with the perceived need to demonstrate the superiority of (US) capitalism, and the growing influence of the Mont Pèlerin Society (Mirowski, 2013), and game theory (Aldred, 2020).

Post-Keynesian scholars were critical of the neoclassical synthesis initiated by John Hicks' IS-LM framework. Arguably, the synthesis facilitated the emergence of New Keynesianism. Post Keynesians have long viewed this path as contentious and unrepresentative of much of Keynes' thinking (for example, Arestis and Sawyer, 2001; Dow, 1995; Wray, 2016). By contrast, Post Keynesianism continues to emphasise endogenous change in capitalist economies, stress effective demand, and reject Say's Law. For them, this leads to pronounced policy differences from the macroeconomic consensus of the 1990s and 2000s (Galbraith, 2008). Post Keynesians, Institutionalists, and

Marxists were among those suspicious of supply-side policy orientation, the spectacular growth of the financial sector, and its deregulation (Crotty, 2009; Galbraith, 2009). Based on their understanding of economic phenomena, most heterodox schools present an alternative policy platform. This chapter traces the evolution of this from the 1940s to date. In doing so, I identify examples of policy associated with recent prominent heterodox contributions: modern monetary theory (MMT) and stratification economics (SE).

The remainder of the chapter is structured: the next section provides an outline of the underpinnings of the mainstream economic approach to policy founded on the Humean guillotine between the positive and normative and shift from class analysis. This is followed by an outline of the possible points of divergence between more heterodox approaches and the standard framing. The "Heterodox Economics and Policy" section then turns to illustrations of heterodox economics and policy. It identifies the post-war Keynesian revolution and Post Keynesianism traceable to the "Cambridge Circus". Two illustrative examples of more recent developments in heterodox thinking are subsequently discussed – MMT and SE. The final section offers some conclusions on the nature of heterodox economic thinking and policy.

Mainstream Economics, Policy, and Differences with Heterodoxy

A standard university economics education usually commences with topics, such as "thinking like an economist" and the division between normative and positive (Mearman and McMaster, 2019). Of course, this establishes the impression that economics is value-free and accordingly that policy advice provided by economists is objective. This stance has attracted a number of challenges and critiques. Arguably one of the most notable is Kenneth Boulding's address to the American Economic Association in 1968:

> I am prepared to … say that no science of any kind can be divorced from ethical considerations … Science is a human learning process which arises in certain subcultures in human society and not in others, and a subculture … is a group … defined by the acceptance of common values … This means that even the epistemological content of science, that is, what scientists think they know, has an ethical component.
>
> (Boulding, 1969: 2)

Boulding's argument has appeal. The advocacy of a "harder science" in the marginal turn at the end of the nineteenth century increased mathematical content and dispensed with the class as part of economic analysis. The Marshallian representative agent solidified a utilitarian influence on notions of well-being and the broader framing of economic problems. Subsequent theoretical development of revealed preferences, Pareto optimality, and Kaldor-Hicks' compensation criterion all reflect the evolutionary path established at the turn of the nineteenth and twentieth centuries (for example, Hodgson, 2001; Yonay, 1998). Power, class, and distribution are diminished in their analytical relevance to the pursuit of optimality. Indeed, following Lionel Robbins, the framing of (neoclassical) economic inquiry as the "science of choice" (Hodgson, 2001) revealed the consequentialist/utilitarian influence in that resources were to be allocated such that as many (unlimited) wants as possible were to be "satisfied". Robbins wrote,

> There are no economic ends, only economical and uneconomical means for achieving given ends ... Economics deals with ascertainable facts; ethics with values and obligations. The only way to associate them is by juxtaposition.
>
> (Robbins, 1935: 148, cited in Skidelsky, 2020: 161)

Following Robbins, the demarcation between economics and political economy, and other social sciences is therefore pronounced. Economics' abandonment of ethics marks its aspirations as a "social physics" as well as a belief that economic analysis presents a higher standard of evidence from which to offer policy advice (for an insightful view on the evolving relationship between standard economics and physics, see, for example, Drakopoulos and Katselidis, 2015). On this returning to Robbins, the means of achieving given ends usually commence with markets. With a few exceptions, markets were widely presumed as conduits of efficiency. Under this reading, then, the state's primary economic function was to correct for market failure, through, for example, Pigovian taxes.

At the macroeconomic level, following the demise of the Keynesian consensus and the rise of Monetarism and Neoliberalism in the 1970s and 1980s, the principal purpose of the state was reduced to ensuring inflationary stability. Indeed, this rubric shaped New Keynesian thinking following the failure of the Monetarist rubric to control the money supply. Despite the abandonment of its central policy, Monetarist theory persisted in its influence on the emergence of a macroeconomic consensus in the 1990s. This centred on the assumed stability of economies; the need for passive fiscal policy (to circumvent inflation and crowding-out), and supply-side oriented employment policies. In short, New Keynesianism embraced Say's Law (Arestis and Sawyer, 2001).

This rather potted history of the broad policy trajectory of mainstream economics raises at least two points of relevance to the argument presented here. First, arguably, since the peak of the socialist calculation debate in the 1940s, the ideological locus of the neoclassical-mainstream framework has steadily shifted. In the 1950s and 1960s, the Keynesian mixed economy dominated. With the increasing influence of the Mont Pèlerin Society and the associated rise of the Chicago and Virginia Schools in the mainstream, the standard approach became increasingly associated with a neoliberal ideology (Mirowski, 2013) further supported by game theory's individualistic orientation and consequentialism (Aldred, 2020). Arguably, this has been the principal success of both Chicago and Virginia. On this, distribution is confirmed as, at best of limited importance in contrast to growth. The mantra being that a rising tide raises all boats (Stiglitz, 2016).

Chicago is perhaps more well-known than the Virginia School; the former is noted for Milton Friedman's monetarism, Gary Becker's extension of standard reasoning to "non-market" aspects of human behaviour, and Richard Posner's economics and law. These approaches typically advocate a *de minimus* role for the state. Prominent Virginia School scholars, such as James Buchanan and Gordon Tullock, presented a similar prospectus. The focus of this school was the "economics of politics". In contrasting democratic institutions and bureaucracy with standard representations of markets, the likes of Tullock highlighted the alleged inefficiencies of the apparatus of the state (see, for example, Muller, 2003).

Both schools influenced national and international policies. Chicago is most obviously in macro. The "Washington consensus" is arguably a further example. Keynesian Bretton Woods institutions and development goals were repurposed in ways that tied developing economies to endorsing and implementing a range of market-oriented reforms, such as privatisation of infrastructure, deregulation of financial systems, and foreign direct investment. Without this, development funding was withheld (Blyth, 2013; Rodrik, 2006). Further instances of Chicago-inspired influence include initiatives such as carbon trading framed under the auspices of the Coase Theorem and deregulation of finance on the basis of the efficient market hypothesis and Black-Scholes model (Mirowski, 2013).[1] The Virginia School was influential in shaping the "new public management" turn in the governance of state bodies from education to health care to welfare reform from the 1980s (Hood, 1991).

Second, notwithstanding Boulding's (and others') noted criticisms, the mainstream's dictum of the Humean dichotomy is remarkably resilient. Standard economic analysis is presumed to be value-free, especially following its increasing employment of mathematical techniques, which enables the generation of testable predictions and theoretical insights (Friedman, 1953; Samuelson, 1952). This may create the impression that the mainstream of the discipline is free of ideology, and hence there is an "objective" scientific basis to policy advice and advocacy. That said, Colander and Kupers (2016) are of the view that this implies a bifurcation in economic practice: the science of economics is confined to formal mathematical logic, and therefore "hard science", whereas policy issues are relegated to "art". I remain unconvinced by this argument in that the framing of economic problems to be solved, such as the impact of government debt on growth rates carries potentially significant moral implications. Reinhart and Rogoff's (2010) work in this area is illustrative of the influence of economics in shaping policy. The authors' study detected that beyond a certain threshold, government debt acts as a drag on growth. This reinforced the politics of austerity. Yet, Reinhart and

Rogoff's analysis was significantly technically flawed (Herndon *et al.*, 2014).[2] Notwithstanding this, their "positive" "ascertainable facts" (Robbins, 1938) arguably contributed to a pronounced ideology in policy.

By contrast, heterodox schools by and large do not make claims to cleave ethics and values from economics. Radical political economics, for example, explicitly embraces much of Marx's humanism and in contrast to the standard approach in economics, emphasises the importance of class, race, and gender in economic activity. Central to this are notions of justice, primarily with a focus on forms of inequality (for example, see URPE, 2021). This is not unique to radical political economists. Original Institutionalists and Post Keynesians are among those expressing similar sentiments (for example, Hodgson, 2021; Wray, 2016). Indeed, the founding principles of the Association for Social Economics challenge the Humean dichotomy (Dolfsma *et al.*, 2012).

> A foundational idea in social economics is that economic problems and processes are integrally connected with other dimensions of social life.
>
> (Dolfsma *et al.*, 2012: 155)

Liberty and justice also underpin Austrian thinking. For instance, Friedrich Hayek is explicit in arguing that liberty is the foundation of all other values. In his *Road to Serfdom*, Hayek (1944) invokes a negative conception of individual freedom – freedom from – as the prerequisite of individual welfare and social harmony. On this, the state is viewed as a force of coercion akin to Thomas Hobbes's *Leviathan*.

John Maynard Keynes also recognised the importance of ethics in economic analysis (Carabelli and Cedrini, 2018). After all, in acknowledging the possibility of a stationary state, Keynes argued,

> If I am right in supposing it to be comparatively easy to make capital-goods so abundant that the marginal efficiency of capital is zero, this may be the most sensible way of gradually getting rid of many of the *objectionable* features of capitalism. For a little reflection will show what enormous social changes would result from a gradual disappearance of a rate of return on accumulated wealth.
>
> (Keynes, 1936: 221, emphasis added)

Therein lies a fundamental difference between heterodox approaches and the mainstream: economics and ethics are intertwined. Despite his Marshallian heritage, Keynes explicitly recognised that economic systems are value-laden. As I understand it, the standard approach does not admit this, beyond conflating value with price. Keynes, by contrast, specifies the duties of the state in a capitalist economy. The most striking is to ensure full employment (Keynes, 1936). I believe there are nuanced differences between this and the mainstream advocacy of state intervention in the event of market failure.

Rather, for Keynes, unemployment was one of the "objectionable" features of capitalism, which therefore possessed a moral dimension independent of an efficiency rationale.

This draws on a broader issue, noted in the Introduction. Classical political economy did not divorce the economy from the rest of society. The former was nested in the latter. Accordingly, economic activity to some extent reflects wider social values. Arguably, this constitutes a fault line between mainstream and heterodox approaches and attitudes to policy. For the former, following Robbins, policy ends are exogenously determined. The economist provides the means to those given ends. By contrast, the cleavage from values is not as evident in heterodox approaches, which lends a normative hue to policy means and ends, or as Colander and Kupers (2016) term it, the "art" of policy issues. Thus, heterodox schools' policy orientation goes beyond the utilitarian framed potential compensation criteria of neoclassical welfare theory. Despite their pronounced differences, one only has to consider Marx's humanism, Hayek's libertarianism (Rodrigues, 2013), and Keynes' disdain for what he sees as the "many" unfortunate features and consequences of capitalism to appreciate this.

Heterodox Economics and Policy

The most obvious post-war heterodox-informed policy suite is the emergence of the Keynesian "administered market". In developed Western economies, the late 1940s and 1950s were typified by the expansion of the peace-time state into aggregate demand management initiatives, such as the privileging of fiscal policy, the management of exchange rates, and the development of Bretton Woods' institutions. Whereas this broadly heterodox orientation emerged as a mainstream consensus from the 1950s to the 1970s, not all heterodox schools were uncritical. The Austrians, for example, argued that the state created economic problems through price distortion and consequent inefficiencies (Hayek, 1944; Rodrigues, 2013), and Marxist scholars contended that the welfare state was inherently contradictory (Glyn, 2006; O'Connor, 2002).

The Keynesian Consensus and the Development of the Keynesian National Welfare State

Keynes advocated the "socialisation of investment" as a means of ameliorating the vagaries of the "animal spirits" of private sector investment decisions, which could lead to sustained unemployment. A potential manifestation of this is state ownership of industry, especially manufacturing. Certainly, the immediate post-war period in many Western economies was typified by programmes of nationalisation (for example, Cumbers, 2012). In the UK, for example, industries that were considered to have strategic value, such as mining, manufacture of steel, and transport were nationalised on a centralised hierarchical model (Cumbers, 2012). That said, neoclassical micro theory presents an efficiency-based case for the regulation, if not ownership of natural monopolies.

Nationalisation of industries and demand management were also accompanied by the emergence of a Keynesian national welfare state (KNWS) (Jessop, 2002). Possibly, in part, this reflected Keynes' concerns about the randomness of laissez-faire outcomes and hence the risks confronting the individual. In the UK, for instance, the Beveridge reforms instituted radically changed arrangements in economic security, education, health, and housing. Arguably, at the centre of these reforms was an expansion in citizenship rights, such that accessing health and education, for example, were no longer to be issues of affordability. Of course, the reality was rather more nuanced with the persistence of pronounced class divisions in education and differences in health care access (for example, Webster, 1998).

Nonetheless, the expansion of *de jure* rights symbolised by the KNWS was an important dimension. It was intended to preserve an individual's dignity in that there was no stigma associated with the receipt of benefits or the exercise of access rights. These were no longer acts of charity but entitlements by virtue of citizenship. The paternalistic state partly assumed the risks of harm associated with a capitalist economy, such as the variabilities of income and employment to which Keynes alluded in the *General Theory*.

Given their ideological breadth, heterodox schools did not universally embrace the KNWS or Keynesian demand management. For instance, the Austrian critique is well-documented and eventually, via the Mont Pèlerin Society became influential in dismantling the KNWS (Jessop, 2002; Mirowski, 2013). Following the breakdown of the Keynesian consensus in the 1980s, Austrian and Chicago school thinking shaped welfare state reform as well as shifting macroeconomic policy in the West. Thus, there was a transfer of risk from the state to the individual, such as shifts from "welfarist" to "workfarist" approaches, where the latter entailed the erosion of benefits and compulsory work schemes (Jessop, 2002). The increasing emphasis on individualism is consistent with Hayek's view of the state as a force of coercion and according to Jessop (2002) transformed the KNWS into a "Schumpeterian competition state". Here the state's role was to encourage individual initiative in the promotion of a "knowledge economy" and entrepreneurship.

The Keynesian macroeconomic consensus and KNWS were also subject to sustained criticism from radical political economists and Marxist scholars. Notably, in the 1970s and 1980s, Ian Gough (1979), James O'Connor ([1973] 2002), and Claus Offe (1984)[3] argued that the welfare state was beset by contradictions. For all three authors, the welfare state is a prerequisite to the survival of capitalism. Gough, for example, writes of progressive reforms that extend rights for the poor through education, social security, and so forth, while acknowledging that by doing so, the welfare state perpetuates the circumstances for capital accumulation. Similarly, O'Connor discusses the function of the capitalist state as the contradiction of ensuring the conditions for social harmony *and* capital accumulation. Following Marxist reasoning, the latter is the antithesis of the former. According to O'Connor's argument, part of state activity and expenditures, which he classifies as "social capital", is directed at labour "productivity improvements" and chiefly benefit the private sector. Education and land development are viewed by O'Connor as examples. By contrast, "social harmony" is promoted by transfer payments for the unemployed, and are not tailored to productivity, rather they legitimate the state. In this way, like Galbraith (1967) and other Institutionalists (for example, Kapp, 1950), O'Connor argues that the fiscal apparatus of the capitalist state ensures the privatisation of benefits, as corporations secure the benefits associated with productivity, and the socialisation of costs as the state assumes responsibility for the unemployment and indigency created by capitalist activity. While there is agreement on this pattern in Western economic policy, Institutionalists and some radical political economists, such as Gough (1979) offer a more evolutionary perspective. In his writings, Gough (1979) acknowledges progressive reform that extends the rights of the working class through the expansion of health care, social security, and education, for example, during the 1950s and 1960s. For Gough (and others, such as Jessop, 2002), the emergence of a paternalistic welfare state also served the needs of capital in that provided the means to ensure demand for the outputs of Fordist mass production.

These criticisms of the Keynesian state are, of course, historically contingent, particularly given the change in trajectory associated with increasingly neoliberal policies, which shifted the burden of risk and responsibility from the paternalistic state to the individual. Indeed, some heterodox economists argue that the period following the KNWS has been typified by state "capture" (Galbraith, 2008; Glyn, 2006; Varoufakis, 2015), as an elite seeks to manipulate the state to its own ends. The socialisation of the costs of the financial crisis, which was at least partly associated with reckless disregard of a substantial proportion of the financial sector, is a very recent potent example (for example, Crotty, 2009; Galbraith, 2009).

In response to the policy environment emerging from the 1980s and the New Keynesian consensus, and "Third Way" (Giddens, 1998) of the 1990s onwards, heterodox schools were sceptical of the impact and effects of these policies (Arestis and Sawyer, 2001). With the 2007–2008 financial crisis, arguably heterodox contributions, gained some traction, especially under the auspices of the "Minsky moment" narrative (McCulley, 2009). The crisis queried the comfortable accord among mainstream economists who "never saw it coming" (Galbraith, 2009), albeit in limited and prescriptive ways (Mirowski, 2013). Nonetheless, the effects of the crisis on state budget positions and the adoption of subsequent austerity policies (Blyth, 2013), and the growing unease, even among standard economics about the impact of persistent wealth and income inequalities (for example, Piketty, 2014; Stiglitz, 2016) raised the profile of two heterodox contributions, MMT and SE, which the remainder of this section discusses.

The Emergence of Modern Monetary Theory

Advocates of MMT acknowledge its antecedents in Abba Lerner's notion of functional finance,[4] Georg Knapp's Chartalism, or state theory of money,[5] and the influences of Wynne Godley, Mitchell Innes, Mikal Kalecki, Keynes, Hyman Minsky, among others (for example, Kelton, 2020; Wray, 2015). In short, MMT is firmly grounded in Post Keynesianism, although not all Post Keynesians endorse it and some are critical (for example, Kregel, 2019; Palley, 2019; Sawyer, 2019).[6]

MMT emerged in the 1990s in a couple of US institutions – University of Missouri at Kansas City and the Levy Economics Institute. Arguably, the MMT "moment" arrived following the period of austerity in the wake of the financial crisis. The adoption of Keynesian fiscal policy by many Western governments combined with the apparent disorientation in the mainstream contributed to the creation of a climate more conducive to Keynesian-informed policy thinking, and attracted attention beyond heterodox economics and the academy, more generally.

In essence, MMT challenges the standard economic Ricardian equivalence account that ultimately state expenditure has no impact on aggregate demand. In short, state deficits are assumed to encourage private sector agents to increase current savings in anticipation of future tax increases to obviate public debt. Current consumption falls thereby counteracting increased state expenditure. This position presumes crowding out and the need for taxation revenues to balance state expenditures. By contrast, Godley's work (for example, 1999) emphasises that following the logic of national income accounting, state budget deficits represent transfers to the private sector.[7] Therefore, far from depleting private wealth, as inferred by Ricardian equivalence, the flow of state deficits can contribute to wealth accumulation. Accordingly, MMT contends that state budgets differ from those of households and firms, especially in circumstances in which the state issues the currency. There are profound differences between the issuers and users of a currency. The former spend money into existence and then impose taxation obligations on households and organisations partly to control inflation, redistribute income, and importantly create and sustain demand for the currency. A state that issues its currency and whose debts are denominated in that currency cannot, in principle default. In other words, the currency issuer cannot run out of money. This implies, *contra* mainstream accounts, there is no budget constraint on a currency issuing state. There are constraints in the form of the scarcity of resources, which if that state continuously operated an expansionary fiscal policy would encounter inflation. Moreover, inappropriately directed expenditure may also cause inflation (Kelton, 2020; Wray, 2015, 2019).

Godley's accounting approach leads Post Keynesians, in general, to argue that state deficits reflect imbalances elsewhere in the economy, and accordingly should not be a policy focus (for example, Arestis and Sawyer, 2004; Galbraith, 2021). Indeed, to some degree, this reiterates Kalecki's conclusion that the goal of sustained full employment "must be based on either a long-run budget deficit policy or on the redistribution of income" (1944: 135). Accordingly, endeavouring to address state debt and deficits as a primary policy objective, especially adopting an austerian orientation is akin to attempting to masking the symptoms without treating the cause. This distinct emphasis further highlights the normative dimension shaping theory and policy recommendations. For Post Keynesians (and other heterodox schools), in general, employment objectives appear to assume priority over inflation goals. This is in mark contrast to more mainstream approaches, which centre on inflation control, with the echo of Say's Law informing thinking on employment.

Yet, there are divergences between MMT advocates and other Post Keynesians. Kelton (2020) and Wray (2015) promote an "employer of last resort" (ELR) function of the state. Indeed, ELR is "inseparable" from MMT (Wray, 2015). The authors contend this resonates with Keynes' thinking on one of the central duties of the state. In short, the state would act as a guarantor of employment, hiring those individuals either unable to gain employment via the labour market, or those unfortunate to be made redundant as a consequence of an economic downturn. Individuals would be employed on a voluntary basis at the legal minimum wage. The proposal is in effect a buffer stock arrangement. This has drawn criticism from other heterodox economists. Sawyer (2019), for instance, identifies major issues with the scheme. By specifying the minimum wage, ELR potentially undermines existing public sector employment contracts, especially if the work offered under ELR is similar to that already undertaken. Moreover, there must be appropriate capacity in the appropriate places – vacancies where needed – to enable employment under ELR, which is a challenging undertaking.

Yet, other proposals, particularly a universal basic (or citizens') income (UBI) do not feature prominently in MMT policy proposals. UBI is not a new proposition; John Stuart Mill was an early advocate (van Parijs and Vanderborght, 2017), and notable mainstream economists, such as Milton Friedman and Gregory Mankiw, for potentially different motivations, have also supported a UBI.[8] Heterodox economists, such as Yannis Varoufakis[9] and philosophers, such as Philippe van Parijs argue that a UBI may be an effective means of partially addressing profound income and wealth inequalities, precarious income, especially in an environment of automation, indigence, and in promoting freedoms. For example,

> A basic income is fully compatible with the view that recognition and esteem are not earned by self-indulgence, but by service to others. A basic income is there to facilitate the search for all of us for something we like to do and do well ….
>
> (van Parijs and Vanderborght, 2017: 27)

While not the sole domain of heterodox schools, and indeed a source of debate within and beyond heterodoxy, aspects of the advocacy of a UBI necessarily entangle the ethical and the economic. Again, this reiterates a central distinction with the mainstream. The emergence of, and increasing interest in SE and its policy implications is a further example.

Stratification Economics and the Quest for Racial Justice

Stratification economics (SE) is associated with US black political economy and is most prominently articulated by William Darity and colleagues. This approach reinvigorates political economy emphasis on groups (including class). For Darity:

> Stratification economics examines the structural and intentional processes generating hierarchy and, correspondingly, income and wealth inequality between ascriptively distinguished groups.
>
> (2005: 144)

The institutional arrangements that enable the persistence of group (dis) advantage and the motivations of powerful elites in maintaining their advantages are primary areas of interest. Darity directly challenges notions, especially advanced by Becker that competitive markets, particularly for labour will end race and sex discrimination. Becker's view rests on the assumption that markets only reflect narrow financial incentives. The economy is separate from society, or indeed, the latter is subordinate to the former. Instead, SE assumes the economy reflects broader social values and power structures; therefore, the economy is embedded in society (Darity, 2005; Davis, 2019). Indeed, Darity and colleagues' empirical work attempts to demonstrate the persistence of African-American relative poverty and the ongoing comparatively limited economic opportunities from access to credit to education to health care, to business ownership, and beyond. Darity and Mullen illustrate the scale of racial wealth inequality in the US:

> Data from the 2016 Survey of Consumer Finances indicates that *median black household net worth ($17,600) is only one-tenth of white net worth ($171,000).*
>
> (2020: 31, original emphasis)

In the context of the US, existing institutional arrangements perpetuate racial wealth and income inequalities. Ongoing equal rights legislation and positive discrimination initiatives in the labour market are insufficient in addressing these historical injustices. The SE literature acknowledges that the US is illustrative of a more general (global) phenomenon of persistent and pronounced inequalities. Yet the US provides a paradigmatic example of the importance of historical and institutional contexts in shaping current socio-economic problems. Like many parts of the World,[10] in the eighteenth and nineteenth centuries, the US economy benefitted enormously from slavery. For some historians, slavery was the "ultimate source" of commercial activity (Darity and Mullen, 2020). One group in society (whites, especially males) almost completely appropriated the benefits of the then prevailing institutional arrangements. Institutional evolution since the US civil war has not sufficiently addressed this profound (dis)advantage. Contra Becker, and the Chicago school, the erosion of rights, and increased flexibility of US labour markets have not ended discrimination and racial inequalities.

According to SE arguments, the pursuit of either or both ELR and UBI, although progressive will not address the substantial injustices arising from persistent disadvantage in the US. Darity is prominent among those advocating reparations for African Americans. For Darity and Mullen, there are three phases of injustice in the history of the US: enslavement; American apartheid (*de jure* discrimination and exclusion); and continuing *de facto* discrimination and exclusion emerging from the previous two phases. SE has investigated and attempted to establish the extent of African Americans' projected losses in net wealth arising from institutional injustices. On this basis, the US federal government should recompense this group in society.

From the perspective of the argument advanced here, I believe that SE demonstrates a broader heterodox characteristic in those groups, as well as individuals, which have theoretical relevance, and socio-economic issues are partly reflective of prevailing social values and historical context. These dimensions are either absent or relegated in standard economics. That said, SE resonates with neoclassical welfare references to loss, and the idea of reparations has some affinities with potential compensation criteria. Yet, ideas of justice are, at best not prominent in welfare economics. Loss is conceived in terms of utility foregone and possible inefficiencies. It is only the *potential* to compensate that appears to matter. By contrast, SE explicitly engages with notions of justice beyond the confines of a utilitarian sculpture.

Some Conclusions

At the outset of this chapter, I referred to Galbraith's (2021) belief that economics is a policy discipline. The way that economists conceive of the economy impacts people's lives. Keynes recognised this and was motivated to write the *General Theory* in part due to the effects of prevailing policy and institutions on the population (Skidelsky, 2020). As economies evolve, so do socio-economic problems, and, to some extent, the theories economists construct to apprehend and understand these phenomena and issues. That said, the mainstream approach in economics had doggedly retained certain characteristics, which to some extent define it. Arguably, equilibrium reasoning, individualism, and *homo economicus* ("Max U") represent at least some of these defining aspects. In some respects, "heterodoxy" is an oppositional response to at least some of these properties. Indeed, the mainstream defines itself in terms of methods (Hodgson, 2019; Lawson, 2006; Skidelsky, 2020). Part of this approach invokes the Humean dichotomy that economics is essentially, or should be value-free. In Section 1, I emphasised how in the teaching of economics, "thinking like an economist" constitutes a significant introductory theme. For me, this represents a significant distinction between the standard approach and heterodoxy. The latter has closer affinities with classical political economy in that ethics is seen as intertwined with the study of the economy. This shapes the policy orientation of schools of thought.

Despite the stated value-neutrality of mainstream analysis, since the fulcrum of the socialist calculation debate and the demise of the Keynesian consensus, conventional theorising has gradually emphasised market-oriented policies, such that it has increasingly been associated with neoliberalism (Mirowski, 2013). There are a number of reasons for this, including the game theoretic restating of selfishness (Aldred, 2020) and the rise of the Chicago school and its influence on New Keynesianism. In some respects, heterodox economic policy advocacy can be viewed as a response to these developments. Arguably, until the 1970s and 80s, what became heterodoxy was dominated by Keynesianism, which until this period appeared as the mainstream in macro. This is not to suggest that there is a uniformity of belief in the policies advocated. The dissent of Marxist and Radical Political Economists as well as Austrianism from rival ideological positions is obvious. More recently, the debate within Post Keynesianism around MMT and ELR is illustrative of important policy and theoretical differences.

Despite the differences within heterodoxy and commonalities between elements of heterodox schools and the mainstream, I return to the common element of an acknowledgement of the entanglement of economics and ethics. Both MMT and SE are grounded in particular value-driven perspectives. Heterodox economic approaches to policy cannot be seen without reference to the evolution in the mainstream as they are in part responses to conventional economics and the effect of its trajectory in the framing of economic problems and subsequent policy advocacy.

Notes

1 Mirowski (2013) provides an interesting and highly critical discussion of the influence of various lobbying groups and think tanks, such as the American Enterprise Institute and Cato Institute, and their relationships with various economists.

2 Thomas Herndon and colleagues (2014) investigated Reinhart and Rogoff's approach, finding substantial flaws, such as coding errors, the selective exclusion of data, the inappropriate weighting of data. Herndon et al accordingly argued that these errors created "serious" measurement issues. Correcting for these errors, authors re-calculated Reinhart and Rogoff's data, finding no significant relationships between debt levels and growth.

3 Rudolf Klein (1993) dubbed the three authors' contributions as "O'Goffe's Tale".

4 Lerner's functional finance proposes that state spending should be goal directed, such as moderating the economic cycle, and that ensuring prosperity should be the overall economic objective of the state, and to this end the seeking to balance state revenues and expenditures is mistaken (Kelton, 2020).

5 Keynes endorsed Chartalism. In the *Treatise on Money*, he wrote: "The evolution of money has been reached … Chartalism – the doctrine that money is peculiarly a creation of the State – is fully realised … Today all civilised money is, beyond the possibility of dispute, chartalist" (1930: 4–5).

6 MMT has also drawn criticisms from mainstream economists. One of which dismisses it as the "magic money tree" (for some examples, see Drumetz and Pfister, 2021; Krugman, 2019).

7 If private and international sectors are in surplus, then of necessity the public sector must be in deficit. Following Godley:

$$G - T = S(Y_f) - I(Y_f) + M(Y_f) - X(WY)$$

(where G is state expenditure; T – taxation receipts; S – private sector savings; I – private sector investment expenditure; M – imports; X – exports; Y_f – domestic income; and WY – world income).

8 Friedman believed that a UBI, or negative income tax, would enable the dismantlement of the KNWS, or as he preferred, reduce state bureaucracy (see, for example, an interview of Friedman in 1968: https://www.youtube.com/watch?v=xtpgkX588nM).

9 See, for example, https://www.yanisvaroufakis.eu/2021/06/11/is-universal-basic-income-a-good-idea-my-debate-with-daron-acemoglou-on-pairagraph/

10 There is increasing recognition of this. For example, to its credit the University of Glasgow acknowledged how it benefitted from slavery. In 2019, it instituted the process of paying reparations (see https://www.nytimes.com/2019/08/24/world/europe/university-of-glasgow-slavery-reparations.html).

Bibliography

Aldred, J. (2020) *Licence to be Bad: How Economics Corrupted Us*, Penguin: London.

Arestis, P. and Sawyer, M. (2001) The economic analysis underpinning the 'Third Way', *New Political Economy*, 6: 255–278.

Arestis, P. and Sawyer, M. (2004) On fiscal policy and budget deficits. *Intervention. Journal of Economics*, 1: 61–74.

Blyth, M. (2013) *Austerity: The History of a Dangerous Idea*, Oxford University Press: Oxford.

Boulding, K. E. (1969) Economics as a moral science, *American Economic Review*, 59: 1–12.

Carabelli, A. M. and Cedrini, M. A. (2018) Great expectations and final disillusionment: Keynes, "My Early Beliefs" and the ultimate values of capitalism, *Cambridge Journal of Economics*, 42: 1183–1204.

Colander, D. and Kupers, R. (2016) *Complexity and the Art of Public Policy: Solving Society's Problems from the Bottom Up*, Princeton University Press: Princeton, NJ.

Crotty, J. (2009) Structural causes of the global financial crisis: A critical assessment of the 'New Financial Architecture', *Cambridge Journal of Economics*, 33: 563–580.

Cumbers, A. (2012) *Reclaiming Public Ownership: Making Space for Economic Democracy*, Zed Books: London.

Darity, W. A. (2005) Stratification economics: The role of intergroup inequality, *Journal of Economics and Finance*, 29: 144–153.

Darity, W. A. and Mullen, A. K. (2020) *From Here to Equality: Reparations for Black Americans in the Twentieth-First Century*, University of North Carolina Press: Chapel Hill.

Davis, J. B. (2019) Stratification as an economics of exclusion, *Journal of Economics, Race and Policy*, 2: 163–172.

Dolfsma, W., Figart, D., McMaster, R., and Starr, M. (2012) Promoting research on intersections between economics, ethics, and social values: Editorial, *Review of Social Economics*, 70: 155–163.

Dow, S. C. (1995) The appeal of neoclassical economics: Some insights from Keynes's epistemology. *Cambridge Journal of Economics*, 19: 715–733.

Dow, S. C., McMaster, R., and Cumbers, A. (2018) *Sine praejudicio*? Economics and the 2014 Scottish independence referendum, *Cambridge Journal of Economics*, 42: 597–615.

Drakopoulos, S. and Katselidis, I. (2015) From Edgeworth to econophysics: A methodological perspective, *Journal of Economic Methodology*, 22: 77–95.

Drumetz, F. and Pfister, C. (2021) The meaning of MMT, *Banque de France*, Working Paper 833, September, 28pp.

Friedman, M. (1953) *Essays in Positive Economics*, University of Chicago Press: Chicago, IL.

Fullbrook, E. and Morgan, J. (eds) (2019) *Modern Monetary Theory and Its Critics*, World Economics Association Books: Bristol.

Galbraith, James K. (2008) *The Predator State: How Conservatives Abandoned the Free Market and Why Liberals Should Too*, The Free Press: New York.

Galbraith, James K. (2009) Who are these economists, anyway? *The NEA Higher Education Journal*, Fall: 85–97.

Galbraith, James K. (2021) What is economics? A policy discipline for the real world, *Real World Economics Review*, 96: 67–81.

Galbraith, John K. (1967) *The New Industrial State*, Penguin: Harmondsworth.

Giddens, A. (1998) *The Third Way: The Renewal of Social Democracy*, Polity: Cambridge.

Glyn, A. (2006) *Capitalism Unleashed: Finance, Globalization, and Welfare*. Oxford University Press: Oxford.

Godley, W. (1999) *Seven Unsustainable Processes: Medium Term Prospects and Policies for the United States and the World*, Jerome Levy Institute Special Report: Annandale-on-Hudson, NY. https://www.levyinstitute.org/pubs/sevenproc.pdf

Gough, I. (1979) *The Political Economy of the Welfare State*, Macmillan: London.

Greenspan, A. (1998) Is there a new economy? https://www.federalreserve.gov/boarddocs/speeches/1998/19980904.htm

Hayek, F. A. (1944) *The Road to Serfdom*, Routledge: London.

Herndon, T., Ash, M., and Pollin, R. (2014) Does high public debt consistently stifle economic growth? A critique of Reinhart and Rogoff, *Cambridge Journal of Economics*, 38: 257–279.

Hodgson, G. M. (2001) *How Economics Forgot History: The Problem of Historical Specificity in Social Science*, Routledge: London.

Hodgson, G. M. (2019) *Is There a Future for Heterodox Economics? Institutions, Ideology and a Scientific Community*, Edward Elgar: Cheltenham.

Hodgson, G. M. (2021) *Liberal Solidarity: The Political Economy of Social Democratic Liberalism*, Edward Elgar: Cheltenham.

Hood, C. (1991) A public management for all seasons? *Public Administration*, 69: 3–19.

Jessop, B. (2002) *The Future of the Capitalist State*, Polity Press: Cambridge.

Kalecki, M. (1944) Three ways to full employment, in *The Economics of Full Employment*, Oxford University Institute of Statistics, Blackwell: Oxford (6–39).

Kapp, K. W. (1950) *The Social Costs of Private Enterprise,* Harvard University Press: Cambridge.

Kelton, S. (2020) *The Deficit Myth: Modern Monetary Theory and the Birth of the People's Economy*, Public Affairs: New York.

Keynes, J. M. (1930) *A Treatise on Money*, Cambridge University Press: Cambridge.

Keynes, J. M. (1936) *The General Theory of Employment, Interest, and Money*, Prometheus Books (1997): Amherst, NY.

Klein, R. (1993) 'O'Goffe's' tale, or, what can we learn from the success of the capitalist welfare state? in *New Perspectives on the Welfare State in Europe*, Jones, C. (ed.), Routledge: London (7–18).

Kregel, J. (2019) MMT: The wrong answer to the wrong question, in *Modern Monetary Theory and its Critics*, Fullbrook, E. and Morgan, J. (eds.), World Economics Association Books: Bristol (182–206).

Krugman, P. (2019) Running on MMT wonkish: Trying to get this debate beyond Calvinball, *New York Times*. https://www.nytimes.com/2019/02/25/opinion/running-on-mmt-wonkish.html

Lawson, T. (2006) The nature of heterodox economics, *Cambridge Journal of Economics*, 30: 483–505.

McCloskey, D. N. (2016) 'Max U vs. Humanomics: A critique of neo-institutionalism', *Journal of Institutional Economics,* 12: 1–27.

McCulley, P. A. (2009) The shadow banking system and Hyman Minsky's economic journey, https://www.pimco.com/en-us/insights/economic-and-market-commentary/global-central-bank-focus/the-shadow-banking-system-and-hyman-minskys-economic-journey/

Mearman, A. and McMaster, R. (2019) Teaching future economists, in *The Ethical Formation of Economists*, Dolfsma, W. and Negru, I. (eds), Routledge: London (24–43).

Minsky, H. P. (1982) *Can "It" Happen Again?* M. E. Sharpe: Armonk, NY.

Mirowski, P. (2010) The great mortification: Economists' responses to the crisis of 2007-(and counting), *Hedgehog Review*, 12: 28–41.

Mirowski, P. (2013) *Never Let a Serious Crisis Go to Waste: How Neoliberalism Survived the Financial Meltdown*, Verso: London and New York.

Morgan, J. and Embrey, J. (2017) Heterodox economics as a living body of knowledge: Community, (in)commensurability, critical engagement, and pluralism, in *The Routledge Handbook of Heterodox Economics: Theorizing, Analyzing, and Transforming Capitalism*, Jo, T.-H., Chester, L., and D'Ippoliti, C. (eds.), Routledge: London (515–534).

Muller, D. C. (2003) *Public Choice III*, Third Edition, Cambridge University Press: Cambridge.

O'Connor, J. ([1973] 2002) *The Fiscal Crisis of the State*, updated edn. Transaction Publishers: New Brunswick, NJ:.

Offe, C. (1984) *Contradictions of the Welfare State*, Hutchinson: London.

Palley, T. I. (2019) Macroeconomics vs modern monetary theory: Some unpleasant Keynesian arithmetic and monetary dynamics, in Fullbrook, E. and Morgan, J. (eds), *Modern Monetary Theory and Its Critics*, World Economics Association Books: Bristol.

Piketty, T. (2014) *Capital in the Twenty-First Century*, Belknap Press for the Harvard University Press: Cambridge.

Reinhart, C. M. and Rogoff, K. S. (2010) Growth in a time of debt, *American Economic Review: (Papers & Proceedings)*, 100: 573–578.

Robbins, L. (1935) *An Essay on the Nature and Significance of Economic Science*, (second edition), Macmillan: London.

Rodrigues, J. (2013) The political and moral economies of neoliberalism: Mises and Hayek, *Cambridge Journal of Economics*, 37: 1001–1017.

Rodrik, D. (2006) Goodbye Washington consensus, hello Washington confusion? *Journal of Economic Literature*, 44: 973–987.

Samuelson, P. A. (1952) Economic theory and mathematics – An appraisal, *American Economic Review* (Papers and Proceedings), 42: 64–65.

Sawyer, M. C. (2019) Modern monetary theory: Is there any added value?, in Fullbrook, E. and Morgan, J. (eds), *Modern Monetary Theory and Its Critics*, World Economics Association Books: Bristol (353–379).

Skidelsky, R. (2020) *What's Wrong with Economics? A Primer for the Perplexed*, Yale University Press: New Haven, CT.

Sloman J., Garrat, D. and Wride, A. (2015) *Economics*, 9th edition, Pearson: London.

Stiglitz, J. (2016) Inequality and economic growth, in *Rethinking Capitalism: Economics and Policy for Sustainable and Inclusive Growth*, Jacobs, M. and Mazzucato, M. (eds.), Wiley Blackwell: Chichester (134–155).

Taylor, N. and Mankiw, N. G. (2017) *Economics*, 4th edition, South-Western CENGAGE Learning: Andover.

Union of Radical Political Economics (URPE) (2021) Principles of radical political economics, https://urpe.org/resource/principles-of-radical-political-economics/

Van Parijs, P. and Vanderborght, Y. (2017) *Basic Income: A Radical Proposal for a Free Society and a Sane Economy*, Harvard University Press: Cambridge.

Varoufakis, Y. (2015) *The Global Minotaur: America, Europe, and the Future of the Global Economy*. Zed Books: London.

Webster, C. (1998) *The National Health Service: A Political History,* Oxford University Press: Oxford.

Wray, L. R. (2015) *Understanding Modern Money*, second edition, Edward Elgar: Cheltenham.

Wray, L. R. (2016) *Why Minsky Matters: An Introduction to the Work of a Maverick Economist*, Princeton University Press: Princeton, NJ.

Wray, L. R. (2019) Alternative paths to modern monetary theory, in Fullbrook, E. and Morgan. J. (eds), *Modern Monetary Theory and Its Critics*, World Economics Association Books: Bristol (8–46).

Yonay, Y. P. (1998) *The Struggle Over the Soul of Economics: Institutional and Neoclassical Economists in America between the Wars*, Princeton University Press: Princeton, NJ.

14 Policy Challenges, Ideologies, and the Evolution of Behavioural Economics

Peter E. Earl

Introduction

Behavioural economists base their analysis on what is known about how people behave, rather than on axioms chosen for their analytical convenience. The knowledge that they use comes primarily from psychology, experiments, interviews, and questionnaires, with introspection and anecdotes playing serious roles in raising questions about the adequacy of conventional economic thinking. Aspects of the behavioural approach date back to Marshall and even to Adam Smith, but it became more noticeable in the 1930s with Keynes's psychologically inspired view of how asset markets function under uncertainty, and with the publication of the first findings of the Oxford Economists Research Group (OERG) via the launch of *Oxford Economics Papers* in 1938. The OERG's work cast doubt on the responsiveness of firms to changes in interest rates (Meade and Andrews, 1938) and suggested that firms set their prices in a take-it-or-leave-it way by adding a mark-up to their costs rather than by equating marginal costs and revenues (Hall and Hitch, 1939). These contributions added weight to the case for using fiscal policy rather than monetary policy to manage aggregate demand and implied that inflation might be explained in terms of changes in costs, as firms would normally tend to respond to increases in demand by raising their output. However, the 'behavioural economics' term only came into use after the end of World War II, so the focus of this chapter is on the intersection between behavioural economics and policy after 1945.

To understand this intersection, it is useful to be aware of the distinction that Sent (2004) has drawn between 'Old' and 'New' behavioural economics. 'Old behavioural economics' (OBE) refers to contributions made prior to 1980, and in a similar vein since then, that have sought to rebuild economics in a way that incorporates ideas from psychology and organizational research and is not anchored to established economic methods. OBE is epitomized by the contributions that earned Herbert Simon the 1978 Nobel Memorial Prize in Economic Sciences, where the notion of 'satisficing' replaces the conventional focus on optimization. 'New behavioural economics' (NBE) refers to contributions from around 1980 onwards that seek to make sense of evidence

DOI: 10.4324/9781003228097-14

at odds with predictions from conventional economics in terms of 'bias-inducing heuristics' that real humans seem prone to use as a means of coping with everyday decision-making challenges. This approach is epitomized by the work that led to the award of Nobel Memorial Prizes to Daniel Kahneman (in 2002) and Richard Thaler (in 2017).

The chapter covers five policy-related areas. The first three are areas addressed in OBE that have practical significance but have been given little attention within NBE. The first case study focuses on the work of George Katona on consumer sentiment and its significance for macroeconomic policymakers. The second case study examines the intersection between the behavioural theory of the firm and the contrasting views taken in Japan and by Western neoliberal politicians about how organizational efficiency can be improved and how rates of national productivity growth can be increased. The third case study shows how ideas from the behavioural theory of the firm were deployed, in conjunction with related thinking in marketing and psychology, to understand how 'non-price factors' could create problems for policymakers. The fourth case study then shifts focus to NBE, where the policy philosophy of Thaler and his followers has attracted the interest of politicians despite being criticized for 'pathologizing' consumers (Mehta, 2013). The fifth and final case study considers the potential role of behavioural insights for policymaking aimed at addressing contemporary environmental challenges such as the existential threat posed by global warming.

Consumer Sentiment and Macroeconomic Management

Uncertainty makes optimizing decisions about saving to fund future consumption inherently problematic. Consequently, in his *General Theory*, Keynes (1936) offered what was essentially a rule-/habit-based view of saving behaviour whereby people accumulate savings from their unspent income at a rate determined by their 'propensity to consume'. He also presumed that the marginal propensity to consume was a decreasing function of income. In the early post-war period, two lines of psychology-based thinking augmented Keynes's view of the consumption function. One was Duesenberry's (1949) 'relative income hypothesis' which drew on social psychology and focused on how consumers' concerns about their social standing could affect their saving behaviour: he envisaged that consumption would display a ratchet effect when income fell, for people would cut back on saving (and, if necessary, draw down their savings) rather than face the social ignominy of being seen to fall behind in terms of status. This section focuses on the other psychological perspective, which came from George Katona (1951, 1960), of the University of Michigan's Survey Research Center. It questioned the short-run stability of the propensity to spend.

Katona recognized that, in a modern affluent society, much consumption is discretionary and can therefore be readily postponed. For example, expensive foreign holidays and restaurant meals are not essential right now and can readily be substituted with something cheaper if one 'needs' a break or a meal but is reluctant to run down one's financial assets. Likewise, consumers enjoy discretion about when they replace their cars, for they mostly replace them to get more recent models rather than because their vehicles are now only fit for a wrecking yard. It might therefore seem that aggregate consumption spending is driven by the social pressures that Duesenberry emphasized, and/or by the power of advertising, as Galbraith (1958) argued. However, Katona argued that such pressures to spend could be overwhelmed or augmented by shifts in consumer sentiment. If consumers became nervous about their prospects, their discretionary spending could suddenly dry up even if their incomes had not fallen and/or they had not run out of opportunities to make credit-financed purchases. A telling example was the 1957–1958 downturn in the USA, which was hard to explain in terms of conventional economic variables and seemed to have more to do with Cold War concerns resurfacing after the USSR demonstrated its technological capabilities by launching its first Sputnik ahead of the USA's first satellite. Conversely, discretionary spending could take off due to non-economic events (even, say, the international success of a national sporting team) that resulted in people feeling good about their prospects. The survey-based index of consumer sentiment that Katona and his colleagues pioneered provided a way of studying the relationship between consumer confidence and spending, with Katona and Strumpel (1976) later showing how, in the mid-1970s US downturn, a fall in consumer sentiment was associated with a fall in spending on consumer durables that preceded the downturn in business investment.

Katona's contribution can be viewed as akin to applying Keynes's (1936, pp. 161–162) view of the significance of 'animal spirits', as a driver of business investment under fundamental uncertainty, to household discretionary spending. It adds weight to Keynes's views about the need for governments to be willing to run fiscal deficits to restore aggregate demand, rather than to pursue austerity policies if the economy is experiencing a major downturn in activity and tax revenue has decreased. However, Katona's view of consumption poses a problem for those Keynesians who (mistakenly, in the analysis of Keynes's thinking offered by Hutchison, 1977) interpret Keynes as implying that macroeconomic policy could aim to keep 'fine tuning' economies to hold them close to full employment yet free of inflationary pressures. If consumer sentiment is prone to instability that is not always well related to changes in key macroeconomic indicators, there is great scope for policymakers to be surprised by sudden downturns in consumer sentiment and for excess aggregate demand to emerge due to unexpectedly buoyant consumer sentiment in the event of a macroeconomic stimulus.

Although the University of Michigan's Index of Consumer Sentiment led to the construction of many similar indices, it continues to be compiled (see www.sca.isr.umich.edu/). However, even though indices of consumer sentiment are reported in primetime TV news, the idea that aggregate consumer spending is driven by confidence has barely penetrated academic macroeconomics: it clashes with mainstream approaches that treat macroeconomics as the aggregation of outcomes of micro-level 'rational' choices.

Organizational Efficiency and Productivity

The best-known pre-1980 behavioural contributions were made by Herbert Simon, Richard Cyert, and James March, whose research team at what became Carnegie-Mellon University (CMU) focused mainly on the internal operations of firms and other organizations (see Simon, 1947, 1959; March and Simon, 1958; Cyert and March, 1963). Simon's early contributions were much inspired by Chester Barnard's (1938) book *The Functions of the Executive*, which emphasized that leadership skills are crucial for organizational performance as an executive's authority is granted by workers rather than being guaranteed by the executive's title. Simon assigned a key role to the 'docility' of workers in allowing firms to run smoothly in the direction that managers wish to take them. He saw this as a key issue since employment contracts often lack detail on the outputs that workers are expected to produce for a given weekly salary (Simon, 1951). Their output thus has a large discretionary element, with the incentive to perform well coming via scope for enhancing one's promotion prospects by being seen to perform well. The salary-recipient's situation is thus very different from, say, that of fruit pickers who are paid per kilo of fruit that they pick, or sales staff whose income is mainly from commissions: in the latter cases, the incentive to perform well comes via the immediate reward of performance-based pay. Simon also challenged the notion that decision-making entails finding optimal solutions; instead, he argued that, because of uncertainty and complexity, people can at best achieve 'bounded rationality' and must 'satisfice', i.e., they get through life by trying to meet aspiration levels that, in the long run, they adjust to align with their attainments. In the short run, however, aspirations are sticky, and actual or expected failures to meet them prompt decision-makers to search (initially locally) until they find something that seems likely to serve as a satisfactory means to meeting the goals to which they aspire.

Cyert and March's behavioural theory of the firm takes these themes further by seeing firms as coalitions of stakeholders who benefit from their association with the firm but who have conflicting interests. Hence, although organizational goals may be set by boards and senior managers and may help with coordination and in shaping expectations regarding acceptable performance levels, what really interests the stakeholders are whether they will be able to meet their personal 'subgoals' regarding what they can extract from the organization. However, none of them knows for sure how far they can push their luck when bargaining for a better deal. As a result, in good times, with aspirations lagging attainments, 'organizational slack' develops, with some stakeholders enjoying returns greater than the minimum they view as acceptable given the alternatives available to them. When the going gets tougher, those who see their returns falling below their transfer earnings may be willing to risk experimenting by demanding concessions from others rather than simply moving elsewhere. If they succeed in restoring their prospective returns to satisfactory levels, organizational slack is thereby reduced. Clearly, an important consideration in determining how pushy to be is what one's opportunities appear to be in the external environment. For example, if managers see their counterparts in other organizations enjoying increasingly lucrative remuneration packages, they may be more inclined to risk things backfiring if they try to extract more from their existing organizations without improving their performance.

Cyert and March argue that the complexity of problems that must be addressed in firms results in rule-based decision-making and failures to work out all the trade-offs that decision options entail. Resource allocation tends to reflect departmental interests rather than organizational goals, and goals are attended to sequentially depending on what currently seems the most urgent issue to address (this idea has also been applied to the behaviour of policymakers: see Mosley, 1976, 1984; Drakopoulos, 2004). The failure to consider the collateral implications of the steps taken to meet whichever goal is being focused upon makes organizations prone to appear to 'go round in circles' as they give sequential attention to goals. The CMU team saw organizations as cautious, reactive entities whose managers engage in 'uncertainty avoidance', often by attempting to achieve a 'negotiated environment' (for example, by lobbying governments for support and protection). Uncertainty about the returns to many activities (notably to marketing and research and development) results in budgets set via established rules playing key resource allocation roles and becoming focal points for attention during intra-organizational bargaining.

The CMU team's work was complemented by more explicitly policy-related contributions of Harvey Leibenstein (1966, 1976, 1989) focused on what he called 'X-inefficiency'. This term essentially refers to what most non-economists would mean if they said that an organization was operating inefficiently, namely that its productivity levels were below those that ought to have been possible given the resources at its disposal. Such a view of efficiency clashes with the conventional economist's presumption that firms maximize their profits, so economists normally view inefficiency in terms of deadweight losses of consumer surplus that result from relative prices being distorted by market imperfections.

Leibenstein argued that economists often underestimated the welfare losses associated with monopolies or protectionist trade policies because they assumed that observed cost levels of firms were the lowest ever possible. He contended that, especially where firms enjoyed monopoly advantages or were shielded by tariffs and/or quotas, they were likely to be operating with higher costs than they might have achieved in the face of stronger competition. Managers are not always aware of current best-practice production methods, and they cannot monitor everything that their subordinates do. Those that report to them may therefore be enjoying a quiet life, taking advantage of the vagueness of their employment contracts while mindful that those who set out to perform conspicuously well risk being ostracized for breaking social norms regarding reasonable performance levels. The same argument applies at any level in an organization with multiple layers of management, so even CEOs and board members might be able to find ways for the firm to do better, to the benefit of shareholders and customers, if they were more motivated to do so.

However, as Loasby (1976) has pointed out, Leibenstein failed to give attention to the benefits of the vagueness in employment contracts: though fuzzy contracts facilitate subgoal pursuit, they are cheap to design, and they provide flexibility when surprises occur. Loasby also notes (as does Martin, 1978) that Leibenstein underplays the distributional issues that a reduction in *X*-inefficiency may entail: many consumers are workers, too, and benefits in terms of cheaper products may come at the cost of long-term unemployment or a more exhausting, more stressful life at work. Reductions in *X*-inefficiency may benefit some, harm others and leave yet others neither better nor worse off once things have settled down, and the adjustment costs may also be significant.

In sum, the behavioural approach to the firm views productivity as depending not merely on the quality of equipment and the capabilities of employees but also on the motivation of employees to concentrate on producing output and discovering better production methods. Rather than viewing productivity growth merely as a matter of buying better equipment and hiring more capable workers, the behavioural perspective implies that there is also potential to achieve it via three types of policy interventions (see also Cyert and George, 1969).

First, there is the 'stick' approach. This entails toughening up the competitive conditions that decision-makers face, thereby forcing them to perform better in some areas to continue to be able to meet their aspirations. The stick approach is evident in neoliberal/conservative/'managerialist' policies that entail:

- market deregulation (e.g., allowing new entry and reducing the amount of bureaucratic 'red tape' that entrants have to deal with).
- removing protectionist trade policies and public sector monopolies (often in conjunction with the corporatization and subsequent privatization of the former monopoly entities).
- opening input sourcing to bids from external suppliers (not just for services that have traditionally been performed in-house but also by filling vacant job slots externally rather than relying on internal labour markets).
- rehiring staff on fixed-term contracts with detailed KPIs (key performance indicators), and measures aimed at breaking the bargaining power of labour unions.

From the behavioural standpoint, these kinds of measures can also be viewed as conducive to increasing productivity and reducing real labour costs by increasing worker docility, especially in conjunction with the tightening up of eligibility requirements for unemployment benefits and reductions in the real value of these benefits: fears about being unemployed for long periods would concentrate the minds of workers on being more cooperative with their bosses.

An alternative 'stick' approach, that goes against the neoliberal mindset, is to use regulations to promote search activity. Indeed, even if regulatory policies are introduced to serve ends other than productivity growth, they may still impact the latter. An example of this is evident in Loasby's (1967) study of industrial location policies in the UK: firms that were prevented from expanding unless they did so in depressed areas were sometimes surprised to discover much cheaper ways of operating when they put their minds to dealing with the restrictions that the policies entailed.

The second way of promoting productivity growth is the 'carrot' approach that involves providing performance-based rewards to motivate employees to perform more with a view to organizational goals rather than their personal subgoals. This has been central to neoliberal/conservative government policy platforms, too, typically in the highly regressive form of cuts in taxes on profits and reforms to personal tax systems that not only reduce marginal rates of income tax but also favour performance-based executive remuneration packages built around stock options. But less regressive systems for aligning employee interests with long-run corporate goals focused on rapid technological change and productivity growth can also be designed. Large firms in Japan devised precisely such a system during the period in which the behavioural theory of the firm was being worked out. It entailed an inclusive system of company-based unions, seniority-based pay, lifetime employment, allowing line workers to participate in decision-making, and paying everyone significant annual bonuses based on the firm's performance (see Adams and Kobayashi, 1969; Dore, 1973; Gao, 1998).

The third approach complements Barnard's (1938) emphasis on the leadership role of executives in creating dynamic organizations. It entails using what we might call 'coaching' methods, akin to those used in sports, to promote a 'We can do better' mentality via education and exhortation that uses examples and benchmarking studies of the success of others whose ambitions and strategies might be emulated. This approach has appealed to social democrats and others who place less faith than neoliberals in 'free' markets. At the government level, it is evident in the creation of government departments that focus on identifying areas where performance could be improved, bringing them to the attention of relevant parties, and trying to coordinate the setting of more ambitious industry-wide targets. Examples include some of the activities of the Ministry of International Trade and Investment in Japan over many decades and the role of the National Economic Development Office in the UK (cf. the start of the next case study in this chapter). However, the earliest instance is probably the use of agricultural extension schemes, whose history long predates the behavioural theory of the firm. Where firms or entire economies are facing major problems, the role of 'coaching' may be extended to include leadership activities aimed at generating hope, to deter an exodus of key personnel whose loss would hamper the potential for recovery (Wallis, Dollery, and Crase, 2009).

Although the examples above align with implications that might be drawn from the work of Simon, Cyert and March, and Leibenstein, there is little evidence to suggest that these policies were inspired by their work. The Japanese management systems were created in parallel with the work at CMU and, according to Gao (1998, pp. 97–98), this was in the context of encouragement from ministerial technocrats whose inspiration (and, sometimes, doctoral training) came from Schumpeter. (In academic economics, the OBE and Schumpeterian literatures on firms and industrial evolution were eventually merged in the seminal 'neo-Schumpeterian' work of Nelson and Winter, 1982, but this synthesis remains outside the mainstream.) In the West, behavioural perspectives on the firm were certainly taught in the 1970s and early 1980s in university courses on industrial economics (cf. the textbooks by Pickering, 1974, especially Chapter 6, and Hay and Morris, 1979, especially pp. 67–70, 248–251). However, the inspiration for the policies introduced after the electoral successes of Margaret Thatcher and Ronald Reagan seems to have been ideas drawn from Adam Smith, Friedrich Hayek, and Milton Friedman about the power of competition for enhancing social welfare in a world of self-interested individuals.

Interest in the behavioural analysis of organizations largely petered out in academic economics while neoliberal 'reforms' were being implemented (the exception was in evolutionary economics, within Nelson and Winter's neo-Schumpeterian synthesis). This occurred despite Herbert Simon being awarded the 1978 Nobel Memorial Prize in Economic Sciences for his work on decision-making in organizations, and despite organizational economics becoming a hot research area in the 1980s and 1990s. In essence what happened was that rather than adopting Simon's satisficing perspective, mainstream economists developed their own analysis of organizations. They accepted that stakeholders differ in their interests and that this can affect organizational performance, but their focus became one of designing optimal incentive structures for self-serving optimizing agents, to ensure that the latter best served the principals that hired them. Examples of this 'agency theory' approach influencing policymakers are easier to find, as with the Harvard PhD-based book by Murray Horn (1995), published while he was Secretary to the New Zealand Treasury. Agency theory was essentially static, for it lost sight of the role of problem-driven search in generating knowledge of better ways of doing things. Decades passed before attempts were made to infuse agency theory with insights from behavioural economics (see, for example, Kaufman and Englander, 2011; Pepper and Gore, 2015).

Non-Price Competition and Non-Compensatory Decision-Making

In the late 1970s, as the UK manufacturing sector was increasingly struggling against competition from Germany and Japan, and as neoliberal ideas were gaining political traction, the UK's National Economic Development Office (NEDO) published a provocative report on research undertaken by a team led by its Economics Director, David Stout (1977). The report argued that the widespread focus on achieving productivity improvements – and hence cost and price reductions relative to overseas rivals – as the solution to the UK's economic malaise was coming at the expense of neglect of the significance of 'non-price factors' in shaping trade in manufactured products. Successful attempts to improve efficiency might increase cost competitiveness without solving the balance of trade problem insofar as the problem with UK exports commonly was not that they were too expensive but that the products themselves were deficient.

At that time, the best-known economic analysis of consumer behaviour that focused on the characteristics of products was the model that Lancaster (1966) had developed. However, Lancaster's model was built around a utility function that assumed consumers have decreasing marginal rates of substitution between characteristics. With relative prices determining how much a budget could buy in terms of characteristics if spent on one product rather than another, or combinations thereof, the model implied that cheaper domestically manufactured products would enable buyers to get a better 'bang for their bucks'. Hence, so long as British workers were prepared to tolerate slower real wages growth than their counterparts in countries whose firms offered products that excelled in non-price terms, a lower exchange rate and productivity improvements would enable the UK to pay its bills by following the maxim that 'If you can't sell good goods, sell cheap goods' (Posner, 1978, p. 51). This line of argument was not conducive to the 1979 Thatcher government taking up NEDO's concern about the significance of non-price factors, or subsequent suggestions that product design needed to be taken much more seriously (Schott, 1984), and that British firms needed to develop a much stronger marketing orientation and focus on finding out what buyers wanted rather than simply offering the products that engineers devised (Doyle, 1985).

From the Lancaster/Posner standpoint, the only way that non-price shortcomings can trump any price reduction is where the cost of *using* the product exceeds the combined capital and operating costs of its technically superior alternatives: in such a situation, no one will have a use for the product even if they are given it for free. This exception has had practical significance in the shift to digital technologies, such as with the switch from analogue Strowger and TXE4 telephone exchange technologies to the digital System X technology from the late 1970s, and the switch from film-based photography to digital imaging as digital camera costs tumbled in the early 2000s. But the

NEDO research can be read as implicitly suggesting that there can be other situations in which policies intended to facilitate relative price adjustments by achieving lower costs would fail, even if they resulted in substantial productivity improvements. To understand what these 'other situations' might be, it helped if one reflects on consumer behaviour mindful of the behavioural theory of the firm.

Like hedonic pricing models that seek to predict prices as an additive function of product characteristics, Lancaster's model abstracted from the cognitive challenges entailed in trading off the non-price characteristics and prices of rival products to arrive at overall scores by which they can be ranked. This could be especially important in situations where many rival products were available and these products differed significantly in terms of many characteristic dimensions. There was an obvious lesson to take from Simon's satisficing analysis and Cyert and March's view of firms as setting aspirations for multiple goals that they pursued sequentially: it might be wise to think of decisions about which product to buy as being made in a satisficing way that involves a hierarchical filtering process in which products are successively eliminated if they fail to meet any of the buyer's targets.

From this standpoint, the product that survives the biggest number of these aspirational tests, in order of priority, is the one that gets purchased. Search continues if the would-be buyer rules that none of the options has survived enough of the tests. If two or more products tie, a further rule is needed to complete the process. This rule might indeed be price-based – such as 'if there is a tie, choose the cheapest of the products that have tied' (which ignores cheaper products that have already been rejected on non-price grounds) – but it might not be. For example, a car buyer might instead choose the product whose range of colour options includes the most appealing paintwork, having already deemed all the tied contenders to be 'cheap enough'. This is rather like making the final choice based on the presence of what marketers nowadays call a 'USP', i.e., a unique selling point (or unique selling proposition), that had not been on the priority list but which appeals to the buyer when drawn to his or her attention (cf. Trout, 2008, Chapter 3).

This view of how consumers deliberate when they suffer from bounded rationality was branded as 'characteristic filtering' in Earl (1983) and then used in Earl (1984, pp. 195–197) as a basis for discussing the NEDO findings. It allows a single substandard area of performance to be a 'deal-breaker', regardless of how well a product performs in higher-priority tests (so long as it passes them) and regardless of how well it would have performed in lower-priority tests from which it is excluded. In terms of conventional economic thinking, it entails irrational intolerance and ignores relevant information, yet it is economical in its demands on the decision-makers' computational and short-term memory capacities. It provides a plausible means towards understanding the UK car industry's loss of market share in the late 1970s insofar as UK-built cars were viewed as, say, too unreliable (especially if reliability had a high priority) or inadequately equipped with 'standard' features compared with Japanese vehicles that may have been only just adequate in areas such as space utilization, ride and handling but 'ticked more boxes' in terms of interior 'bells and whistles'. Similarly, the collapse of the UK toy industry in the early 1980s might plausibly be explained in part by non-price shortcomings that resulted from UK toy designers not appreciating what children were expecting products to offer. For example, most children may have had rather low aspirations regarding how accurately scale-model cars represented their full-size counterparts; instead, their main concern may have been with how the models performed in school playgrounds. If so, Meccano's decision not to license the 'hot wheels' technology (Brown, 1993, p. 599) to make its Dinky Toys models roll faster, and for longer distances, would have been a big mistake, even though this technology made model cars look less realistic.

If potential buyers are rejecting products because of their non-price shortcomings, the implication for suppliers is simple: they need to bring the quality of their products up to the standards that the buyers set; cutting prices will not change the behaviour of these buyers. If non-price factors are causing balance of trade problems, tariffs or currency depreciations may only be effective if they result in imported rival products becoming viewed as 'too expensive', leading consumers to forego some of their non-price aspirations if they are to purchase products that come into their budget ranges. More effective policies may entail the use of quotas and bureaucratic hurdles for importers, or the imposition of local design rules that local products can already meet but which imported rivals will only be able to meet after their manufacturers have incurred significant costs. But the significance of deal-breaker elements in decision-making has wider ramifications for policymakers, as in the following four examples (see also Brooks, 1988).

First, deal-breaker elements may make it impossible to form effective political coalitions or resolve industrial relations problems. Secondly, such elements may arise on both sides of the labour market: for example, if jobs are considered 'too dangerous', 'too remotely located', etc., offering more pay may not increase the rate of applications from applicants who have the specific skills that are required. Thirdly, consider the difficulty of undertaking cost–benefit analysis on new infrastructure projects if those whose properties would have to be demolished to make way for them say, without attempting to extort more compensation, that they 'would not move for the world' because they believe that 'money can't buy' an acceptable alternative to the life they have built for themselves at their current location. Finally, note that deal-breaker rules may be manifestations of personal operating principles that embody normative views of the world that have policy significance, as with the behaviour of those who were generating externalities for the wider population and sometimes even had to give up their jobs, because they refused, on principle, to be vaccinated against the COVID-19 virus.

The 'characteristic filtering' view of choice complemented a neglected view of consumer behaviour proposed by Ironmonger (originally in 1961, but not published until 1972) to make sense of observed changes in patterns of consumer behaviour after the introduction of new commodities. His analysis had some features in common with Lancaster's work but viewed consumer choices as based on a hierarchically ordered set of satiable wants. It was not inspired by Simon's thinking and instead can be viewed as having formalized a long-standing hierarchical view of choice, shifting that view's focus to product quality and what makes consumers switch to new products. (For surveys of hierarchical perspectives on choice and the place of hierarchical perspectives in the history of economic thought, see Drakopoulos, 1994; Drakopoulos and Karayiannis, 2004.) However, Ironmonger had not explored the significance of his analysis for international trade policy and focused mainly on changing patterns of demand for generic categories of products rather than on the demand for the different within-genre varieties that manufacturers offered.

It is important to note that the 'characteristic filtering' perspective owed much to Simon-inspired thinking in marketing (notably Bettman, 1979) that focused on the information-processing heuristics that buyers use. Within the latter literature, on what is labelled 'non-compensatory' decision rules, it is acknowledged that there are several other ways by which buyers can end up operating in an intolerant manner. One is to use a 'conjunctive' approach, which entails rejecting any product that does not match up to a complete set of requirements. This approach might function as a shortlisting technique, with a Lancaster-style trade-off then being applied to the more computationally manageable set of options that 'tick all the boxes' but differ in how they over-achieve, whereas characteristic filtering obviously provides a way of dealing with cases where nothing is adequate in conjunctive terms. The marketing perspective also admits the possibility of buyers taking a 'disjunctive' approach, i.e., being obsessed with finding the best performer in terms of a single characteristic, regardless of how it performs in other areas. If this produces a tie, the buyer may switch to a 'lexicographic' heuristic that works hierarchically, like characteristic filtering, but does not entail the use of performance targets. Instead, it operates like a stack of disjunctive tests, with the buyer taking options that tie as best on the top-priority test on to the characteristic with the second-highest priority, and on to the third-highest priority, etc., if there is another tie between any of the options that had tied in terms of higher-priority characteristics. (The 'lexicographic' notion is commonly mentioned briefly in microeconomics to illustrate alternative, questionable preferences in the good space: the consumer is portrayed as looking for the bundle that contains the biggest quantity of the first-priority good regardless of whatever else is in the bundle; if there is a tie, bundles are ranked according to which dominates in terms of the second-priority good, and so on. See, for example, Malinvaud, 1972, p. 20; Deaton and Muellbauer, 1980, p. 27.)

Characteristic filtering is easy to confuse with the notion of 'elimination by aspects' (EBA) explored by Tversky (1972). EBA works in a filtering way, too, but the decision-maker is viewed as assigning weights to characteristics based on their importance, with these weights determining the *probabilities* of characteristics coming to mind first, second, third, and so on, in the filtering process. In other words, the decision-maker choosing via EBA does not apply decision criteria based on a hierarchical ordering of requirements, and the choice process may be highly path-dependent, with the outcome depending on what triggers the order in which characteristics come to mind.

However, despite the long-standing interest of some economics and marketing scholars in hierarchical/non-compensatory ways of taking decisions, mainstream economists remain impervious to such thinking, maintaining their core principle that 'everyone has their price'. It seems as though they are not merely unaware of research by leading marketing scholars that finds strong evidence of non-compensatory decision-making, especially when people are under cognitive pressure (the classic study is Payne, Bettman, and Johnson, 1993); it also seems that their habits of thought are so ingrained they fail to notice widespread evidence in everyday life that can be taken to imply that the substitution principle is a gross over-generalization – evidence such as people referring to 'box-ticking' ways of choosing, products that they rejected due to having 'too much' or 'not enough' of particular features, claiming that they simply 'do not like' some products, making principles-based choices (such as 'becoming a vegetarian') or seeming to experience satiation in some areas and then shifting their focus to commodities with different kinds of characteristics regardless of changes in relative prices.

Nudging Decision-Makers and Boosting Decision-Making Capabilities

As Thaler (2015) has recounted, the origins of his remarkably successful version of behavioural economics came via a fortuitous chain of events that began in the mid-1970s with his interest in how people make decisions about high-risk job opportunities. He thereby came across research on risk-taking that had been conducted by Kahneman and Tversky and their colleagues via lab-based experiments focused mainly on hypothetical lottery choices (see Tversky and Kahneman, 1974; Kahneman, Slovic, and Tversky, eds, 1982). They found that people assess risks and choose in ways that differed systematically from the dominant subjective expected utility (SEU) model: it appeared that people dealt with the cognitive challenges of taking decisions by using a large set of heuristics that 'biased' their behaviour away from what SEU theory asserted a 'rational' decision-maker should do – rather, we might say, in the way that a vehicle with poor wheel alignment will pull to one side. The heuristics in question included using gain/loss reference points rather than comparing overall values (and assigning losses roughly twice the score, in disutility, that they would assign, in utility, to a similarly sized gain), factoring sunk costs into their choices, allowing evaluations to be unduly affected by initial anchor points and how options were framed, generalizing from very limited knowledge, and overweighting low probability outcomes while underweighting high probability outcomes. Systematic incompetence in the handling of statistics was widespread (e.g., in handling compound probabilities). Kahneman and Tversky's (1979) prospect theory incorporated many of these behavioural regularities and thereby posited an *S*-shaped utility function that is steeper for losses than for gains and whose inflexion point is at the reference point used in dividing gains from losses.

Thaler realized that the prospect theory utility function had many interesting applications for risk-free choices. His research programme (outlined in Thaler, 2015) explored these applications and focused on exposing other aspects of everyday life that were anomalous in terms of conventional economic thinking and which could be explained as resulting from the use of specific heuristics. The only notable point of intersection between his work and research of the kind considered in the previous two sections of this chapter was that he saw people as using heuristic methods in choosing due to the cognitive challenges they faced. The Simon-inspired contributions to behavioural economics focus on heuristics in terms of the sets of decision rules that people experiment with on a personal basis and/or share socially – operating rules whose impacts range from those that are highly effective (as in Gigerenzer, Todd, and the ABC Research Group, 1999) through to needless underachievement. By contrast, Thaler-style behavioural economics focuses on heuristics that are inherited dysfunctional aspects of human nature – hence Mehta's (2013) accusation that the approach 'pathologizes' consumers. Moreover, the dysfunctionality of the heuristics that are studied is relative to what a 'fully rational' economic agent is expected to do, rather than in terms of, say, attainment levels that can readily be achieved amid the pressures and constraints of the decision environment. But Thaler's methodology has proved fertile, and its findings have been both engaging and hard for mainstream economists to ignore. As a result, courses on this kind of behavioural economics have been incorporated with great success into university curricula.

Growing insight into the predictable effects of these aspects of human nature did not lead Thaler to advocate policies that sought to use regulatory interventions to protect people from their decision-making shortcomings; rather, he started to design policies that exploited human shortcomings in ways that would improve welfare. Most notably, Thaler and Benartzi (2004) devised the 'Save More Tomorrow' plan for increasing retirement savings. Instead of requiring Americans to lock up a percentage of their income in a retirement saving fund (in the way that, say, Australians have been required to do), the plan took account of default bias by offering workers plans that they were enrolled in by default, so that they had to make the (small) effort of ticking the opt-out box if they did not wish to participate. The likelihood of opting out due to loss aversion was countered by subtracting savings from increases in income rather than from the level of income being received at the time the decision to accept the default or opt out had to be made. It was simple, left Americans to make their choices, and it worked.

Around the same time, with his lawyer colleague, Cass Sunstein, Thaler came up with the term 'libertarian paternalism' to describe this approach to policy, which they framed in a popularizing way in their book *Nudge* (Thaler and Sunstein, 2008) as entailing designing 'choice architecture' to prompt – but not require – behaviour that would be welfare-enhancing. The thinking here was that whenever a choice is presented to decision-makers, it must be framed somehow, so it should be framed in a way that the policymaker has reason to believe will be beneficial to the target group rather than prone to result in them making needlessly poor choices.

Thaler and Sunstein accept that nudge-style policies warrant ethical scrutiny given that such policies are designed to shape behaviour without the underlying strategy being explained. They envisaged that this could be part of a pilot phase of using randomized control trials to test whether planned nudges are effective. The subjects who had been in the nudge treatment groups would be informed about what had been going on and asked how they felt about it in light of how they ended up behaving. One could also inform subjects in control groups that they had been part of an experiment, explain how those in the nudge group tended to behave differently and ask the control subjects how they would have felt to have been nudged. Insofar as the dominant view of participants in the experimental trial is that being nudged in the manner in question is not a problem and produced benefits, then the policy would be said to have passed the subjects' 'as judged by themselves' ethical test and be suitable to implement as intended. All this sounds fine in principle, but we might, like Sugden (2018), be concerned that governments will fail to follow this procedure in practice, especially where they stand to benefit from changing their constituents' behaviour. This was precisely the situation in the first nudge-based policy designed by the UK's Behavioural Insights Team, which sought to increase the submission rate of personal income tax returns via a letter that played upon the social conformity heuristic by informing the recipients that they were in a small minority who were running late with their tax returns (see Thaler, 2015).

Although nudges may (as with the late tax letter) be very cost-effective means for producing some of the behaviour changes that policymakers seek, there is a risk that focusing on them will divert attention from potential payoffs to investing in enabling people to make better decisions. For example, if people are by nature prone to be very inept when gathering data and attempting to draw inferences from data, we might be wise to consider training them in statistics as part of the school curriculum and supply them with data (or knowledge about how they may easily find relevant data) that a statistician would see as providing a basis for drawing reliable inferences to inform their choices (see further Gigerenzer, 2015). Likewise, if we can discover what Gigerenzer, Todd, and the ABC Research Group (1999) call 'fast and frugal' heuristics for taking decisions in particular contexts, we might be able to build policies around informing people about these heuristics. In other words, instead of taking human shortcomings as given by nature, we may be able to help people by, in effect, providing them with new apps to add to the repertoires of rules and heuristics that comprise their personal operating systems for coping with life. Instead of covertly seeking to manipulate people in a paternalistic manner, we may openly seek to 'boost' their decision-making capabilities (see further, Grüne-Yanoff and Hertwig, 2016).

Countering Environmentally Destructive Lifestyles

The four proceeding sections all yield behavioural insights that are relevant for policymakers who are wrestling with contemporary environmental challenges. Some of these insights come from a single area. For example, the behavioural approach to the firm implies that, in the absence of regulatory policies, firms that can meet their aspirations via their existing techniques and products may delay making environmentally helpful changes that would lead them to discover ways to increase their productivity and profitability (cf. the 'Porter hypothesis': see Porter and van der Linde, 1995a, 1995b; Ambec *et al.*, 2013). In other cases, diverse behavioural insights can be used together when designing and sequencing sets of policy measures.

Consider the uptake of battery electric vehicles (BEVs). Range anxiety and ambitious range aspirations may be a major non-compensatory impediment to consumers switching to BEVs even if they have the funds to do so. If so, it is better for governments to invest in battery-charging infrastructure rather than to provide subsidies to such consumers. Governments should expect discontinuities in the BEV uptake trajectory as popular range targets (say, 400 km/charge) are met by vehicles that are deemed cheap enough. Thaler's (1985) insights regarding 'mental accounting' may be applicable, too, in relation to managing views about how expensive electric vehicles are, as people may tend to keep the purchase and running costs of their cars in separate mental compartments. A $70,000 BEV could thus seem unacceptably expensive to those who are used to spending $45,000 on a car and $100 per week on fuel. However, such thinking might not be an impediment to BEV adoption if the product can be sold on a 'battery not included' basis for $45,000 and the battery leased separately for less than $100 per week. However, we should recognize, via Katona, that consumers will hold back from making investments in expensive environmentally friendly durables if they lack confidence about their financial situations and whether it is wise to invest in such products now rather than waiting for technological improvements. Yet there is the risk that strong consumer sentiment will merely fuel spending that increases environmental footprints if policymakers do not devise effective ways to ensure that consumers keep in mind the environmental consequences of their lifestyles.

There is considerable scope for policies designed to do the latter by triggering emotions such as fear, anxiety, and guilt (for example, in parents whose environmental choices will affect their children's lives). However, although marketing has long taken account of the psychology of emotions, most behavioural economics have been slow to give attention to emotions (despite suggestions in Earl, 1983). Meanwhile, marketing-savvy politicians (such as Australia's then-Prime Minister, Scott Morrison in the 2019 federal election) have been able to cultivate support by using fear appeals based on the losses that voters will incur in a transition to more sustainable living. Seen from the standpoint of Thaler-style behavioural economics, such conservative ruses are likely to get traction via both loss aversion and present bias (i.e., gross overweighting of immediate benefits and costs due to people tending to discount in a quasi-hyperbolic manner rather than exponentially).

There is plenty of scope, too, for using nudges and boosts to reduce human environmental impacts. Indeed, some public utilities worked out how to do this before *Nudge* was published: for example, during the 2007 Queensland drought, the water supply utility in Brisbane did not use the regressive strategy of raising prices to conserve water; instead, it successfully nudged and coached customers to be more careful with their water use. Water bills were designed to show customers whether they were exceeding socially normal rates of usage, as well as indicating that 'please explain' letters would be sent to those whose usage rates seemed unreasonable; informative leaflets on ways of reducing demand were also sent with bills.

However, there is the risk that in the face of complexity, policymakers and the general population will anchor their views of the environmental challenge on reducing carbon emissions and avoiding water shortages, and thereby lose sight of many of the lifestyle changes that are necessary if life on Earth is to become sustainable while inequality is reduced as per capita incomes are increased in developing countries. Consumers in affluent nations will need to learn how to enjoy life by taking more leisure and consuming less. 'Happiness economics', an area of behavioural economics not considered in this chapter, has a vital role to play here on the way to appropriate policymaking, as does an enhanced understanding of how people form their aspirations and how their views of acceptable behaviour evolve (see further Earl, 2022, Chapter 13).

Conclusion

Some readers may be surprised by how much of this chapter has been devoted to areas of behavioural economics that have not achieved the widespread currency among both policymakers and academic economists that has been achieved by the kind of behavioural economics that Thaler fostered from 1980 onwards. If so, they should consider whether they are implicitly assuming that the market for economic knowledge functions efficiently rather than being distorted by the operating heuristics that economists employ to cope with the impossibility of reading everything that economists have written. These heuristics result in contributions remaining unknown because they are not picked up by search rules or get dismissed if they conflict with core axioms and operating rules. The non-fashionable behavioural perspectives covered here (and others that a longer work would also have covered) have not been rejected empirically and they can be useful for policymakers. But they will continue to have limited impact if those who practise the currently fashionable approach to behavioural economics do not incorporate them in an integrative approach to behavioural economics (as is offered in Earl, 2022) and instead concentrate on identifying and explaining behaviour that is at odds with what a 'fully rational' agent would supposedly do. If they gave up anchoring their research to that reference point and sought also to understand effective ways of behaving in the real world in terms of rules and heuristics, they would have a wider range of areas in which they could offer behavioural insights to policymakers.

Bibliography

Adams, T. F. N., & Kobayashi, N. (1969). *The World of Japanese Busines.* London: Ward Lock.

Ambec, S., Cohen, M. A., Elgie, S., & Lanoie, P. (2013). The Porter hypothesis at 20: Can environmental regulation enhance innovation and competitiveness? *Review of Environmental Economics and Policy,* 7(1), 2–22.

Barnard, C. I. (1938). *The Functions of the Executive.* Cambridge, MA: Harvard University Press.

Bettman, J. R. (1979). *An Information Processing Theory of Consumer Choice.* Reading, MA: Addison–Wesley.

Brooks, M. A. (1988). Toward a behavioral analysis of public economics. In P. E. Earl (ed.), *Psychological Economics: Development, Tensions, Prospects* (pp. 169–188). Boston, MA: Kluwer Academic Publishers.

Brown, K. D. (1993). The collapse of the British toy industry, 1979–1984. *Economic History Review, New Series, 46*(3), 592–606.

Cyert, R. M., & George, K. D. (1969). Competition, growth and efficiency. *Economic Journal, 79*(313), 23–41.

Cyert, R. M., & March, J. G. (1963). *A Behavioral Theory of the Firm.* Englewood Cliffs, NJ: Prentice-Hall.

Deaton, A., & Muellbauer, J. (1980). *Economics and Consumer Behaviour.* Cambridge: Cambridge University Press.

Dore, R. P. (1973). *British Factory, Japanese Factory: The Origins of National Diversity in Industrial Relations.* Berkeley and Los Angeles: University of California Press.

Doyle, P. (1985). Marketing and the competitive performance of British industry: Areas for research. *Journal of Marketing Management, 1*(1–2), 87–98.

Drakopoulos, S. A. (1994). Hierarchical choice in economics. *Journal of Economic Surveys, 8*(2), 133–153.

Drakopoulos, S. A. (2004). Satisficing and sequential targets in economic policy: A politico-economic approach. *Contributions to Political Economy, 23*(1), 49–64.

Drakopoulos, S. A., & Karayiannis, A. D. (2004). The historical development of hierarchical behaviour in economic thought. *Journal of the History of Economic Thought, 26*(3), 363–378.

Duesenberry, J. S. (1949). *Income, Saving and the Theory of Consumer Behavior.* Cambridge, MA: Harvard University Press.

Earl, P. E. (1983). *The Economic Imagination: Towards a Behavioural Analysis of Choice.* Brighton: Wheatsheaf.

Earl, P. E. (1984). *The Corporate Imagination: How Big Companies Make Mistakes.* Brighton: Wheatsheaf.

Earl, P. E. (2022). *Principles of Behavioral Economics: Bringing Together Old, New and Evolutionary Approaches.* Cambridge: Cambridge University Press.

Galbraith, J. K. (1958). *The Affluent Society.* London: Hamish Hamilton.

Gao, B. (1998). Efficiency, culture, and politics: The transformation of Japanese management 1946–66. In M. Callon (ed.), *The Laws of the Markets* (pp. 84–115). Oxford: Blackwell/The Sociological Review.

Gigerenzer, G. (2015). On the supposed evidence for libertarian paternalism. *Review of Philosophy and Psychology, 6*(3), 361–383.

Gigerenzer, G., Todd, P. M., & the ABC Research Group (1999). *Simple Heuristics That Make Us Smart.* New York: Oxford University Press.

Grüne-Yanoff, T., & Hertwig, R. (2016). Nudge versus Boost: How coherence are policy and theory? *Minds and Machines, 26*(1–2), 149–183.

Hall, R. L., & Hitch, C. J. (1939). Price theory and business behaviour. *Oxford Economic Papers, 2*(May), 12–45.

Hay. D. A., & Morris, D. J. (1979). *Industrial Economics: Theory and Evidence.* Oxford: Oxford University Press.

Horn, M. (1995). *The Political Economy of Public Administration: Institutional Choice in the Public Sector.* Cambridge: Cambridge University Press.

Hutchison, T. W. (1977). *Keynes Versus the Keynesians…? An Essay in the Thinking of J. M. Keynes and the Accuracy of Its Interpretation by His Followers.* London: Institute of Economic Affairs.

Ironmonger, D. S. (1961). *New Commodities and Quality Change in the Theory and Measurement of Consumer Behaviour.* PhD Thesis, University of Cambridge.

Ironmonger, D. S. (1972). *New Commodities and Consumer Behaviour. University of Cambridge, Department of Applied Economics Monographs, No. 20.* Cambridge: Cambridge University Press.

Kahneman, D., Slovic, P., & Tversky, A. (eds.). (1982). *Judgement under Uncertainty: Heuristics and Biases.* Cambridge: Cambridge University Press.

Kahneman, D., & Tversky, A. (1979). Prospect theory: An analysis of decision under risk. *Econometrica, 47*(2), 263–291.

Katona, G. A. (1951). *Psychological Analysis of Economic Behavior.* New York: McGraw-Hill.

Katona, G. A. (1960). *The Powerful Consumer: Psychological Studies of the American Economy.* New York: McGraw-Hill.

Katona, G. A., & Strumpel, B. (1976). Consumer investment versus business investment. *Challenge, 18*(6), 12–16.

Kaufman, A., & Englander, E. (2011). Behavioral economics, federalism, and the triumph of stakeholder theory. *Journal of Business Ethics, 102*(3), 421–438.

Keynes, J. M. (1936). *The General Theory of Employment, Interest and Money.* London: Macmillan.

Lancaster, K. J. (1966). A new approach to consumer theory. *Journal of Political Economy, 75*(2), 132–157.

Leibenstein, H. (1966). Allocative efficiency vs. "X-efficiency". *American Economic Review, 56*(3), 392–414.

Leibenstein, H. (1976). *Beyond Economic Man: A New Foundation for Economics.* Cambridge, MA: Harvard University Press.

Leibenstein, H. (1989). *The Collected Essays of Harvey Leibenstein, Volume 2: X-Efficiency and Microeconomic Theory (edited by K. Button).* Aldershot: Edward Elgar.

Loasby, B. J. (1967). Making location policy work. *Lloyds Bank Review, 83*(January), 34–47.

Loasby, B. J. (1976). Review of *Beyond Economic Man: A New Foundation for Microeconomics,* by Harvey Leibenstein. *Economic Journal, 86*(344), 913–915.

Malinvaud, E. (1972). *Lectures on Microeconomic Theory.* Amsterdam: North-Holland.

March, J. G., & Simon, H. A. (1958). *Organizations.* New York: Wiley.

Martin, J. P. (1978). X-inefficiency, managerial effort and protection. *Economica, 45*(179), 273–286.

Meade, J. E., & Andrews, P. W. S. (1938). Summary of replies to questions on effects of interest rates. *Oxford Economic Papers, 1* (October), 14–31.

Mehta, J. (2013). The discourse of bounded rationality in academic and policy arenas: Pathologising the errant consumer. *Cambridge Journal of Economics, 37*(6), 1243–1261.

Mosley, P. (1976). Towards a 'satisficing' theory of economic policy. *Economic Journal, 86*(341), 59–72.

Mosley, P. (1984). *The Making of Economic Policy: Theory and Evidence from Britain and the United States since 1945.* Brighton: Wheatsheaf.

Nelson, R. R., & Winter, S. G. (1982). *An Evolutionary Theory of Economic Change.* Cambridge, MA: Belknap Press of Harvard University Press.

Payne, J. W., Bettman, J. R., & Johnson, E. J. (1993). *The Adaptive Decision Maker.* Cambridge: Cambridge University Press.

Pepper, A., & Gore, J. (2015). Behavioral agency theory: New foundations for theorizing about executive compensation. *Journal of Management, 41*(4), 1045–1068.

Pickering, J. F. (1974). *Industrial Structure and Market Conduct.* London: Martin Robertson.

Porter, M. E., & van der Linde, C. (1995a). Green and competitive. *Harvard Business Review, 73*(5), 120–134.

Porter, M. E., & van der Linde, C. (1995b). Towards a new conception of the environment-competitiveness relationship. *Journal of Economic Perspectives, 9*(4), 97–118.

Posner, M. V. (1978). Wages, prices and the exchange rate. In M. J. Artis & A. R. Nobay (eds.), *Contemporary Economic Analysis.* London: Croom Helm.

Schott, K. (1984). Economic competitiveness and design. *Journal of the Royal Society of Arts, 132*(5338), 648–659.

Sent, E.-M. (2004). Behavioral economics: How psychology made its (limited) way back into economics. *History of Political Economy, 36*(4), 735–760.

Simon, H. A. (1947). *Administrative Behavior.* New York: Macmillan (3rd edition 1976, Free Press).

Simon, H. A. (1951). A formal theory of the employment relationship. *Econometrica, 19*(3), 293–305.

Simon, H. A. (1959). Theories of decision-making in economics and behavioral science. *American Economic Review, 49*(3), 253–283.

Stout, D. K. (1977). *International Price Competitiveness, Non-Price Factors and Export Performance.* London: National Economic Development Office.

Sugden, R. (2018). Better off, as judged by themselves: A reply to Cass Sunstein. *International Review of Economics, 65*(1): 9–13.

Thaler, R. H. (1985). Mental accounting and consumer choice. *Marketing Science, 4*(3), 199–214.

Thaler, R. H. (2015). *Misbehaving: The Making of Behavioral Economics.* New York: W. W. Norton.

Thaler, R. H., & Benartzi, S. (2004). Save more tomorrow: Using behavioral economics to increase employee saving. *Journal of Political Economy, 112*(1, pt. 2), S164–S187.
Thaler, R. H., & Sunstein, C. R. (2008). *Nudge: Improving Decisions about Health, Wealth and Happiness.* New Haven, CT: Yale University Press.
Trout, J. (2008). *Differentiate or Die: Survival in Our Era of Killer Competition* (2nd edition). Hoboken, NJ: Wiley.
Tversky, A. (1972). Elimination by aspects: A theory of choice. *Psychological Review, 79*(4), 281–299.
Tversky. A., & Kahneman, D. (1974). Judgement under uncertainty: Heuristics and biases. *Science, New Series, 185*(4157): 1124–1131.
Wallis, J., Dollery, B., & Crase, L. (2009). Political economy and organizational leadership: A hope-based theory. *Review of Political Economy, 21*(1), 123–143.

15 Fiscal Policy after the Crisis

What Is the Role of Fiscal Policy in Times of Crisis, Low Interest Rates and High Public Debts?*

Arne Heise

Introduction

Post-2007, the global financial crisis sparked a revival of Keynesian economics. On the one hand, the financial instability hypothesis of the post-Keynesian economist Hyman P. Minsky gained considerable prominence well beyond heterodox circles, as it appeared to provide an early prediction (see Minsky 1986) and *ex post* explanation of what mainstream economics found so difficult to reconcile with its postulate of self-regulation: the occurrence of an almost complete economic breakdown. On the other hand, Keynesian economic policy – i.e. expansionary monetary and fiscal measures – not only dominated the immediate governmental responses all over the world but also conquered an institution which was for many decades at the forefront of non-Keynesian policy advice: the International Monetary Fund (IMF; see Ban 2015a and 2015b). Although the policy responses might have been simply pragmatic rather than following a genuine policy reorientation, the revival of Keynesian thinking was only short-lived and the IMF's apparent paradigm shift insubstantial on closer inspection, the discussion about the importance of fiscal policy and its particular stance as a tool of economic management has nonetheless been reopened.

Stabilisation policy as a way to mitigate business cycle fluctuations and a form of macroeconomic demand management is inextricably linked to Keynesian economic thinking: only after the Great Depression of the 1930s did governments assume responsibility for targeted macroeconomic interventions (see e.g. Middleton 1985; Hall 1993) and they did so based on the principles associated with Keynes's new economics as set out in his *General Theory* or, rather, the interpretations put forward by prominent early Keynesians such as John Hicks, Paul Samuelson and Alvin Hansen in the famous IS–LM model.[1] This interpretation of Keynes – commonly known as 'standard Keynesianism' or the 'neoclassical synthesis' – was based on the assumption of price and wage rigidities that explained the distortion of the otherwise fast, perfectly functioning process of self-regulation and readjustment towards a general equilibrium after an exogenous shock had hit the economy. Moreover, it also provided the policy tools to cope with these

DOI: 10.4324/9781003228097-15

kinds of disequilibrium states, which were the source of substantial welfare losses to society and, at least potentially, of political unrest: 'easy money' and 'deficit spending' policies could be implemented in an almost hydraulic fashion to readjust the economy. As monetary policy may be caught in a 'liquidity' or 'investment' trap and, perhaps more important, is not always at the indiscriminate disposal of political actors (especially when the central bank is granted autonomy), fiscal policy became the centre of attention and, consequently, standard Keynesian economic demand management was dubbed 'fiscalism' (see e.g. Coddington 1976: 1264).

However, starting in the early 1970s, both Keynesian economics and Keynesian demand management came under pressure and lost much of their appeal: in the 'monetarist counter-revolution', Keynesian models were criticised for their lack of microeconomic foundations for macroeconomic relations, the '*ad hoc*' nature of expectations and the assumed stability of functional relations, such as a stable Phillips curve (see e.g. Lucas and Sargent 1979). Post-Keynesian authors completely rejected the IS–LM model as an adequate representation of Keynes's new economics (see e.g. Davidson 1972; Weintraub 1972; Chick 1983), yet could not – until today – form a coherent alternative. And the co-existence of stagnation and inflation in the 1970s and early 1980s (which led to the coining of the expression 'stagflation') appeared difficult to reconcile with Keynesian 'inflationary' and 'deflationary' gaps and was instead seen as the outcome of Keynesian demand management gone amok (see e.g. Hall 1993: 285). Robert Lucas and Thomas Sargent's paper 'After Keynesian Macroeconomics' (1979) was taken by many economists as the death knoll for Keynesian economics and Keynesian demand management, as it suggested that the business cycle can be an equilibrium process based on rational decisions by the microeconomic actors confronted with unexpected shocks rather than indicating a situation of disequilibrium. This also implies the ineffectiveness of Keynesian stabilisation policies, which in Sargent and Wallace's view can only cause transitory disequilibrium based on unexpected policy measures ('tricking the public'; see Sargent and Wallace 1976: 178). If these policy measures become apparent to the market actors, they will be included in these actors' decisions and equilibrium will be re-established, possibly at higher nominal values (prices and wages) but at unchanged real values (something that came to be known as the 'natural rate hypothesis'[2]). Of course, denying the long-term stabilisation effects of monetary and fiscal policy does not mean that these policies will not be pursued but that they need a certain stance oriented towards reinforcing the economy's self-regulating processes. In order to anchor the expectations of market participants and prevent time-inconsistent policy behaviour, both policy areas should be rule-based: monetary policy should follow a simple, non-feedback rule such as the simple Friedmanian money supply rule ('sound monetary policy'), while fiscal policy should follow a balanced-budget rule ('sound fiscal policy').[3]

In his presidential address to the American Economic Association in 2003, Lucas (2003: 12) still rejected macroeconomic stabilisation policies 'that go beyond the general stabilization of spending that characterizes the last 50 years'. With regard to the post-WWII period, which has effectively seen only a short period of 'Keynesian' demand management followed by a long neoliberal era (see e.g. Harvey 2005), it remains unclear whether this claim is entirely in line with the view that emerged after a decade-long dispute between 'new classical' and 'new Keynesian' economists (see e.g. Klamer 1983) and became known as new consensus macroeconomics (NCM). NCM combines the monetarist idea of economic fluctuations being an equilibrium phenomenon ('real business cycles') with the new Keynesians' introduction of market imperfections that mean policy interventions are sometimes nonetheless permitted.

Fiscal Policy and New Consensus Macroeconomics in the Great Moderation Period (Mid-1980s–2007)

After more than a decade of economic turmoil (comprising two oil price crises and a period known as stagflation) and a phase of disputes between 'Fiscalists' and 'Monetarists' (see e.g. Friedman and Heller 1969), western economies entered a period of relative economic stability known as 'Great Moderation' and of a sort of conciliation between the former antagonists dubbed new consensus macroeconomics (NCM).

NCM is based on general equilibrium theory. This means that both new classical economics (NCE) and new Keynesian economics (NKE) take it for granted that the 'natural' position of an economy – i.e. the position when markets are perfect – is one of full-employment equilibrium. Thus, cyclical fluctuations are either due to external shocks (technological or policy shocks) or transitory due to nominal or real rigidities stemming from imperfect labour, commodity or financial markets which impede quick adjustment and, thus, serve as propagation mechanisms for business cycles. In the former case, shocks that are merely expected pose no problems, as economic agents will adapt to them in advance, while if they are unexpected they cannot be helped in the sense that they either form 'real' business cycles (which are not subject to stabilisation policies) or are politically motivated. In the latter case, the rigidities cause distortions in the short term (until they are overcome) and hence prompt rule-based stabilisation measures to mitigate welfare losses.

On this theory, stabilisation policy is always designed to reduce aggregate output volatility, i.e. to flatten upturns and downturns, but not to impact the growth path, which is determined by supply-side factors only. This seems, from a mainstream point of view, quite trivial; however, it means neglecting sustainability issues (for instance in the fiscal policy), which may be important once macroeconomic policy intervention becomes permanent. By comparison with the 'we are all Keynesians now' consensus of the IS–LM model, NCM has a far more solid foundation in microeconomic decision rules,[4] incorporates expectations and grossly downplays the role of fiscal policy.[5] While in standard Keynesianism, fiscal policy – for theoretical reasons mentioned above – took the lead in the macroeconomic policy mix, NCM models primarily rely on monetary policy to shoulder stabilisation needs. This emphasis on monetary policy can be explained by reference to its dominant role during the period of relative economic stability between the mid-1980s and 2007 known as the Great Moderation (see e.g. Ahmed, Levin and Wilson 2002; Bernanke 2004) and by highlighting the role central banks' research departments played in developing and laying the groundwork for such models (see e.g. Blanchard 2009: 210). Moreover, fiscal policy also had ever less room to manoeuvre due to rising public indebtedness and, finally, timing problems for fiscal policy in democratic societies (see e.g. Solow 1999: 286) can be pointed out as a comparative disadvantage of fiscal policy. However, there is also a more theoretical aspect to the neglect of fiscal policy in NCM.

As mentioned above, fiscal policy in NCM is about allocation rather than stabilisation issues (see e.g. Chari and Kehoe 2006: 16–17), a feature inherited from NCE (see e.g. Lucas 2003: 1ff.). But why did NKE not pass on more of its stabilising genes to NCM? The answer is twofold: on the one hand, why should fiscal policy take all the risks associated with mistiming, misspecification due to the democratic process and, potentially, shrinking its own room for manoeuvre if the interest share in public spending increases, when the job can be done by monetary policy? Monetary policy works more quickly, is less dependent on vested interests and, additionally, keeps fiscal capabilities intact. On the other hand, fiscal policy tends to drive monetary policy into a policy stance that counteracts fiscal policy intentions: if fiscal policy were successful in increasing effective demand, this would be accompanied by a rise in inflation, which the central bank would have to offset through its monetary reaction function (Taylor 2000: 27). If we presume different inflation–unemployment targets for the fiscal policy actor (the government) and the monetary policy actor (the central bank) – which is not unrealistic if we assume central banks' independence from governments – there is likely to be a conflict in the pursuit of monetary and fiscal policy, as William Nordhaus (1994) showed. Under these conditions, an optimal policy mix will encumber monetary policy with the dual task of safeguarding price and output stability[6] under a Taylor rule, while fiscal policy is supposed to refrain from any discretionary measure (i.e. keeping the budget structurally balanced) and merely allow for the automatic stabilisers to take effect.

Alternative Views on Fiscal Policy

NCM emerged after a long, intense debate between 'freshwater' and 'saltwater' economists.[7] Is there still room today for different perspectives on fiscal policy? The answer to this question is positive only if an entirely different – heterodox – paradigmatic approach is taken which does not rest on general equilibrium theory. If unrestricted economic action is conceived not as an allocative process by decentralised decision-makers regarding intertemporal markets which, if no market failures occur, will generate optimal welfare results, but instead understood in such a way that the action of a collective actor may increase society's welfare, it will be possible to develop an alternative conception of fiscal policy. Keynes appears to have had a paradigm shift of this sort in mind when writing the *General Theory*; at any rate, this idea is central to a post-Keynesian school broadly termed 'fundamentalist Keynesianism' (see Coddington 1976).[8] But before we take a closer look at the fiscal policy implications of this form of post-Keynesianism based on Keynes's idea of 'capital budgeting', we will have to consider Abba Lerner's concept of 'functional finance', which is clearly opposed to the neoclassical concept of 'sound finance' and often seen as related to Keynes's fiscal policy concept (see e.g. Colander 1984).

Lerner's 'Functional Finance'

It is sometimes claimed (see e.g. Colander 2003: 37) that standard Keynesian fiscal policy is actually based on Abba Lerner's concept of 'functional finance'. By 'functional finance', Lerner meant that fiscal policy – roughly speaking, the balance between public expenditures and revenues – should be set with a view to ensuring full employment and price stability.[9] In line with standard Keynesianism, this implies a public deficit in times of unemployment and a public surplus in times of overemployment and inflation. The size of the public deficit (and, also, the surplus) is supposed to be related to the level of unemployment (or overemployment) and, thus, is 'functional' in the sense of being directed solely towards restoring full employment. Any potential conflict between employment stimulation and inflation was ruled out, as Lerner apparently assumed a stable and horizontal Phillips curve (until full employment is reached). Assuming a standard Keynesian framework, all the reservations of monetarists and new classical economists apply, and it seems hard to see how 'functional finance' offers any alternative.

However, Lerner did admit the need for permanent fiscal policy interventions (see Lerner 1943: 42ff.), which was not in line with the transitory, anti-cyclical fiscal policy stance of standard Keynesianism. Unfortunately, the theoretical basis for Lerner's ideas remained unclear. David Colander, a former collaborator of Lerner, suggests that the rejection of a unique (Walrasian) general equilibrium is necessary in order to revive Lerner's concept of functional finance (Colander 2003: 43ff.). If multiple equilibria are allowed for – depending on the institutionalised, conventionalised agency of individual and collective actors in a complex, adaptive world – fiscal policy will shape the particular position of equilibrium and, thus, could be seen as 'functional' in the sense that it contributes to the selection among multiple equilibria according to pre-established goals: 'The government must establish policies which stabilize the price level and coordinate both the money supply rule and the aggregate total spending rule with this stable price level at the unemployment level it prefers' (Colander 2003: 48).

Thus, taking complexity or agent-based computational economics (ACE) as its paradigmatic foundation,[10] 'functional finance' may offer an alternative to NCM's concept of 'sound finance'. However, in this sense, 'functional finance' differs from 'sound finance' primarily in being a means (not an end) while the latter has become an end in itself. As long as we do not know what fiscal policy stance follows from ACE, it is impossible to argue that 'functional finance' also includes an alternative fiscal policy rule. But why should we not be able to establish such a policy stance? On the one hand, ACE has so far been concerned with theoretical rather than policy issues. On the other, the policy stance is obviously dependent on the targeted equilibrium position – there simply is no 'general' rule to be followed. Moreover, even if, as seems reasonable, we aim for a full employment–price stability equilibrium, the best fiscal policy to achieve this target crucially depends on the agency assumptions on which the model is built. Although it is always, on any type of model, the case that outcomes depend on inputs (assumptions), agent-based complexity modelling is different from reductionist modelling because it does not accept a general rule for a human agency such as the *homo economicus*–representative agent assumption of reductionism. Instead, the macroeconomic outcome – and the effect of fiscal policy – depends on built-in *ad hoc* algorithms and must, therefore, be rated as highly contingent or difficult to trace, and macroeconomic-oriented ACE in particular must be kept very simple in structural terms.

Taking the *ad hoc* algorithms to be 'rooted in empirical and experimental micro-economic evidence' (Fagiolo and Roventini 2017: 5.6), initial attempts to evaluate fiscal policy in ACE models suggest that allowing an unrestricted play of the automatic stabilisers is the best way to dampen economic fluctuations (see Dosi et al. 2015) – something that is, admittedly, entirely compatible with NCM results. A more expansionary fiscal policy stance that goes beyond merely allowing automatic stabilisers to take effect and is more in line with Lerner's functional finance is not simulated by, but could well be supported on the basis of, ACE modelling as – at least in the Dosi et al. version – there are no negative feedback algorithms (expectations, interest rates, inflation) that could counterbalance targeted growth and employment effects. However, and this is the basic problem with ACE policy modelling, such feedback algorithms could easily be introduced, making ACE models' virtue of flexibility (see e.g. Fagiolo and Roventini 2017: 7.2) a vice and rendering discretionary fiscal policy in ACE utterly opaque.

Keynes's Capital Budgeting

It is interesting to note that there is no chapter on economic policy in general or fiscal policy in particular in Keynes's magnum opus, *The General Theory.* The concept of 'deficit spending' being inextricably linked to 'Keynesian economic policy' is actually based on Samuelson's idea of 'inflationary' and 'deflationary (income) gaps', as shown in his 'Keynesian cross' diagram; fiscal policy is supposed to fill these gaps by means of public deficits and surpluses respectively. Accepting Walras's law, inflationary and deflationary gaps are only temporary in nature, since the business cycle and public budget deficits and surpluses would, to a certain extent, cancel each other out over the business cycle, leaving no room for sustainability issues. Protracted public budget deficits that increase public indebtedness must, on this mindset, be politically motivated, as the extensive literature on the political economy of fiscal policy suggests.[11]

Keynes's approach was different, as he rejected Walras's law and explained permanent involuntary unemployment either from a static perspective or, from a dynamic perspective, in terms of an equilibrium growth path below full utilisation of production factors without any 'natural' tendency for self-correction. In later work after the publication of the *General Theory*, Keynes distinguishes three different stages in the development of modern capitalist economies, characterised by particular constellations of savings and investment (see Keynes 1943a). Stage 1 is characterised by an overshooting of planned investment over the amount of savings that would be generated by a full-employment income. At this stage, inflation would be the most pressing problem. Stage 2 is characterised by equality of planned investment and savings out of full-employment income – this would be the stage mainstream economics sees as 'natural'. The third stage is characterised by a lack of planned investment compared with savings out of full-employment income, so permanent unemployment becomes the most pressing problem. In any of these stages, the amount of investment and savings that is achieved will always be equal and, therefore, no process to equilibrate the two parameters is required. Taking the lack of self-regulation as the essence of the 'Keynesian revolution', the objective of any fiscal intervention in a 'fundamentalist Keynesian approach' is not to smoothen the business cycle but to raise the growth path until all factors of production – and in particular labour – are fully utilised. There are different measures that could be employed: the average propensity to save could be lowered by redistributing income from higher-income, higher-savings households to lower-income, lower-savings households. Or the incentive to invest could be increased by reducing interest rates – which would involve monetary policy being pursued by the central bank, which is often primarily responsible for price stability but not for employment and economic growth. Therefore, fiscal policy on Keynes's approach needs to fill the gap between planned private investment and full-employment savings by means of deficit-financed public expenditure – and as the investment–savings gap can be permanent, so must public deficits. Permanent deficit spending must, of course, raise concerns about the sustainability of such a policy stance and draws attention to the composition (i.e. investment or consumption spending) of deficit-financed public expenditure.

In his writings on public finance, Keynes distinguished between current and capital budgets (see Keynes 1945; Heise 2002). The current budget comprises all public consumption spending and ought to be balanced by tax income over the business cycle: thus, in order to allow the automatic stabilisers to take effect, the current budget will be in deficit in economic downturns and in surplus in economic upturns. The capital budget, however, comprising all public investment outlays, can and should be deficit-financed to a degree depending on economic circumstances (in stages 1 and 2 of capitalist development, deficits would only crowd out private investment; in stage 3, a balanced capital budget would not do the job) and fiscal sustainability considerations. In order to take the latter into account, fiscal sustainability must be defined. Most commonly, a public budget is considered to be sustainable when all future obligations can be met. However, this is not an operational definition, as future obligations may not only be highly uncertain but the ability to meet future obligations – i.e. to create income and control expenditures – involves a high level of discretion. Therefore, fiscal sustainability is often operationalised as the ability to stabilise a given public debt ratio (debt to GDP) over the business cycle, i.e. ever-increasing debt ratios are regarded as unsustainable.[12] This compels us to determine a (desired, optimal or imposed) debt ratio and makes it possible to specify 'sustainable' public deficit and primary budget ratios. The (desired, optimal or imposed) debt ratio to be stabilised over the business cycle can be taken as exogenously given – determined by political considerations as the 60% threshold level of the European Stability and Growth Pact (ESGP)[13] or as some kind of 'optimal' ratio[14]; the 'sustainable' deficit and primary budget ratios can thus be derived using Domar's fiscal arithmetic (see Domar 1944).

The calculation of functional (in Lerner's sense, of which Keynes seemingly approved[15]) and sustainable budget deficits[16] not only rests on uncertain expectations (about medium-term growth, inflation and interest rate developments) but also on the fact that both variables – budget deficits and economic growth – are endogenously and recursively determined, the pursuit of fiscal policy in accordance with Keynes's capital budgeting approach should not be pressed into a sanctionable policy rule (as, for instance, in the case of the ESGP) but rather be taken as what has been termed a 'fiscal standard'.[17]

Contrasting Orthodox and Heterodox Perspectives on Fiscal Policy

Orthodox and heterodox fiscal policy perspectives can be neatly contrasted by referring to the ESGP. The ESGP is clearly based on orthodox economic theory and was influenced, firstly, by the neoliberal ideas that dominated at that time and, secondly, by German interests in curtailing fiscal policy space for governments which the Germans[18] expected not to be financially prudent. A balanced-budget rule (structurally or cyclically adjusted fiscal balance) with a sanction-free threshold deficit level of 3% of GDP to allow automatic stabilisers to take effect (cyclically unadjusted fiscal balance) mirrors the insights from NCM. Moreover, sanctions applied in the event of non-compliance account for the moral hazard behaviour of actors (governments) in the political arena. Finally, the institutionalised pressure to pursue austerity policies after major economic shocks is in line with the dominant literature on 'non-Keynesian' effects of fiscal policy[19] and the much-criticised claim by Carmen Reinhart and Kenneth Rogoff that economic growth will be harmed if a debt threshold level of about 90% of GDP is exceeded (see Reinhart and Rogoff 2010) – implying that austerity measures to bring public debts quickly below that threshold level after a major economic downturn will be growth-enhancing.[20]

On heterodox grounds that are entirely neglected in the formulation of European fiscal policy, the ESGP would allow the cyclically unadjusted public budget to oscillate around a structural deficit of close to 3% of GDP in order to finance public investment (capital budget). While the 3% deficit ceiling of the ESGP imposed on orthodox reasoning represents a maximum below which no sanctions are imposed and is (if at all) based on empirically measured fiscal elasticities,[21] the 3% threshold level for structural deficits in heterodox, post-Keynesian approaches reflects sustainability considerations based on the assumption of a politically determined 'desired' debt ratio of 60% and a cyclically adjusted, long-term nominal GDP growth rate of 5%.[22] While the 'orthodox' fiscal policy stance – if applied – would drive down the public debt level in the (very) long run to (close to) zero and violate the 'golden rule' according to which public investment should not be paid out of the current budget (and hence should be deficit-financed), the heterodox 'fiscal standard' – if applied – would stabilise the debt ratio at the desired 60% and not only comply with the 'golden rule' but potentially open fiscal space for the public investment needed to transform economies in the direction of ecological sustainability and digitalisation, as well as keeping them on a higher growth path.[23]

Fiscal Policy, the Global Financial Crisis and High Public Debts

As mentioned above, the consensus in macroeconomic policy modelling came to an abrupt end in the aftermath of the global financial crisis and the ensuing 'euro crisis'. First, the monetary policy proved unable to achieve economic stabilisation when nominal interest rates hit zero. Second, there was no longer any consensus on whether excessively lax fiscal policy prior to the global financial crisis caused or, at least, contributed to the euro crisis or whether excessively restrictive fiscal policy (due to the regulations of the ESGP) aggravated the economic downturn after the global financial crisis. Third, non-Keynesian effects of fiscal retrenchment were no longer undisputed in academic discussions, and a distinction between 'normal' business cycles and exceptionally deep recessions was proposed that would allow for a strong divergence in terms of fiscal multipliers and, thus, the effects of public spending decisions.

Although all EU and Eurozone governments reacted pragmatically in the wake of the deepest depression in 80 years by enacting huge bank rescue and economic stabilisation programmes in 2008 and 2009, these programmes were not designed to meet the different impacts of the crisis on EU and Eurozone member states but rather to address the different fiscal spaces left under ESGP regulations and the conditions imposed by the IMF, the European Stability Mechanism (ESM) and the European Central Bank (ECB), which were in some cases subject to particular borrowing requirements.[24] The austerity programmes that most EU and Eurozone member states were forced to implement from 2009 onwards procyclically hampered economic recovery, by contrast with the US and the UK, which did not fall under ESGP regulations and allowed fiscal policy to be more expansionary (see e.g. Heise 2012; Gechert et al. 2016). However, this experience was apparently necessary to demonstrate the flaws of the approach, as proponents of fiscal orthodoxy and 'expansionary austerity' were dominant up until empirical evidence to the contrary became overwhelming. For instance, Alberto Alesina, widely considered a world-leading expert on fiscal policy and fiscal adjustments, wrote in a paper prepared for a meeting of the European Union's Economic and Financial Affairs Council (Ecofin) in April 2010:

> The conventional wisdom about the political economy of fiscal adjustments goes more or less as follows. Deficit reduction policies cause recessions which (in addition to the direct political costs of tax increases and spending cuts) create political problems for incumbent governments. The latter therefore see fiscal adjustments as the kiss of death. They postpone them and when they implement them then they pay at the polls. … This view, which is a combination of textbook Keynesianism with 'conventional' notions of naive voters' behavior, is largely imprecise to say the least. … Fortunately the accumulated evidence paints a different picture. First of all, not all fiscal adjustments cause recessions. Many even sharp reductions of budget deficits have been accompanied and immediately followed by sustained growth rather than recessions even in the very short run. These are the adjustments which have occurred on the spending side and have been large, credible and decisive. Second and this is most likely a consequence of the first point, it is far from automatic that governments which have reduced deficits have been routinely not reappointed. Governments which have initiated thorough and successful fiscal adjustment policies have not systematically suffered at the polls.
>
> (Alesina 2010: 2–3)

Such claims, in combination with Reinhart and Rogoff's aforementioned study recommending a public debt ceiling of around 90% of GDP, did, even if not accepted as absolute consensus,[25] at least lend strong support to those who saw fiscal imprudence as the trigger for the euro crisis, who wanted the ESGP to be strengthened (as happened in the Fiscal Compact) and who called for austerity policies in the aftermath of the global financial crisis, when public debts soared to extraordinarily high levels.

The opposite position of 'contractionary austerity' (see e.g. Delong and Summers 2012; Guajardo, Leigh and Pescatori 2014; Blinder 2016) was based on the belief that fiscal multipliers – their definite magnitude being dependent among other things on the composition (revenue increases versus expenditure cuts, consumption versus investment spending cuts), size and credibility of the austerity measures, the state of public indebtedness at the time of their introduction and general economic circumstances (boom or slump) – are much higher than expected and simulated in many policy models.[26] This led to a new approach to fiscal policy, described by Jason Furman, then chair of the US Council of Economic Advisers, as follows:

> 1. Fiscal policy is often beneficial for effective countercyclical policy as a complement to monetary policy. 2. Discretionary fiscal stimulus can be very effective and in some circumstances can even crowd in private investment. To the degree that it leads to higher interest rates, that may be a plus, not a minus. 3. Fiscal space is larger than generally appreciated because stimulus may pay for itself or may have a lower cost than headline estimates would suggest; countries have more space today than in the past; and stimulus can be combined with longer-term consolidation. 4. More sustained stimulus, especially if it is in the form of effectively targeted investments that expand aggregate supply, may be desirable in many contexts. 5. There may be larger benefits to undertaking coordinated fiscal action across countries.
>
> (Furman 2016: 2–3)

What sounds like a complete reversal of positions when compared with the words of Alesina (and Martin Eichenbaum; see endnote 25) only a few years earlier is merely a shift in perspective, not in theoretical underpinnings: the 'new view' is basically another swing in the pendulum from NCE, with its focus on rational expectations and equilibrium situations, to NKE, which emphasises short-term disequilibria and frictions that can be overcome by governmental interventions. Jason Furman (2016: 1) is thus correct to describe this approach as the '"New View" of fiscal policy (with, admittedly, the core of this theory being an "Old Old View" that dates back to John Maynard Keynes and the liquidity trap)'. As we have seen, the reference to Keynes is misleading, as Keynes's 'capital budgeting approach' is about far more than the use of discretionary fiscal interventions that go beyond the automatic stabilisers in times of severe economic depressions; rather, it combines Lerner's 'functional finance' with the 'golden rule' and sustainability considerations at any moment in the business cycle.

Fiscal Policy in Times of Low Interest Rates

One last aspect of modern-day fiscal policy needs to be addressed: does the phenomenon of close-to-zero (and even below-zero in some countries) interest rates on public bonds present any new challenge to the stance and orientation of fiscal policy? Very basically, the answer depends on whether the phenomenon of very low interest rates is assumed to be temporary or permanent. If it is taken as temporary, no challenge would arise for fiscal policy theory based on general attitudes or 'standards' in the sense described above. If, on the other hand, it is taken as permanent or, at least, as a phenomenon that will be with us for the foreseeable future, perspectives on public deficits and debts might change.

As long as we do not know why (real) interest rates are as low as they are at the moment, predictions about future levels become difficult. And although there are some suggestions (see e.g. Bean et al. 2015; Thwaites 2015; Hall 2016), they do not boil down to a common prediction. However, most authors assume (or attribute high likelihood to) low interest rates for the foreseeable future. In that case, not only will the load of interest payments on governmental debts be reduced but, if the interest rate falls below the growth rate (i.e. in the event of a negative interest rate–growth rate differential), the sustainable primary balance may even turn into a deficit, thereby considerably increasing the financial room for manoeuvre.[27] Moreover, if a negative interest rate–growth rate differential were to last permanently independent of the fiscal stance, the trade-off between today's and tomorrow's financial room for manoeuvre would be nullified as any incentive (based on time-preference considerations of the government or public) to restrict deficit spending.[28]

Even if the interest rate–growth rate differential was not independent of the fiscal stance and growing indebtedness would have adverse effects on the interest rate (causing it to increase) and growth rate (causing it to decrease), eventually turning the differential positive with increasing deficits,[29] the 'desired' public debt ratio would certainly increase, as deficits and ensuing debts come virtually without cost.[30]

Concluding Remarks: Fiscal Policy – Looking to the Future

It appears safe to predict that the 'old fiscal orthodoxy', which assigns fiscal policy a passive role in stabilising an unstable economy and arguing for 'expansionary austerity', has lost much of its appeal and support in the academic community. With monetary policy becoming less effective in times of low inflation and low interest rates and a higher fiscal multiplier than expected, fiscal policy is back at the heart of stabilisation policy, and with the recognition that major economic crises are part of capitalist development and may be around the corner any time, sanction-based fiscal policy rules primarily inaugurated to tie governments' hands are seen by ever more economists as outdated and harmful.

Fiscal policy in modern times can, however, not simply return to a discretionary stance that neglects all insights from the 'policy games' and 'golden rule' literature and pretends that deficit spending is a 'free lunch'. Instead, fiscal policy must follow a standard which links deficits to public investment, introduces a sustainability cap and allows coordination with monetary and wage policies to prevent macro conflicts (see Heise 2008). This insight may either translate into a balanced-budget stance with investment-oriented discretionary leeway for extraordinary circumstances – as authors such as Della Posta and Tamborini (2021) and Furman (2016) appear to be proposing. Or it might further a 'capital budgeting' stance that functionally relates the deficit-financed capital budget to the medium-term output gap. In this case, the structural deficit will have to be constrained by a sustainability cap that is determined by growth expectations and a predetermined debt ratio taken as 'desired'. The option chosen will depend on which economic paradigm we find most compelling, what the empirical evidence shows or will merely follow political considerations.

Notes

* The author would like to thank Stavros A. Drakopoulos and Ioannis Katselidis for valuable comments. The usual caveats apply.

1 It is now common wisdom that the IS-LM model neglects many features important to Keynes such as the formation of expectations under uncertainty.

2 Olivier Blanchard (2018: 98) confirms that the natural rate hypothesis was 'widely accepted, and has been the dominant paradigm in macroeconomics ever since'.

3 For a comprehensive account of how macroeconomics lost control of stabilisation policy, see Chatelain and Ralf (2020).

4 Some regard these rules as the principles of the economic theory that is to be followed. For a critique see Solow (2008).

5 See e.g. Snowdon and Vane (1999a, 1999b: 88) and Fontana (2009). In some articles surveying macroeconomic policy in NCM, fiscal policy is no longer discussed as a stabilising measure but rather in relation to intertemporal distortions; see e.g. Chari and Kehoe (2006). Hall (1993) therefore takes the two as completely different policy paradigms – something I would disagree with, as they are both based on the same economic paradigm.

6 According to the Tinbergen rule, there must be as many policy instruments as independent policy targets. To make NCM monetary policy compatible with the Tinbergen rule, both targets (inflation and output stabilisation) must be causally dependent.

7 This commonly made distinction between new classical and new Keynesian economists is based on the geographic locations of the two theoretical approaches' proponents: the former being primarily concentrated near the USA's Great Lakes, the latter on the country's east and west coasts. This distinction thus reflects the US hegemony in the current development of macroeconomics.

8 For an introduction to this particular post-Keynesian approach see Heise (2019).

9 'The central idea is that government fiscal policy, its spending and taxing, its borrowing and repayment of loans … shall all be undertaken with an eye only on the *results* of these actions on the economy and not to any established traditional doctrine about what is sound or unsound.' (Lerner 1943: 39; italics in original).

10 For a detailed description of complexity economics/ACE as a paradigmatic alternative to NCM, see Fagiolo and Roventini (2017).

11 Nordhaus (1975), Hibbs (1977), Tabellini and Alesina (1990) and Alesina and Perotti (1995), among many others, made significant contributions to this field of research, which describes public deficits and debts not as functional devices of stabilisation policies in the economic sphere but as optimisation behaviours by actors in the political sphere.

12 In a recent paper, Furman and Summers (2020) propose using the share of interest payments or the primary budget balance as a better indicator of fiscal sustainability, as the public debt ratio may lose informative value in times of low interest rates. However, in order to translate the primary budget balance into an operative policy variable (using Domar's fiscal arithmetic), we need to estimate three determinants – the real interest rate, the real growth rate and the inflation rate – while in the case of the public debt ratio, it is only the real growth rate and the inflation rate (or, in short, the nominal growth rate) which need to be estimated. And, of course, the interest rate is particularly hard to predict in the medium term. I therefore believe the debt ratio to be superior, although the particular threshold level (if determined by time-preference considerations) is likely to increase with lower interest rates.

13 There are rumours about the 60% threshold level being either the average debt ratio in the EU at the time of drafting the Maastricht Treaty or the projected debt ratio of Germany and France at the time the Maastricht convergence criteria were expected to be evaluated, so as to guarantee both countries could join the European Monetary Union.

14 Such 'optimal' debt ratios have been studied with respect to GDP growth (see e.g. Reinhart and Rogoff 2010) or the welfare of society (see e.g. Heise 2002).

15 In a letter to James Meade, Keynes not only mentions Lerner's famous article of 1943 but also remarks that '(h)is argument is impeccable' (Keynes 1943b: 320).

16 It is sometimes argued that Modern Monetary Theory (MMT) provides an alternative to 'sound finance' based on Lerner's 'functional finance' (see e.g. Forstater 2003) – however, MMT has no definite role for 'fiscal sustainability' (see e.g. Ehnts 2017: 127) as governments – in this view – can borrow without clearly definable limits and cannot become insolvent if issuing a sovereign currency. These ideas make MMT interesting to policy-makers, yet have aroused much criticism from proponents of all economic paradigms (see e.g. Palley 2015; Davidson 2019; Mankiw 2020).

17 'Rules and standards are alternative ways of writing down legal norms that regulate behavior. … The difference between them is in the degree to which legal content is defined ex post, at the point of application, rather than ex ante. The limit case of a rule is a legal norm in which all legal content is defined ex ante, such as "Do not drive faster than 55 miles an hour". The limit case for a standard is a norm in which all legal content is defined ex post, such as "do not drive at excessive speed". What "excessive speed" means exactly is left to the driver (and in the event of a dispute, to a court), based on social norms and legal precedent.' (Blanchard, Leandro and Zettelmeyer 2021: 22–23).

18 Conservatives led German governments over most of the past 30 years when European fiscal policy regulations were being discussed and enacted. However, the German Social Democrats and Greens can also be seen as fiscally conservative – far more so than their political counterparts elsewhere in Europe; see e.g. Eisl (2020: 14).

19 These 'non-Keynesian' effects pertain to the claim that deficit spending is not only ineffective in the long but also the short run. This view has been championed in particular by Giavazzi and Pagano (1990) and Bertola and Drazen (1993).

20 The study has been heavily criticised for its technical and methodological flaws (see Herndon, Ash and Pollin 2014). In the aftermath of the 'Reinhart–Rogoff

controversy', as it was known, various studies tried to replicate Reinhart and Rogoff's result, ending up with threshold debt ratios between 20 and 115% of GDP.

21 The 3% threshold deficit ratio of the ESGP goes back to the convergence criteria of the Maastricht Treaty. It is rumoured to be an 'invention' of two French bureaucrats, with no economic significance (see Schubert 2013). However, it can be shown that 3% is just about the margin the Eurozone countries need for the automatic stabilisers to take effect, assuming a balanced budget in a 'neutral' position of the business cycle is achieved and the trough of the business cycle does not exceed −2% of GDP (see e.g. Buti, Franco and Ongena 1997; Dalsgaard and de Serres 1999; Mourre, Poissonnier and Lausegger 2019). Once this trough is exceeded (as, for instance, during the global financial crisis or the coronavirus pandemic), the stipulations of the ESGP concerning the deficit cap are suspended.

22 Both the 60% debt ratio and the 5% nominal GDP growth expectations (a combination of 2% inflation and 3% real GDP growth) were the assumptions of the European Commission in the early 1990s when the Maastricht Treaty was drafted. According to Domar's fiscal arithmetic, this results in a 'sustainable' structural deficit of 3%!

23 The 'golden rule' has undergone something of a revival over the past decade, as there are indications that fiscal conservatism and austerity, which are associated with balanced-budget rules, are a main explanatory factor for the tendency of the public investment share to fall (see e.g. Oxley and Martin 1991; de Haan, Sturm and Sikken 1996; Perée and Välilä 2005). Most simulations and empirical studies (see e.g. Greiner and Semmler 2000; Straub and Tchakarov 2007; Creel, Monperrus-Veroni and Saraceno 2009) hold there to be a positive correlation between the golden rule and economic growth, but Minea and Villieu (2009) show that this is not in line with the predictions of orthodox theory – which, of course, puts this theory in doubt and favours Keynes's capital budgeting as an alternative theoretical foundation.

24 See e.g. Horton (2011) and Schelkle (2012) for a comparison of EU and US fiscal stimulus packages.

25 In 1997, Martin Eichenbaum wrote in this vein: 'There is now widespread agreement that countercyclical discretionary fiscal policy is neither desirable nor politically feasible.' (Eichenbaum 1997: 236).

26 See e.g. Gechert and Rannenberg (2018). Jordà and Taylor (2013) propose a method which may explain the wide-ranging magnitudes of fiscal multipliers that were empirically observed prior to the global financial crisis, and come to the conclusion: 'Generally, in the slump, austerity prolongs the pain, much more so than in the boom.' (Jordà and Taylor 2013: 36).

27 This is what some southern European countries experienced when they entered the Eurozone and their high (nominal and real) interest rates on governmental bonds quickly converged towards the much lower German federal bonds.

28 Today's financial room to maneouvre is determined by the sustainable structural public deficit ratio, while tomorrow's financial room to maneouvre is determined by the sustainable primary deficit ratio. For a post-Keynesian model of 'optimal debts' and 'sustainable deficits' based on the time-preference considerations of governments (agents) and voters (principals), see Heise (2002).

29 Of course, there are good reasons why both interest and growth rates could be adversely affected by growing public (structural) deficits (e.g. expectations of inflation developments and the unsustainability of public debts impacting on the behaviour of private financial market actors and central banks) and it would be risky to assume a negative interest rate–growth rate differential as a

normal or even permanent state of affairs. On the basis of data from 1950 to 2018, Blanchard (2019) takes a negative interest rate–growth rate differential to be the normal position rather than an exception – but this result is driven by the long 'golden era of capitalism' after WWII, which surely cannot be taken as 'normal'. John H. Cochrane (2021: 2), a proponent of NCE, says that the idea of a negative interest rate–growth rate differential as the 'normal' scenario is 'ridiculous' because 'it seems there are no fiscal limits at all. If our government can borrow, and never worry about paying back debts, why should any of us pay back debts? Why should the government not borrow, and repay our student debts, mortgage debts, business debts; bail out state and local pension promises, and more. Why should we pay taxes? Why should we work? Let the government just send us money and we can order stuff from Amazon.'

30 Or to put it another way: assuming a certain primary budget balance to be sustainable, the more negative the interest rate–growth rate differential is (or the smaller the interest rate–growth rate differential in the event of interest rates being higher than growth rates), the higher the corresponding ('optimal' or 'desired') debt ratio will be.

Bibliography

Ahmed, S., Levin, A., Wilson, B. A. (2002); 'Recent U.S. Macroeconomic Stability: Good Policies, Good Practices, or Good Luck?'; International Finance Discussion Paper 2002–730, Board of Governors of the Federal Reserve System, Washington, DC.

Alesina, A. (2010); 'Fiscal Adjustments: Lessons from Recent History'; paper prepared for the Ecofin meeting in Madrid, 15 April 2010 (accessible at: Definition of the episodes (psu.edu)).

Alesina, A., Perotti, R. (1995); 'The Political Economy of Budget Deficits'; *IMF Staff Papers* 42(1), pp. 1–31.

Ban, C. (2015a); 'From Designers to Doctrinaires: Staff Research and Fiscal Policy Change at the IMF'; in Morgan, G., Hirsch, P., Quack, S. (eds); *Elites on Trial* (Research in the Sociology of Organizations, vol. 43); Emerald, Bingley, pp. 337–369.

Ban, C. (2015b); 'Austerity versus Stimulus? Explaining Change on Fiscal Policy at the International Monetary Fund since the Great Recession'; *Governance: An International Journal of Policy, Administration, and Institutions* 28(2), pp. 167–183.

Bean, C., Broda, C., Ito, T., Kroszner, R. (2015); 'Low for Long? Causes and Consequences of Persistently Low Interest Rates'; Geneva Report on the World Economy 17, Centre for Economic Policy Research, Geneva, and CEPR Press, London.

Bernanke, B. S. (2004); 'The Great Moderation', Remarks at the meetings of the Eastern Economic Association, Washington, DC, February 20, 2004 (accessible at: https://www.federalreserve.gov/boarddocs/speeches/2004/20040220/)

Bertola, G., Drazen, A. (1993); 'Trigger Points and Budget Cuts: Explaining the Effects of Fiscal Austerity'; *American Economic Review* 83(1), pp. 11–26.

Blanchard, O. (2009); 'The State of Macro'; *Annual Review of Economics* 1, pp. 201–228.

Blanchard, O. (2018); 'Should We Reject the Natural Rate Hypothesis?'; *Journal of Economic Perspectives* 32(1), pp. 97–120.

Blanchard, O. (2019); 'Public Debts and Low Interest Rates'; *American Economic Review* 109(4), pp. 1197–1229.

Blanchard, O., Leandro, A., Zettelmeyer, J. (2021); 'Redesigning the EU Fiscal Rules: From Rules to Standards'; *Economic Policy* 36(105), pp. 3–42.

Blinder, A. (2016); 'Fiscal Policy Reconsidered'; Hamilton Project Policy Proposal 2016-05, Washington, DC.

Buti, M., Franco, D., Ongena, H. (1997); 'Budgetary Policies during Recessions – Retrospective Application of the Stability and Growth Pact to the Post-War Period'; *Louvain Economic Review* 63(4), pp. 321–366.

Chari, V. V., Kehoe, P. J. (2006); 'Modern Macroeconomics in Practice: How Theory Is Shaping Policy'; *Journal of Economic Perspectives* 20(4), pp. 3–28.

Chatelain, J.-B., Ralf, K. (2020); 'How Macroeconomists Lost Control of Stabilization Policy: Towards Dark Ages'; *European Journal of the History of Economic Thought* 27(6), pp. 938–982.

Chick, V. (1983); *Macroeconomics after Keynes: A Reconsideration of the General Theory*; Philip Allan, Oxford.

Cochrane, J. H. (2021); 'Comments on "The Constraint on Public Debt when r < g but g < m" by Ricardo Reis'; comments delivered at the conference NBER Economic Fluctuations and Growth, 19 February 2021 (accessible at: cochrane_comments.pdf (nber.org)).

Coddington, A. (1976); 'Keynesian Economics: The Search for First Principles'; *Journal of Economic Literature* 14(4), pp. 1258–1273.

Colander, D. (1984); 'Was Keynes a Keynesian or a Lernerian?'; *Journal of Economic Literature* 22, pp. 1572–1575.

Colander, D. (2003); 'Functional Finance, New Classical Economics and Great-Great Grandsons'; in Nell, E. J., Forstater, M. (eds); *Reinventing Functional Finance: Transformational Growth and Full Employment*; Edward Elgar, Cheltenham, pp. 35–51.

Creel, J., Monperrus-Veroni, P., Saraceno, F. (2009); 'On the Long-Term Effects of Fiscal Policy in the United Kingdom: The Case for a Golden Rule'; *Scottish Journal of Political Economy* 56(5), pp. 580–607.

Dalsgaard, T., de Serres, A. (1999); 'Estimating Prudent Budgetary Margins for 11 EU Countries: A Simulated SVAR Model Approach'; OECD Economics Department Working Paper No. 216, Paris.

Davidson, P. (1972); *Money and the Real World*; Macmillan, London.

Davidson, P. (2019); 'What Is Modern about MMT? A Concise Note'; *Real-World Economics Review*, 89, pp. 72–74.

Della Posta, P., Tamborini, R. (2021); 'The Existential Trilemma of EMU in a Model of Fiscal Target Zone'; EconPol Working Paper No. 65, Munich.

DeLong, J. B., Summers, L. H. (2012); 'Fiscal Policy in a Depressed Economy'; *Brookings Papers on Economic Activity* 43(1), pp. 233–297.

Domar, E. D. (1944); 'The "Burden of Debt" and the National Income'; *American Economic Review* 34, pp. 798–827.

Dosi, G., Fagiolo, G., Napoletano, M., Roventini, A., Treibich, T. (2015); 'Fiscal and Monetary Policies in Complex Evolving Economies'; *Journal of Economic Dynamics & Control* 52, pp. 166–189.

Ehnts, D. H. (2017); *Modern Monetary Theory and European Macroeconomics*, Routledge, Abingdon.

Eichenbaum, M. (1997); 'Some Thoughts on Practical Stabilization Policy'; *American Economic Review* 87(2), pp. 236–239.

Eisl, A. (2020); 'The Ambiguous Consensus on Fiscal Rules: How Ideational Ambiguity Has Facilitated Social Democratic Parties' Support of Structural Deficit

Rules in the Eurozone'; MaxPo Discussion Paper 20/4, Max Planck Science Po Center on Coping with Instability in Market Societies, Paris.

Fagiolo, G., Roventini, A. (2017); 'Macroeconomic Policy in DSGE and Agent Based Models Redux: New Developments and Challenges Ahead'; *Journal of Artificial Societies and Social Simulation* 20(1), Article 1.

Fontana, G. (2009); 'The Transmission Mechanism of Fiscal Policy: A Critical Assessment of Current Theories and Empirical Methodologies'; *Journal of Post Keynesian Economics*, 31(4), pp. 587–604.

Forstater, M. (2003); Towards a New Instrumental Macroeconomics: Abba Lerner and Adolph Lowe on Economic Method, Theory, History and Policy; in: Nell, E.J., Forstater, M. (Eds.); *Reinventing Functional Finance. Transformational Growth and Full Employment*, Edward Elgar, Cheltenham, pp. 52–65.

Friedman, M., Heller, W. (1969); *Monetary versus Fiscal Policy*, W.W.Norton & Co., New York.

Furman, J. (2016); 'The New View of Fiscal Policy and Its Application'; paper given at the conference Global Implications of Europe's Redesign, New York, 5 October 2016.

Furman, J., Summers, L. (2020); 'A Reconsideration of Fiscal Policy in the Era of Low Interest Rates'; discussion draft/unpublished manuscript (accessible at: furman-summers-fiscal-reconsideration-discussion-draft.pdf (brookings.edu)).

Gechert, S., Hughes Hallett, A., Rannenberg, A. (2016); 'Fiscal Multipliers in Downturns and the Effects of Eurozone Consolidation'; *Applied Economics Letters* 23(16), pp. 1138–1140.

Gechert, S., Rannenberg, A. (2018); 'Which Fiscal Multipliers Are Regime-Dependent? A Meta-Regression Analysis'; *Journal of Economic Surveys* 32(4), pp. 1160–1182.

Giavazzi, F., Pagano, M. (1990); 'Can Severe Fiscal Contractions Be Expansionary? Tales of Two Small European Countries'; *NBER Macroeconomics Annual* 5, pp. 75–111.

Greiner, A., Semmler, W. (2000); 'Endogenous Growth, Government Debt and Budgetary Regimes'; *Journal of Macroeconomics* 22(3), pp. 363–384.

Guajardo, J., Leigh, D., Pescatori, A. (2014); 'Expansionary Austerity: New International Evidence'; *Journal of the European Economic Association* 12(4), pp. 949–968.

de Haan, J., Sturm, J.-E., Sikken, B. (1996); 'Government Capital Formation: Explaining the Decline'; *Review of World Economics* 132, pp. 55–74.

Hall, P. A. (1993); 'Policy Paradigms, Social Learning, and the State: The Case of Economic Policymaking in Britain'; *Comparative Politics* 25(3), pp. 275–296.

Hall, R. E. (2016); 'The Role of the Growth of Risk-Averse Wealth in the Decline of the Safe Real Interest Rate'; NBER Working Paper No. 22196, Washington, DC.

Harvey, D. (2005); *A Brief History of Neoliberalism*; Oxford University Press, Oxford.

Heise, A. (2002); 'Optimal Public Debts, Sustainable Deficits, and Budgetary Consolidation'; *Empirica* 29(4), pp. 317–337.

Heise, A. (2008); *Economic Governance and Employment: Policy, Polity and Politics of Economic Rise and Decline*; LIT Verlag, Münster.

Heise, A. (2012); 'Governance without Government or, The Euro Crisis and What Went Wrong with European Economy Governance'; *International Journal of Political Economy* 41(2), pp. 42–60.

Heise, A. (2019); 'Post-Keynesian Economics – Challenging the Neoclassical Mainstream'; *Efil Journal of Economic Research* 2(8), pp. 8–29.

Herndon, T., Ash, M., Pollin, R. (2014); 'Does High Public Debt Consistently Stifle Economic Growth? A Critique of Reinhart and Rogoff'; *Cambridge Journal of Economics* 38(2), pp. 257–279.

Hibbs, D. (1977); 'Political Parties and Macroeconomic Policy'; *American Political Science Review*, 71(4), pp. 1467–1487.

Horton, M. A. (2011); 'Comparing Transatlantic Responses to the Financial Crisis: The Fiscal Policy Response'; in Pisani-Ferry, J., Posen, A., Saccomanni, F. (eds); *An Ocean Apart? Comparing Transatlantic Responses to the Financial Crisis*; Peterson Institute for International Economics, Brussels, pp. 111–145.

Jordà, Ò., Taylor, A. M. (2013); 'The Time for Austerity: Estimating the Average Treatment Effect of Fiscal Policy'; NBER Working Paper No. 19414, Washington, DC.

Keynes, J. M. (1943a); 'The Long-Term Problem of Full Employment'; in Moggridge, D. (ed.); *The Collected Writings of John Maynard Keynes*, vol. 27; Macmillan, London, 1980, pp. 320–325.

Keynes, J. M. (1943b); 'Letter to James E. Meade on 25th of April 1943'; in Moggridge, D. (ed.); *The Collected Writings of John Maynard Keynes*, vol. 27; Macmillan, London, 1980, p. 320.

Keynes, J. M. (1945); 'National Debt Inquiry: The Concept of a Capital Budget (Memorandum by Lord Keynes)'; in Moggridge, D. (ed.); *The Collected Writings of John Maynard Keynes*, vol. 27; Macmillan, London, 1980, pp. 405–413.

Klamer, A. (1983); 'A Background for the Conversations'; in Klamer, A.; *Conversations with Economists: New Classical Economics and Their Opponents Speak Out on the Current Controversy in Macroeconomics*; Rowman & Littlefield, Savage, pp. 1–25.

Lerner, A. P. (1943); 'Functional Finance and the Federal Debt'; *Social Research* 10(1), pp. 38–52.

Lucas, R. E., Jr (2003); 'Macroeconomic Priorities'; *American Economic Review* 93(1), pp. 1–14.

Lucas, R. E., Jr, Sargent, T. J. (1979); 'After Keynesian Macroeconomics'; *Federal Reserve Bank of Minneapolis Quarterly Review* 3(2), pp. 1–16.

Mankiw, G. N. (2020); A Skeptic's Guide to Modern Monetary Theory; *American Economic Review*, 110, Papers and Proceedings, pp. 141–144.

Middleton, R. (1985); *Towards the Managed Economy: Keynes, the Treasury and the Fiscal Policy Debate of the 1930s*; Methuen, London.

Minea, A., Villieu, P. (2009); 'Borrowing to Finance Public Investment? The "Golden Rule of Public Finance" Reconsidered in an Endogenous Growth Setting'; *Fiscal Studies* 30(1), pp. 103–133.

Minsky, H. P. (1986); *Stabilizing an Unstable Economy*; Yale University Press, New Haven, CT.

Mourre, G., Poissonnier, A., Lausegger, M. (2019); *The Semi-Elasticities Underlying the Cyclically-Adjusted Budget Balance: An Update & Further Analysis*; European Economy Discussion Paper No. 098, Luxembourg.

Nordhaus, W. D. (1975); 'The Political Business Cycle'; *Review of Economic Studies* 42(1), pp. 169–190.

Nordhaus, W. D. (1994); 'Policy Games: Coordination and Independence in Monetary and Fiscal Policies'; *Brookings Papers on Economic Activity* 2, pp. 139–216.

Oxley, H., Martin, J. (1991); 'Controlling Government Spending and Deficits: Trends in the 1980s and Prospects for the 1990s'; *OECD Economic Studies* 17, pp. 145–189.

Palley, T. I. (2015); 'The Critics of Modern Money Theory (MMT) Are Right'; *Review of Political Economy*, 27(1), pp. 45–61.
Perée, E., Välilä, T. (2005); 'Fiscal Rules and Public Investment'; European Investment Bank Economic and Financial Report No. 02–2005, Luxembourg.
Reinhart, C. M., Rogoff, K. S. (2010); 'Growth in a Time of Debt'; *American Economic Review* 100(2), pp. 573–578.
Sargent, T. J., Wallace, N. (1976); 'Rational Expectations and the Theory of Economic Policy'; *Journal of Monetary Economics* 2(1), pp. 169–183.
Schelkle, W. (2012); 'Good Governance in Crisis or a Good Crisis for Governance? A Comparison of the EU and the US'; *Review of International Political Economy* 19(1), pp. 34–58.
Schubert, C. (2013); 'Wie das Maastricht Kriterium im Louvre entstand'; *Frankfurter Allgemeine Zeitung*, 26 September 2013 (accessible at: 3-Prozent-Defizitgrenze: Wie das Maastricht-Kriterium im Louvre entstand – Wirtschaftswissen – FAZ).
Snowdon, B., Vane, H. R. (1999a); 'Interpreting Modern Macroeconomics: From Tobin to Romer'; in Snowdon and Vane (1999b); Conversations with Leading Economists: Interpreting Modern Macroeconomics; Edward Elgar, Cheltenham, pp. 1–90.
Snowdon, B., Vane, H. R. (1999b); *Conversations with Leading Economists: Interpreting Modern Macroeconomics*; Edward Elgar, Cheltenham.
Solow, R. M. (1999); 'Robert M. Solow'; in Snowdon and Vane; *Conversations with Leading Economists: Interpreting Modern Macroeconomics*; Edward Elgar, Cheltenham, pp. 270–291.
Solow, R. M. (2008); 'The State of Macroeconomics'; *Journal of Economic Perspectives* 22(1), pp. 243–246.
Straub, R., Tchakarov, I. (2007); 'Assessing the Impact of a Change in the Composition of Public Spending: A DSGE Approach'; ECB Working Paper No. 795, European Central Bank (ECB), Frankfurt.
Tabellini, G., Alesina, A. (1990); 'Voting on the Budget Deficit'; *American Economic Review* 80(1), pp. 37–49.
Taylor, J. B. (2000); 'Reassessing Discretionary Fiscal Policy'; *Journal of Economic Perspectives* 14(3), pp. 21–36.
Thwaites, G. (2015); 'Why Are Real Interest Rates So Low? Secular Stagnation and the Relative Price of Investment Goods'; Bank of England Working Paper No. 564, London.
Weintraub, S. (1972); Classical Keynesianism, Monetary Theory, and the Price Level; Greenwood Press, Westport.

Name Index

Note: Page numbers followed by "n" denote endnotes.

Subject Index

Note: Page numbers followed by "n" denote endnotes.

FSC
www.fsc.org
MIX
Papier | Fördert
gute Waldnutzung
FSC® C083411

Kolibri 360 GmbH
Ferdinand-Jühlke-Straße 7
99095 Erfurt, Deutschland
produktsicherheit@kolibri360.de